Holy Places in the Israeli–Palestinian Conflict

This book addresses the major generators of conflict and toleration at holy places in Palestine and Israel. Examining the religious, political, and legal issues, the authors show how the holy sites have been a focus of both conflict and cooperation between different communities.

Bringing together the views of a diverse group of experts on the region, *Holy Places in the Israeli–Palestinian Conflict* provides a new and multi-faceted approach to holy places, giving an in-depth analysis of relevant issues. Themes covered include legal regulation of holy places; nationalization, and reproduction of holy space; sharing and contesting holy places; identity politics; and popular legends of holy sites. Chapters cover in detail how recognition and authorization of a new site come about; the influence of religious belief versus political ideology on the designation of holy places; the centrality of such areas to the surrounding political developments; and how historical background and culture affect the perception of a holy site and relations between conflicting groups.

This new approach to the study of holy places and the Israeli–Palestinian conflict has great significance for a variety of disciplines, and will be of great interest in the fields of law, politics, religious studies, anthropology, and sociology.

Marshall J. Breger is a Professor of Law at the Columbus School of Law, The Catholic University of America, where he teaches Administrative Law, Church and State, International Law, and Legal Issues of the Peace Process.

Yitzhak Reiter teaches at the Conflict Studies Program of the Hebrew University of Jerusalem and is a Senior Lecturer at the Department of Political Science of Ashkelon Academic College.

Leonard Hammer is Associate Professor at Middle East Technical University, Northern Cyprus Campus. He lectures in the fields of public international law and international human rights, and has published books, articles, and chapters pertaining to these areas.

Routledge Studies in Middle Eastern Politics

1 Algeria in Transition
Reforms and development prospects
Ahmed Aghrout with Redha M. Bougherira

2 Palestinian Refugee Repatriation
Global perspectives
Edited by Michael Dumper

3 The International Politics of the Persian Gulf
A cultural genealogy
Arshin Adib-Moghaddam

4 Israeli Politics and the First Palestinian Intifada
Political opportunities, framing processes and contentious politics
Eitan Y. Alimi

5 Democratization in Morocco
The political elite and struggles for power in the post-independence state
Lise Storm

6 Secular and Islamic Politics in Turkey
The making of the justice and development party
Ümit Cizre

7 The United States and Iran
Sanctions, wars and the policy of dual containment
Sasan Fayazmanesh

8 Civil Society in Algeria
The political functions of associational life
Andrea Liverani

9 Jordanian–Israeli Relations
The peacebuilding experience
Mutayyam al O'ran

10 Kemalism in Turkish Politics
The Republican People's Party, secularism and nationalism
Sinan Ciddi

11 Islamism, Democracy and Liberalism in Turkey
The case of the AKP
William Hale and Ergun Özbudun

12 Politics and Violence in Israel/Palestine
Democracy versus military rule
Lev Luis Grinberg

13 Intra-Jewish Conflict in Israel
White Jews, Black Jews
Sami Shalom Chetrit

14 Holy Places in the Israeli–Palestinian Conflict
Confrontation and co-existence
Edited by Marshall J. Breger, Yitzhak Reiter, and Leonard Hammer

Holy Places in the Israeli–Palestinian Conflict

Confrontation and co-existence

**Edited by
Marshall J. Breger, Yitzhak Reiter,
and Leonard Hammer**

LONDON AND NEW YORK

First published 2010
by Routledge
2 Park Square, Milton Park, Abingdon, Oxon OX14 4RN

Simultaneously published in the USA and Canada
by Routledge
270 Madison Ave, New York, NY 10016

Routledge is an imprint of the Taylor & Francis Group, an informa business

© 2010 editorial selection and matter, Marshall J. Breger, Yitzhak Reiter, and Leonard Hammer; individual chapters the contributors

Typeset in Times New Roman by Taylor & Francis Books
Printed and bound in Great Britain by
CPI Antony Rowe Ltd, Chippenham, Wiltshire

All rights reserved. No part of this book may be reprinted or reproduced or utilised in any form or by any electronic, mechanical, or other means, now known or hereafter invented, including photocopying and recording, or in any information storage or retrieval system, without permission in writing from the publishers.

British Library Cataloguing in Publication Data
A catalogue record for this book is available from the British Library

Library of Congress Cataloging in Publication Data
Holy places in the Israeli-Palestinian conflict : confrontation and co-existence / edited by Marshall J. Breger, Yitzhak Reiter, and Leonard Hammer.
　p. cm. – (Routledge studies in Middle Eastern politics; 14)
Includes bibliographical references and index.
1. Arab-Israeli conflict-1993-Religious aspects. 2. Religion and politics–Palestine. 3. Sacred space-Political aspects-Palestine. I. Breger, Marshall J. II. Reiter, Yitzhak. III. Hammer, Leonard M.
　DS109.95.H65 2009
　956.04–dc22
　　　　　　　　　　2009017682

ISBN 978-0-415-54901-1 (hbk)
ISBN 978-0-203-86745-7 (ebk)

Contents

	Notes on contributors	ix
	Acknowledgments	xi
1	Introduction MARSHALL J. BREGER, YITZHAK REITER, AND LEONARD HAMMER	1
2	The legal regulation of holy sites MARSHALL J. BREGER AND LEONARD HAMMER	20
3	Protection of holy places in international law: objective and subjective approaches LEONARD HAMMER	50
4	Wars and sacred space: the influence of the 1948 War on sacred space in the state of Israel DORON BAR	67
5	The three kinds of holy places in Jewish law: the case of Nachmanides' Cave in Jerusalem as a third kind MICHAEL WYGODA	92
6	The *waqf* in Israel since 1965: the case of Acre reconsidered YITZHAK REITER	104
7	Holy places in urban spaces: foci of confrontation or catalyst for development? RASSEM KHAMAISI	128
8	The pessimist's guide to religious coexistence RON E. HASSNER	145
9	Contest or cohabitation in shared holy places? The Cave of the Patriarchs and Samuel's Tomb YITZHAK REITER	158

10 Treatment of antiquities on the Temple Mount/*Al-Haram al-Sharif* 178
JON SELIGMAN

11 The Shihab Al-Din Mosque affair in Nazareth: a case study of
Muslim–Christian–Jewish relations in the state of Israel 192
DAPHNE TSIMHONI

12 Holy shrines (*maqamat*) in modern Palestine/Israel and the politics
of memory 231
MAHMOUD YAZBAK

13 Self-empowerment through the sacred culture and representation in
the urban landscape: the Mosque of Hassan Bey and the Arab
community of Jaffa 249
NIMROD LUZ

14 The head of Husayn Ibn Ali: its various places of burial and the
miracles that it performed 264
KHALID SINDAWI

Bibliography 274
Index 297

Notes on contributors

Doron Bar heads the Land of Israel Studies at the Schechter Institute of Jewish Studies. He also teaches at the department of Theory and History, Bezalel Academy. His work examines the ways in which pilgrimage and holy space influenced Palestine's geography throughout history.

Marshall J. Breger is a Professor at the Catholic University of America. He has published extensively on a wide variety of legal and social issues, including matters pertaining to the holy places in Israel. He is involved in a number of initiatives concerning issues of faith and inter-state dialogue.

Leonard Hammer is an Associate Professor at Middle East Technical University, Northern Cyprus Campus. He lectures in the fields of public international law and international human rights, and has published books, articles, and chapters pertaining to these areas. He has received a number of fellowships and grants to conduct research on international law, freedom of religion and conscience, migrant workers, and holy places.

Ron E. Hassner is an Assistant Professor of Political Science at the University of California, Berkeley. His publications have focused on the role of perceptions in entrenching international disputes, the causes and characteristics of conflicts over sacred places, the characteristics of political-religious leadership and political-religious mobilization, and the role of national symbols in conflict. He is the author of *War on Sacred Grounds* (Cornell University Press, 2009), a book on the causes and mitigation of conflicts over holy places.

Rassem Khamaisi is an Associate Professor at the Department of Geography and Environmental Studies, Haifa University. He has published a number of books and articles on the urban and regional planning and human geographic and development of Arab Palestinians and Israeli cities and towns. He is also a senior research fellow at the Van Leer Institute and senior planner and researcher at the International Peace and Cooperation Center (IPCC), Jerusalem.

Nimrod Luz is a Senior Lecturer at the Department of Sociology and Anthropology, Western Galilee College. He studies the dialectics of the built environment in the Middle East and Islamic Societies, past and present, within an interdisciplinary approach, using multidisciplinary methodologies. His recent project is concerned with politics of sacred places in Palestinian communities in Israel and myriad phenomena connected to the production, reproduction, and experience of these places among Palestinians as part of processes of resistance, collective identity, and memory formation and self-empowerment.

Yitzhak Reiter is an Associate Professor at the Department of Political Science, Ashkelon Academic College and teaches at the Hebrew University of Jerusalem. He is also a research fellow at the Jerusalem Institute for Israel Studies and the Harry S. Truman Research Institute for the Advancement of Peace.

Jon Seligman is the Jerusalem Regional Archaeologist for the Israel Antiquities Authority. He received his education at the Hebrew University and at the Institute of Archaeology of the University of London. He has directed numerous excavations, mainly at Beth Shean, Mt. Carmel, and especially Jerusalem. Together with Dr Gideon Avni he has co-directed work in the Holy Sepulchre and has worked on ancient Georgian remains in Jerusalem. He has been involved in the composition of archaeological master plans for Jerusalem and its Old City. He has authored numerous excavation reports, a series of master plans, a book on the Holy Sepulchre and a number of articles analyzing the position of the holy sites in archaeological research and management.

Khalid Sindawi is a Senior Lecturer on Islamic studies at the Department of Multidisciplinary Studies, The Academic College of Emek Yezreel and Tel Aviv University. His research focuses on Shi'ite Studies, and he has written extensively on different aspects of Shi'a and Shi'ism.

Daphne Tsimhoni is Professor of Modern Middle East History at the Department of Humanities and Arts at the Technion – Israel Institute of Technology and is Research Fellow at the Truman Research Institute, Hebrew University of Jerusalem. Her research focuses on ethnicity and ethnic relations in the modern Middle East with special reference to Christians and Jews. She has written extensively on these topics and is the author of the book *Christian Communities in Jerusalem and the West Bank Since 1948* (Greenwood, 1993). She is active in the promotion of interfaith relations in Israel and is a member of the Israel Interfaith Association.

Michael Wygoda serves as Department Chief of the Jewish Law Division in the Israel Ministry of Justice. He addresses all issues of Jewish Law for the Ministry of Justice.

Mahmoud Yazbak is a Senior Lecturer teaching Palestinian history in the Department of Middle Eastern History at the University of Haifa. He publishes works on different aspects of Palestine's social history. Most of his social studies make use of the *Sijill* of the *Shari'a* courts.

Acknowledgments

This volume grew out of the conference "Confrontation and Co-existence in Holy Places: Religious Political and Legal Aspects in the Israeli–Palestinian Context." The conference was held January 3–4, 2006 at the Jewish–Arab Center of the University of Haifa and the Al-Qasemi Academy – Academic College of Education in Baqa al-Gharbia. We are grateful to the Head of the Jewish–Arab Center, Professor Faisal Azaiza, the President of Al-Qasemi Academy – Academic College of Education, Dr. Muhammad Issawi, as well as to the Rector of the University of Haifa, Professor Yossi Ben-Arzi, for hosting the conference.

We are glad to acknowledge a debt of gratitude to the Royal Norwegian Ministry of Foreign Affairs and to the United States Institute of Peace for the material support that allowed this book to come to fruition.

In addition:

Marshall J. Breger wishes to thank his wife, Jennifer Stern Breger, for her unflagging support: "*in cui la mia speranza vige,*" *Paradiso*, Canto XXXI: 79.

Yitzhak Reiter expresses his thanks to the three institutes that were the venues of his research activity during the period he worked on this book: the Jerusalem Institute for Israel Studies – and particularly Professor Yaacov Bar-Siman-Tov, Head of the Institute and the Institute's Director Ora Ahimeir; Ashkelon Academic College, headed by its President Professor Moshe Mani, Vice-President for Academic Affairs, Professor Shimon Sharvit, the General Director, Adv. Pinchas Haliva, and the Chair of the Political Science Department, Dr. Shmuel Tzabag; and to the Hebrew University's Truman Institute that supported his studies for about two decades.

Leonard Hammer would like to acknowledge his parents, Dr. David and Florence Hammer, and his in-laws, Ernest and Linda Hirsch, who have served as constant positive forces for his family and himself.

We thank Dr. Esther Cohen, Lauder School of Government, IDC, Herzliya, Israel for her editorial assistance in the preparation of this volume and Ms. Julie Kendrick, Columbus School of Law, Catholic University of America for her secretarial assistance.

Marshall J. Breger, Yitzhak Reiter, and Leonard Hammer

1 Introduction

Marshall J. Breger, Yitzhak Reiter, and Leonard Hammer

The interplay of politics and religion

Holy places play an important and oftentimes central role in matters not only of religion, but also of politics. The topic raises significant issues regarding national identity, treatment of minorities and approaches towards coexistence. Indeed, debates surrounding holy places are a metaphor for how we deal with the religious elements of a conflict. They impact and reflect issues of identity and underscore the religious as opposed to the political characteristics of the conflict.

Contemporary ethnic and national conflicts often involve the struggle over holy places[1] or the employment of holy sites as a symbol of group identity[2] and even as a source of political consolidation versus a rival group. As an indication of a new modern phenomenon, one has only to look at the following examples that have recently occurred: the destruction by radical Sunnis of the Shi'ite Al-Askari Mosque in Samarra during the internecine warfare in Iraq in 2006;[3] the destruction of Orthodox churches during the 1999 conflict in Kosovo[4] and of mosques in Bosnia, between 1992 and 1996,[5] as well as the destruction of religious property in the siege of Dubrovnik, Croatia by the Yugoslav People's Army ("JNA") in 1991[6] during the armed conflicts in former Yugoslavia; the destruction of statues of Buddha by the Taliban Government of Afghanistan in 2001;[7] the destruction of the Babri Mosque in Ayodhya during the Hindu–Muslim conflict in India and Kashmir in 1992;[8] and the torching and destruction of Joseph's Tomb in Nablus by Palestinians in 2000.[9] While existing literature on holy places refers to issues such as their spatial importance in the geography of the sacred[10] or their manifestation of the human perception of the divine,[11] there is little research on the cultural and political aspects of holy sites.[12] This book aims at filling the gap.

Surprisingly, in the age of interdisciplinary research, few studies (at least in the Middle Eastern context) have attempted to consider how both politics and culture affect the status of holy places. Further, discussions regarding the holy places provide an inroad into understanding the importance attached to religious belief and the manner by which the faithful perceive and interpret the actions of other individuals or groups, thereby paving the way for possible coexistence and further dialogue. Focusing on holy places can demonstrate how a conflict can be transformed from a political and nationalist dispute to a religious *Kulturkampf* and may hopefully allow us to analyze ways of diffusing that dangerous development.[13]

This book will grapple with issues that are both generic and region-specific and will pursue answers to questions such as the following: What are the indicia of holy places and who is authorized to designate such sites? What influences the recognition of a new site and how does recognition come about? Do the designations of holy places reflect political ideology alone or are they truly manifestations of religious beliefs? And how do religious beliefs regarding holy places impact on political considerations? To what extent does culture shape and identify the perception or significance of a holy site? How central are holy places to the surrounding political developments, especially in areas of conflict or dispute? Has the historical background affected the manner by which conflicting ethnic or religious groups relate?

Holy places as an effective cultural element of modern nationalism

Emile Durkheim made a fundamental distinction between the "sacred" and "profane" in religious life. Durkheim submits that "[i]f religious life is to develop, a special place must be prepared for it, one from which profane life is excluded ... [t]he institution of temples and sanctuaries arise from this."[14] Durkheim's explication of a special (or what we would call sacred) place is apparently based on his approach to the sacred as something which emanates from human nature and from society, and which is superimposed on specific geographical properties.[15] This approach, however, has proven only partially useful. For example, a study by Dawn Mari Hayes of medieval churches in Europe found that the intermingling of the sacred and the profane was in fact the integral reality of Christian sacred places.[16]

Mircea Eliade has discussed the role of human—as opposed to divine revelation—in determining the sanctity and status of a particular holy site.[17] In his 1959 book *The Sacred and the Profane*, Eliade explores how profane space is converted into sacred space and suggests that this symbolic process reflects the spiritual characteristics associated with both the physical features and the deeper, abstract implications of delimiting a particular site as sacred. Designation of a site as sacred is generally a response to one of two types of events. Some events ("hierophanic") involve a direct manifestation on earth of a deity, whereas in other ("theophanic") events, someone receives a message from the deity and interprets it for others.[18] Nonetheless, Eliade was referring mainly to the spiritual significance of such sanctification rather than to the earthly aspects of the phenomenon.

Writing in 1979, Harold Turner developed a phenomenological approach to holy places, particularly with regard to those sites that serve as places of worship. He stressed their function as "the center of the world" and as community meeting places in addition to their function as "Houses of God." In addition, he highlighted their role as representing a microcosm of the heavenly realm and as an immanent-transcendent presence of God everywhere.[19]

The phenomenological approach was criticized by succeeding scholars who called for an empirical approach. In his 2004 study of holy cities, Gerard Wiegers distinguished between "profane" urban spaces containing one or more important holy places (such as Jerusalem) and "holy" urban spaces in which holy places or sanctuaries may be found, such as Mecca and Al-Madina for Muslims and Varanasi for Hindus.[20] In the latter, the entire city is holy, not simply specific sites within that city.

In their insightful 1995 book *American Sacred Space*,[21] Chidester and Linenthal developed ideas presented earlier by Dutch theologian Gerardus Van der Leeuw (whose phenomenological theory was adopted by Eliade). In his 1933 seminal work,[22] Van der Leeuw addressed the politics of sacred space, arguing that the very definition of a place as sacred is a political act whose purpose is the "conquest of the space." Sacred places are, indeed, characterized by a politics of ownership and possession. From the time that a site is defined as sacred, it undergoes expropriation and a change of ownership. Sacred space is also a religious symbol that is mobilized for purposes of political authority. Another political aspect of the holy site is its exclusivity. That is, whoever is outside of its boundaries is excluded from it. And finally, the sacred space is also connected to the politics of exile—that is, the loss of the sacred space or nostalgia for it on the part of those who were connected to it in the distant past and are now, in the modern era, severed from it.[23]

Chidester and Linenthal expanded upon Van der Leeuw's thesis and emphasized the secular forces which come into play with regard to the holy site. In their view, a sacred space exists not merely in the heavenly dimension but also on the plane of reality, hierarchical power relations between rulers and ruled, exclusion, and inclusion, ownership and the loss of ownership. They adopt Michel Foucault's theory of power[24] in order to explain the various functions exerted upon a holy site. Sacred space is, first and foremost, a venue for ritual activity. It is a place that radiates meaning to man. Thus, it is the focus of an unavoidable competition or struggle over ownership, legitimacy and sacred symbols. Because sacred space is also a place over which ownership or possession may be claimed and which may be used by human beings seeking to further specific ends, it is also an arena in which various players engage in a power struggle.

Most interestingly, Chidester and Linenthal suggest that a holy place is usually considered most sacred by those who had originally sanctified it, when it is perceived as being in danger of secularization by economic, social and political forces or of seizure by some other entity which is liable to defile it. Competing religious groups view Jerusalem, for example, as endangered sacred space. Some have argued that the city received special attention by the Muslim Umayyad Dynasty, which moved its capital to nearby Al-Sham (Greater Syria) which Jerusalem was part of, as well as by the Ayyubids after its conquest by the Crusaders. All of them followed the city's sanctification by the Holy Scriptures from Abraham's Mount Moriah, via David's City and Solomon's Temple, Jesus' encounters and Muhammad's Night Journey.[25] The historical stories involving holy men inspires current peoples and nations and, as witnessed after Israel conquered East Jerusalem in 1967, the city has become a major focus of struggle between Israeli Jews and Palestinian and Arab Muslims.[26] Holy places, then, take on greater sanctity when people are willing to fight and die for it. People are willing to die in struggles over holy places, because the holy place is an inexhaustible source of meaning and a symbol of their ethnic and religious identity.[27]

Chidester and Linenthal based their conclusions concerning the meanings attached to sacred places on research conducted in Hawaii and on the American mainland. Nevertheless, their conclusions are particularly relevant with regard to the status of the Holy Land in the eyes of the followers of the three great Abrahamic faiths. That status is elevated due to the very fact of its being the epicenter of a political conflict.

The virtue of a holy place in the eyes of believers and its political importance are interrelated.[28] In ancient periods and during medieval times, religious conviction and religious affiliation, and sometimes even interreligious association, were the major axes around which internal politics as well as intercommunal relations were organized. A ruler's or a ruling elite's decision about the location of its central site of worship was clearly motivated by political considerations. One only need consider King David's decision to move the Ark of the Covenant from Kiriat Ye'arim and to place it in ancient Jebus—today's Jerusalem, a decision that turned a small urban place into the political capital of his kingdom.[29] Or consider the prophet Muhammad who had to leave Mecca because of mounting opposition from the Quraysh—the ruling clan—who were in charge of the Ka'ba as a center of a pagan ritual. In 630 CE, Muhammad and his followers returned to Mecca as conquerors and, after eliminating all pagan idols, rededicated the Ka'ba as an Islamic house of worship. Henceforth, the traditional annual pilgrimage, the Hajj, was to Mecca.[30] One thus cannot avoid the political consequences of sanctifying a site or a city.

For a long time "modernization theory" assumed that in modern society religious affiliations would lose their value as a source of political identity and affiliation in favor of civic and national identities.[31] Thus, one would expect that in modern society struggles over holy places would vanish or at least become rare. In fact, however, the political reality is just the opposite. Notwithstanding the conventional academic wisdom[32] religious emotions still play a central role in ethnic conflicts around the globe, while religious heritage and religion in general constitute a large part of the ethnic and national ethos of many modern societies.[33]

In constructing a modern national ethos, politicians and intellectuals draw on the framework of popular culture and consciousness, which was mainly religious in the past, and exploit holy sites in order to buttress projects of national or ethnic identity.[34] Religion and holy places are thus an effective cultural element of modern nationalism.[35] Places where military battle occurred, national heroes, and areas of the military front are all effective tools through which nationalist elites, consciously or unconsciously, imagine narratives that 'sanctify' the nation and refer to the homeland as "sacred territory."[36]

The Palestinian–Israeli conflict is a good example of this process. For the Zionist movement, albeit a secular national movement, religious symbols were an important asset for acquiring legitimacy.[37] Religious affiliation and its territorial significance were the foundations of consolidating legitimacy for the "Return to Zion," i.e., to the holy Jerusalem and Eretz Yisrael. When the Zionist movement began at the end of the nineteenth century, the majority of the Jewish people lived in the Diaspora—outside their historical cradle, the Land of Israel. The movement required religious identity as a common denominator for the unification of the people and for its new political goal of rejuvenating political life in the Holy Land. This link between religion and politics helps explain why modern Israel, as a secular, democratic nation state, is defined as a Jewish state, and why the newborn state in 1948 insisted on declaring Jerusalem as its capital even though the Old City and its holy places were in the eastern part of the city, which was not then under Israel's control. Here the symbol was much more important than the reality.[38] For Jewish Israel, Jerusalem and the Temple Mount serve as a source of national inspiration.

The same could be said regarding the Arabs who lived in the Ottoman Empire *vilayets* (or provinces) of "Palestine" who found themselves in the late nineteenth century confronting a Jewish national movement which strove to establish a political and national entity on land that had been under the Ottoman Empire for five centuries. The Arabs who lived in those *vilayets* were among the weakest of Arab peoples. Unlike Egyptians and Syrians, they lacked a historical record as a coherent, unified or identifiable ethnic or political group. When the new national boundaries for the Middle East were delineated by the imperial powers during and after World War I, they found themselves included within the British Mandate. According to the Balfour Declaration, the British were committed to the establishment of "a national home for the Jewish people" in that very territory. Consequently, Islam, in addition to Pan-Arabism, would become the strongest source of religious and national identity for the Palestinians, lending strategic depth to their struggle against Zionism. It was Mohammad Amin al-Husseini, the Grand Mufti of Jerusalem from 1922 to 1948, who realized the unifying potential of religious symbols in his struggles with the incipient Zionist movement. After his plans for a Greater Syria were foiled by the British and the French in 1920, Al-Husseini turned from Damascus-oriented Pan-Arabism to a specifically Palestinian ideology centered on Jerusalem.[39]

Under al-Husseini's tutelage, in an effort to recruit the aid of the Muslim World, Palestinian leadership employed the religious symbols of holy places, calling muslim communities to rescue Islamic domain and the divine blessed land (*ard al-baraka*) from non-Muslim (Jewish and Christian British) control.[40] Their highest political leader held such religious titles as "the Grand Mufti" and "the President of the Supreme Muslim Council." Indeed, the first serious violent clash between Zionist Jews and Palestinian Muslims erupted in 1929 on the issue of the holy places—the Western Wall affair. For Jews, the Western Wall (or as it was historically known, the "Wailing Wall"), the last remnant of the Jewish Temple, was a place of religious ritual for centuries while the Temple Mount is the holiest site in Judaism. For Muslims, the Temple Mount compound which they refer to as Al-Haram al-Sharif is revered as the location of the prophet Muhammad's night journey to Jerusalem and ascent to heaven and is associated with other local Muslim figures of antiquity. The site is the location of the al-Aqsa Mosque and the Dome of the Rock, the oldest extant Islamic structure in the world. In 1929, when Jews opted to extend their rights and religious access at the Western Wall and when the Muslims acted to prevent it and to glorify the Al-Haram al-Sharif and the Al-Aqsa Mosque, it was only a question of time before a clash would take place.

Similarly, the Second Intifada, triggered by the public visit of then Defense Minister Ariel Sharon to the Temple Mount on 28 September 2000, was infused with religious significance.[41] And Israeli Islamists, such as Sheikh Ra'id Salah, head of the Northern branch of the Islamic movement, successfully deployed the slogan, "al-Aqsa is in Danger," to rally supporters to the defense of Muslim interests.[42] Once again, national politics dictated that the Holy Places of Jerusalem would be the trigger of violent strife.

In the Palestine case, we can see a coupling of the process of recruiting sacred places for political ends with a process of elevating the sacredness of holy places and their value.[43] Hence, the level of sacredness is strongly connected to the political centrality of the holy places, even in a modern and non-religious context. Both in pre-modern times, where there was no separation between religion and politics or between Church and State, and in modern times, where these realms are separate, political considerations continue to influence the centrality of a holy place both in religious conviction, as well as in inter-communal relations, and politicians often exploit the emotional intensity a holy place generates.[44]

This phenomenon can be seen in modern Israel even with secular 'holy sites' such as Masada which achieved iconic centrality during the 1948–67 period when Israel lacked a foothold in the Old City of Jerusalem. During that time Israeli officers took their oath on Masada's heights, affirming in a torchlight swearing-in ceremony that "Masada shall not fall again."[45] Similar efforts were made during that period to consecrate Mount Zion, which was then the closest point in Jewish Jerusalem to the Western Wall.[46] After the Israeli conquest of the Old City in 1967, the symbolic significance of both Masada and Mount Zion diminished in favor of the Western Wall.

The special situation of Palestine/Israel

While issues surrounding holy places arise in a variety of countries and national conflicts, certainly few could deny that the one area of the world

Introduction 7

where issues of holy places have clear political significance is the Middle East. Most discussion of the holy places in Israel and Palestine[47] has focused on the Temple Mount or the historical issues related to the so-called Ottoman "Status Quo." Granted these are important issues, but they focus either on the relevance of antiquarian political questions or on immensely important theological considerations. There has been little discussion of the politics of sacred space in Israel and Palestine.

Yet it is abundantly clear that holy places in Israel and Palestine have political ramifications. Just to consider some examples: the virulent dispute between PLO Chairman Yasser Arafat and the Israeli negotiating team at the Camp David Summit in July 2000 over his comment that the Jewish Temple had never been located on the Al-Haram al-Sharifa that caused the failure of those negotiations;[48] the 2000 conflagrations set off by Sharon's ill-timed visit to the Temple Mount; the tragic massacre on February 25, 1994 of Muslim worshipers executed by Baruch Goldstein at the Tomb of the Patriarchs in Hebron; and the destruction of Joseph's Tomb and the continual confrontations at Rachel's Tomb during the Second Intifada.

These are not mere intramural debates. For example, the Joseph's Tomb issue was raised in the US Human Rights Report of 2002.[49] The 2001 Mitchell Report called specifically for joint action by the parties to protect the Holy Places[50] as did the January 2002 Alexandria Declaration of the Religious Leaders of the Holy Land.[51] The intense dispute in Israel during the 2005 Gaza Disengagement regarding how to "dispose" of abandoned synagogues and graves in Gaza simply underscores the deleterious policy consequences of ignoring this issue.[52] Moreover, whenever there is a resumption of final status talks, it should be clear that explosive issues surrounding the Antiquities Law's application to excavations on the Al-Haram al-Saharif and Jewish access to the Temple Mount are likely to require issue management.[53]

As we have seen, the situation of holy places in Israel and Palestine is especially complex. One city, Jerusalem, contains space sacred to the narrative of each of the three Abrahamic religions. In many cases, most prominently at the Temple Mount/Al-Haram al-Sharif, claims to sacred space overlap. The competing religious narratives have in many ways shaped the political conflict. In the 1920s, the Supreme Muslim Council focused attention on the Al-Haram al-Sharif in order to build political support for Palestinian aspirations throughout the Muslim world.[54] The late Yasser Arafat's comment at Camp David, that the Jewish Temple had never been on the Al-Haram al-Sharif was considered by Israelis, both religious and secular alike, as a rejection of any Jewish claim to the Temple Mount and to Israel itself—a rejection of the entire Jewish narrative regarding Eretz-Yisrael.[55] Indeed, in both Israel and Palestine we have seen a proliferation of sacred space used by partisans to buttress their own national narrative.[56] Palestinians have asserted Canaanite roots, infusing ancient Philistine festivals in Sebastia with nationalist ideology.[57] Israelis have "discovered" numerous holy sites in Judea and Samaria, all serving to legitimate and reinforce the Jewish presence.[58] For both Palestinians and Israelis, archeology has been the handmaiden of politics.[59] One can only note the resumption of Har Dov as a Jewish pilgrimage site the very day it was reported that the United Nations had asked Israel to discuss with Lebanon the future of Har Dov, known to the Lebanese as "Shabaa Farms."[60]

Another issue prominent in the Holy Land is that of the management of holy places.[61] Israel faces issues concerning the recognition and listing of sites and the operational significance of sites denominated as sacred or holy. The problem of access to holy places runs up against problems of security and of national sovereignty. Even the possibility of peace raises issues of holy site management as, for example, the challenge of how to manage the large number of Muslim pilgrims who would likely visit the Al-Haram al-Sharif after a peace settlement.[62] Lessons from Saudi pilgrimage management of the *Hajj* may be relevant.[63]

Sacred space in the Holy Land raises unique international law issues. For one, the so-called "Status Quo" agreements with the Ottomans are still drawn upon by the Christian denominations to validate their claims.[64] Indeed, the Vatican–Israel Fundamental Agreement of 1993 refers specifically to those agreements in relation to the Holy Places.[65] Issues such as "access" to holy places are often raised by Palestinians and Christians in international law contexts on the grounds of freedom of religion under, for example, Article 18 of the International Covenant of Civil and Political Rights (pilgrimage and access as a manifestation of a religious belief). Interestingly, as a result of the Israeli disengagement from Gaza in 2005, Israeli settlers referred to international law principles as grounds for preserving their abandoned synagogues.[66] While that argument was innovative, if not speculative given the lack of any specific grounding of the claim in international human rights, any response demands a deeper understanding of the international legal materials related to holy places.

We cannot ignore the extent to which the United Nations Educational, Scientific and Cultural Organization (UNESCO) stresses the protection of "cultural heritage," having concluded the Convention on the Protection of Cultural Property in the Event of Armed Conflict,[67] and prepared its two protocols[68] and the UNESCO World Heritage List (which includes, for example, the Old City and its walls),[69] along with other instruments impacting on holy sites.[70]

The book raises the profound problem of sharing sacred space by considering the experience of shared holy sites beginning with case studies of such shared sites as the Tomb of the Patriarchs (Cave of Machpelah) in Hebron and the Tomb of Samuel (Nebi Shmuel) outside Jerusalem. Indeed, any study of sacred space in the Holy Land raises concrete issues of shared holy space—the problem of how one manages the religious claim of two religions to the same sacred space. The experience at the Tomb of the Patriarch (Ibrahim Mosque) in Hebron has been particularly unsuccessful in suggesting any possibility of coexistence, while that of the Tomb of Samuel is less discouraging.[71] Nevertheless, sharing has proved to be more successful in certain minor holy places, for example, at the Tomb of Hulda the Prophetess on the Mount of Olives[72] and at the Cave of Elijah on Mount Carmel.[73]

Themes under discussion

Legal regulations of holy places

Domestic considerations

It is natural for a state to address conflicts concerning holy sites through its domestic law. Once the legal regime of the state enters the fray, questions abound concerning the desired scope of regulation, the means by which the state will continue to engage the issue of holy places and the unavoidable social and political factors that enter into such legal decisions. Marshall Breger and Leonard Hammer[74] address these issues in the context of approaches that a state might take when designating certain places as holy. They note the intentionally ambiguous nature of domestic laws concerning holy places and the difficulties encountered by the authorities in meshing previously existing legal systems into the framework of the existing legal system.

International approaches

The international community and its institutions maintain a dual responsibility that reflects an inherent contradiction. On the one hand, UNESCO is assigned to protect places of universal heritage interest. On the other hand, the UN is engaged in protecting the rights and freedoms of individuals and groups including their religious freedom. If one group seeks exclusive control of a universal heritage site, the general interest of society may be ignored. Alternatively, holy places as forms of cultural assets recognizes their role as part of the universal cultural heritage separate from the interest of specific religious groups.

The international framework is operating within a particular context, adopting specific perspectives that tend to influence the scope and breadth of protection (and understanding) created for holy places. Leonard Hammer[75] concludes that, depending on the interests at stake, the international framework might adopt an object-oriented approach that tends to protect a specific object or place, as opposed to a subject-orientation reliant on assertions of individual or group rights. Different international legal instruments are employed for different purposes, thereby suggesting a variety of possibilities and approaches. What merits further examination, however, is an analysis of the importance of these international frameworks to the domestic legal system and whether there is any possibility of synergy between the domestic and international.

Nationalizing holy space

Considering as well the social and political aspects of holy places, one turns to the means by which social and political forces play a role in their protection and development, especially when accounting for the nationalizing of holy places by the State of Israel. How have political and social forces dealt with regulation and control of holy places during power shifts and regime changes? What about perceptions of holiness as deriving from religious sources—might they also have some persuasive effect? Further, given the seemingly inherent bias by a controlling state entity and its apparatus, can there still exist some form of actualization and categorization for holy places?

Clearly holy places are victims of the overriding nationalist doctrine, becoming inherent links in the nationalist chain, helping to strengthen and entrench the dominant social and political forces. Doron Bar[76] discusses how the Israeli authorities tended to "create" and use sacred space for social and political purposes following the 1948 War and the establishment of the state. He contends that sacred space was manipulated, becoming part of the internal political, nationalist doctrine to entrench the state and its new populace. Many sites were deemed significant, not because they were accorded lofty positions in the pantheon of sacred space, but because they served a specific nationalist purpose for the public at large.

Inherent in this analysis are the unavoidable political considerations that go into designating and protecting holy places. Michael Wygoda[77] considers the controversy surrounding Nachmanides' Cave, a seemingly harmless site that nevertheless encompasses the panoply of problems confronting the state when considering methods for regulation and control over holy places. Oral tradition that serves as a basis for deeming the site holy, contrasts with the actual historical use at the site. While the matter is still pending before the courts, the manner by which the court-appointed reviewing committee deemed the site as a Jewish holy place, comparing it to a functioning synagogue, is rather compelling. It gives us an insight into the perceptions adopted by various parties operating in these contexts, demonstrating the lengths that some will go to broaden the protection accorded to holy places.

A contrasting example is the operation of the *waqf* in Acre. Yitzhak Reiter[78] discusses the problems presented by the huge amount of *waqf* land present in Israel and the avenues utilized by the state for regulation and control of such lands. The state essentially labeled many *waqf* lands as absentee property, thereby subjecting the areas to state control. Reiter goes on to analyze the means by which the local religious authorities in Acre dealt with this designation, by utilizing forms of administration designed primarily to limit internal corruption rather than to narrow the scope of governmental oversight.

Sharing/contesting holy places

Recognizing that holy places are forms of actual physical space, it is necessary to take into account broader economic and social considerations of development as well as more focused issues of coexistence and cohabitation among different population groups. Do holy places act as a boon for urban development, serving as a means for economic development by attracting pilgrims or other tourists? What of places with a strong minority presence or those that have been "shared" by a number of religions? Is there a possibility for some form of coexistence at holy places or are external political forces too great to prevent such results?

Rassem Khamaisi[79] discusses the advantages and disadvantages of having holy places in the vicinity, converting them from economic barriers to assets subject to social and economic planning. The key linchpin here is the importance of including the full panoply of existing social and political interest in the decision-making process such to ensure for effective development. In a country rife with political balancing that tends to skewer policy choices, achieving the right decision and allowing for proper inclusion of all relevant parties proves to be quite a difficult task.

Of course, holy places tend to serve as grounds for fomenting conflict. Recognizing this, Ron Hassner[80] proposes that one can reduce the impact of broader religious forces by deferring to localized interest groups. Because religious leaders tend to cloak their assertions in nationalist rhetoric that pleases the ears of their supporters and followers, Hassner asserts that local leaders serve as a better source for ameliorating conflict, even if it results in separation from religious and political actors. He proposes moving the issue away from the broader religious political arena towards the context of parties closer to the source of the conflict.

Nonetheless, one cannot ignore the operation of some form of "shared" holy places at places like Samuel's Tomb (shared by Muslims and Jews) or Hebron, as discussed by Yitzhak Reiter,[81] or the Temple Mount/Al-Aqsa area, as discussed by Jon Seligman.[82] Reiter accounts for the advent of a shared existence at a holy site pointing to such factors as the site's religious and political importance, its actual location and the role of shifting political regimes that serve to influence a given religious group. As such, Samuel's Tomb is more conducive towards coexistence, whereas Hebron certainly requires greater governmental oversight and involvement to keep the sides at bay. Seligman discusses the roles of the archaeological authorities in maintaining some form of cooperative atmosphere at the Temple Mount. He notes that such relations are subject to constantly changing political winds. He concludes that cooperative activity at the Temple Mount has waned in recent years owing to the tendency of the Palestinian Authority to become more active and assertive in the area.

Daphne Tsimhoni[83] considers a situation where cooperation and coexistence have failed miserably. Discussing the matter of building a mosque in the historically Christian city of Nazareth, she outlines the involvement of not only the local and national authorities, both religious and political, but also of external elements, such as other states and international religious institutions, such as the Holy See. She concludes that much of the conflict could have initially been avoided had the Israeli authorities handled the affair differently, taking into account all minority interests at stake.

Identity politics and holy places

The treatment accorded by the state towards its holy places serves as a form of microcosm for the treatment of its minority sects. As noted in some of the aforementioned chapters, Israel's treatment of the holy places of minorities has been problematic, and at times, egregious. In the broader sense, what has been the treatment accorded to minority groups within the State of Israel, particularly the Arab minority? What have been the inherent problems that go along with protecting and preserving the holy places of such groups and have there been instances whereby initiative was taken by the minority group to preserve its holy places? Mahmoud Yazbak[84] provides a broad outline of the problems associated with Israel's treatment of its Arab minority since 1948. He notes the problems of disappearing Muslim holy places and the overall lack of support accorded to minority groups and their holy places. By contrast, Nimrod Luz[85] describes how a group of local Arab Muslims suceeded in preserving a historically important mosque in Tel Aviv-Yaffo that presently serves the needs of the immediate local community.

Popular legends of holy sites

The discussions thus far concerning holy places have been linked to political, religious and social forces, but sources that are more esoteric can also serve as the basis for denominating holy places. In many instances, holy places emerge from legend generated by popular myths and folklore, at times coinciding with, and at times diverging from, state policy or developmental measures. The notion of legend is an important consideration for holy places and serves as a starting point for examining the inherent amalgamation of myth and physical space. How did these legends emerge and what was their importance to the local population? How do they fit into the traditional narrative and what forms of veneration derived from these legends? Khalid Sindawi[86] traces the legend of Husayn's head (the head of Husayn ibn Ali ibn Talib). Sindawi attributes the large number of places where the head has been located and has "performed" miracles, to the importance of Husayn and the perception of him as a figure equivalent to that of a saint. This status served as the basis for the creation of the Shi'ia legend surrounding his head.

Conclusion

Sacred space, and particularly sites holy to more than one religious denomination, are in many cases the focus of inter-communal conflict. Hence, it is surprising that the theoretical literature in religious studies and in the social sciences is almost silent about the political aspects of holy places. With the growing number of case studies dealing with the political reality in sacred spaces in which this book seeks to contribute, there is a need to relate to conflicts involving holy places as a separate realm of study. We have argued in this Introduction that a holy place is by definition a place of a political theatre in large measure because of the exclusivity that religious groups seek to attach to what they view as "their" place.

Often, parties in a political conflict over land or group identity employ claims over holy space to enhance their position. In turn, these claims tend to elevate the significance of that site in both the religious and political realms. In light of this phenomenon, we are in need of more field studies and empirical studies of political engagement at holy sites in order to develop, models and theories of what are the factors that influence inter-communal relations at holy places, what drives groups to the use of violence, as well as the utilization of religious symbols of sacred space for political ends. We also suggest a closer examination of those holy places and where "convivencia" and co-existence prevail.

No place better exemplifies the struggles concerning the sanctification of space than the Holy Land. Case studies from this specific region are, thus, immensely important particularly those which touch on the current political strife between Israelis and Palestinians. However, some case studies from India and other parts of Asia and from the Balkans unfold similar processes regarding political behavior involving sacred places. Students of both comparative religion and conflict resolution are hungry for cross-regional comparative studies that discuss holy places. We trust that this volume will go some way to satisfy that need.

Notes

1 *See* Seligman, Chapter 10 in this volume.
2 This is a central point in Bar, Chapter 4 in this volume.
3 *See* R. Worth, "Blast at Shiite Shrine Sets Off Sectarian Fury in Ira1," *New York Times*, 23 Feb. 2006, Online. Available: http://www.nytimes.com/2006/02/23/international/middleeast/23iraq.html?_r=1&oref=slogin; The San Francisco Bay Area Independent Media Center, "Al Askari Mosque Destroyed Sparking Sectarian Violence," Online. Available: http://www.indybay.org/newsitems/2006/02/28/43052.php (accessed 2 Sept. 2008).
In sharp contrast, consider the extensive debate in Allied circles before the bombing of Monte Cassino Monastery during World War II. Only after the Allies concluded incorrectly that German artillery used the Monte Cassino Monastery in Italy as a forward base for shelling American troops was it ordered destroyed. The entire story is well told in D. Hapgood and D. Richardson, *Monte Cassino*, NY: Congdon and Weed, 1984, pp. 52–53, 77, 158, 162; F. Majdalany, *The Battle of Cassino*, Cambridge, Mass.: Riverside Press, 1957, pp. 134–66; R. Trevelyan, *Rome '44: The Battle For the Eternal City,* New York: Viking Press, 1981, pp. 122–42. Later in the war the Allies divided Italian cities into three categories based on the historic or religious artifacts they contained. The first category, which was not to be bombed without direct orders, included the cities of "Rome, Fiesole, Florence, Venice and Torcello." Trevelyan, *Rome '44*, pp. 233–34.

4 A. Herscher and A. Riedlmayer, "Monument and Crime: The Destruction of Historic Architecture in Kosovo," Grey Room (Autumn 2000), vol. 1, pp. 108–22.
5 A. Hadzimuhamedovic, "Transnational Meaning of the Bosnia-Herzegovinian Architectural Heritage and Its Post-War Reconstruction." Online. Available: http://www2.units.it/~vplanet/atti/Hadzimuhamedovic.doc (accessed 2 Sept. 2008); M. Sells, *The Bridge Betrayed: Religion and Genocide in Bosnia*, Berkeley, Calif.: University of California Press, 1996; R. Mahmutcahajic, *Bosnia the Good: Tolerance and Tradition*, Budapest: Central European University Press, 2000; Asim Zubcevic, "Islamic Sites in Bosnia: Ten Years After," in *Islamica Magazine*, 2007, http://www.islamicamagazine.com/issue-15/islamic-sites-in-bosnia-10-years-after-the-war.html (accessed 2 Sept. 2008); J. Armatta, "Systematic Destruction of Cultural Monuments," in *Bosnia Report*, new series 35 (Aug.–Sept. 2003). Online. Available: http://www.bosnia.org.uk/bosrep/report_format.cfm?articleid=1010&reportid=160 (accessed 2 Sept. 2008).
6 For Dubrovnik *see* Press Release, International Criminal Tribunal for the Former Yugloslavia (ICTY), "Full Contents of the Dubrovnik Indictment Made Public," 2 Oct. 2001. Online. Available: http://www.un.org/icty/pressreal/p625-e.htm (accessed 2 Sept. 2008). Four military officers were indicted by the ICTY for charges including, " ... destruction or wilful damage done to institutions dedicated to religion and to historic monuments ... destruction or wilful damage done to institutions dedicated to education or religion." *Ibid*. Damage assessment found "that, of the 824 buildings in the Old Town, 563 (or 68.33 per cent) had been hit by projectiles in 1991 and 1992." *Ibid*. The officers indicted were Pavle Strugar, Miodrag Jokic, Milan Zec and Vladimir Kovacevic. Pavle Strugar was sentenced to eight years in prison. Press Release, International Criminal Tribunal for the Former Yugloslavia, Pavle Strugar Case Concludes (20 Sept. 2006) http://www.un.org/icty/pressreal/2006/p1112-e.htm (accessed 2 Sept. 2008). Miodrag Jokic was sentenced to seven years in prison. *Prosecutor v. Miodrag Jokic*, Case No. IT-01-42/1-A, (30 Aug 2005). Online. Available: http://www.un.org/icty/jokic/appeal/judgement/index.htm (accessed 2 Sept. 2008). Milan Zec's indictment was withdrawn for the present. Press Release, 29 July 2002, International Criminal Tribunal for the Former Yugloslavia, "Indictment against Milan Zec Withdrawn." Online. Available: http://www.un.org/icty/pressreal/p691-e.htm (accessed 2 Sept. 2008). Finally, Vladimir Kovacevic was declared unfit to stand trial due to mental illness. Press Release, International Criminal Tribunal for the Former Yugloslavia, Vladimir Kovacevic Declared Unfit to Stand Trial (12 Apr. 2006). Online. Available: http://www.un.org/icty/pressreal/2006/p1069-e.htm (accessed 2 Sept. 2008).
7 Online. Available: http://en.wikipedia.org/wiki/Buddhas_of_Bamyan (accessed 2 Sept. 2008). The story is well laid out in Kanchanca Wangkoo, "Monumental Challenges: The Lawfulness of Destroying Cultural Heritage During Peacetime," *Yale Journal of International Law*, 2003, vol. 28, pp. 183, 243–63.
8 R. Friedlander and R. Hecht, "The Bodies of Nations: A Comparative Study of Religious Violence in Jerusalem and Ayodhya," *History of Religions*, Nov. 1998, vol. 2, pp. 38, 101–49. The Ayodhya example is of special interest as the same site was the venue for a prequel in the mid-1800s. *See* Juan Cole, *Sacred Space and Holy War: The Politics, Culture, and History of Islam*, London: I.B. Tauris, 2002, pp. 8–9, 161–72.
9 Palestine Facts, "What Happened at Joseph's Tomb in October 2000?" Online. Available: http://www.palestinefacts.org/pf_1991to_now_alaqsa_josephstomb.php (accessed 2 Sept. 2008). For a summary of recent efforts by Israelis to visit Joseph's Tomb on a regular basis, *see* Isabel Kershner, "Pilgrimage to Roots of Faith and Strife," *New York Times*, 24 Oct. 2008, A5. Although Israeli settlers once visited the tomb located in the Palestinian city of Nablus sporadically (like "thieves in the night"), settlers are now working to organize monthly and even

weekly bus convoys of pilgrims. *Ibid.* The pilgrimages are carefully orchestrated in conjunction with the Israeli army, which secures the tomb in advance and stations military vehicles along the route. *Ibid.*
10 L. Kong, "Ideological Hegemony and the Political Symbolism of Religious Buildings in Singapore," *Environment and Planning D: Society and Space*, 1993a, vol. 11, pp. 23–45; Chris C. Park, *Sacred Worlds: An Introduction to Geography and Religion*, New York: Routledge, 1994.
11 M. Eliade, "The Sacred and the Profane," in W.C. Beane and W. G. Doty (eds.) *Myths, Rites, Symbols: A Mircea Eliade Reader*, vol. 1, New York: Harper & Row, 1976, p. 155. On sanctification, *see generally*, J. Scott and P. Simpson-Housley, *Sacred Places and Profane Spaces: Essays on the Geographics of Judaism, Christianity, and Islam*, New York: Greenwood Press, 1991.
12 *See*, however, R.M. Hayden, "Antagonist Tolerance: Competitive Sharing of Religious Sites in South Asia and the Balkans," 2002, *Current Anthropology*, 205. (Hayden explores the cultural and political factors that motivate the control of competitively shared holy sites, suggesting that competitive sharing is akin to the passive meaning of tolerance—i.e., non-interference with religious activities, as opposed to active tolerance where competing religious groups embrace and accept the other.)
13 *Compare* Reiter, Chapter 8, *with* Hassner, Chapter 7, both in this volume.
14 Emile Durkheim, *The Elementary Forms of the Religious Life*, trans. K. Fields, New York: The Free Press, 1995, p. 312.
15 *Ibid.*, pp. 208–31.
16 *See* D.M. Hayes, *Body and Sacred Place in Medieval Europe, 1100–1389*, New York: Routledge, 2003, p. xxi.
17 Eliade, "The Sacred and the Profane," n. 11, pp. 155–56.
18 C. C. Park, *Sacred Worlds: An Introduction to Geography and Religion*, London, Routledge, 1994, p. 245.
19 H.W. Turner, *From Temple to Meeting House: The Phenomenology and Theology of Places of Worship*, The Hague, Mouton, 1979.
20 G.A. Wiegers, "Holy Cities in the Perspective of Recent Theoretical Discussions in the Science of Religions," in Alain Le Boulluec (ed.) *A la recherche des villes saintes: actes du Colloque franco-néerlandais "Les villes saintes," Collège de France, 10 et 11 mai 2001: colloque honoré d'une subvention du Ministére de la rechérche,* Turnhout, Brepols, 2004, p. 6.
21 D. Chidester and E.T. Linenthal (eds.) *American Sacred Space*, Bloomington, Ind.: Indiana University. Press, 1995.
22 G. Van der Leeuw, *Religion in Essence and Manifestation*, trans. J.E. Turner, Princeton, N.J.: Princeton University Press, 1986 (first ed. 1933).
23 Chidester and Linenthal, *American Sacred Space*, n. 21, pp. 7–9.
24 Power for Foucault is a transgressive notion that moves beyond a form of assertive relationship between entities. Power is distributed throughout social actions and discourse, creating an inter-linked operation of influences and change between all relating parties. Power then "is everywhere, not because it embraces everything but because it comes from everywhere." M. Foucault, *The History of Sexuality*, New York: Pantheon Books, 1978, p. 93.
25 U. Rubin, *Between Arabia and the Holy Land: A Mecca–Jerusalem Axis of Sanctity,* Jerusalem: Jerusalem Studies in Arabic and Islam, vol. 34, forthcoming 2008.
26 E. Sivan, *Arab Political Myths*, Tel Aviv: Am Oved, 1988 [Hebrew]; Y. Reiter, *From Jerusalem to Mecca and Back: The Islamic Consolidation of Jerusalem, Jerusalem:* The Jerusalem Institute for Israel Studies, 2005 [Hebrew].
27 Chidester and Linenthal, *American Sacred Space*, n. 23, pp. 15–20.
28 This issue is more fully discussed in Hassner, Chapter 8 in this volume.
29 II Samuel 6:1–19.

30 U. Rubin, "The Direction of Prayer in Islam: On the History of a Conflict between Rituals," 6 *Historia* (2000), pp. 5–29 [Hebrew].
31 *See* the discussion in J.K. Hadden, "Toward Desacralizing Secularization Theory," *Social Forces*, Mar. 1987, vol. 65, pp. 587–611; R. Walters and S. Bruce, *Secularization: The Orthodox Model* in Steve Bruce (ed.), *Religion and Modernization: Sociologists and Historians Debate the Secularization Thesis*, London: Oxford University Press, 1992, pp. 8–30: "modernization (itself no simple concept) brings in its wake (and may itself be accelerated by) 'the diminution of the social significance of religion.'"
32 "At least since the Enlightenment, most modern intellectuals have anticipated the death of religion." Rodney Stark and William S. Bainbridge, *The Future of Religion*, Berkeley and Los Angeles, Calif.: University of California Press, 1985, p. 1.
33 Tsimhoni in Chapter 11 of this volume typifies this problem.
34 H. Ben Israel, "Hallowed Land in the Theory and Practice of Modern Nationalism," in B.Z. Kedar and R.J. Zvi Werblowsky (eds) *Sacred Space: Shrine, City and Land*, Macmillan and the Israel Academy of Sciences and Humanities 1998, p. 278.
35 This device was employed during the pre-modern era as well. Sindawi, in Chapter 14 of this volume, makes use of such examples.
36 Ben Israel, "Hallowed Land in the Theory and Practice of Modern Nationalism", n. 34, pp. 283, 291.
37 *See* the discussion in the introduction to: Y. Reiter (ed.) *Sovereignty of God and Man: Sanctity and Political Centrality on the Temple Mount*, Jerusalem: Jerusalem Institute for Israel Studies 2001 [Hebrew]. *See also* Bar, Chapter 4 of this volume, for a discussion of Israeli use of symbols in this regard.
38 Bar, in Chapter 4 of this volume, demonstrates this point.
39 *See* U.M. Kupferschmidt, *The Supreme Muslim Council: Islam under the British Mandate for Palestine*, The Hague: E.J. Brill, 1987, pp. 129–39.
40 *See* Y. Reiter, *Jerusalem and Its Role in Islamic Solidarity*, New York: Palgrave Macmillan, 2008, pp. 93–95.
41 *See* "Palestinians and Israelis In a Clash at Holy Sites," *New York Times*, 28 Sept. 2000, at A6; Joel Greenberg, "Unapologetic: Sharon Rejects Blame for Igniting Violence," *New York Times*, 5 Oct. 2000, A10.
42 *See* "Salah Calls for Fund to 'Liberate' Al-Aksa Mosque, [sic]" *Jerusalem Post*, 19 Aug. 2007, 2007 WLNR 16169024. In addition, Sheikh Raed Salah has held twelve annual "Aksa in danger" [sic] conventions in Umm el-Fahm. *See* "Raed Salah Promises Israel Will 'Disappear,'" *Jerusalem Post*, 9 Sept. 2007, 2007 WLNR 17731062.
43 *See* Reiter, *From Jerusalem to Mecca and Back*, n. 26.
44 *See* Khamaisi, Chapter 7 of this volume, who attests to the political forces at work and Tsimhoni Chapter 11 of this volume, who describes the emotional intensity and the historical sources from which it is drawn.
45 *See* D. Williams, "Masada—Symbol of Resistance or Overblown Myth?" *Jewish News Weekly of Northern California*, Online. Available: http://www.jewishsf.com/content/2-0-/module/displaystory/story_id/16528/edition_id/324/format/html/displaystory.html (accessed 27 July 2001). Masada now only hosts the ceremony for the engineering corps. *See also*, A. Shapira, *Israeli Identity in Transition*, New York: Greenwood/ Praeger, 2004, pp.15–16; J. Telushkin, *Jewish Literacy: The Most Important Things To Know About The Jewish Religion, Its People, and Its History*, New York: HarperCollins 1991, p. 140.
46 *See* Bar, Chapter 4 of this volume.
47 In this volume the term "Palestine" refers to the biblical land of Eretz Yisrael, which the Arabs refer to as "Filastin."
48 D. Ross, *The Missing Peace: The Inside Story of the Fight for Middle East Peace*, New York: Farrar, Straus, Giroux, 2004, p. 694 ("Solomon's Temple was not in

Jerusalem, but Nablus. Arafat was challenging the core of Jewish faith, and seeking to deny Israel any claim in the Old City."); M. Klein *The Jerusalem Problem: The Struggle for Permanent Status*, Coral Gables, Fla.: University Press of Florida, 2003, p. 72. The Palestinian position, publicly and officially, was that all of East Jerusalem should to returned to Palestinian sovereignty; the Jewish quarter and Western Wall should be placed under Israeli authority, not Israeli sovereignty; and an open city and cooperation on municipal services should be maintained. The Palestinians rejected a proposal for "custodianship," though not sovereignty, over the Temple Mount, and they demanded complete sovereignty over East Jerusalem's Islamic holy sites, in particular, the Al-Aqsa Mosque. *See also* Reiter, n. 40, p. 38.

49 Bureau of Democracy, Human Rights, and Labor, U.S. Dep't of State, *Israel and the Occupied Territories*, (4 Mar. 2002). Online. Available: http://www.state.gov/g/drl/rls/hrrpt/2007/100597.htm (accessed 2 Sept. 2008).

50 Bureau of Near Eastern Affairs, U.S. Dept of State, *Sharam El-Sheikh Fact-Finding Committee Report* (30 Apr. 2001) http://www.state.gov/p/nea/rls/rpt/3060.htm.

51 *See* United States Institute for Peace, *First Declaration of Alexandria of the Religious Leaders of the Holy Land*, Jan. 2002, Online. Available: http://www.usip.org/religionpeace/alexandria_declaration.html (accessed 2 Sept. 2008).

52 *See e.g.*, M. Wagner, "High Court, Rabbis on Collision Course," *Jerusalem Post*, 31 Aug. 2005; D. Izenberg, "State Insists on Dismantling Gaza Synagogues," *Jerusalem Post*, 8 Sept. 2005, p. 3; M. Wagner, "Rabbis: Jews Don't Destroy Synagogues," *Jerusalem Post*, 12 Sept. 2005, p. 2; M. Wagner and T. Lagoroff, "Government Determined to Raze Gaza Shuls Despite Growing Opposition," *Jerusalem Post*, 4 Sept. 2005. *See also*, "What Will Be the Fate of Gaza Synagogues After the Withdrawal?" 26 Apr. 2005. Online. Available: http://web.israelinsider.com/Articles/AntiSemi/5391.htm (accessed 2 Sept. 2008).

53 Many of the issues surrounding the Temple Mount as well as issues connected to the general issue of "sacred space" are discussed in M. J. Breger and O. Ahimeir (eds) *Jerusalem: A City and Its Future*, New York: Syracuse University Press, 2003.

54 Thus, the Supreme Muslim Council in the 1920s raised funds for repair of the *Haram* from as far as British India and used this international effort to develop support for the Palestinian cause. Kupferschmidt, *The Supreme Muslim Council*, n. 39, p. 129.

55 Reiter, *From Jerusalem to Mecca and Back*, n. 26, Ch. 3.

56 This is one of Khamaisi's key points in Chapter 7 of this volume.

57 *See* Ehud Ya'ari, "The New Canaanites," 7 *Jerusalem Report*, 19 Sept. 1996, p. 320.

58 The tomb of Othniel Ben Knaz near Hebron and the tomb of Avner Ben Ner are two examples.

59 *See* M. Benvenisti, *Sacred Landscape: Buried History of the Holy Land Since 1948*, trans. M. Kaufman-Lacusta, Berkeley, Calif.: University of California Press, 2002 (describing the Israelization of Arab place names, sacred and otherwise). For a controversial argument critiquing Israeli archaeology for its service in "nation-building," *see generally*, N. Abu El-Haj, *Facts on the Ground: Archaeological Practice and Territorial Self-Fashioning in Israeli Society*, Chicago, Ill.: University of Chicago Press, 2002.

60 E. Ashkenazi, "Group Holds Torah Reading at Disputed Har Dov in North," *Haaretz*, 21 Oct. 2007. Some Jewish groups believe that Har Dov/ Shabaa Farms is the location at which God promised Abraham the Land of Israel. In recent years, Hezbollah has claimed Shabaa Farms as Lebanese territory and the return of Shabaa to Lebanese possession is one of the stated justifications of its confrontation with Israel. *See* C.S. Smith, "Lebanon's Three-Sided Postwar Game: Who Gets Shabaa Farms?" *New York Times*, 24 Sept. 2006.

61 Breger and Hammer consider this issue in Chapter 2 of this volume.

62 M. Dumper, *The Politics of Sacred Space: The Old City of Jerusalem in the Middle East Conflict*, Boulder, Col.: Lynne Reinner, 2003, pp. 147–56, 160–61
63 D. Long, *The Hajj and Its Impact on Saudi Arabia and the Muslim World*, Saudi–US Relations Information Service, 16 Dec. 2007. Online: Available: http://www.saudi-us-relations.org/articles/2007/ioi/071216-long-hajj.html (accessed 30 Nov. 2008).
64 L.G.A. Cust, *The Status Quo in the Holy Places*, reprint of 1929 ed., Ariel Pub. House, 1980; M. Eordegian, "British and Israeli Maintenance of the Status Quo in the Holy Places of Christendom," *International Journal Middle Eastern Studies*, 2003, vol. 35, pp. 307–28.
65 *See* Fundamental Agreement between the Holy See and the State of Israel, 30 Dec. 1993, Vatican-Israel, 33 *ILM* 153 (1994) [hereinafter Fundamental Agreement] Art.4, para. 1; Leonard Hammer, "Israel's Understanding of the Fundamental Agreement with the Holy See," in Marshall J. Breger (ed.) *The Vatican-Israel Accords*, Notre Dame, Ill.: University of Notre Dame Press, 2004, pp. 78–81.
66 For the international implications of the status of the synagogues given their location in occupied territory. *See e.g.*, Y. Ronen, "The Demolition of Synagogues in the Gaza Strip," *ASIL Insight* of 17 Oct. 2005. Online. Available: http://www.asil.org/insights/2005/10/insights051017.html (accessed 12 Sept. 2008).
67 Convention for the Protection of Cultural Property in the Event of Armed Conflict, 14 May 1954, 249 *U.N.T.S.* 240.
68 *See* Protocol for the Protection of Cultural Property in the Event of Armed Conflict, 14 May 1954, 249 *U.N.T.S.* 358; Second Protocol to the Hague Convention for the Protection of Cultural Property in the Event of Armed Conflict, 26 Mar. 1999, 38 *I.L.M.* 769.
69 The World Heritage Convention List. Online. Available: http://whc.unesco.org/en/list (accessed 2 Sept. 2008).
70 Some of these instruments include the 25 Nov. 1981, UN Declaration on the Elimination of All Forms of Intolerance and of Discrimination Based on Religion or Belief, see 35 *Ybk. United Nations*, New York: United Nations, 1985, pp. 879–83; the 1972 UNESCO Convention on the Protection of World Cultural and Natural Heritage, Doc. No. 17 C/106, 15 Nov. 1972, cited in 11 *ILM* (1973), p.1358), and the 1976 Recommendation Concerning the Safeguarding and Contemporary Role of Historic Areas, 29 Nov. 1976, in UNESCO, *Conventions & Recommendations of UNESCO Concerning the Protection of the Cultural Heritage*, Geneva: UNESCO, 1985, p. 191. *See* Hammer's discussion in Chapter 3 of this volume.
71 Reiter develops this point in Chapter 9 of this volume.
72 J. Seligman and R. Abu Raya, "A Shrine of Three Religions on the Mount of Olives: Tomb of Huldah the Prophetess; Grotto of Saint Pelagia; Tomb of Rabi'a Al-'Adawiyya," *Atiqot Holy Places*, 2001, vol. 42, pp. 221–36.
73 The Elijah's cave "compromise" is discussed in U. Bialer, *Cross the Star of David: The Christian World in Israel's Foreign Policy*, Bloomington, Ind.: Indiana University Press, 2005, pp. 136–37. We should recognize that there have been well-documented examples of the practice of joint Muslim-Jewish veneration of (usually Jewish) saints in the Maghreb, as discussed in L. Voinot, *Pèlerinages judéo-musulmans du Maroc*, Paris: Larousse, 1948, pp. 1–20. Issuchar Ben-Ami has identified at least 126 saints venerated by both Jews and Muslims in Morocco. *See* Isachar Ben-Ami, *Saint Veneration Among the Jews in Morocco*, Detroit, Wisc.: Wayne State University Press 1998, pp. 131 42. Examples exist in the medieval period in the Levant, including the Tomb of the Prophet Ezekiel in al-Kifl, Iraq and the Shrine of Ezra in Basra. *See* J.W. Meri, *The Cult of Saints Among Muslims and Jews in Medieval Syria*, Oxford and New York: Oxford University Press 2003, pp. 231–34. *See also* J. Wilkinson, "Visits to Jewish Tombs by Early Christians," in *Jahrbuch Fur Antike Und Christentum Erganzungsband*,

Munster: Aschendorffsche Verlagsbuchhandlung, 1995, vol. 20, pp. 425–65. *See also* the contributions of Reiter, Yazbak and Hassner, Chapters 9, 12, and 8 in this volume.
74 *See* Chapter 2 in this volume.
75 *See* Chapter 3 in this volume.
76 *See* Chapter 4 in this volume.
77 *See* Chapter 5 in this volume.
78 *See* Chapter 6 in this volume.
79 *See* Chapter 7 in this volume.
80 *See* Chapter 8 in this volume.
81 *See* Chapter 9 in this volume.
82 *See* Chapter 10 in this volume.
83 *See* Chapter 11 in this volume.
84 *See* Chapter 12 in this volume.
85 *See* Chapter 13 in this volume.
86 *See* Chapter 14 in this volume.

2 The legal regulation of holy sites*

Marshall J. Breger and Leonard Hammer

Because the topic of this essay is the legal regulation of holy sites, it will deal only indirectly with issues related to the religious and social aspects of holiness. The essay raises some general definitional questions and focuses specifically on legal structures that define and regulate sacred space in Israel and within the Palestinian Authority (PA).

Some general issues regarding legal protection of holy places

Some countries have laws that specifically protect holy places, focusing on holy cities or regions. Others have laws that protect historical buildings and cultural heritage property including sacred space.

Holy Cities

Mecca and Medina

In some religions, entire cities, not simply the holy places within them, are considered as sacred space. Examples are Mecca and Medina, the holy cities of Islam, located in Saudi Arabia.[1] As protectors of these holy cities, Saudi law encompasses Shari'a requirements which forbid non-Muslims from entering them. Indeed, Saudi statutes specifically forbid non-Muslims from owning property in these cities.[2]

Qum and Mashad

These holy cities – more correctly cities of pilgrimage – are located in Iran. There are no special laws of the Islamic Republic of Iran that apply to them and there are no restrictions for foreigners.

Vatican City

The 1929 Vatican Concordat between the Vatican and the Government of Italy refers to the sacred character of Rome: "In consideration of the sacred character of the Eternal city, Episcopal See of the Sovereign Pontiff, center of the Catholic world, and goal of pilgrimages, the Italian government will take precautions to prevent the occurrence in Rome of everything that might be contrary to this sacred character."[3] Article 2.4 of that treaty now states that the Italian Republic recognizes the "particular significance" that Rome has for Catholicism.[4]

Holy Regions

Mount Athos

An example of a legally denominated holy region is Mount Athos, which while not a holy city may be described as a holy region or peninsula that has been granted special autonomous status in Greece and even in the European Union. Mount Athos is a wooded peninsula in Northern Greece about thirty-five miles long and from two to five miles wide.[5] It is home to more than twenty Orthodox monasteries and more than 1,500 monks.[6] It is under formal Greek sovereignty, but "in accordance with its ancient privileged status," the Greek constitution grants Mount Athos self-government under a "Holy Community," or religious council, which consists of representatives of the 20 monasteries, and an Epistasia, vested with executive power and composed of four members of the "Holy Community."[7] This arrangement is based on a charter drawn up in 1924 by the Athonite community, the political aspects of which the Greek government subsequently ratified, while the Greek Orthodox Patriarchate in Istanbul ratified its "spiritual" aspects.[8]

The autonomous status of Mount Athos was first institutionalized in the Treaty of Berlin (1878),[9] and was reiterated in the Treaty of Sèvres (1920),[10] which acknowledged Greek sovereignty on Mount Athos and asserted the obligation of Greece "to recognize and preserve the traditional rights and liberties enjoyed by the non-Greek monastic communities on Mount Athos." This language was incorporated, as well, into the Treaty of Lausanne (1923), the peace treaty between Turkey and Greece.[11] Further, in the Agreement Providing for the Accession of Greece to the European Community (1979), the European Economic Community agreed that the special status of Mount Athos would be "taken into account in the application and subsequent preparation of provisions of community law, in particular in relation to customs franchise privileges, tax exemptions, and the right of establishment."[12]

Aboriginal/native "holy" regions

Aboriginal and native holy regions as well as Holy Places are protected in a variety of countries including the United States,[13] Canada,[14] New Zealand,[15] Australia,[16] and the Philippines.[17] As an example, the US law protects Native American Holy Places, but this protection is not absolute and must be balanced against public necessity.[18] Thus, specific identifiable Holy Places are considered as sacrosanct under US law whereas holy forests, holy shorelines, or deserts which encompass large swathes of land, are less protected.

Protecting holy sites as historical antiquities

Most legal protection of holy places is not accomplished by specific laws regulating holy places, but by more general laws protecting architectural cultural heritage property. These general laws often protect houses of worship and cemeteries and pilgrimage sites.[19] In Albania for example, buildings older than 100 years are protected.[20] New holy places would also be afforded this protection. In Egypt, a historical commission certifies sites as cultural property important to Egypt's heritage.[21] This includes mosques and churches. Some years ago the commission certified the gravesite of Rabbi Abu Hasira in the village of Demitioh in the Nile Delta province of Beheira that was the site of Jewish pilgrimage as a "historic site." Villagers around the shrine protested, claiming that the Jewish visitors aggravated the locals with their drinking. In response, the Egyptian Administrative Court found that Jewish sites cannot be part of Egypt's heritage.[22] On January 5, 2004, the Supreme Administrative Court upheld the decision to cancel the annual festival for Jewish pilgrims.[23]

American law protecting cemeteries is complex and depends on the law within each individual state. What is striking however is that it is not the existence of graves that creates a cemetery but rather the dedication of the gravesite as a cemetery under state law.[24] One example of this is the Glorieta gravesite in New Mexico. In 1987, a construction crew working on the Siler's family property found a mass grave containing the remains of Confederate soldiers killed in the Battle of Glorieta during the Civil War (March, 1862).[25] The Confederates lost 48 soldiers during the fighting, 31 of whom were buried in the grave on the Siler family land.[26] Because the Confederates buried their soldiers in great haste the day after the battle, there was never a dedication of the site as a graveyard.[27] The Silers informed the Museum of New Mexico of the discovery. They agreed to allow the excavation of the area and signed over the remains to the Museum, but retained the rights to any artifacts found during excavation.[28] The Attorney General of New Mexico advised that the remains could be removed without any state involvement because the property did not have the legal status of a cemetery.[29] Word soon spread that the Confederate soldiers had been located.[30] In response, the Federal Government passed legislation authorizing the acquisition of land to create a national park at the battlefield, including a cemetery for the dead.[31] Unfortunately, the federal solution came too late as most of the Confederate soldiers had already been reinterred in the National Cemetery in Santa Fe, New Mexico.[32]

Of course, whatever the law, politics can intervene. In the early 1990's, gravesites of slaves from the eighteenth century were discovered in New York City during construction of a federal office building.[33] Notwithstanding the legal position, public pressure caused building plans to be modified so as to prevent further construction over the graves.[34]

Palestine archaeology law under the British mandate made a distinction between historical sites that have sacred aspects and sacred sites that are still in use (or "living" sites).[35] The 1929 Antiquities Ordinance distinguished between historical monuments "whether movable or immovable or part of the soil" and "antiquities of religious use or devoted to a religious purpose which are the property of a religious or ecclesiastical body."[36] The effort was to distinguish, in the words of a British Government memorandum, between monuments "that are not of a merely archeological character, but are also ... 'living' monuments, that is to say monuments still in use for religious purposes."[37]

Israel passed its own antiquities act in 1978.[38] The legislation defines an antiquity in Article 1 as an object, either detached or attached, which was made by a person prior to 1700 CE, including anything added to it that constitutes an integral part of it. In the spirit of the times, a change was made in this definition in Article 2, according to which an object made in 1700 CE or thereafter could be an antiquity if it possessed historical value and the Minister of Education had declared it to be an antiquity. There is no written definition of what constitutes "an object of historical value," and thus its definition is left exclusively in the hands of the Minister, who is responsible for the implementation of this law.[39] The Minister acts through the Director of the Department of Antiquities who has authority to declare a particular place an antiquity site.[40]

The classification of holy places

The remainder of this essay will suggest some of the problems of dealing with the regulation of holy places in Israel and Palestine and will address the following points: 1) Is there a specific definition of holy places distinct from churches, religious institutions, and cemeteries? 2) Should the list of holy places be open (i.e. changeable) or closed (i.e. fixed)? 3) What are the criteria for classifying a holy place? 4) How are holy places regulated in Israel and Palestine?

Is there a specific definition of holy places?

The Encyclopedia of Public International Law defines holy places as "geographically determined localities to which one or more religious communities attribute extraordinary religious significance or consider a subject of divine consecration. Holy places may consist of man-made structures (churches, temples, graves, etc.) or natural objects (trees, groves, hills, rivers, etc.)."[41]

Traditionally, the Holy Places in Israel and Palestine were understood as those sites listed in the so-called Ottoman Status Quo, whose goal was to ensure protection for a variety of key Christian sites and lessen tension among the religious populace. In the eighteenth and nineteenth centuries, the Ottoman

Empire issued *firmans* providing Christian denominations with rights over selected holy places. Most important of these were the *firmans* of 1757 and 1852. These *firmans* collectively became known as the Status Quo. They were enshrined in international law through various legal instruments and affirmed by the British in 1923 after they took over the Mandate.[42]

In an effort to better understand the Status Quo, the British Military Administration tasked L.G.A. Cust, a British soldier with a classical education, to compile and classify the elusive Status Quo arrangements as they had evolved over the centuries. In 1929, *The Status Quo and the Holy Places* was published, rapidly becoming the definitive statement of the Status Quo.[43]

It is important to note that the Mandate interpreted holy places in a broader sense than did the 1757 and 1852 Ottoman *firmans*. While the British adhered to the Status Quo, they extended the Status Quo principles to the Western Wall and Rachel's Tomb.[44] Cust, himself, noted the application of regulations tracking the Status Quo beyond the five Christian Status Quo sites to include the Milk Grotto, Shepherds' Field, the Western Wall and Rachel's Tomb.[45] The Status Quo was also affirmed in the 1993 Vatican-Israel Fundamental Agreement which noted:

> "§ 1. The State of Israel affirms its continuing commitment to maintain and respect the "*Status quo*" [sic] in the Christian Holy Places to which it applies and the respective rights of the Christian communities there under. The Holy See affirms the Catholic Church's continuing commitment to respect the aforementioned "*Status quo*" [sic] and the said rights."[46]

We should note, however, that there is no definition of a holy pace in Israeli law. The term is referred to in the 1967 Law for the Protection of Holy Places[47] without explanation.

There have, however, been many informal attempts to identify and list holy places, both for the Jewish population (usually via governmental channels) and for other religions (through non-governmental organizations and religious groups). One also can glean relevant criteria from court opinions and other governmental sources.

Should the list of holy places be open or closed?

There are several approaches to defining which sites and places are considered as holy. Under one approach it is the state which classifies them. The definition of a holy place can be closed – a bounded list of specific holy places, or it can be open – a list that changes according to sociology, politics or religion. Under an open approach, each religion is given the task of defining its holy sites and the state can then accept their definition. The Israeli Law for the Protection of Holy Places reflects all of these approaches in varying degrees.

Professor Ruth Lapidoth has suggested (at least regarding Jerusalem and the West Bank) a closed list amended only by agreement between Israel and the Palestinian Authority.[48] Of course, a closed list could create obvious identification problems given the different approaches and perceptions of sacred space, thereby complicating the issue of achieving any form of agreement between the various political and religious parties involved. It could also forestall any allowance for change or socio-political developments that at times is necessary in high-tension areas.

In contrast, David Guinn urges that a list should be open in the sense that it can change according to religious views and approaches.[49] Guinn has proposed a set of four criteria for designating a place as holy: 1) the historic character (whether its significance dates back to the founding of a religion); 2) the relationship to major religious figures connected with a religious faith; 3) the extent to which a site provides "a home to a living community of believers" serving as a place of cultic practice; and 4) whether the site is "a public space associated with or in proximity to a building or structure."[50] Guinn further offers status classifications based on iconic sites, cultic sites, latent sites, cemeteries, historical and archeological sites and contested sites.[51] In 2003, the Foundation for the Culture of Peace also proposed a similar open-ended list, pursuant to the norms of the common heritage of mankind.[52]

There are specific lists of holy places in the Peace Treaty with Jordan,[53] the various Oslo Accords[54] and the Vatican-Israel Fundamental Agreement.[55] But these lists are certainly not exclusive and do not exhaust the possible holy places in Israel and the Palestinian Authority controlled areas. For example, the Israeli Holy Places Authority lists over 140 sacred places,[56] yet does not include the site known as Har ha-Bayit (the Temple Mount) to Jews or Al-Haram al-Qudsi al-Sharif (the Jerusalem Noble Sanctuary) to Muslims.[57]

In our view, Guinn's classificatory scheme is both over- and under-inclusive. It is over-inclusive by including in the category of "holy" all sites of historical significance, without concern for other indicative factors. Further, Guinn incorporates cemeteries and archeological sites in the holy site category without allowing for varying degrees of importance or reverence.[58] On the other hand, Guinn is under-inclusive in that he fails to include more recently imbued holy sites. For example, the graves in Israel of Rabbi Yisrael Abuhatzeira, known as Baba Sali, or other revered rabbis maintain some form of holiness beyond the mere fact that they are graves. In addition, Guinn's categories and criteria are less analytic and somewhat descriptive. Contested sites, for example, are less a separate analytic category than a description of a historical or sociological reality. There is nothing unique about contested sites other than their contestation. The fact that they are contested does not bear any implications regarding their authenticity or standing as such. Calling a site iconic or cultic does not provide any insight as to how to treat the site in law, regulation, or practice.

Nonetheless, some of Guinn's other classifications have proven useful in practice. History and custom, for example, are central aspects in the determination of a site's holy place stature under Israeli jurisprudence. While Guinn is correct that political and sociological circumstances can affect one's view of holy sites, Lapidoth's concerns ring true from a juridical standpoint. Leaving the definition of holy sites to popular (or even expert) opinion will lead to an increase in the number of holy sites that require special legal attention. Lapidoth has acutely noted that the lack of a general definition or authorized list of holy places has led to an unreasonable increase in their number.[59] The Ottoman Status Quo listed five Christian holy places.[60] Lionel Cust, however, in his exhaustive study of holy places for the Mandate authorities, added two Jewish sites to the Status Quo, namely the Western Wall and Rachel's Tomb, but did not address Islamic sites given the Mandate's policy of noninterference with Muslim institutions.[61] A 1949 UN map enumerated 30 holy places in the Jerusalem area.[62]

A 1950 Israeli inter-ministerial committee, established to study the manner by which the new State of Israel might protect the Holy Places, listed at least 300 holy sites for the Christian, Muslim, and Jewish religions, although this was an expansive list including all places of worship and cemeteries.[63] The ensuing regulations that were issued following the 1967 Holy Places Law included 15 Jewish holy sites.[64] On an informal level, however, the Department for Holy Places deems itself responsible for close to 160 Jewish sites throughout the country. According to a list prepared in 2000 by three authors, an Israeli Jew, an American Christian, and a Palestinian Muslim, there were 326 noted Holy Places.[65] The Islamic organization Al-Aqsa Association for Protection and Maintenance of Islamic Waqf Properties has catalogued hundreds of abandoned and disused Muslim sites throughout the country.[66] There is no "official" list of Christian sites as the Custos of the Holy Land (the Franciscan order charged with custody of holy sites for Catholics) considers a formal list to be inappropriate as it may "close off" additions in the future.

In light of these disparate classifications, one can best understand the identification of holy places, not in terms of a dichotomy, namely "holy" and "unholy," but rather as a continuum.

This theoretical framework recognizes that there are different types (or levels) of sacred spaces—ranging from heritage sites to religious institutions to religious schools to places of worship, to cemeteries, to seminal holy places, and to Status Quo sites. Embracing a continuum of "holiness" recognizes not only the sacredness of sites, but also the fact that public attitudes can influence a site. This model accounts for sites contained in the law, holy sites compiled in both official lists (such as prepared by the Holy Places Authority) and unofficial lists (prepared by relevant religious organizations or NGOs), sites receiving heightened protection (such as those falling under the Order-in-Council – like Mount Tabor) and of course the Status Quo sites. Moreover, a major advantage of envisioning a continuum of holy places is that it actually allows for changes in line with altered perceptions and practice (religious or otherwise), surrounding political and social changes and legal adjustments in a natural and evolving manner. Thus, a heritage site or synagogue could alter its place on the continuum over time, due to a specific event or even as a result of intended political focus.

The status of Mount Zion provides an illustrative example. At the founding of the State of Israel, Mount Zion was the closest site under Israeli sovereignty to the Temple Mount and became a key focus of nationalist and religious activity until 1967.[67] Its place on the so-called continuum before 1967 might have been quite high, given the reverence and focus by the general Israeli populace towards the site, yet now it does not maintain any special or unique status, save the existence of a yeshiva and a holocaust museum founded by holocaust survivors (and even that receives rather scant attention). What Mount Zion demonstrates, however, is that the concept of holiness is ongoing and ever shifting.

Historically, holy places have undergone constant change in status and protection. The important Ottoman *firman*s of 1757 and 1852 that entrenched the Status Quo were meant to freeze the rights of all Christian religious communities in Palestine.[68] Article 62 of the Treaty of Berlin reaffirmed this notion, declaring the "Status Quo of the Holy Places" as inviolable. Since the Status Quo dealt with administration of the Holy Places and not necessarily the principle of free access or the maintenance of public order in these places, the Mandate incorporated other sites into the ambit of the Status Quo, including the Western Wall and Rachel's Tomb, as discussed above. Thus, sites like the Holy Sepulchre or the Western Wall maintain an elevated status given their central religious role.

Beyond the listed Status Quo sites are additional sites that merit specific attention and sensitivity, in some instances going beyond the jurisdiction of the court. Holy places such as the Tomb of the Patriarchs or Mount Tabor are more than mere places of worship, as they also possess seminal religious, historical, and social aspects relevant to the site. Thus while Jethro's Grave is not a Status Quo site, the reverence afforded it by the Druze community merits its protection as an exalted place.[69] Another example, the Cenacle, a key Christian holy site held by Muslims since the 1500s, is not a Status Quo site even though it is recognized as an important holy place.[70]

A third point on the continuum would be places of worship or graves that have no special associations. They acquire some form of sanctity and access, as well as prevention of destruction, simply by virtue of what they are. The level of protection accorded would, however, be geared to preventing desecration as provided by law and not due to the elevated "holy" status.

What are the criteria for classifying a holy place?

The problem of an open or closed list has plagued judicial consideration of holy places. In treating this issue, the Mandate courts decided that calling a site holy does not necessarily make it so. In the 1940 case of *Mudir*, the court noted:

> Although a cemetery may be holy in the sense that it is consecrated ground, or is so regarded by the friends and relations of those buried in

it, we do not think that it is a holy place unless there are special facts to make it so. We infer that an illustration of such 'special facts' is that provided where there exists in relation to a 'site' some fact or facts of special religious and historical importance to one or more of the three predominant faiths.[71]

At the same time, a Mandate era commission of inquiry found that Mount Tabor – a site historically and continually associated with the transfiguration of Christ-was a "unique" sacred site with "universal characteristics" and thus was worthy to be considered as having holy place status even though it was not part of the historical Status Quo.[72]

After the creation of the state in 1948, Israel inherited the Status Quo obligations, but the issue was largely moot as the key Christian and Jewish sites were situated in the Jordanian-occupied sector of Jerusalem and the West Bank. With the conquest of Jerusalem in 1967, Israel came to control the holy sites. Soon after, the Knesset passed the 1967 Protection of Holy Places Law.[73]

The 1967 law codified the Jewish right of access to previously denied holy sites, thus altering the Status Quo.[74] The Knesset attempted to step gingerly in making such changes, noting that the purpose was to emphasize the importance of holy places to all three major religions and to uphold the holiness of the sites by allowing for access and internal administration via the relevant state authorities. While the law does not provide any formal definition of a sacred site, it focuses on aspects of upholding the dignity and sanctity of all holy places, deeming any violation of the law as criminal.

The application of these limiting principles concerning decorum and behavior as derived from the 1967 law is difficult. Consider the case of Nachmanides' Cave (the Cave of the Ramban), where the noted medieval scholar allegedly worshiped when he came to Jerusalem in 1267 and was possibly also buried there as well.[75] Apparently the cave had been used as a cattle shed and then by vagrants and drug users. The cave came to public attention when a group of Jewish settlers in Wadi Joz, led by MK Benny Elon, a leader in the Moledet Party (a radical right-wing party), sought to pray there. The Arab owners thereupon fenced off the area to prevent access. At that point, the Jewish settlers petitioned the Supreme Court to grant them access.

In accordance with the 1924 Order in Council, then Minister of Religion, Yossi Beilin, requested that the government appoint a committee to determine whether in fact the cave was to be considered a holy site.[76] The committee reviewed rabbinical sources that mentioned the cave and testimony that Jews had frequented the cave for prayer and study as evidence of continuity.[77] Despite the fact that the cave was not listed as a holy site in the Ministry of Religion's regulation nor in certain important sources,[78] such as Rabbi Isaac Luria's (the ARI),[79] the committee decided that there were enough historical references to justify deeming the cave a holy site. In doing so, it gave "points" to the importance of the personality involved and accepted the assertion that there had been extended use of the cave through continuous and ongoing visits and prayer.[80]

The committee's decision highlights the problems associated with certifying holy places. There was ample testimony contradicting the assertions of the Jewish groups regarding the cave. Indeed, the very location of the cave was controversial, a host of sources (Jewish and otherwise) referring to different locations for the cave. Besides that, the cave had not really been subject to "continuous" use but only sporadic visits (the Arab owners had held the property in their family for over 100 years and had only witnessed recent interest in the cave). The committee began by treating the cave as equivalent in status to a synagogue, but then elevated its status to that of a Holy Place on par with unique areas protected by the Holy Places Law and its attendant regulations.

How are holy places regulated?

At the commencement of the Mandate the generally accepted idea was that holy places should be regulated through an inter-religious commission. In their first report to the Council of the League of Nations in December of 1923, the British affirmed that they were maintaining the Status Quo pending the appointment of such a commission.[81]

But neither the League of Nations nor the British could work out the composition of such a commission, in large measure owing to disputes between the various Christian denominations as to how the commission would be organized and who would participate. By 1924, however, the British had essentially given up on the idea of a commission.[82] Lacking a commission to resolve disputes over the holy places, the British promulgated an Order-in-Council on July 25, 1924 stating that, "no cause or matter in connection with the Holy Places or religious buildings or sites in Palestine or the rights or claims relating to different religious communities in Palestine shall be heard or determined by any court in Palestine." The Order-in-Council referred all matters regarding the holy places to the High Commissioner, "pending the constitution of a commission charged with jurisdiction over the matters set out in the said Article."[83] The High Commissioner's decisions were final and binding on all parties.[84] In other words, the British came to the conclusion that issues related to the holy places were too controversial for the courts to handle. They were "political" decisions to be made in the political realm. As a result, whenever disputes arose over the holy places, the High Commissioner would constitute an ad-hoc commission of enquiry whenever appropriate.

The Order-in-Council remains part of Israeli law today, except where specific Israeli statutes have been passed which supersede the previous legislation. How does this work? In the 1971 dispute between the Copts and Ethiopians concerning the Monastery Deir-al-Sultan (near the Church of the Holy Sepulchre),[85] the Supreme Court of Israel decided that it lacked jurisdiction over the substantive issues and left the final decision in the hands of the government.[86] In the Coptic case, control over particular chapels and passageways in the Monastery Deir-al-Sultan had changed hands between the parties a number of times throughout the previous two centuries.[87] In 1961, the Jordanian government declared Ethiopian "ownership" of the contested chapels and passageways, but the decision was later suspended, and the status quo restored.[88] Although the Copts maintained ownership and control over the Church, the Ethiopians held daily services in the Chapel of the Four Living Creatures in Deir-al-Sultan.[89] The Copts, however, traversed the central square of Deir-al-Sultan down to the entry of the Church for their solemn Easter processions.[90] Then, in 1970, while the Copts were praying in the main chapel of Church of the Holy Sepulchre, the Ethiopians changed the locks on the doors to the passage of Deir-al-Sultan. This prevented the Copts from using the passage for their procession.[91] While the Supreme Court agreed in principle with the Copts,[92] relying on the 1924 Order-in-Council, it decided to leave the matter to the government which appointed a governmental committee ostensibly for negotiations.[93] The committee's efforts have yet to meet success.[94]

Protecting holy places after 1967

Directly after the conclusion of the Six Day War, Israel passed the Protection of Holy Places Law in 1967. That law states:

1. The Holy Places shall be protected from desecration and any other violation and from anything likely to violate the freedom of access of the members of the different religions to the places sacred to them or their feelings with regard to those places.
2. a. Whosoever desecrates or otherwise violates a Holy Place shall be liable to imprisonment for a term of seven years.
   b. Whosoever does anything likely to violate the freedom of access of the members of the different religions to the places sacred to them or their feelings with regard to those places shall be liable to imprisonment for a term of five years.
3. This law shall add to and derogate from any other law.[95]

The regulation of holy sites in Israel has been a virtual kaleidoscope. The Minister of Religious Affairs was originally charged with the implementation of the 1967 law. After consultation with representatives of the religions concerned, the Ministry was to draft regulations for various sites that the Ministry of Justice must then approve. At the demand of the secular Shinui Party, the Ministry of Religious Affairs was dissolved in early 2004 and its functions distributed among the other ministries and the National Authority for Religious Services located in the Prime Minister's office.[96] But by early January 2008, the political map had changed once again, and in what many saw as a nod to the Shas religious party, the cabinet approved the resurrection of the Ministry of Religious Affairs.[97]

Further, while the 1967 statute declared that holy places were protected, it did not provide a list of the protected sites. The Ministry of Religion was charged with developing such a list. In 1968, the Ministry began the process of drafting regulations regarding holy sites, starting in Meron with the grave of Rabbi Shimon Bar Yochai (one of the most eminent disciples of Rabbi Akiva), attributed by many with the authorship of the *Zohar* ("The Brightness"), the chief work of Jewish mysticism during the Roman period after the destruction of the Second Temple in 70 CE. In 1981, the Ministry promulgated regulations designating the Western Wall and surrounding sites as holy places.[98] Additionally, after 1967, the Organization for Holy Places[99] was created and funded by the Ministry of Religion to care for and tend to Jewish holy sites. In 1988, the Ministry reorganized this body into the Office of Religious Affairs, which in 1989 went on to create a public organization, the Organization for the Development of the Holy Places. The list prepared by the Organization in 1989 is informal and includes any site with a link to a Jewish personality, synagogues, and places of historical significance to the Jewish people. It now lists 162 sites and where necessary tends to their upkeep.[99] Based on this criterion, it would be difficult to "create" a new holy site if the place has not been in continuous use or was not recognized as such.[100]

In 2000, the Ministry of Religion attempted to delineate criteria for designating holy sites, recognizing the potential for abuse by political and nationalist-religious forces. Although the regulations were never promulgated, the draft notes that not all synagogues or graves are automatically deemed holy;[102] there must be specific reference to the site in the rabbinic literature. Furthermore, even with such a reference, the site must be subject to some form of continuous "use," such as for prayer and pilgrimage. The basic policy was to reduce the number of holy sites to places frequented throughout the year owing to the importance of the place or the figure associated with the place. The report notes that it is not meant to belittle other sites and that graves and ancient synagogues demand respect, but that a distinction must be made between such sites and more particular holy sites that speak to the nation as a whole. In short, without so stating, the report proposes a continuum.[103]

Inexplicably the Ministry has never issued – in draft or otherwise – a list of Muslim holy sites. The reasons for failure of the Israelis to develop a list is clearly political. Many Muslim holy sites were treated by the Israeli government as abandoned property after 1948 and were often (legally or otherwise) converted to other purposes. Israeli officials fear that listing Muslim holy sites will open a pandora's box of claims related to decisions under the Abandoned Property Law.[104] In November 2004, Adalah, an NGO operating on behalf of the Arab minority in Israel, filed a petition before the Israel Supreme Court requesting that the Ministry of Interior (the replacement for the disbanded Ministry of Religion) draft regulations concerning Muslim Holy Places.[105] The petition contended that the absence of such regulations is discriminatory to the minority Arab population and a violation of the Basic Law: Human Dignity, of freedom of religion and the concept of equality.[106]

More recently, the Citizens' Accord Forum between Jews and Arabs in Israel has been working with Knesset members to urge the promulgation of regulations to protect a number of important Muslim holy sites.[107] On May 28, 2007, two Knesset members, Rabbi Michael Melchior and Dr. Hana Sawid, sent a letter requesting the Minister for Religious Affairs, Rabbi Y. Cohen, to draft regulations protecting a number of key Muslim holy places.[108] The letter stressed that they had the support of a number of noted rabbis, including the Sephardic Chief Rabbi, Rabbi Shlomo Amar, and that the issue was important given the number of neglected abandoned sites.[109] Later that year, Rabbi Melchior sponsored legislation to establish an authority responsible for preserving Muslim mosques and cemeteries abandoned in the 1948 Arab-Israeli conflict and designating eight million NIS annually to that effort.[110]

Access to holy places and the right of prayer

There have been a number of contentious issues related to the interpretation of the 1967 law and the regulations implementing it. One is the extent to which "freedom of access" in Section 2 relates to an individual's ability to pray at a holy place according to his or her personal prayer ritual. This personal devotion might well conflict with Section 1 of the Act protecting the Holy Places from "desecration" or activities that might upset "feelings. ... [of members of a religion] ... towards such places."

An example of this conflict is the dispute concerning the Women of the Wall (WOW), a feminist group, who in the late 1980s, in contravention of Orthodox Jewish custom (some would say law), engaged in group prayer at the Western Wall plaza (or *Kotel*) in the women's section, reading from the Torah and wearing the traditional prayer garb of *tallit*, *tefillin* and *kippah*. In Orthodox Judaism, only men can form a quorum for prayer (or *minyan*) and wear the traditional prayer garb.

Regulations had been promulgated in 1981 designating the Western Wall plaza (the *Kotel*) as a Holy Place under the 1967 Protection of Holy Places Law and detailing the rules of behavior there. The 1981 regulation also appointed a rabbi in charge of the Wall.[111] However, in 1989, after WOW began to pray publicly at the Western Wall, the Ministry of Religious Affairs amended those regulations to expressly "prohibit the conduct of a religious ceremony which is not according to the custom of the place and which injures the sensitivities of the worshiping public towards the place."[112]

The ensuing controversy concerning the rights of the WOW group to pray at the *Kotel* led to a number of lawsuits (and legislative initiatives) that WOW eventually lost. The women's prayer group was eventually moved to an area next to Robinson's Arch which is adjacent to the Western Wall, albeit not traditionally seen as part of the prayer area.[113] The matter had a rather drawn out history in the Israel Supreme Court. In its first decision, the Supreme Court recognized the right of the Women of the Wall to pray in the women's section of the main *Kotel* plaza; however, the Court could not agree whether such a right applied and requested the Government to take action.[114] Four days later, Haredi political parties introduced several bills to overturn the decision, including a bill that would have made it a criminal offense for women to pray in non-traditional ways at the Western Wall, punishable by up to seven years in prison. Although the bill did not pass, the Israeli Supreme Court reconsidered its earlier decision, as the State claimed that it had provided a place of prayer, albeit one outside the confines of the Western Wall. The Court in this instance called on the Government to appoint a committee to look into the matter and reach a proper solution.[115] The Governmental Committee, following many delays, offered an alternative site for WOW at Robinson's Arch, citing the public danger involved in having the women pray at the Western Wall.[116] In response, the Court held that the Committee essentially ignored the existing right of the women to pray at the Western Wall, noting that the alternative site simply does not possess the same level of importance and significance as the Western Wall. The Court, in a rather divided decision, ordered the Government to find the means for providing prayer capacities at the Western Wall, noting quite clearly that this was a matter beyond the competencies of a court.[117] Following further inaction by the Government, the Court, on April 6, 2003, deferred to the interests of the Government, recognizing its limitations as a court to create and impose policy, holding that Robinson's Arch site should be used as an alternative site within 11 months; if that proved to be unsuccessful, then the Government must allow for prayer at the Western Wall.[118] The Robinson's Arch site was subsequently completed by October, 2003.

The Women of the Wall issue also raised issues as to the meaning of "desecration of a holy place." In the first case,[119] the Supreme Court interpreted desecration as turning something holy into secular, so that, for example, building another mosque on the Temple Mount was not considered a desecration to Judaism since Muslims have always prayed there. Justice Elon, in interpreting a regulation concerning the protection of decorum as "the custom of the place, at the Western Wall," understood the reference to custom "as one pertaining to religious conventions, thus enabling him to give deference to the Chief Rabbi, who had obviously rejected altogether the women's initiative."[120] In this instance, then, the meaning of desecration was left in the hands of the Rabbis controlling the area.[121]

A second issue is the relationship between the right of access and the right to pray. Does the first right encompass the second? In the *Nationalist Circles* case, Justice Simon Agranat attempted to maintain the analytic distinction between the right of access and the right to pray.[122] In his view, the freedom of access promised in the Protection of the Holy Places Law extends only to entry onto the Temple Mount, but does not include the right to pray. Access is based on the above referenced statute which provides that, "[t]he Holy Places shall be protected from desecration and any other violation and from anything likely to violate the freedom of access of the members of the different religions to the places sacred to them or their feelings with regard to those places."[123] Since the 1967 statute does not include prayer, that "right" must be laid down by the executive, not the courts. In the same case, Justice Alfred Witkin advanced an even more gossamer distinction, suggesting that the right of Jews to pray on the Temple Mount is certain, but that does not mean that there exists also a right to request police protection to enforce it.[124]

As Justice Izhak Englard suggested, courts have shifted ideologically from rejecting outright an enforceable right to pray on the Temple Mount to the recognition of an abstract right subject to the needs of public order.[125] Thus, in one recent case, *Gershon Solomon v. Yair Yitzchaki*, the Supreme Court wrote, "The petitioner, like any other person in Israel, enjoys the freedom of conscience, belief, religious observance and practice. This framework provides him with the privilege of gaining access to the Temple Mount for purposes of worship."[126] In principle, then, Jews have the right to pray on the Temple Mount, but it is understood as a limited form of right,[127] especially when weighed against the danger to public security.[128]

According to this view, the law would ensure access contingent upon an executive (i.e., police) decision that permitting access would not cause a breakdown in public order. The question is, of course, what constitutes public order. The courts have generally taken a very deferential view of the term leaving it to the judgment of the police as experts. Thus, public order considerations have included not only exigencies of the moment (for example, the inability to protect worshippers at the time of the request), but also deference to police priorities regarding the deployment of their forces throughout the city.[129] From the perspective of legal doctrine rather than of public policy, in some respects the law is unstable. Can one say fairly that there is a right to pray if one is never allowed to effectuate it? Can one have the right to pray "in one's heart" (i.e. to oneself) but make no visible intimation of praying? Apparently so. The Minister of Internal Security recently opined that one can pray on the Temple Mount as long as one does so silently, moving neither the lips nor the body.[130] One must wonder if this legal position can be sustained.

Regulation of holy places in the West Bank and Gaza

The regulation of sacred space in the West Bank and Gaza is a complex issue. There are a number of international instruments and bilateral agreements that apply.[131] The relevant international agreements include the Hague Convention of 1954,[132] the UNESCO World Heritage Convention,[133] and the International Covenant on Civil and Political Rights (ICCPR).[134] Israel also has bilateral agreements with both the PA and Jordan.

As regards Israel and the PA, the Oslo Accords gave the PA full control of Area A (circa 3 per cent of the land area). In Area B, control of around 25 per cent of the land area is shared with Israel while Area C (circa 70 per cent of the area) is under full Israeli control.[135] The Agreement on the Gaza Strip and the Jericho Area of May 4, 1994, provides that the "Palestinian Authority shall ensure free access to all holy sites in the Gaza Strip and the Jericho Area."[136] The Israeli Palestinian Interim Agreement, signed on the White House lawn on September 28, 1995, deals with the status of two *specific* places holy to Jews, Joseph's Tomb in Nablus and a synagogue in Jericho.[137] Article 32 of Appendix I in Annex III of that Agreement calls for both sides to respect relevant holy sites, provide protection, free access and worship, and proper coordination to allow for pilgrimage.[138] While the Oslo Accords are still formally in place, the political situation in the West Bank has left their applicability uncertain. In any event, there has never been much evidence of Palestinian adherence to those clauses.

As regards Israel and Jordan, the Jordan-Israel Peace Treaty of October 26, 1994 requires that "Each party will provide freedom of access to places of religious and historical significance." The Treaty further notes that:

> In this regard, in accordance with the Washington Declaration, Israel respects the present special role of the Hashemite Kingdom of Jordan in Muslim holy shrines in Jerusalem.
> When negotiations on permanent status will take place, Israel will give high priority to the Jordanian historic role in these shrines.[139]

The body of domestic law governing Palestinians in the occupied territories is, formally at least, a complex quilt of pre-1967 Jordanian law, Israeli military orders, and rules and regulations laid down by the Palestinian Authority.[140] Throughout the West Bank, the Israeli military administration applies pre-1967 Jordanian law unless superseded by Israeli military regulations.[141] In terms of regulating archeology, Jordanian Temporary Law no. 51 on Antiquities 1966 governs.[142] The situation of Gaza is more complicated. While at present Hamas is in *de facto* control, *de jure* Palestinian law applies.[143] In Gaza, this means that the British Mandate Antiquities Ordinance of Antiquities of 1929 is operative.[144]

In regulating holy places, the Israeli military promulgated a specific directive[145] that essentially mirrors that of the relevant Israeli law.[146] Thus, the military will not automatically recognize a site as holy simply because it is a place of prayer. Designating a holy site[147] requires proof by an authorized body (such as a military officer for religious affairs) concerning the holiness of that site.[148] Nonetheless, it is clear that there has been a proliferation of holy sites in the West Bank and that the military gives significant credence to settlers' claims in that regard.

The Jordanian Antiquities Law of 1966[149] was adopted by the PA with only a single technical change – the designation "Director" (of the Department of Antiquities) was replaced by the term 'Staff Officer for Archaeology in Judea and Samaria.'[150] The Jordanian law defined antiquities as objects or buildings that date from 1700 or before.[151] Antiquities are deemed to be owned by the state and are heavily regulated by the government, especially with regard to sales and inspection of sites by the government.[152] In 1986 two Antiquities law decrees were promulgated (Nos. 1166 and 1167) by the Israeli authorities. While they largely kept the Jordanian Law of 1966 intact, the result of these regulations was to allow the Staff Officer to conduct excavations throughout the West Bank without oversight by "anyone in the Civil Administration or in the Israeli Government."[153]

One should also note that the 1924 Order-in-Council remains in force in the West Bank and Gaza. It is on that basis that Yasser Arafat, in July 1997, ordered the eviction of a group of clerics from a church in Hebron, located at the Oak of Mamre.[154] The church had been controlled by the Russian Orthodox Church Abroad (the so called "White" Church) and for political reasons, the PA presented the church building to representatives of the Moscow patriarch (the so-called "Red" Church),[155] notwithstanding that Jordan had recognized 'White' Russian property rights. In 2002, the PA, on Arafat's orders, evicted White Russian nuns from a monastery in Jericho to hand it over to the "Red" Church.[156] In June 2008, the PA transferred three lots in Jericho to the 'Red' Russian Church on the occasion of a visit by Abu Mazen to Moscow.[157]

Access to holy places in the West Bank and East Jerusalem

Contrary to Israeli claims that access to Christian holy sites is assured without impediment, the Christian population argues that if there is free access, it is only for tourists, not for Christian residents of Israel and the West Bank. Due to the security fence, residents of Jerusalem cannot travel to Bethlehem easily to pray (if at all). And residents of Bethlehem cannot go without permits to the Church of the Holy Sepulchre in East Jerusalem. The Israeli response is that this is all the result of security considerations, which are a legitimate concern. Still, Palestinians find that statements about free access are largely irrelevant if security concerns prevent them from ever visiting their holy places.

Two of the most well-known Jewish sites in the West Bank have engendered radically different experiences with the Muslim population.[158] Administration of the Tomb of the Patriarchs (or Cave of Machpelah) in Hebron has been particularly problematic, causing violent disputes between the Muslim and Jewish worshippers.[159] The Cave is divided into different sections forming a mosque in one area and a synagogue in another. (Here we cannot forget the 1994 massacre of 29 Muslims carried out by Dr. Baruch Goldstein.) The Cave is under the control of the Military Administration.[160] In contrast, the Tomb of Samuel, north of Jerusalem, is under the Civil Administration. Even though it also includes a mosque and a synagogue, it has had a relatively successful (or at least nearly livable) relationship between Muslim and Jewish religious attendees.[161]

Other holy places have been rife with conflict. Joseph's Tomb in Nablus was burnt to the ground during the Second Intifada on 7 October, 2000. Now under Israeli military control, it is generally off limits to Jews.[162] However, Bratslav Chasidim often evade Israeli troops and pray there.[163] Rachel's Tomb, located in Bethlehem, has become a symbol for Jewish settlers and has been transformed into a shrine-fortress for Jewish worshippers, notwithstanding that before 1967 both Muslims and Jews prayed there.[164] In 2002, after fire bombings and gunfire resumed at Rachel's Tomb, the Israeli cabinet decided to include the site, by then fortified with barbed wire and concrete structures, within the boundaries of a security zone to be constructed around Jerusalem.

While not specifically holy places, the treatment of archeological sites in the West Bank and particularly East Jerusalem (many of which have religious significance) has been a source of continuous controversy. An example is the dispute over Silwan in East Jerusalem, "considered by Jews to be the site of the City of David, where King David established his capital."[165]

In the spring of 2008, however, a group of senior Israeli and Palestinian archeologists developed an "Israeli-Palestinian Cultural Heritage Agreement" to address this and other cultural heritage issues. In its discussion of "immobile heritage," the Agreement stated that each party will be obliged to treat equally all archeological sites in its territory "regardless of their ethnic, national or cultural affiliation."[166] It further requires the creation of a "Heritage Zone" to include the Old City and additional sites, and specifies that "archeological sites in the zone would be accessible to anyone, and any research would have to be done with full transparency."[167]

Conclusion

The challenge of ascertaining the status of holy places is more than a theoretical one. The dispute over the fate of the Gaza synagogues during the unilateral disengagement of 2005 makes that clear, particularly in light of the controversy surrounding the treatment to be accorded the synagogues and the rallying cry to preserve them. As shown above, there have been various definitions of a holy place put forward in recent years. Whatever one thinks of the debate over definitions, what is indisputable is that the number of holy places in Israel and Palestine is steadily increasing.

Israeli law needs to make clear distinctions between holy places and other places of sacred activity, such as churches, cemeteries and schools. Whether there is the political will in the Knesset or the Courts to clarify and enforce these distinctions remains to be seen.

Israelis need as well to address the failure to develop any mechanisms – even at this late date – to regularize the protection of Muslim holy places. Whatever excuses were made in the early years of the state no longer exist. It is not sufficient to argue that the Palestinians are using this problem for political purposes. Israel's obligation to work to provide free access exists whether or not Arab Israeli political movements are seeking to turn this into a nationalist political issue.

At the same time attention should be paid to the administrative mechanisms established to regulate holy places. The desire for state regulation will always be in tension with the desire for internal autonomy of the custodians of the holy places who seek to fulfill their responsibilities free from state control. More work is required in providing the proper balance.

Finally, Israel must not allow the mantra of security to keep Palestinians from visiting their Christian and Muslim holy places. Innovative solutions including pre-screening group visits seem possible.[168] Like so many other solutions related to the problem of the West Bank holy places, this is a question of will and of priorities.

In summary, the challenge of the holy places is to disentangle questions of access and protection from politics. This can only be done if there is recognition of the value and imperative of religious freedom as an autonomous value, one that should be sustained whatever the political costs, however conceived. Internalizing such an approach could go a long way to change the underlying dynamics of the Arab-Israeli conflict.

Notes

* Research for this essay was supported by grants from the Royal Norwegian Ministry of Foreign Affairs and the United States Institute for Peace. Note that the terms holy places and holy site are used interchangeably.

1 For a probing discussion of the Holy City as a typology with special reference to Mecca, *see* Francis E. Peters, *Jerusalem and Mecca: The Typology of the Holy City in the Middle East*, New York: New York University Press, 1986, pp. 6–8. Peters discusses a process of anthropomorphosis, by which God is made to dwell beside His worshippers in cities and houses. For Muslims, God dwells in a simple structure in Mecca, the Ka'ba, or "House of the Lord." *Ibid.*, p. 6. Peters surmises that nomadic followers of Islam once carried with them the "black rock" that was to become the stone of Mecca: "[I]t was only when its devotees had begun to become sedentary at Mecca that it was housed there in Ka'ba." *Ibid.* Similarly, the Bible chronicles the journeying Israelites, carrying the Ark of the Covenant, and temporarily housing the Ark in tents throughout their journey through the Sinai. The God of Israel, however, also came to dwell among his worshipers in the Temple, or for Muslims *Bayt Allah*: "Both the Temple Scroll and the biblical books that preceded it are redolent with images of the city, to the point indeed that if the *Bayt Allah*, the House of the Lord, shared its sanctity with the city, the city gave shape and form and intelligibility to the Temple." *Ibid.* at pp. 7–8.

2 Non-Muslims may not enter Mecca and Medina because of the "special religious significance" of the cities. Royal Embassy of Saudi Arabia, Washington, D.C., "Traveler's Information" (2003). Online. Available: http://www.saudiembassy.net/Travel/Travel.asp (accessed 25 Aug., 2008). Regulation of Ownership and Investment in Real Estate by Non-Saudis, Art. 5, Royal Decree No. M/15, 17/4/1421H (19 July, 2000). However, a law passed in 2000 allows foreigners to buy real estate in other parts of Saudi Arabia. Saudi Arabian General Investment Authority, Real Estate Law (2004). Online. Available http://www.sagia.gov.sa/english/index.php?page=relevant-laws (accessed 4 Sept., 2008).

3 The Concordat between the Holy See and Italy, 11 Feb., 1929, Art. 1, *repr. in* Hyginus Eugene Cardinale, *The Holy See and the International Order*, Great Britain: The Macmillan Company of Canada, 1976, p. 329. Note however that the effect of this article was open to interpretation. *See* D.A. Binchy, *Church and State in Fascist Italy*, London: Oxford University Press, 1941 (hereinafter Binchy) p. 365. In his address to the Chamber of Deputies Mussolini declared:

... the Italian Government shall impede in Rome anything disrespectful to that [sacred] character. But this does not mean that Rome, which has always been and must still be the mother and the standard-bearer of civilization, is to remain closed to the currents of new ideas and to the acquisition of modern thought. All that is intended and all that is necessary is to defend Rome's devout, sacred character, spreading out from the Catacombs to her four hundred churches, against those utterances and manifestations which lack the serene composure of thought and the reverent consciousness of the solemnity of the place.

Message of His Excellency the Honorable Benito Mussolini, Prime Minister, to the Chamber of Deputies, (30 April, 1929), *repr. in* National Catholic Welfare Conference, *Treaty and Concordat between the Holy See and Italy: Official Documents*, Baltimore, Md.: The Belvedere Press, Inc., 1929, p. 30. Mussolini assured worried Protestants that their churches would remain open and Roman inhabitants that recreational opportunities in the city would remain. Binchy, p. 366.

An example of the legal significance of this clause protecting "sacred character," is the 1965 play "The Deputy." The play, written by Rolf Hochhuth, was a savage criticism of the role of the Church and Pope Pius IX in World War II and was therefore banned in Rome as sacrilegious under the sacred character clause. M. E. de Francisis, *Italy and the Vatican: The 1984 Concordat Between Church and State*, New York: Peter Lang, 1989 (hereinafter de Francisis), p. 56. The state had allowed the performance of sexually suggestive plays and movies over the objections of the Church. Binchy, p. 367. "The Deputy" was notably different because of its political content. Thus prosecutions that could be brought in Rome owing to the sacred character of the city would not be brought, for example, in Milan. The provision detailing Rome's sacredness was amended and given more limited scope in the 1984 Concordat. de Francisis, p. 146.

4 Concordat between the Holy See and Italy, Art 2.4, 18 Feb., 1984, *repr. in* de Francisis, *supra* note 3, p. 226.
5 Mt. Athos, unlike Israel, was never a sovereign state. It was part of the *territorium* first of the Byzantine and then of the Ottoman Empire, Charalambos K. Papastathis, "The Status of Mount Athos in Helenic Public Law," in Anthony-Emil N. Tachraos (ed.) *Mount Athos and the European Community*, Thessalonika: Institute for Balkan Studies, 1993 (hereinafter Papastathis), p. 56.
6 *See* John Julius Norwich and Rersby Sitwell, *Mount Athos*, New York: Harper and Row, 1966 (hereinafter Norwich and Sitwell). *See also*, Philip Sherrard, *Athos: The Holy Mountain*, Woodstock, N.Y.: Overlook Press, 1982.
7 Article 105 of The Greek Constitution of 1975 is most easily accessible as an appendix in Charalambos K. Papastathis, 'The Hellenic Republic and the Prevailing Religion,' *Brigham Young University Law Review* 815, 1996, p. 851 . *See also* Norwich and Sitwell *supra* note 6, pp. 87–9.
8 These institutional arrangements are described in Philip Sherrard, *Athos: the Mountain of Silence*, London: Oxford University Press, 1960, pp. 22–26.
9 Papastathis, *supra* note 5, pp. 55–75. *See* Treaty of Berlin, Art. 62, *repr. in*, F.L. Israel, *Major Peace Treaties of Modern History 1648–1967*, New York: Chelsea House, 1967, p. 975.
10 The Treaty of Sèvres specifically made reference to the Treaty of Berlin's protection of the rights and liberties of the monastic communities in Article 13. *See* Treaty of Sèvres, Art. 13, 1920 *United Kingdom of Great Britain Treaty Series* (UKTS) No. 11 (Cmd. 961), in 15 *American Journal of International Law*, pp. 179–295. In 1923 the Treaty of Sèvres was superseded by the Treaty of Lausanne. *Encyclopædia Britannica*, 11th edn, 1911, s.v. "Treaty of Sèvres."

11 Treaty with Turkey and other Instruments Signed at Lausanne, Art. 16, 24 July, 1928 *UNTS* 12, in *American Journal of International Law,* 18 Supp., pp. 1–115.
12 *Official Journal of the European Community*, L 291, vol. 22, 19 Nov., 1979, p. 186.
13 25 USC §§ 3001–13 (2000). The Native American Graves and Reparations Act (NAGPRA) was the result of extensive lobbying of many years. Ryan M. Seidemann, "Bones of Contention: A Comparative Examination of Law Governing Human Remains from Archaeological Contexts in Formerly Colonial Countries," 64 *Louisianan. Law Review* 545–46 2004 (hereinafter Seidemann).
14 Constitution Act 1982, RSC (1985), App. II, No. 44, Sched. B, Pt. II, s. 35(1). The Act defines "aboriginal people" to include "the Indian, Inuit, and Métis peoples of Canada." *Ibid.* § 35(2).
15 Historic Places Act 1993. "The purpose of this Act is to promote the identification, protection, preservation, and conservation of the historical and cultural heritage of New Zealand." *Ibid.* § 4.
16 Heritage Protection Act 1984 § 4 (intending "preservation and protection from injury or desecration of areas and objects in Australia and in Australian waters, being areas and objects that are of particular significance to Aboriginals in accordance with Aboriginal tradition.").
17 Philippine Constitution (1987) Art. XIV, sec. 16 ("All the country's artistic and historic wealth contributes to the cultural treasure of the nation and shall be under the protection of the state which may regulate its disposition.").
18 *See* Seidemann, *supra* note 13. Other statutes that bear on the position of Native American holy places are the Antiquities Act, 16 U.S.C. § 431–33, the Archeological Resources Protection Act, 16 U.S.C. § 470aa-mm, the National Historic Protection Act, 16 U.S.C. § 470a(d)(6)(A), and the American Indian Religious Freedom Act, 42 U.S.C. § 1996.
19 *See e.g.*, Marilyn Phelan, "A Synopsis of the Laws Protecting Our Cultural Heritage", 28 *New England Law Review*, 63, 1993, pp. 67–78.
20 *See* The People's Assembly for the Republic of Albania, "For the Cultural Heritage," Nr. 9048, 07.04.2003. Online. Available http://www.unesco.org-al_forcultheritage2003_engtof.pdf (accessed 21 Nov., 2008).
21 *See* Egyptian Law on the Protection of Antiquities No. 117 (1983). Online. Available: http://www.unesco.org/culture/natlaws/index (accessed 21 Nov. 2008); *see also, United States v. Schultz*, 178 F. Supp. 2d 445, 446 (2002) *aff'd* 333 F. 3d 393 (2d Cir. 2003) (using the Egyptian law as the basis for a federal smuggling indictment).
22 The Egyptian State Information Service, "Court Bans Controversial Jewish Festival," 9 Sept., 2001; *see* Court Rules that Rabbi's Tomb Not Sacred Shrine, *Al-Wafd*, 6 Jan., 2004, *repr. in* BBC Monitoring Middle East, 2004 WL 63908827 (10 Jan., 2004) ("Jews lived in Egypt 250 years and worked as shepherds at a time when Egypt had the greatest civilization on earth [sic] and that whatever the Jews left behind in this country should not be considered ancient monuments because the time they spent in Egypt was not sufficient to establish a new culture."). *See also*, N. El-Aref, "Culture Back in Court: The Culture of Ministry is Appealing a Court Decision to Remove from Egypt's List of Protected Monuments the Tomb of a Man Revered by Jews as Holy," *Al-Ahram Weekly*, no. 551, 13–19 Sept., 2001. Online. Available: http://weekly.ahram.org.eg/2001/551/eg5.htm (accessed 19 May, 2008).
23 *See* Egyptian MPs: Stop Israeli Pilgrimages, *Jerusalem Post*, Online. Available: http://www.jpost.com/servlet/Satellite?cid=1228728140237andpagename=JPost%2FJPArticle%2 (accessed 10 Dec., 2008). Despite the ruling, the government does not seem to have implemented that decision. *See* US Dept. of State, *Egypt, International Religious Freedom Report*, 2007, (stating that despite the ruling, Jewish pilgrims have celebrated the Abu Hasira festival since 2005).

24 *See e.g., Wana the Bear v. Com. Constr., Inc.*, 180 Cal. Rptr. 423, 426 n. 7 (Cal. Ct. App. 1982) (describing the dedication requirement of a cemetery in order to obtain legal status).
25 C. Mitchell, *The Second Battle of Glorieta*. Online. Available: http://www.nmcultu renet.org/heritage/civil_war/essays/4.html (accessed 6 Oct., 2008) (hereinafter Mitchell). The Siler family had owned the land since 1926. *Ibid*. The Battle of Glorieta was considered a "key battle" of the American Civil War because it ended the Confederate advance in the far west. R.B. Cunningham, *Archeology, Relics, and the Law* 2nd ed, Durham, N.C.: Carolina Academic Press, 2005 p. 561 (hereinafter Cunningham).
26 *The Handbook of Texas Online, Battle of Glorieta*. Online. Available: http://www.tshaonline.org/handbook/online/articles/GG/qfg2.html (last accessed 25 Aug., 2008).
27 *Ibid*. In contrast to other cemeteries at Civil War battlefields, most notably Gettysburg where President Lincoln himself dedicated the cemetery in his Gettysburg Address. *See* Mitchell, *supra* note 25; *see also,* New Mexico Att'y Gen'l Op. No.87-31, available at 1987 WL 27033087.
28 Mitchell, *supra* note 25.
29 Cunningham, *supra* note 25, p. 560.
30 Mitchell, *supra* note 25. Historians had been searching for the Confederate dead for 100 years prior to Siler's discovery. *Ibid.*
31 16 U.S.C. § 41 (2000).
32 Cunningham, *supra* note 25, p. 573. One of the identified soldiers was buried in his family cemetery in Kentucky. *Ibid.*
33 *See* David W. Dunlap, "African Burial Ground Made Historic Site," New York Times, 26 Feb., 1993, p. B1.
34 *See ibid.* p. B3. For current information regarding the site, *see* "African Burial Ground: Return to the Past to Build the Future" Online. Available: http://www.africanburialground.gov (accessed 25 Aug. 2008). *See also* Cunningham, *supra* note 25, pp. 669–78, reprinting an article with extensive background information on the case and discussing how the case changed the field of African-American archeology.
35 Antiquities Ordinance 1929, 1 *Laws of Palestine* 28.
36 *Ibid.*
37 *See* Naidha Abu El-Haj Producing (Arti) Facts: Archeology and Power During the British Mandate of Palestine, 7 *Israel Studies* 33, 2002, p. 41.
38 Art.29(iii), 885 *Sefer Chukim* 76, 1978 (in Hebrew).
39 *See e.g.*, M. Benvenisti, *Sacred Landscape: The Buried History of the Holy Land Since 1948*, Berkeley and Los Angeles, Calif.: University of California Press, 2000, p. 19. *See also* S. Berman, *Antiquities in Israel in a Maze of Controversy*, 19 *Case Western Reserve Journal of International Law* 343, 1987, pp. 346–47.
40 1978 Antiquity Law at § 49(b). *See also* Benvenisti, *supra* note 39, p. 346.
41 Christian Rumpf, "Holy Places" in R. Bernhardt (ed.), *Encyclopedia of Public International Law*, vol. 2, 1995, pp. 863–66.
42 For the intricacies of the Status Quo, *see e.g.* M. Eordegian, "British and Israeli Maintenance of the Status Quo in the Holy Places of Christendom," 35 *International Journal of Middle East Studies*, 2003, 307 (hereinafter Eordegian); P. Berger, "The Internationalization of Jerusalem," 10 *Jurist* 357, 1950, pp. 362–68.
43 *See generally*, L.G.A. Cust, *The Status Quo in the Holy Places*, London: HMSO, 1929, reprinted as facsimile edition by Ariel, Jerusalem 1980 (hereinafter Cust).
44 Eordegian *supra* note 42, p. 311.
45 Cust, *supra* note 43.
46 Fundamental Agreement between the Holy See and the State of Israel, 30 Dec., 1993, Vatican-Israel, *ILM*, 1994, vol. 33, p. 153 (hereinafter Fundamental

Agreement). It was also reaffirmed in the Basic Agreement between the Holy See and the Palestine Liberation Organization on 15 Feb., 2000, Art. 4.
47 Protection of Holy Places Law 1967, trans. in R. Lapidoth and M. Hirsch, *The Jerusalem Question and Its Resolution: Selected Documents,* Dordrecht, Boston, London: Kluwer, 1994, p.169.
48 *See* R. Lapidoth, "Freedom of Religion and Conscience in Israel," in M. Breger, ed. *The Vatican-Israel Accords: Political, Legal, and Theological Contexts,* Indiana: Notre Dame Publishing, 2003, p. 249 (hereinafter Lapidoth).
49 D.E. Guinn, *Protecting Jerusalem's Holy Sites: A Strategy for Negotiating Sacred Peace,* Cambridge: Cambridge University Press, 2006 (hereinafter Guinn) pp. 123–27.
50 *Ibid.* pp. 131–33.
51 *Ibid.* pp. 133–41.
52 *Holy Places – Common Heritage of Mankind,* 27 Sept., 2003, Foundation for the Culture of Peace Madrid, Spain, at Annex III, para's. 1–3 (on file with authors).
53 Treaty of Peace between Israel and the Hashemite Kingdom of Jordan, 26 Oct., 1994 Online. Available http://www.mfa.gov.il/mfa (accessed 4 Sept., 2008).
54 Israeli-Palestinian Interim Agreement on the West Bank and Gaza Strip, Annex III, Schedule 4.
55 *See* Fundamental Agreement, *supra* note 46.
56 Official list compiled by the Holy Sites Authority as of 12 April, 2003 (on file with authors).
57 *But see,* 3338/99 *Pakovich v. State of Israel* 54 (3) *Piskei Din* 667 (2000) (in Hebrew) where the Israeli High Court found that it was obvious that the Temple Mount was a holy place, even if not listed as such.
58 Guinn, *supra* note 50, pp. 138–40.
59 *See* Lapidoth, *supra* note 48, p. 255.
60 Cust, *supra* note 43.
61 *Ibid.*
62 "Central Portion of the Jerusalem Area: Principle of Holy Places," *United Nations Map,* no. 229 (Nov. 1949); *See also,* Elihu Lauterpacht, *Jerusalem and the Holy Places,* London, The Anglo-Israel Assoc'n, 1968, p. 5, n. 1.
63 Israeli Archives 2397/3 – Holy Places, 25/5/50. The list was compiled to determine the viability of certain structures that had been abandoned and the financial possibilities for protecting the sites. The authorities closed many churches and mosques due to problems of decay or abandonment, with the remainder receiving some form of protection or having posted guards.
64 The first regulations drafted in 1968 related to the manner of decorum to be imposed at the gravesite of Rabbi Shimon bar Yochai in Meron, *Kovetz Takanot* 2182, from 9/2/68, p. 828, followed in 1969 by additional sites where the rules of decorum were to apply – Cave of Simon the Just and the Small Sanhedrin in Jerusalem, Graves of Rabbi Ovadiah of Bartenura, Zechariah the Prophet and Absalom in Jerusalem, the Cave of Elijah in Haifa, and the Grave of Maimonides, Cave of Rabbi Akiva, Cave of Rabbi Chiya and Sons all in Tiberias, *Kovetz Takanot* 2387, from 8/5/69 (in Hebrew), p. 1438.
Additional regulations with similar directives were passed in 1972 concerning the Western Wall and its plaza area, *Kovetz Takanot* 2803, from 11/1/72 (in Hebrew), p. 609, and in 1981 when the Western Wall was designated a holy area requiring proper decorum, *Kovetz Takanot* 4282, from 21/1/81 (in Hebrew), p. 2197, and the aforementioned sites were listed in *Kovetz Takanot* 4252, from 16/7/81(in Hebrew) p. 1212. Another regulation was passed in 1989 in response to the Women of the Wall case where the Knesset attempted to bypass the legal challenge by issuing a regulation under this law that disallows any form of religious ceremony that deviates from customary practices at the site and insults the public sphere. *See Kovetz Takanot* 5237, from 1989 (in Hebrew), p. 190.

65 *See* Y. Reiter, M. Eordegian and M. Abu Khahuf, "The Holy Places: Introduction" and "Between Divine and Human: The Complexity of Holy Places in Jerusalem," in M. Maoz and S. Nusseibeh (eds) *Jerusalem: Points of Friction – and Beyond*, Leiden: Brill Academic Publishing, 2000, pp. 95–97, 109–10. They use two criteria to develop a definition of holy places: first, "the relationship between the public and the place," and second, "the function of the place itself." With these criteria they have prepared an exhaustive list. The authors distinguished between different levels of sites and concluded that Holy Places should be split into five groups: sanctuaries, holy sites, places of worship, religious buildings and religious sites.
66 *See* discussion *infra*. *See also*, N. Collins-Kreiner, "Pilgrimage Holy Sites: A Classification of Jewish Holy Sites in Israel," 18 *Journal of Cultural Geography*, 57, 2000.
67 D. Bar, "Recreating Jewish Sanctity in Jerusalem: Mount Zion and David's Tomb, between 1948–67," 23 *Journal of Israeli History*, 233, 2004.
68 For the Status Quo, *see* Cust, *supra* note 43.
69 *See e.g.*, N. Dana, *The Druze in the Middle East: Their Faith, Leadership, Identity, and Status*, Brighton: Sussex Academic Press, 2003, p. 27.
70 The Cenacle houses both an ancient synagogue and what is purported to be David's Tomb, along with a Chapel commemorating the site of the Last Supper.
71 28/1940 *Mudir el Awkaf v. Keren Kayemet of Israel et al.*, 7 *PLR* 242 (1940).
72 CSO B/3/41 *Mount Tabor–Settlement of Title* (Israel Archive 30/3).
73 Protection of Holy Places Law, June 27, 1967. Online. Available http://www.mfa.gov.il/mfa/peace%20process/reference%20documents (accessed 4 Sept., 2008).
74 *Ibid*.
75 *See also* Guinn *supra* note 49, p. 11.
76 The committee was composed of individuals experienced in these issues including rabbinic officials, the Rabbi of the Holy Places and the Legal Adviser to the Ministry of Religion.
77 They did not resort to modern Arabic scholarship.
78 An example of an important source would be the responsa, known as *She'elot u-Teshuvot* "questions and answers" that comprise the body of written decisions and rulings given by poskim ("decisors of Jewish law").
79 *See* 11 *Encyclopædia Judaica*, 1972, s.v. "Luria, Isaac Ben Solomon," pp. 572–78, for extensive background on Rabbi Isaac Ben Solomon Luria (1534–72). While in Safed "he often took long walks with his closest disciples in the neighborhood ... pointing out to them the graves of saintly personages not hitherto known, which he discovered through his spiritual intuition and revelations." *Ibid*. pp. 573–74.
80 The case is still pending before the court.
81 Report by His Britannic Majesty's Government on the Palestine Administration, 31 Dec., 1923, Online. Available http://domino.un.org/unispal.nsf/d80185e9f0c69a7b85256cbf005afeac/cc87d3bf6e0759f3052565e800573851!OpenDocument (accessed 28 Oct., 2008).
82 S. I. Minerbi, *The Vatican and Zionism*, Arnold Schwartz, trans., Oxford: Oxford University Press, 1990, p. 89. This seems to have occurred at the beginning of the Mandate in 1923.
83 The Palestine (Holy Places) Order in Council, 25 July,1924, *repr. in* Enrico Molinaro, *Negotiating Jerusalem*, Jerusalem: PASSIA Pub., 2002, Annex 2.
84 *See* The Palestine (Holy Places) Order in Council of 1924, in Cust, *supra* note 43, p. 65–66. *Ibid.*, annex 2.
85 *Coptic Patriarchate v. Minister of Police* 25(1) *Piskei Din* 226 (1971), (in Hebrew).
86 The Supreme Court's ruling issued an order of eviction to the Copts. Enforcement was postponed to allow the government to make determinations as to substantive rights under the 1924 Order in Council. *See* "Palestine (Holy Places) Order in

Council," *supra* note 83, annex 2. *See also, 222/68 Nationalist Circles et al. v. Minister of Police*, 24(2) *Piskei Din* 142 (1970) (in Hebrew).
87 *See e.g., Guinn supra* note 49, pp. 33–34 (noting the problems Jordan had with the Copts and Ethiopians at this site); W. Zander, "Jurisdiction and Holiness: Reflections on the Coptic-Ethiopian Case," 17 *Israel Law Review* 1982, 245 (hereinafter Zander), pp. 248–49 .
88 Zander, *supra* note 87, pp. 251–52. *See also,* Raymond Cohen, *Saving the Holy Sepulchre*, New York: Oxford University Press, 2008 (hereinafter: Cohen), p. 194.
89 Zander, *supra* note 87, pp. 248–49.
90 *Ibid.* p. 248. *See also,* Cohen *supra* note 88, p. 194 for a discussion of the dispute with special reference to the diplomatic maneuvering that led to the crisis.
91 Zander, *supra* note 87, p. 252.
92 *Ibid.* pp. 252–53 (showing the Court's distaste for the Ethiopians' behavior because it was akin to "taking the law into their own hands.")
93 The Copts filed another petition which was summarily dismissed in deference to the actions of the government. *Coptic Patriarchate v. Government of Israel* 33(1) *Piskei Din* 225 (1979) (in Hebrew).
94 Zander, *supra* note 87, pp. 255–57. *See also,* Eordegianat *supra* note 42, p. 320 (noting that despite attempts at negotiations, the government has to this day not taken any action on this matter). At different times, both the Egyptian and the Ethiopian governments have intervened on behalf of their "charges." *See generally,* Zander *supra* note 87.
95 Protection of Holy Places Law 1967, *supra* note 73. The first paragraph of this law was adopted in the Basic Law: Jerusalem, Capital of Israel, 1980. *See generally,* R. Lapidoth and M. Hirsch, eds, *The Basic Law: Jerusalem, Capital of Israel,* repr. in *The Arab-Israel Conflict and its Resolution*, Boston, Mass.: Martinus Nijhoff Publishing 1999, p. 255.
96 *See* Z. Zruhiya, "It's Official-Religious Affairs Ministry to be Dissolved Sunday," *Haaretz*, 3 Mar., 2004, page A1 col. 2 (in Hebrew) which states: "Responsibility for non-Jewish groups will be transferred to the Interior Ministry, while the department that deals with religious councils will be moved to the Prime Minister's Office. The Organization for the Development of Holy Sites will be the responsibility of the Tourism Ministry, the rabbinic courts will be under the control of the Justice Ministry, and the Rabbi of the Holy Sites and the Western Wall will be under the supervision of the Chief Rabbinate. Civil Service Commissioner Shmuel Hollander called the move historic, saying it was correct from an administrative point of view." *Ibid. See also,* A. Dayan, "Carving Up the Religious Affairs Ministry," *Haaretz,* 23 Dec., 2003; Gideon Alon, Knesset Votes to Dismantle Religious Affairs Ministry, *Haaretz,* 25 Dec., 2003 (in Hebrew).
97 R. Sofer, "Ministry of Religious Affairs Reestablished," Online. Available: http://www.YnetNews.com (accessed 6 Jan., 2008).
98 Including, e.g., the Cave of Simon the Just, the small Sanhedrin Cave (near the former), the Tomb of Rabbi Ovadiah of Bartenura (at the Mount of Olives cemetery), and Zechariah's Tomb and Absalom's Monument in the Kidron Valley.*See, Kovetz Takanot* 4252 from 16/7/81 (in Hebrew), p. 1212 for a list of the "officially declared" sites in the regulations. *See also,* Appendix 1 to Regulations for Protection of Jewish Holy Places 1981, where sites are listed for Jerusalem, Haifa, Tiberias, Meron, and Peki'in. These designated sites are a far cry from the over 160 sites that the Organization for the Development of Holy Places oversees on an unofficial basis. *See also,* R. Lapidoth, *The Basic Law: Jerusalem, Capital of Israel,* Jerusalem: The Harry and Michael Sacher Center for Legislative Research and Comparative Law, the Hebrew University of Jerusalem, 1999, p. 56 (in Hebrew).

The legal regulation of holy sites 45

In 1995, the Ministry of Religious Affairs proposed to add to the list: David's Tomb on Mount Zion, the Cave of the Prophets Haggai and Malachi (on the western slopes of the Mount of Olives), the Tomb of the Prophetess Hulda (at the top of the Mount of Olives), Jehoshaphat's Cave and the Grave of the Sons of Hezir in the Kidron valley, the Siloam Tunnel and spring, the large Sanhedrin Cave (in the Sanhedrin Tombs Garden), Jeremiah's Cave (*Hatzar Hamatarah*) near the central bus station of East Jerusalem), Zedekiah's Cave (near the Nablus Gate), the Kings' Tombs in Saladin Street and synagogues in the Old City. This proposal was not approved. Guinn *supra* note 49, pp. 120–21.

99 Sometimes this is translated as "the Observer of Holy Places."
100 Official list compiled by the Organization for Holy Sites as of 12 April, 2003 (on file with authors). The Organization actively tends to around 140 sites.
101 Of course, disputes arise, such as over the Grave of Rachel, the wife of Rabbi Akiva. Various Tiberias Rabbis pressured the Organization to include the grave in the list of official holy sites.
102 The draft, prepared on 23 July, 2000 (hereinafter Draft Report), was submitted by Rabbi Shmuel Rabinowitz, then the Rabbi of the Holy Places in Israel and now the Rabbi of the Western Wall.
103 *Ibid.* p. 2.
104 Abandoned Property Law, 1950, *Sefer Ha-Chukim*, 14/3/50, p. 86 (in Hebrew).
105 *See* "Press Release: Adalah Petitions Supreme Court in Name of Muslim Religious Leaders Demanding Legal Recognition for Muslim Holy Sites in Israel," Online. Available http://www.adalah.org/eng/pressreleases/pr.php?file=04_11_23 (accessed 23 Nov., 2004) (hereinafter: Adalah Press Release). The petition was officially filed on 21 Nov. 2004. For a copy of the petition (in Hebrew) *see* Adalah Newsletter, vol. 39, Online. Available: http://www.adalah.org/newsletter/eng/aug07/6.php (accessed 21 Nov., 2004) (hereinafter: Adalah Newsletter).
106 *See* Adalah Press Release *supra* note 105. The petition further states that due to the lack of regulations "many mosques and holy sites have been converted, for instance, into bars, night clubs, stores and restaurants." Additionally, many of the concerned sites carry religious significance to the worldwide Muslim community which should add pressure on the Israeli government to act. *Ibid.* The pending case is named *Sheikh Abdallah Darwish and others v. Minister for Religious Affairs, Ministry of Justice and others*. The most recent development occurred in August 2007 when the Israel Supreme Court gave an order to the State to explain why there was no protection for Muslim Holy Sites and to give appropriate funding for the protection. For a copy of the Order, *see* Adalah Newsletter, *supra* note 105.
107 The approach of the Citizens' Accord Forum was to use well known rabbis to lobby at the Knesset concerning the importance of protecting those Holy Places.
108 Letter from Rabbi Michael Melchior and Dr Hana Sawid to Rabbi Yitzchak Cohen, Minister for Religious Affairs, 28 May, 2007 (on file with authors). The letter listed twelve Muslim holy places worthy of protection (seven mosques in Tiberias, Palmachim, Nahariya, Safed, Amuka, Shlomi, and Yavneh, as well as five graveyards in Tiberias, Beer Sheva, Herzliya, Azor, and Ashkelon) and requested regulations for seven out of the twelve.
109 *Ibid.*
110 Y. Stern, "Bill Would Create Body to Preserve Muslim Holy Sites," *Haaretz*, 29 Dec., 2007, p. 2 (English ed.). Among the mosques that would benefit are Dahr al-Omar, a mosque in the center of Tiberias; Masjad al-Basa, near Shlomi in the north; and Sidna Ali, near Herzliya. *Ibid.*
111 *Kovetz Takanot* 4252 from 16/7/81, p. 1212 (in Hebrew).
112 The Regulation on the Protection of Sacred Spaces for the Jewish People (Amendment), *Kovetz Takanot* 5237 from 1989 (in Hebrew), p. 190, which added in the wording "which is not according to the custom of the place". *See also,* R.

Halperin-Kaddari, "Women, Religion and Multiculturalism in Israel", 5 *UCLA Journal of International Law and Foreign Affairs* 339, 2000 (hereinafter: Halperin-Kaddari) p. 358.
113 The history of the litigation (and attendant legislative activity) is laid out in F. Raday, *Culture, Religion and Gender*, 1 *International Journal Constitutional Law*, 663, 2003, pp. 668–69. *See also*, D. Izenberg, "Court Rules Women of the Wall Should Pray Elsewhere," *Jerusalem Post*, 7 Apr., 2003. The women's perspective was laid out in P. Chesler and R. Haut, *Women of the Wall: Claiming Sacred Ground of Judaism's Holy Sites*, Woodstock, Vt.: Jewish Lights Publishing, 2002. *See also*, F. Raday, "Claiming Equal Religious Personhood: Women of the Wall's Constitutional Saga," in W. Brugger and M. Karaynni (eds) *Religion in the Public Sphere: A Comparative Analysis of German, Israeli, American and International Law*, Berlin and New York: Springer, 2007, pp. 243–52.
114 257/89 *Hoffman v. Israel*, 48(2) *Piskei Din* 265 (in Hebrew). In concurring opinions, Justice Elon compared the Western Wall to a synagogue, such that the local customs must be respected (thus deferring to the rabbinic authorities to deny prayer in the area) along with the public interest and security factors that make it difficult to allow for such prayer. Justice Levin held that the Western Wall is a national area and should remain pluralist (thereby favoring the WOW) but he also placed responsibility on the Government to uphold security and public order, something clearly reserved for the Legislature to address and not the Court. Justic Shamgar similarly called on the Government to attain a compromise with the WOW, noting as well the right of the WOW to pray in the area.
115 882/94 *Alter et. al. v. Government of Israel*, decided 12 June, 1994, not published.
116 The Committee decision is referred to in the third case, 3358/95 *Hoffman v. Israel*, 54(2) *Piskei Din* 345 (2000) (in Hebrew).
117 3358/95 *Hoffman v. Israel*, 54(2) *Piskei Din* 345 (2000). Justice Maza called for a balancing between the rights of the women and the governmental interests involved (such as security and public order), Justice Turkel agreed with Justice Maza, and Justice Englard asserted the previous position of Justice Elon, that the area was a holy site and that pursuant to the regulations, the Orthodox character of the site had to be maintained. *Ibid.*
118 4128/00 *Hoffman v. Israel*, decided 4 Apr., 2003, not published.
119 257/89 *Hoffman v. Israel*, 48(2) *Piskei Din* 265 (in Hebrew).
120 Halperin-Kaddari *supra* note 112, pp. 339, 360–61. Elon's decision was the last in the Women of the Wall cases.
121 *Compare* Justice Englard who noted at the time that to preclude the question of whether Jewish access to a site will be deemed desecration by Muslims, the definition of desecration must be a secular, not a religious definition. Izhak Englard, *The Legal Status of the Holy Places in Jerusalem*, 28 *Israel Law Review* 589, 1994, 593.
122 222/68 *Nationalist Circles v. Minister of Police*, 24(2) *Piskei Din* 142 (1970) (in Hebrew) pp. 194–228 (J. Agranat).
123 *The Protection of the Holy Places Law, 1967* is restated in the 1980 Jerusalem Basic Law; see *Basic Law: Jerusalem, Capital of Israel*, in *LSI*, 30 July 1980, vol. 34, p. 209, sec. 3. Supporters of Jewish prayer on the Temple Mount argued that their freedom of access to the Temple Mount was violated.
124 222/68 *Nationalist Circles. v. Minister of Police*, 24(2) *Piskei Din* 142 (1970) (in Hebrew), pp. 160–68 (J. Witkin). *See also* Claude Klein, *The Temple Mount Case*, 6 *Israel Law Review*, 263, 1971.
125 *See* Englard *supra* note 121, pp. 596–97.
126 3374/97, *Gershon Solomon v. Yair Yitzchaki, Officer in Charge of East Jerusalem and the Israeli Police* (decided 10 June, 1997) (in Hebrew). Online. Available: http://elyon1.court.gov.il/files/97/740/033/E03/97033740.e03.pdf (accessed 6 Aug., 2008).

127 *See e.g.,* 2697/04 *Solomon v. Commander of East Jerusalem,* 58(4) *Piskei Din* 572 (2004) (in Hebrew), 67/93 *Kach Movement v. Minister of Religion,* 47(2) *Piskei Din* 1 (1993) (in Hebrew).
128 4776/06 *Solomon v. Commander for East Jerusalem,* decided 28 Dec., 2006, not published (in Hebrew) (must balance right of prayer against a justified limitation for public security concerns). Note as well the jurisdictional limitation imposed on the Court as a result of the Mandate Law. *See e.g.,* 10450/07 *Temple Mount Faithful v. Police et al.,* decided 11 Dec., 2007, not published (in Hebrew) (court refrained from deciding whether the Temple Mount Faithful may light Hanukah candles on the Temple Mount due to lack of jurisdiction); 8666/99 *Temple Mount Faithful v. Attorney General,* 54(1) *Piskei Din* 199 (2000) (in Hebrew); 7128/96 *Temple Mount Faithful v. Israel,* 51(2) *Piskei Din* 509 (1997) (in Hebrew).
129 Similar considerations are made when addressing the issue of digging on the Temple Mount by the *waqf* authorities. Coupled with the issue of jurisdictional limitations imposed on the Court as a result of Mandate Law and governmental policy concerning the *waqf*'s control of the area, the Court also defers to the relevant authorities including the Police and the Antiquities Authority. 8666/99 *Temple Mount Faithful v. A. Rubinstein,* decided 11 Jan., 2000, not published, (in Hebrew) (Justice Cheshin noting as well the need for deference to the government as the Court is an inappropriate place for these decisions); 1868/07 *Temple Mount Faithful v. Israel,* decided 4 June, 2007, not published, (in Hebrew) (Court recognized presence of archaeologists working with *waqf* to supervise digs)
130 *See* N. Shragai, *"No moving Jewish lips in prayer on Temple Mount, says Dichter" Haaretz,* 2 Jan., 2008, p. 1. Public Security Minister Avi Dichter opined, "[I]t is possible to carry out an arrest for expressions of outward and demonstrative signs of prayer." *Ibid.*
131 These documents are discussed in more detail in Chapter 3 in this volume by Leonard Hammer.
132 *See* 1954 Hague Convention for the Protection of Cultural Property in the Event of Armed Conflict, 249 *UNTS* 215 (24 May, 1954).
133 UNESCO World Heritage Convention. Online. Available http://whc.unesco.org/en/conventiontext (accessed Aug. 2008).
134 *See* Art.18, 999 *UNTS* 171 (16 Dec., 1966). The Human Rights Committee, the body charged with oversight of the treaty, applies the convention to areas under control by Israel, including the West Bank. *See* Human Rights Committee, General Comment 31, Nature of the General Legal Obligation on States Parties to the Covenant, U.N. Doc. CCPR/C/21/Rev.1/Add.13 (2004). Online. Available: http://www1.umn.edu/humanrts/gencomm/hrcom31.html (accessed 4 Aug., 2008). *See also,* Universal Declaration of Human Rights, Art.18, UNGA Res. 217 (III 1948). Online. Available: http://www.un.org/Overview/rights.html (accessed 29 May, 2008).
135 Geoffrey R. Watson, *The Oslo Accords,* Oxford University Press, 2000, pp. 107–10.
136 Agreement on the Gaza Strip and the Jericho Area, Signed 4 May, 1994, Cairo, UN Doc. A/49/180 S/1994/727 (Annex) of 20 June 1994. Repr.in 33 *ILM* (1994), pp. 626–720, also in 28 *Israel Law Review,* 452, 1994.
137 Israeli–Palestinian Interim Agreement on the West Bank and the Gaza Strip, 1995. Signed 28 Sept., 1995. Excerpted in 36 *ILM* (1997), pp. 551–647. Online. Available: http://www.mfa.gov.il/MFA/Peace+Process/Guide+to+the+Peace+Process/THE+ISRAELI-PALESTINIAN+INTERIM+AGREEMENT.htm (accessed 23 Jun., 2008)
138 *Ibid.*
139 Israel-Jordan Treaty of Peace (26 Oct., 1994), Art.9, 34 *ILM* 43–66 (1995). One should note that in the Jordan-Israel Armistice Agreement of 1949, Jordan agreed to allow Israel "free access for the Holy Places and cultural institutions and use of the cemetery on the Mount of Olives." That agreement was never adhered to.

Hashemite Jordan Kingdom-Israel General Armistice Agreement, 3 Mar., 1949, 42 *UNTS* 304 (1949).
140 *See e.g.*, Country Reports on Human Rights Practices-2000 Released by the Bureau of Democracy, Human Rights and Labor, 23 Feb., 2001, U.S. Dept. of State, "The Occupied Territories (Including Areas Subject to the Jurisdiction of the Palestinian Authority)" Online. Available: http://www.state.gov./g/drl/rls/hrrpt/2000/nea/882.htm (accessed 17 Jan., 2009).
141 Israel adheres to Article 43 of the 1907 Hague Convention concerning the Laws and Customs of War on Land, 18 Oct., 1907, Reg. 42, 36 Stat. 2277, 1 *Bevans* 631, deeming it reflective of customary international law. *See e.g.*, 610/78 *Oiev v. Minister of Defense*, 33(2) *Piskei Din* 113 (1978) (in Hebrew). Article 43 requires an occupying state to respect the laws in force, unless absolutely prevented from doing so.
142 *See* M. M. Kersel, The Trade in Palestinian Antiquities, *Jerusalem Quarterly*, vol. 33, at 27, Online. Available: http://www.jerusalemquarterly.org/pdfs/33_kersel.pdf (accessed 17 Jan., 2009) (hereinafter Kersel). This statute "formed the basis of the fifth draft of the Palestinian Cultural Heritage Legislation 2003." *Ibid.*, pp. 27–28.
143 Prior to the 2005 Israeli withdrawal, Military Order No. 462 (1973) applied. "The order forbade the sale or transfer of any antiquity to a person who does not reside in the Gaza Strip, without permission from the director of the DOA." Kersel *supra* note 142, p. 28.
144 Antiquities Ordinance No. 51 of 1929, Online. Available: http://audit2.clio.it/legaldocs/Palestine/palestina%20web/ANTIQUITIES%201929.htm (accessed 17 Jan., 2009).
145 Military Directive No. 327 "On the Matter of Protecting Holy Places," 12 July, 1969 and subsequent updates. Online. Available: http://augtofi2.birzeit/legislation/PDFPre.asp27?=1969&ID = 11549. According to Article 2, the Directive will operate in a similar manner to Israeli domestic law (the Holy Places Law of 1967), thereby permitting the military authorities to address matters of civilian concern, such as rules of behavior at holy sites. *Ibid.*
146 *See* Article 5 of Military Directive No. 327.
147 Military Directive No. 327.
148 Interview with Commander Ehud Barosh, Military Legal Division for Judea and Samaria, 19 Sept., 2004.
149 The Antiquities Law, No. 51 for the year 1966, as cited in R. Greenberg and A. Keinan, *The Present Past of the Israeli-Palestinian Conflict: Israeli Archeology in the West Bank and East Jerusalem Since 1967*, Tel Aviv: S. Daniel Abraham Center for International Religious Studies, Tel Aviv University, July 2004, Research Paper No. 1 p. 49 (hereinafter Greenberg and Keinan).
150 *Ibid.*, *supra* note 149, p. 16.
151 *Ibid.*, *supra* note 149. *See also*, Jordanian *Official Gazette*, 16 July, 1966 (in Arabic).
152 *Ibid.* at Chapters 3 and 4 of the Law.
153 Greenberg and Keinan, *supra* note 149, p. 17. The decrees are published in *ibid.* p. 49.
154 *See Genesis* 18: 1–8 (where Abraham and Sarah offered hospitality to the three strangers)
155 *See* Serge Schmemann, "Arafat Enters Into a New Fray Over a Russian Church," *New York Times*, 11 July, 1997, at A3.
156 Interestingly, one of the evicted nuns was the sister of George Stephanopoulos which turned the PA effort to placate Russia into an international incident. *See*, Barbara Berick, "Jericho Monastery Beholds a Small-Scale Cold War Crisis," *Philadelphia Inquirer*, 27 Jan., 2000; Philip Reeves, One Nun Defies the Long Reach of the Russian Church, *The Independent*. (U.K.) 24 Jan., 2000; Bernard Wasserstein, Red Alert for White Russians, *Jerusalem Post*, 31 Jan., 2000.
157 *See* Sarah Honig, "The Sergei Connection", *Jerusalem Post*, 19 Sept., 2008.

158 *See* Chapter 9 of this volume, Y. Reiter, *"Contest or Cohabitation in Shared Holy Places: the Cave of the Patriarchs and Samuel's Tomb."*
159 *Ibid.*
160 *Ibid.*
161 *Ibid.*
162 In February 2005, at the urging of MK Meir Porush, Prime Minister Olmert asked the Palestinian Authority to restore the grave and treat it "with respect as a holy site." Matthew Wagner, "Prime Minister Asks PA to Renovate Joseph's Tomb," *Jerusalem Post*, 5 Feb., 2008.
163 *See* E. Wohgelernter, "Worshipers Indicted After Entering Palestinian Areas," *Forward*, 19 Dec., 2003. We should note that Muslims believe that Joseph is buried with the Patriarchs in Hebron and that the grave is that of Sheikh Yusuf Dukat, a "locally venerated Moslem ... who lived about 150 years ago." S. Waxman, "They Knew Not Joseph," *Jerusalem Post,* 24 Nov., 2000.
164 *See* E. Prince-Gibson, "Who Weeps for Rachel?" *Jerusalem Post*, 24 Nov., 2000. *See also,* N. Shragai, "The Palestinian Authority and the Jewish Holy Sites in the West Bank, Rachel's Tomb as A Test Case," *Jerusalem Viewpoints* No. 559, Dec. 2007, for an articulation of the Jewish 'narrative' regarding Rachel's Tomb. A more nuanced view is put forward in F. Strickart, *Rachel Weeping: Jews, Christianity and Muslims at the Fortress Tomb*, Collegeville, Minn.: Liturgical Press, 2007. For recent political disputes *see ibid.* pp. 128–37.
165 For a critical view see, Y. Bronner and N. Gordon, "Beneath the Surface: Are Jerusalem's Digs Designed to Displace Palestinians?" *Chronicle of Higher Education*, 21 Apr., 2008, B5–6.
166 M. Rapoport, "A Separate Peace," *Haaretz*. Online, 14 Apr., 2006; *see also* Israeli-Palestinian Archaeology Working Group Agreement, Online. Available: http://www.usc.edu/dept/LAS/religion/arc/sh/agreement.pdf (accessed 10 Oct., 2008), p. 2.
167 J. Bohannon, "Team Unveils Mideast Archaeology Peace Plan," 320 *Science*, No. 5874, 18 Apr., 2008, p. 302; *see also* Israeli-Palestinian Archaeology Working Group Agreement. Online. Available: http://www.usc.edu/dept/LAS/religion/arc/sh/agreement.pdf (accessed 10 Oct., 2008), p. 5.
168 One creative example was the decision in December 2007 to establish "a special passage to Bethlehem for Christian pilgrims before and after Christmas." Y. Azoulay and I. Rosenbaum, "Pilgrims to Get Quick Entry into Bethlehem," *Haaretz*, Dec. 21, 2007, p. A3 (in Hebrew). Former British Prime Minister Tony Blair made a special request to ease the passage of the thousands of Christians planning to attend Christmas mass in Bethlehem. Due to the numerous security checks at the checkpoint leading to Bethlehem, visitors typically braved long lines when entering the West Bank. Unfortunately, the 'fast-track' checkpoint was open only to Christian pilgrims from abroad. *Ibid.* Similarly, between 1947–67, Israeli Christians enjoyed passage to Bethlehem during the Christmas and New Year season. *See* R. Israeli, *Jerusalem Divided: The Armistice Regime 1947–1967*, Portland, Oreg.: Frank Cass, 2002, pp. 101–3. Because Jordanian officials would not accept Israeli passports, Israeli citizens received acceptable documents from the government—called *laissez passer*—in advance of the holiday. *Ibid.* By allowing Israeli Christians to participate in Christmas celebrations in Bethlehem, Jordanian officials complied, at least in part, with Article VIII of the Armistice Agreement providing for free access to religious sites. *Ibid.* The Christmas crossings also eased tensions on both sides: "If on normal days an abnormal vigilance prevailed on both sides, lest someone trespassed into no man's land, on the abnormal day of the Christmas crossing, the place suddenly became normal: people wandered about the square in large numbers, completely unmindful of their proximity to the armistice lines." *Ibid.* p. 101.

3 Protection of holy places in international law
Objective and subjective approaches

Leonard Hammer

Introduction

While addressing the need to protect and preserve areas of cultural interest, including holy places, there is no internationally acknowledged definition or designation of a holy place.[1] The lack of a specific focus on holy places as such necessitates an understanding of the general perspective adopted by the international system towards holy places, especially since such insight can provide assistance and direction regarding domestic law as well as create binding obligations on states.

In reviewing a variety of treaties and resolutions, the pertinent aspect for holy places within international law is the framework by which the international system applies protections. Protection for holy places derives either from the system's desired ends concerning a particular site or object, or the use of the site following the implementation of a human right. The identified approaches within the international system may be divided into an object-oriented approach, whereby the integrity of the object is what compels the protection of a holy place, as opposed to a more subjective, functional, aspect of the place, where the focus lies within assertions by individuals or groups who require a holy place for a specific purpose. The two approaches diverge due to the desired ends for creating the protection in the first place. This in turn leads to a difference in the scope of accorded protection.

An object-oriented approach

The object-oriented approach focuses on the protection of the structure, with the central driving aspect being protection of the common cultural heritage. The desire is to preserve a particular site or building given its importance to the world at large. One can incorporate holy places into this object-oriented realm given their status as cultural property that merits specific protection because of a holy place's representative cultural status. The determination of protection does not necessarily involve use of the object as such, but rather the object's intrinsic importance because of its status as a monument, or even its serving as part of a historical record of what once existed in the area, similar to an historical artifact or museum.

The protection of holy places during times of conflict

A key example of this approach is the way in which holy places are protected during times of conflict. This issue is firmly anchored in international law. For example, the 1874 Brussels Convention prohibits military action against "institutions dedicated to religion ... " holding the parties responsible for marking their protected landmarks and implying that there is no immunity if use of the area is for military purposes.[2] The 1880 Institute of International Law's *Laws of War on Land* (referred to as the Oxford Manual), which was meant to serve as a guidebook that codified customary international law, requires that warring parties spare buildings dedicated to religion, art or science. Article 27 of both the 1899 Convention with Respect to the Laws of Custom of War on Land[3] and the 1907 Hague Convention with Respect to the Laws and Customs of War on Land[4] impose a similar requirement, along with a visible sign of their status; these buildings are to be spared provided they are not being used for military purposes.[5] Articles 25 and 26 of the 1923 Hague Convention on the Rules of Air Warfare, although never ratified, provides protection zones around buildings dedicated to public worship, provided they are not used for military purposes.[6]

The approach taken in all these documents is one of preservation, given the importance of such sites as cultural monuments. The defining factor is the focus on the property, usually as determined by the state party, given the requirement for some form of designation (again indicating an object-oriented approach towards cultural preservation).

Another more recent example is the 1954 Hague Convention for the Protection of Cultural Property in the Event of Armed Conflict.[7] Article 1 provides protection for cultural property, which is defined as "moveable or immoveable property of great importance to the cultural heritage of every people such as monuments of architecture, art or history, whether religious or secular. ... "[8] The key term "cultural heritage of every people" can either be interpreted restrictively, i.e., that it refers to an object or place of world renown,[9] or broadly, i.e., that it refers to each contracting state's national cultural heritage, as defined by the state.[10] In either form of interpretation,[11] however, the focus is on the object as grounds for protection and is subject to the designation of such property by the state.[12] The approach is an object-oriented understanding with the underlying goal of preserving a national cultural heritage that has significance for the world at large. Here, the state in essence holds the property in trust for the international community (thereby turning the issue into one of international concern).[13]

At one time, the protection of the Hague Convention had been invoked between warring parties, illustrating the mode of protection accorded under the Convention. Following Israel's 1967 occupation of various territories, including the Old City in Jerusalem, UNESCO acted under Article 23 of the Convention,[14] and appointed two commissioner generals (one for Israel and one for the surrounding Arab states).[15] Particular concern surrounded the Israeli-occupied Temple Mount, a place of paramount importance to Jews and Muslims, especially in view of the ensuing excavations of the area by Israel. While Article 23 mandates that the appointed officials are to offer technical assistance to implement the Convention, the states interpreted it in a narrow sense to mean scientific technical assistance. The commissioner generals operated until 1977, when UNESCO terminated their mandates. UNESCO did not subsequently appoint any officials, although the organization continued to remind the parties of their obligations under the Convention. Cambodia underwent a similar, albeit less formalized, action for the Angkor Wat area. UNESCO sent in ongoing missions to remove valuable cultural property and engage long-range protection plans.[16] In each instance, the fact that the sites were of global cultural importance triggered concern from UNESCO.

Article 53 of Additional Protocol I to the Geneva Conventions of 1977 also prohibits acts of hostility against " ... places of worship which constitute the cultural or spiritual heritage of peoples."[17] Similarly, Article 16 of Additional Protocol II prohibits any acts of hostility directed against " ... places of worship which constitute the cultural or spiritual heritage of peoples. ... "[18] Both prohibit the use of such buildings to support the military effort. Pursuant to their terms, these treaties also apply to occupied territory. Even though Israel never signed or ratified the Additional Protocols, owing to the customary nature of the Hague Convention of 1907 and owing to the fact that Israel is a signatory to the Fourth Geneva Convention, it has recognized that it is bound to apply the Hague Regulations and the humanitarian provisions of the Fourth Geneva Convention.[19]

Cultural heritage

A variety of UNESCO documents also highlight the object-oriented approach with a focus on preserving the site given its overall importance to the world generally. A key document demonstrating this approach is the 1972 World Heritage Convention.[20] The Preamble explicitly states that cultural heritage of outstanding interest "need[s] to be preserved as part of the world heritage of mankind as a whole" and that disappearance of cultural heritage constitutes a "harmful impoverishment of the heritage of all the nations of the world." It goes on to define cultural heritage as including "monuments ... which are of outstanding universal value from the point of view of history, art or science."[21] The Convention accords the state the capacity to submit what it deems to be of universal value within its territory, with UNESCO determining what it will adopt from the submitted list as meriting World Heritage status pursuant to the "general interests of the international community." The state (along with the international community) is obliged to protect, conserve and present such cultural heritage using its maximum resources.[22] While there is no enforcement of the World Heritage list, placement on the list merits the attention of the international community.[23] The Convention engages in a delicate balancing act that must accord deference to the state as the actor that designates such sites[24] as well as recognize the role of the international community at large whose heritage merits protection.[25]

Demonstrating the object-orientation of UNESCO's approach reminiscent of the 1954 Hague Convention, UNESCO termed the Old City of Jerusalem and its Holy Places as "an issue for all of mankind because of their artistic, historical and religious value."[26] UNESCO imposed sanctions on Israel, excluding the state from participating in UNESCO activities.[27]

In all of the following UNESCO documents, the focus is on the object itself, linking the protection to the state as a means of designating and preserving the variety of sites. The 1968 Recommendation concerning the Preservation of Cultural Property Endangered by Public or Private Works refers to the importance of cultural property and tradition as reflecting the personality of the peoples of the world. The 1972 Recommendation concerning the Protection, at National Level, of the Cultural and National Heritage defines cultural heritage in a manner similar to the 1972 World Heritage Convention, noting in the Preamble the importance of preserving heritage for all mankind. The 1976 Recommendation concerning the Safeguarding and Contemporary Role of Historic Areas[28] recommends national regional or local authorities to preserve historic areas in the interests of all citizens and the international community.[29] In addition, the 1976 Recommendation on Participation of People At Large in Cultural Life and Their Contribution to It recommends that states adopt legislation to protect and enhance the heritage of the past and particularly ancient monuments.[30] A 1997 Declaration on the Responsibilities of the Present Generations Towards Future Generations imposes a responsibility to identify, protect and safeguard cultural heritage and transmit it to future generations.[31] More recent documents include a 2001 Universal Declaration on Cultural Diversity requiring states to preserve cultural heritage[32] and a 2003 Declaration Concerning the Intentional Destruction of Cultural Heritage calling on states to cease all forms of heritage destruction[33]

Similarly, a number of General Assembly resolutions provide for the protection of religious sites, with the focus on the collective heritage overall. Principally among these are General Assembly Resolutions 55/254 on the Protection of Holy Sites (2001) and 58/128 on Promotion of Religious and Cultural Understanding, Harmony and Cooperation (2004).[34]

Part of the problem with the object-oriented approach is the constant tension between international desires to uphold what can be deemed culturally important sites to all, as opposed to state assertions and selective applications of such protections when it reflects particular interests. Indeed, the very notion of a common cultural heritage is, on the one hand, the human community's overall relationship with cultural property, and, on the other hand, its recognition of the importance of cultural property's role for specific national cultures and their peoples.[35]

Furthermore, there has not been enough activity or definition regarding the shape and scope of cultural protection. For example, Article 15 of The International Covenant on Social Economic and Cultural Rights of 1966 provides for the right of everyone to take part in cultural life.[36] While there is no general comment to this article and it has not been subject to much analysis,[37] "the right of everyone to take part in cultural life" can serve as grounds for asserting protection of holy sites. As stated in section 2 of the above article, "The steps to be taken by the States Parties to the present Covenant to achieve the full realization of this right shall include those necessary for the conservation, the development and the diffusion of science and culture." Such steps would therefore allow for participation in the cultural life of the community as well as access to holy sites and for the preservation and protection of holy sites as an implicit means of ensuring participation and access to such sites.[38] Thus, the Committee on Economic Social and Cultural rights has noted a duty to protect cultural heritage from vandalism or theft[39] as well as a duty to prohibit its deliberate destruction.[40] Yet implementation of the right proves problematic when factoring in political and ideological tensions, the conflict between the identity of a group or individual and that of the collective or national identity, and identifying what exactly is a "cultural" right.[41]

One system that merits mention here is the General Framework Agreement for Peace in Bosnia and Herzegovina of 1995[42] that formed a Commission to Preserve National Monuments[43] to receive and decide on petitions to designate property having cultural, historic, religious or ethnic importance as national monuments.[44] This was a necessary measure given the widespread destruction of holy places during this conflict, especially when accounting for the policy of deliberate destruction to historical, cultural and religious property.[45] After acting under the auspices of UNESCO for the first five years,[46] the Government of Bosnia and Herzegovina passed implementing legislation in 2001 to make the Commission an independent government entity.[47] In the past several years the Commission has met 38 times[48] with surprising success[49] given the seething ethnic conflicts in the former Yugoslavia. The Commission secured funds for their restoration projects from international organizations and foreign countries, religious organizations and private investors.[50] It also received cooperation from the federal government and local governments for the enforcement of its promulgations.[51] There is resistance from some local groups who object to their sites being designated as a national monument because the designation prevents them from making changes to the site.[52] Aside from insisting on enforcement, the Commission has also held bilateral talks with prominent members of the Islamic community, the Catholic and Orthodox Churches and the Jewish community "to find a better way to ensure that the basic needs of the religious communities are not hindered, while fully honoring the protection measures prescribed by the decisions to designate these properties as national monuments."[53]

The subjective approach

By contrast, the subjective approach towards holy places merits protection for a site as a function of its relevance to individuals or groups who desire to access and use the site for a specific purpose. In this instance, the determination that a holy site merits protection derives from assertions by an individual or group, pursuant to a specific right. Here the designation is in one sense outside the realm of the state; it is centered around the needs of an individual or group pursuant to practices mandated by their belief system or religious creed.

Human rights law protection

An example of the subjective approach is Article 18 of The International Covenant on Civil and Political Rights of 1966[54] regarding freedom of religion or belief. To minimize the scope of protection accorded under the right, the capacity to exercise the right is through the manifestation of a religion or belief via worship, observance, practice and teaching. Manifestation then implies an external action conducted pursuant to the edicts of a religion or belief that mandates a particular form of observance or practice. Given the manifestation via some form of worship, a general requirement in most religions, and the right to practice a belief, Article 18 also can include protection for places of worship or practice when an individual or group lays claim to such a right of manifestation. Thus, if the religion or belief mandates a particular form of practice at a given site, such as a holy site, the site itself will be protected as a means of allowing for the manifestation of the right. The driving force, however, is the claim to exercise the right, and not the fact that the site itself deserves protection.

The Human Rights Committee bolstered this interpretation of Article 18, as it has specifically included the protection of places of worship within the mandate of the article. Human Rights Committee General Comment No.22[55] states that places of worship come under the rubric of Article 18. Included within the right to manifest a religion or belief is the protection of places of worship, given the importance of places of worship to the exercise of the right. It follows that such protection would incorporate religious places, sites, and shrines. Note, however, that the scope of protection under Article 18 relates to specific manifestations in accordance with the directives of the right.[56] Thus, the need for observance or worship, while mandating protection for places of worship, refers to active forms of use. It is not a matter of preserving a site or object for the benefit of the common cultural heritage (although that could be a secondary benefit), but rather of ensuring the right to worship or to engage in a specific ritual. Access and pilgrimage have been understood as falling, to a limited extent, within this right,[57] thus providing for the use of places of worship or other holy sites when mandated by the religion or belief. By way of example, the European Court of Human Rights was confronted with the matter of Greek Cypriots who sought to visit holy sites in North Cyprus.[58] Although the parties did not make reference to freedom of religion (Article 9 of the European Convention on Human Rights), the Court held that denying access to religious sites violated the human right to freedom of religion. The court made this ruling despite the fact that there was insufficient proof concerning the denial of access to Maronite Christians of their sites in North Cyprus. Manifestation, then, refers to a specific link between the external action of the believer in accordance with the directives of the religion or belief.[59]

The Commission on Human Rights (CHR) Resolution from 2004[60] also reflects the notion of a rights-based approach towards holy sites as derived from a subjective understanding of their importance pursuant to the assertions of an individual or group. The CHR called on states to ensure religious places and sites, especially where they are vulnerable. The CHR Special Rapporteur on Freedom of Religion or Belief, in her 2005 report, also designated an attack on a religious building as a violation of the rights of individuals and groups.[61] This elevates the importance and status of a holy site for a group as being on a par with the rights of individuals who lay claim to a holy site.

Upon comparison to the object-oriented approach noted above, the subjective interpretation broadens the scope of protection. In the object-oriented approach, some form of connection to a particular site is created due to a common heritage or a determination in a general sense as to whether the site itself is the center of importance. Under the subjective approach, some form of connection to a particular site is created due to the subjective evaluations of an individual or group who deem a particular site important for manifesting their religious beliefs.

Indigenous peoples

Another example of the subjective approach towards holy places is that of rights associated with indigenous peoples. While indigenous peoples operate with some form of autonomous control over the use of their lands, the derivation of the importance of the lands and the associated holy places comes from the indigenous peoples themselves and their need to manifest their beliefs via worship and observance.[62] This is particularly so regarding ancestral lands and other holy areas like burial grounds or places of worship.[63] For instance, Article 13 of The Draft Declaration on the Rights of Indigenous Peoples that has been subject to discussion in the United Nations for quite some time,[64] provides for maintaining, protecting and affording access to religious sites as well as the need to preserve, respect, and protect such sites.[65] The Commission on Human Rights also proposed guidelines for protecting the heritage of indigenous peoples, noting the importance for them of maintaining control over their heritage and traditional territories[66] including, inter alia, sacred sites and significant burial places.[67]

Protection of holy places in international law 57

In a 2003 report, the Special Rapporteur on the Situation of Human Rights and Fundamental Freedoms of Indigenous Peoples[68] referred to the general problems associated with the holy sites of indigenous peoples as being issues of external construction and development that destroy religious or holy places. While economic development generally gains the upper hand, there have been some allowances for preserving such holy sites.[69] What is important is that indigenous peoples have been the source for determining that a place is holy or part of their tradition.[70] Even within the context of privacy and family rights, indigenous peoples have successfully protected ancestral burial grounds given that the group deemed the connection to their ancestors (via the burial ground) as an essential element of their identity and in their family life.[71]

Other examples of this approach towards indigenous peoples includes General Comment No. 23 of the Committee to Eliminate Racial Discrimination, referring to the right of indigenous peoples to practice and revitalize their cultural traditions pursuant to the common heritage and history linked to specific groups and their rights;[72] International Labor Organization Convention No. 169 ensuring control by indigenous peoples over their internal structures;[73] and Operational Directive 4.10 of the World Bank[74] relating to important sites of indigenous peoples, including holy sites.

Combining approaches

The international system's subjective approach towards holy places reflects a notion of designation and protection that emanates from the individual (such as one asserting a right to manifest a religion or belief) or the group (like indigenous peoples). Unlike the object-oriented framework, where the goal is to preserve an object as such, the subjective approach offers an operative method towards preservation and use of holy places derived from the actual use by the group itself. In this way, it avoids problems of state bias that could lead a state to ignore a minority faction or, in the face of an established state religion, exclude other religions and their holy places. Rather, the group or individual assertions can provide the basis for development and protection.

This is not to discount the object-oriented approach. Indeed, focusing on the object serves to uphold holy places where there is no presence of a practicing group. There are many instances where the international system must act based on the object to preserve cultural heritage, such as the Bamiyan Buddhas in Afghanistan, where essentially the sole claim for protection was derived from international sources.[75] When confronting problems such as abandoned property or state expropriation of former religious buildings, it is possible that an argument on cultural and historical grounds will carry greater weight than a contention linked to other human rights, such as freedom of religion. Thus, the right to culture and cultural preservation might provide a stronger case for minority groups to preserve and protect religious structures, especially when abandoned, upon examining the various international instruments. There are many instances of holy places that deserve protection even if they are not in actual use or the subject of a particular claim, especially when considering a site's historical importance or a previously existing ethnic group that does not presently reside in the state.[76]

It also is important to consider contexts where there is an emerging confluence of the subjective/objective approaches. This can allow for a more complete form of protection, by upholding the rights of individuals or a specific group while also preserving the object. Recent activities in UN-sponsored military tribunals[77] have begun to reflect this form of synergy.

In particular, recent decisions of the International Criminal Tribunal for the Former Yugoslavia (ICTY) have included the notion of persecution,[78] the discriminatory intent to destroy institutions of religion in the Former Yugoslavia. Notably the 2004 *Kordic* case[79] states that destroying mosques for no military purpose can be understood as an intent to destroy a particular population (holding that in the town of Ahmici, a holy place symbolizing Muslim culture in Bosnia and the birthplace of many imams and mullahs, there was such an intent to destroy).[80] The *Krstic* case from 2001[81] also involved an attack on religious property, where the court upheld the attack as evincing intent to destroy a group.[82] Similarly, the indictment against Milosevic includes the destruction of mosques and religious buildings in various towns as evidence of intent to destroy an entire population group (one of the key grounds for finding genocide).[83]

In a sense, then, the focus has shifted from the 1954 Hague Convention of object-orientation to also account for the underlying importance of specific holy sites and their relevance to the particular group associated with these sites. The result is that the ICTY in essence blurs the distinction between crimes during conflict against objects as such and crimes against persons.[84] One can find a similar approach in the Rome Statute of the International Criminal Court of 1998 where "serious violations of the laws and customs applicable in international armed conflict" include intentional attacks on religious buildings.[85]

Conclusion

The subject-oriented approach reflects forward movement for designating holy sites and their protection. With the emergence of other international players maintaining an important role in the global framework, such as NGOs who are equipped to deal with assertions of a group or individual rights, the subject-oriented approach towards holy sites can provide the means for further definition of what is a holy site and how it is to be protected. Additionally, the shift away from a state-centric understanding and application of designating holy places bodes well for holy site protection. Even claims based on objective cultural protection can be strengthened when incorporating other human rights, for example minority protection, which maintains an obvious focus on culture and its protection. This is important for properties like *waqf*-designated mosques and cemeteries that have fallen outside the control of the relevant authorities, as well as holy sites that are not in use or have been abandoned. One may claim that these sites maintain some type of cultural value, due to their historical or cultural role in the development of the surrounding population. The claim to minority protection can be used as a means of ensuring the protection of additional aspects of minority rights (especially preservation of culture and heritage) along with cases involving access and upkeep of various holy sites.

Notes

1 Part of the problem is the danger of over- and under-inclusiveness inherent in any form of designation, a similar problem associated with defining a religion or belief in the international human rights context. *See e.g.*, A Krishnaswami, *Study of Discrimination in the Matter of Religious Rights and Practices* E/CN.4/Sub.2/ 200/ Rev.1 (1960), p. 1 at n. 8 (study served as the basis for drafting the right to freedom of religion or belief in the International Covenant on Civil and Political Rights); GA Third Committee, 15th Sess., mtgs.10212–1027 (1960), at 17.
2 Article 8. Online. Available: http://www.icrc.org/ihl.nsf/FULL/135?OpenDocument (accessed 10 July 2008). *See also*, the Lieber Code of 1863 that referred to a prohibition of harming cultural property, pursuant to General Order Number 100, 14 Apr. 1863, in 3 US Dept. of War, *The War of the Rebellion: A Compilation of the Official Records of the Union and Confederate Armies* (ser. III) 148, 151–53 (1902).
3 Article 34. Online. Available: http://www.icrc.org/ihl.nsf/FULL/140?OpenDocument (accessed 10 July 2008).
4 Article 27. Online. Available: http://www.icrc.org/ihl.nsf/FULL/195?OpenDocument (accessed 10 July 2008).
5 Note that Israel has deemed the 1907 Convention as reflecting customary international law. The Convention only applies to instances of international armed conflict, unlike the 1954 Hague Convention discussed *infra* to which Israel also is a party.
6 While not referring to holy places as such, the Treaty on the Protection of Artistic and Scientific Institutions and Historic Monuments (Roerich Pact), Washington, DC, 15 Apr. 1935, protects, at Article 1, "The historic monuments, museums, scientific, artistic, educational and cultural institutions shall be considered as neutral and as such respected and protected by belligerents. The same respect and protection shall be due to the personnel of the institutions mentioned above. The same respect and protection shall be accorded to the historic monuments, museums, scientific, artistic, educational and cultural institutions in time of peace as well as in war." Online. Available: http://www.icrc.org/ihl.nsf/FULL/325?OpenDocument (accessed 10 July 2008).
7 A. Roberts and R. Guelff (eds.) *Documents on the Laws of War*, Oxford: Clarendon Press, 1989, Doc. no. 22, p. 339. Note that pursuant to Article 19, the Convention also applies to conflicts not of an international character, binding all parties to the conflict. In that sense, the Convention attempted to codify customary international law as it stood at that point, as well as adopt a progressive approach to future conflicts. A. Poulos, "The 1954 Hague Convention for the Protection of Cultural Property in the Event of Armed Conflict: An Historic Analysis," 2000, 28 *International Journal of Legal Information*, p. 1, at 37.
8 This Convention also applies to non-international conflicts.
9 R. O'Keefe, "The Meaning of 'Cultural Property' under the 1954 Hague Convention," 1999 *Netherlands International Law Review*, p. 26, at 28–29; S. Eagen,

"Preserving Cultural Property: Our Public Duty: A Look at How and Why We Must Create International Laws that Support International Action," 2001, 13 *Pace International Law Review*, p. 407, at 422, 443. See also L.C. Green, *The Contemporary Law of Armed Conflict*, Manchester: Manchester University Press, 1993, p. 145, n. 184; K. Partsch, "Protection of Cultural Property," in D. Fleck (ed.) *The Handbook of Humanitarian Law in Armed Conflicts,* Oxford: Oxford University Press, 1995, p. 382; K. Detling, "Eternal Silence: The Destruction of Cultural Property in Yugoslavia," 1993, 17 *Maryland Journal of International Law and Trade*, 41, p. 52, referring to the Preamble that provides a focus on a broader approach to cultural property of the world.

10 O'Keefe, "The Meaning of 'Cultural Property' under the 1954 Hague Convention," p. 29, adopting this approach over the restrictive approach, contrary to the majority of other writers who prefer a restrictive approach.

11 Some refer to this as an internationalist approach versus a nationalist approach. Eagen, "Preserving Cultural Property: Our Public Duty," n. 9, pp. 416–17, noting that in each instance, the object being protected takes center stage and merits protection. O'Keefe, "The Meaning of 'Cultural Property' under the 1954 Hague Convention," at pp. 36–38, refers to the travaux préparatoires of the Convention as grounds for demonstrating that the property under protection is to be considered by each state in accordance with its own national cultural heritage. O'Keefe also compares the terms "cultural heritage" as found within the Convention and notes UNESCO documents discussed *infra* with "common heritage of mankind" found in other documents like the 1982 Convention on the Law of the Sea, noting the similarities between the terms as referring to the obligations of the state to serve as a trustee of sorts. *Ibid.*, pp. 42–43. *Cf. Proposed Legal System for the Holy Places – Common Heritage of Mankind*, 27 Sept. 2003, Foundation for the Culture of Peace Madrid, Sapin, (on file with the author) at paras 4–7, for a broad-form approach to the variety of references to a common culture or heritage.

12 According to Eagen, "Preserving Cultural Property: Our Public Duty," n. 11, pp. 426–27, a key problem with the Convention is the deference to military necessity as it is subject to a broad interpretation and application by states. *See also*, C. Forrest, "The Doctrine of Military Necessity and the Protection of Cultural Property During Armed Conflicts," 2007, 37 *California Western International Law Review*, p. 177 (critiquing "protection" given inherent deference to military necessity to destroy objects used for military advantage); Poulos, op. cit., at 15–16. G. Corn, "Snipers in the Minaret—What is the Rule? The Law of War and the Protection of Cultural Property: A Complex Equation," 2005, *2005 Army Lawyer*, p. 28 ("necessity" defined as no other viable alternative)

13 O'Keefe, "The Meaning of 'Cultural Property' under the 1954 Hague Convention," n. 9, p. 43.

14 Article 23 provides for technical assistance from UNESCO in organizing the protection of their cultural property or in connection with any other problem arising out of the application of the Convention.

15 The appointment was based on the Regulations for the Execution of the Convention for the Protection of Cultural Property in the Event of Armed Conflict, Articles 2 and 4. Online. Available: http://www.icomos.org/hague/hague.regulations.html (accessed 10 July 2008).

16 Detling, "Eternal Silence," n. 9, pp. 63–64.

17 A. Roberts and R. Guelff (eds) *Documents on the Laws of War*, Oxford: Clarendon Press, 1989, Doc. no. 26, p. 387.

18 *Ibid.*, Doc. no. 27, p. 447.

19 Israel signed the Fourth Geneva Convention on 8 Dec. 1949 and ratified it on 6 July 1951, Online. Available: http://www.icrc.org/ihl.nsf/WebSign?ReadForm&id=375&ps=P (accessed 10 July 2008).

See e.g., 7957/05, *Ma'arava v. Prime Minister of Israel*, decided 15 Sept. 2005 (not pub.); *Shahin et al. v. Commander of IDF Forces in the Area of Judea and Samaria*, 41(1) PD 197 (1987); *Kwasama v. Minister of Defense*, 35(1) PD 617 (1981) [in Hebrew]. *See also*, S. Berkovitz, *How Dreadful is this Place: Holiness, Politics, and Justice in Jerusalem and the Holy Places in Israel*, Jerusalem: Karta Publishing, 2006, pp. 326–29.
20 Israel acceded to this Convention on 6 Dec. 1999. Online. Available: http://whc.unesco.org/pg.cfm?cid=246 (accessed 10 July 2008).
From the list it submitted to the Intergovernmental Committee, the following have been inscribed on the World Heritage List: Jerusalem, the Old City of Acre, Massada, and the Bauhaus style buildings in Tel Aviv.
21 Article 1 of the Convention. The understanding is that the object maintains a cultural significance "which is so exceptional as to transcend national boundaries and to be of common importance for present and future generations of all humanity." Intergovernmental Committee for the Protection of the World Cultural and Natural Heritage Operational Guidelines for the Implementation of the World Heritage Convention WHC.05/2, (UNESCO, 2/2/05), para. 49.
22 Articles 4 and 5 of the Convention.
23 *Cf.* F. Francioni and F. Lenzerini, "The Destruction of the Buddhas of Bamiyan and International Law," 2003, 14 *European Journal of International Law*, p. 619, at 635, deeming the Convention as reflective of customary international law and equivalent to the *opinio juris* of states, with R. O'Keefe, "World Cultural Heritage: Obligations to the International Community as a Whole?" 2004, 53 *International Comparative Law Quarterly*, 189, pp. 202–5, noting that the there is no compelling evidence regarding a state's obligations concerning cultural heritage protection. O'Keefe reaches this conclusion since the various documents lack any fundamental norm-creating language and the governmental statements are not clear evidence of *opinio juris*. In addition, deeming cultural heritage as a common heritage does not mean there is an obligation to preserve this heritage (even though the documents do support grounds for diplomatic efforts and statements to preserve such cultural heritage).
24 Article 5(5) of the Convention. Eagen, n. 9, p. 443, notes that this is one of the key weaknesses of the Convention as source nations might not have any connection or interest in a particular cultural property, thereby undermining the very reason for developing some form of cultural preservation of common heritage objects.
25 Article 6, with Article 7, calling for international cooperation in assisting state parties to "conserve and identify that heritage."
26 UNESCO General Conference 15th sess., Res. 3.343, 1968. *See also* S. Ferrari, "The Future of Jerusalem: A Symposium: The Religious Significance of Jerusalem in the Middle East Peace Process: Some Legal Implications," 1996, 45 *Catholic University Law Review*, p. 733.
27 *See also*, UNESCO Res. 3.422 of 17 Oct to 21 Nov. 1972, Seventeenth sess., at p. 61.
28 UNESCO Doc 19C/Annex I Records of the General Conference, Nineteenth Sess., Nairobi, 26 Oct. to 30 Nov. 1976, p. 20, 26 Nov.1976, ISBN 92-3-101496-X, Online. Available: http://unesdoc.unesco.org/images/0011/001140/114038e.pdf#page=136 (accessed 10 July 2008).
29 *Ibid.*, at Article 2.
30 UNESCO Doc 19C/Annex I Records of the General Conference, Nineteenth Sess., Nairobi, 26 Oct. to 30 Nov. 1976, p. 29, 26 Nov.1976, ISBN 92-3-101496-X. *See* Article 4, Online. Available: http://unesdoc.unesco.org/images/0011/001140/114038e.pdf#page=136 (accessed 10 July 2008).
31 UNESCO Doc. 29C/Res. 44, 12 Nov. 1997, at Article 4.
32 UNESCO Doc. 31C/Res. 25, 2 Nov. 2001, at Article 7. In addition, Res. 26, "Acts Constituting as Crime Against the Common Heritage of Humanity" called on

states to prevent destructive acts against the cultural heritage of humanity. UNESCO Doc. 31C/Res. 26, Nov. 2001, at Article 1.
33 UNESCO Doc 32C/25, 17 July 2003, at Articles 3 and 4.
34 A/RES/55/254 and A/RES/58/128. Note as well a number of GA and CHR Resolutions concerning the destruction of Bamiyan Buddhas in Afghanistan. GA Resolutions 1998: 53/165, 1999: 54/185 and 2000: 55/119, along with CHR Resolutions 1998/70, 1999/9 and 2000/18 all addressed generally the situation of human rights in Afghanistan, and noted the shared responsibility for the common heritage of cultural artifacts, appealing to the international community to prevent such destruction.
35 D. Thomason, "Rolling Back History: The United Nations General Assembly and the Right to Cultural Property," 1990, 22 *Case Western Reserve Journal of International Law*, p. 47, p. 65.
36 The Article is based on Article 27 of The Universal Declaration of Human Rights, 10 Dec.1948: "the right to participate freely in the cultural life of the community." The Committee has interpreted this as a positive right of the state. *See e.g.*, E/1993/22, para. 186.
37 Note the 1995 report from the World Commission on Culture and Development calling for additional drafting on cultural rights: *Our Cultural Diversity—Report of the World Commission on Culture and Development 1995*, at p. 281.
38 M. Komurcu, "Cultural Heritage Endangered by Large Dams and its Protection under International Law," 2002, 20 *Wisconsin International Law Journal*, p. 233, at 277–78.
39 E/1993/22, para. 186.
40 E/1995/22, para. 136.
41 H. Niec, *Cultural Rights: At the End of the World Decade for Cultural Development in Intergovernmental Conference on Cultural Policies for Development*, UNESCO 1998, CLT-98/Conf.210/Ref.2 at 4, noting as well the problem of cultural relativism and that identifying the precise content of the right to culture remains unclear. The author also notes the separate development of the notion of cultural heritage, referring to L. Prott, "Cultural Rights as Peoples Rights in International Law," in J. Crawford (ed.) *The Rights of People*, Oxford: Oxford University Press, 1988, p. 93. *See also*, Komurcu, "Cultural Heritage Endangered by Large Dams and its Protection under International Law," n. 38, p. 279.
42 The General Framework Agreement, 14 Dec. 1995. Online. Available: http://www.ohr.int/dpa/default.asp?content_id=380 (accessed 10 July 2008).
43 *Ibid.*, at Article 6. Online. Available: http://www.ohr.int/dpa/default.asp?content_id=376 (accessed 10 July 2008). Article 6 of Annex 8 states, "The following shall be eligible for designation as National Monuments: movable or immovable property of great importance to a group of people with common cultural, historic, religious or ethnic heritage, such as monuments of architecture, art or history; archaeology sites; groups of buildings; as well as cemeteries."
44 *See e.g, Application of the Convention on the Prevention and Punishment of the Crime of Genocide (Bosnia and Herzegovnia v. Serbia and Montenegro)* decided 26 Feb. 2007. Online. Available: http://www.icj-cij.org/docket/index.php?p1=3&p2=3&k=f4&case=91&code=bhy&p3=4 (accessed 10 July 2008). Although the actions of Serbia did not reach the level of intent to constitute genocide as required by the Genocide Convention, the Court found sufficient evidence of deliberate destruction of holy places.
45 Press Conference following the Seventh Session.
46 Decision on the Commission to Preserve National Monuments, adopted by the Presidency of Bosnia and Herzegovina, 21 Dec. 2001. Online. Available: http://www.aneks8komisiga.com.ba/main.php?id_struct=82&lang=4 (accessed 10 July 2008). This legislation was passed in accordance with Article 9 of Annex 8 which provides, "Five years after this Agreement enters into force, the responsibility for the

Protection of holy places in international law 63

continued operation of the Commission shall transfer from the Parties to the Government of Bosnia and Herzegovina." n. 3, at Article 9.

47 *See e.g.*, Bosnia and Herzegovina Commission to Preserve National Monuments, 38th Sess. of the Commission. Online. Available: http://www.aneks8komisija.com.ba/main.php?id_struct=66&lang=4 (accessed 10 July 2008).
48 Thus far 196 sites have been designated national monuments including mosques, Catholic and Orthodox churches, synagogues, monasteries and other sites of religious significance. For list of monuments, *see* Bosnia and Herzegovina Commission to Preserve National Monuments, National Monuments. Online. Available: http://www. aneks8komisija.com.ba/main.php?id_struct = 50&lang = 4 (accessed 16 July 2004).
49 Press Conference following the Twelfth Sess., 6 Jan. 2004. Online. Available: http://www.aneks8komisija.com. ba /main.php?id_struct = 68&lang = 4 (accessed 10 July 2008).
50 Press Conference following the Eleventh Sess., 10 Dec.2003. Online. Available: http://www.aneks8komisija.com. ba /main.php?id_struct = 68&lang = 4 (accessed 16 July 2004). *See e.g.*, Press Conference following the Tenth Sess., 11 Oct. 2003. Online. Available: http://www.aneks8komisija.com.bamain.php?id_struct=68&lang=4 (accessed 10 July 2008).
51 Press Release, Carsija Mosque in Prijedor. Online. Available: http://www.aneks8komisija.com.ba /main.php?id_struct = 68&lang = 4 (accessed 16 July 2004).
52 Press Conference following the Eleventh Sess., n. 50.
53 Adopted by General Assembly Resolution 2200 A (XXI) 16 Dec. 1966
54 CCPR/C/21/Rev.1/Add.4, 30 July 1993, at para. 4.
55 *Ibid.*, noting that worship for example extends to "giving direct expression to belief."
56 Pilgrimage is not a right as such given states' capacities to limit the right of access by foreigners. G. Watson, "Progress for Pilgrims? An Analysis of the Holy See–Israel Fundamental Agreement," 1997–98, 47 *Catholic University Law Review*, 497, p. 525, although it could be perceived as a form of manifestation. *See e.g.*, P. Mason, "Pilgrimage to Religious Shrines: An Essential Element in the Human Right to Freedom of Thought, Conscience and Religion," 1993, 25 *Case Western Reserve Journal of International Law,* p. 619. The Islamic Hajj, for example, is an obligatory action required by all Muslims and as such could fall within the purview of manifestation. G. Watson, "Progress for Pilgrims? An Analysis of the Holy See—Israel Fundamental Agreement," in M. Breger (ed.) *The Vatican–Israel Accords: Political, Legal, and Theological Contexts*, Bloomington, Ind.: University of Notre Dame Press, 2004, 203, p. 213, discussing as well the associated right to freedom of movement and travel as a basis.
57 *Cyprus v. Turkey* (Merits), Appl. 2578/94, 10 May 2001, ECtHR, Reports 2001-IV 284. Note that the Court deemed as a violation the expropriation by Turkey of various property interests that had been in abeyance until 1989.
58 Greek Orthodox churches continue to be converted into mosques, vandalized or turned into entertainment centers while priceless treasures and works of art are smuggled out of the country or destroyed, in defiance of the relevant resolutions and calls of European and International Organizations (such as the European Parliament, the Council of Europe, UNESCO, etc.) to stop the destruction and cooperate for the protection of the ancient and religious monuments of Cyprus. Among recent examples of this policy, are:

- the attempt to sell to foreigners the Church of Chrysotrimythiotissa;
- the destruction of the paintings of the Convent of Christ Antiphonetes near the village of Kalograia in the Pentadaktylos mountain and the complete destruction of the historic Armenian Convent of Saint Makarios, also in the Pentadaktylos;

- the looting and desecration of the Church of the Apostle Andreas near Kyrenia, the Church of the Holy Virgin in Pano Zodia, the Church of Saints Sergios and Paraskevi near the ruins of ancient Salamis, the Church of the Holy Virgin (Melandrina) near the villages of Ayios Amvrosios and Kalogrea, the Church of Saint Anastasia in Lapithos, the Church of Saint Irene in Karavas and the Church of Saint George, also in Karavas;
- the conversion of the Convent of the Holy Virgin Eleousa (in occupied Karpasia) into a restaurant and the conversion of the Church of the Archangel Michael in Kyrenia into a museum;
- the conversion into mosques of the Church of Saint George in the village of Prastio in the Famagusta area, the Church of Saint Paraskevi in Lapithos, the Church of the Holy Virgin in Karavas, the Church of Saint Amvrosios in the village of Ayios Amvrosios, the Church of the Holy Virgin Chrysopolitissa in Kyrenia and the Church of Saint George in Kyrenia;
- Illegal archeological works in Kyrenia, Famagusta, Salamina and in the occupied peninsula of Karpasia;
- destruction of churches or conversion into mosques, hospitals, barns or cinemas;
- illegal exportation and sale of priceless mosaics, frescos and icons, such as the ones from the Church of Kanakaria, the Church of St Themonianos, the Convent of Christ Antiphonetes and 12 more convents.

Over 500 churches have been destroyed in an effort to give the occupied areas a Turkish character and the United Nations Peacekeeping Force (UNFICYP) is pursuing the matter with the Turkish side, so far unsuccessfully. Besides outright looting, the occupation authorities have allowed many archaeological sites and religious monuments to be gradually eroded and destroyed through neglect, such as the ruins of ancient Enkomi, the monastery of the Apostle Andreas in Karpasia etc. Online. Available: http://greekembassy.org/Embassy/Content/en/Article.aspx?office=6&folder = 44&article = 89 (accessed 4 June 2008).

Concerning other examples of state practice, note as well the freedom of access and worship provided by the 1994 Agreement on the Gaza Strip and the Jericho Area. *See* Agreement on the Gaza Strip and the Jericho Area between Israel and the Palestine Liberation Organization, 4 May 1994, U.N. Doc. A/49/180-S/1994/727 (Annex) of 20 June 1994, reprinted in 1994, 33 *International Legal Materials*, 622, and the 1995 Israeli–Palestinian Interim Agreement on the West Bank and the Gaza Strip, *Kitvei Amanot* vol. 33, no. 1, reprinted in 1997, 36, *International Legal Materials*, p. 551 (excerpts). In the 1995 Interim Agreement, mention is made of the status of graves sacred to Jews in the territories that were to be handed over to the Palestinian Authority (i.e., those in Area A). According to the agreement, "The present situation and the existing practices shall be preserved" (Article V.b.). Similar concerns are addressed in the 1997 Protocol Concerning the Redeployment in Hebron. *See Protocol Concerning the Redeployment in Hebron and Note for the Record*, 17 Jan. 1997, 1997, 36 *International Legal Materials*, 650. Access rights also are discussed in the Jordan–Israel Peace Agreement noting: "Each Party will provide freedom of access to places of religious and historical significance." Article 9, para. 3, *Peace between the State of Israel and the Hashemite Kingdom of Jordan*, 26 Oct. 1994, Online. Available: http://www.mfa.gov.il/MFA/Peace+Process/Guide+to+the+Peace+Process/Israel-Jordan+Peace+Treaty.htm (accessed 10 July 2008).
59 CHR Resolution 2004/36—Elimination of all Forms of Religious Intolerance 55th meeting 19 April 2004, Ch. XI.–/2004/23–E/CN.4/2004/127.
60 Report by Special Rapporteur, E/CN.4/2005/61 at paragraphs 49–51, referring as well to the Human Rights Committee's General Comment 22.
61 *See e.g.*, C. O'Faircheallaigh, "Negotiating Cultural Heritage? Aboriginal-Mining Company Agreements in Australia," 2008, 39 *Development and Change*, 25.

62 *See e.g.*, L. Prott, "The Development of Legal Concepts Connected with the Protection of the Cultural Heritage" in R. Blanpain (ed.) *Law in Motion*, Hague: Kluwer Law International,1997, 600, p. 618.
63 *See e.g.*, J. Burger, *The Draft United Nations Declaration on the Rights of Indigenous Peoples*, International Council on Human Rights Policy, February Workshop, 2005, Online. Available: http://www.ichrp.org/paper_files/120_w_05.doc (accessed 10 July 2008).
64 Article 13 has generally remained the same throughout the drafting process. *See e.g.*, E/CN.4/2005/WG.15/2 for the most recent draft.
65 *Ibid.*, at para. 6.
66 Commission on Human Rights, Principles, and Guidelines for the Protection of the Heritage of Indigenous Peoples, E/CN.4/Sub.2/2000/26, at paragraphs 6 and 13.
67 Report of the Special Rapporteur on the Situation of Human Rights and Fundamental Freedoms of Indigenous Peoples, E/CN.4/2003/90, at paragraphs 50 and 75.
68 K. Wangkeo, "Monumental Challenges: The Lawfulness of Destroying Cultural Heritage During Peacetime," 2003, 28 *Yale Journal International Law*, 183 (while economic development generally favored in state practice, there is an emerging notion of mitigating damages and making good faith efforts to preserve cultural relics); S. Wiessner, "Rights and Status of Indigenous peoples: A Global, Comparative and International Legal Analysis," 1999, 12 *Harvard Human Rights Journal*, p. 57, at 93 (state practice indicating some form of deference to indigenous peoples, recognizing their spiritual connection to the land).
69 D. Rivera, "Taino Sacred Sites: An International Comparative Analysis for a Domestic Solution," 2003, 20 *Arizona Journal of International and Comparative Law*, 443, pp. 474–81; 511/1992 *Lansmann v. Finland*, UN HRC, CCPR/C52/D/511/1992 (1994) (relying on Article 27 of the ICCPR, which has been understood to include the rights of indigenous peoples along with minorities).
70 549/1993 *Hopu and Bessert v. France UN HRC.*, CCPR/C/60/D/549/1993/Rev.1 (1997) (no destruction of burial ground given interference with right to privacy and family).
71 General Comment No.23 of the Committee to Eliminate Racial Discrimination, 51st. sess., 18 Aug. 1997.
72 Convention No.169 Concerning Indigenous and Tribal Peoples in Independent Countries, adopted 1989, reprinted in 1989, 28, *International Legal Materials*, p. 1382, at Article14.
73 World Bank Operational Policy 4.10, Indigenous Peoples, July 2005. Online. Available: http://wbln0018.worldbank.org/Institutional/Manuals/OpManual.nsf/0/0F7D6F3F04DD70398525672C007D08ED?OpenDocument (accessed 10 July 2008). It provides at para.16 that a borrower must pay specific attention to Indigenous Peoples' customary laws, values, customs, and traditions pertaining to lands or territories that they traditionally owned, or customarily used or occupied, and where access to natural resources is vital to the sustainability of their cultures and livelihoods, including "(c) the cultural and spiritual values that the Indigenous Peoples attribute to such lands and resources." Bank Procedure BP 4.10, *Indigenous Peoples*, July 2005. Online. Available http://wbln0018.worldbank.org/Institutional/Manuals/OpManual.nsf/B52929624EB2A3538525672E00775F66/DBB9575225027E678525703100541C7D? OpenDocument (accessed 10 July 2008). It provides for ongoing consultation and involvement by indigenous peoples in the proposed project.
74 *Compare* F. Francioni and F. Lenzerini, *supra* note 23 (concluding that a customary international obligation exists to protect significant cultural heritage) *with* O'Keefe (2004) *supra* note 23 (no customary obligation exists given the lack of any binding international instrument). Various UN bodies, such as the General Assembly, did issue some non-binding resolutions condemning the destruction. *See e.g.*, GA Res. 55/119 (2000), at paragraph19.

75 Such as the situation in Northern Cyprus, discussed *supra*.
76 Note as well that the post-Second World War trials also alluded to this approach in finding that the burning and demolishing of synagogues was indicative of the intent to persecute Jews. See *US v. Goering*, 1946, 1 *International Military Tribunal*, p. 293, at 295. Israel made a similar claim against Eichmann in his trial before the Israeli domestic court. *See* 1961, 36 *Israel Law Review* (1961), p. 5, para. 57, *Attorney General of the Government of Israel v. Adolf Eichmann*, District Court Jerusalem, 1961, p. 5.
77 H. Abtahi, "The Protection of Cultural Property in Times of Armed Conflict: The Practice of the International Criminal Tribunal for the Former Yugoslavia," 2001, 14 *Harvard Human Rights Journal*, p. 1, at 28, noting that persecution is a crime deemed more serious than a crime against humanity and maintaining similar elements to genocide (albeit not at the same level).
78 *Prosecutor v. Kordic and Cerkez* [2001] ICTY Trial Chamber III, (26 Feb. 2001), at para. 809. Online. Available: http://www.un.org/icty/kordic/trialc/judgement/index.htm (accessed 10 July 2008). The court noted that the accused had "deliberately targeted mosques and other religious and educational institutions. This included the Ahmici Mosque which the Trial Chamber finds was not used for military purposes but was deliberately destroyed by the HVO." *Ibid.*, at para. 807.
79 Note as well *Prosecutor v. Blaskic* [2004] ICTY 11 (29 July 2004) where the initial indictment, at Article 14, included the destruction of religious property as grounds for finding an intent to destroy the Muslim population. On appeal, this part of the indictment was vacated, as the trial court did not engage in any discussion of this charge. Online. Available: http://www.un.org/icty/blaskic/appeal/judgement/index.htm (accessed 10 July 2008). *See* section 530.
80 *Prosecutor v. Krstic* [2001] ICTY 8 (2 Aug. 2001). Online. Available: http://www.un.org/icty/krstic/TrialC1/judgement/index.htm (accessed 10 July 2008). The decision was upheld in *Prosecutor v. Krstic* [2004] ICTY 7 (19 Apr. 2004). Online. Available: http://www.un.org/icty/krstic/Appeal/judgement/index.htm (accessed 10 July 2008).
81 *Krstic Trial Chamber* at para. 207 noting that "This act, [destruction or damage of religious and educational institutions] when perpetrated with the requisite discriminatory intent, amounts to an attack on the very religious identity of a people. As such, it manifests a nearly pure expression of the notion of crimes against humanity, for all of humanity is indeed injured by the destruction of a unique religious culture and its concomitant cultural objects. The Trial Chamber therefore finds that the destruction and wilful damage of institutions dedicated to Muslim religion or education, coupled with the requisite discriminatory intent, may amount to an act of persecution." Online. Available: http://www.un.org/icty/krstic/TrialC1/judgement/index.htm (accessed 10 July 2008).
82 *Prosecutor v. Milosevic* [2004] ICTY 8 (16 June 2004). Online. Available: http://www.un.org/icty/milosevic/trialc/judgement/index.htm (accessed 10 July 2008).
83 *See e.g.*, *Abtahi*, n.75, at 31.
84 Article 8.2 states that "Other serious violations of the laws and customs applicable in international armed conflict, within the established framework of international law, namely, any of the following acts ... (ix) Intentionally directing attacks against buildings dedicated to religion, education, art, science or charitable purposes, historic monuments, hospitals and places where the sick and wounded are collected, provided they are not military objectives;" and the same at Article 8.e (iv) for conflicts of a non-international character. Rome Statute of the International Criminal Court, adopted and opened for signature on 17 July 1998, by the United Nations Diplomatic Conference of Plenipotentiaries on the Establishment of an International Criminal Court, A/CONF.183/9 of 18 July 1998, 2187 *UNTS* 3, EIF: 1 July 2002, Signatories: 139, Parties: 106 (as of 1 June 2008).

4 Wars and sacred space

The influence of the 1948 War on sacred space in the state of Israel

Doron Bar

The process by which holy places are created and turn into pilgrimage sites has been the focus of considerable research in recent years. Numerous scholars representing a variety of disciplines have turned their attention to this fascinating phenomenon and to the way in which it affects the spaces in question. In the Holy Land the sites identified as sacred have always been of great importance and their influence on local history has been extensive. Due to the region's status as the cradle of the three great monotheistic religions, tens of holy sites have emerged here, some of which have been revered jointly by local residents of differing faiths. These sacred places developed via a process that extended over many generations—a process that was frequently affected by the interplay of social, cultural and political forces in the region.

There is a clear connection between the way in which the map of the Holy Land's sacred sites developed and the various regime changes that took place there. The region's successive occupiers and rulers continually redrew the outlines of this map, and the many wars that raged in Palestine over the centuries were crucial to the glorification of the holy places or, alternatively, to their disappearance. It appears that, of all the wars that took place in the region, the 1948 Arab–Israel War was the one that had the most far-reaching consequences for sacred space in the Holy Land. Surprisingly, despite the fact that this conflict has been investigated from a number of perspectives,[1] its effects on the distribution and status of the holy sites have never yet been addressed: this issue will be the focus of the present article. The geopolitical changes to which the Holy Land's inhabitants were subjected after the territorial partition of 1948, and the fact that many of the holy sites at which the region's Jews worshiped prior to 1948 became inaccessible thereafter, led to a reshaping of sacred space within the State of Israel and to the creation of an alternative map of Jewish holy sites, most of which had not existed before the land was divided. Although it is true that the adherents of other religions in the area were also deeply affected by the outcome of the war and were also unable at times to visit their sacred sites, this situation nevertheless appears to have had a particularly strong impact on the Jews who were cut off from such sites of historical and religious centrality as the Western Wall, Rachel's Tomb, and the Cave of the Patriarchs.

Elsewhere I have addressed the development of sacred Jewish space during the 1950s and 1960s, and the ways in which observant Jews coped with the post-1948 reality. During the nineteen years in which the land was divided, Jewish sacred space developed under the guidance of Dr. Shmuel Zanwil Kahana, Director General of Israel's Ministry of Religious Affairs during this period, who devoted himself to the task of redesigning the Jewish holy places.[2] In this essay I shall be focusing on the impact of the 1948 War on the region's sacred space and on the way in which the Israeli establishment, as well as Jewish religious believers, coped with the fact that many of the Jewish holy sites that were developed during this period were actually part of a venerable Muslim tradition. The discussion below will also focus on the process by which numerous sacred places that had been jointly revered in the past by Muslims and Jews were appropriated and Judaized once they came under Israeli sovereignty.

Distribution of the Jewish holy sites prior to 1948

Although our knowledge about the existence and status of Jewish holy sites during the first millennium C.E., after the destruction of the Temple in Jerusalem, is insufficient, it is clear that after the Crusader period, from the twelfth century on, a distinctly Jewish sacred space began to emerge. It appears that the Crusader regime in the region, and the area's later reoccupation by the Muslims, presented Palestinian Jewry with a complex religious challenge and led to the development and expansion of an array of Jewish holy places that were based on ancient myths relating mainly to the Biblical, Mishnaic and Talmudic periods. During the later Muslim period, from the thirteenth century on, holy sites were points of destination both for Jewish inhabitants of the region and for the relatively numerous Jewish pilgrims who came to Palestine from elsewhere in the Middle East, and from Europe. After the Ottoman conquest of Palestine, the Galilee took on a role of central importance in the Ziara ceremonies of the Palestinian and Diaspora Jews. Toward the end of Ottoman rule in Palestine, prior to the arrival of the British, Jewish sacred space in the region consisted of several pilgrimage sites scattered across various areas within Palestine. However, this period actually appears to have seen a relative decline in Jewish interest in these sites. Zionist immigration to Palestine, and the emergence of alternative myths such as Tel-Hai, Massada and Modi'in, led to a significant weakening of the status of the historical holy places, which continued to attract residents of the Old Yishuv and religiously observant pilgrims.

One particularly salient issue regarding the Jewish holy sites before 1948 was the fact that most of them were under Muslim control.[3] Sites such as the Cave of the Patriarchs, King David's Tomb, Elijah's Cave, many of the *kivrei tzadikim* (graves of the righteous) in the Galilee, and, to a certain extent, the Western Wall in Jerusalem, were not administered by the Jews of Palestine, but rather by the region's Muslim inhabitants. The historical reality and the fact that in later generations the Jews were a minority in Palestine, while the Muslims accounted for the majority of the population, led to a state of affairs in which only a small number of the Jewish holy places were under the direct proprietorship of local Jews. Jews were generally permitted to visit the sites under Muslim control, but they were usually required to pay entrance fees, and were granted entry only during certain times. The Cave of the Patriarchs, for example, was generally off limits to Jews, who were obliged to content themselves with standing and praying on the staircase outside the compound. During the course of the nineteenth century, after many generations during which Jews were forbidden to visit King David's Tomb, they were permitted to enter the site, but were restricted to a dummy exhibit on the structure's top floor rather than being admitted to the historical tomb displayed on the ground floor. The Galilee, where holy places passed from one religion to another throughout history, was one of Palestine's more "crowded" regions in terms of the prevalence of these sites, but many of them were under the control of the local Muslim population.[4] Thus, despite the fact that during the generations prior to 1948 the Jews of the Galilee made extensive efforts to gain control of many sacred gravesites, even enjoying a certain amount of success,[5] most of the Jewish sacred space still remained under Muslim proprietorship. During this period the local Muslims still controlled numerous sacred burial sites which were located within, or near, their villages. The grave of Rabbi Shimon bar Yochai, for instance, was revered as a holy site by the residents of the nearby Muslim village of Meron, along with many tens of other burial sites in the area. The Jews regarded these sites as the graves of the Tannaim and Amoraim, while the Muslims associated them with local holy men and sacred personages.

Visiting these places frequently involved obtaining a permit and even having to pay the Muslim village families who controlled them. Thus, for example, the grave of Rabbi Yochanan Hasandlar, near Meron, was identified as that of *Abu Bakr*; the grave of *Muhammad Almazov* was confounded with that of Rabbi Yose of Yokeret, and the tomb of *Tzadik a-Toachin* (the Holy Man of the Mills) was identified with that of Rabbi Yose of Peki'in. The tomb of the prophet Habakkuk was identified as that of *Sheikh Hassan*, and the shrines in the village of Chananya, bordering the Upper and Lower Galilee, mainly served the local Muslims prior to the State of Israel's founding. These sites consisted of heaps of stones, caves, and old coffin fragments which the Muslims identified as the tomb of *Banat Yaqub* (the Father of the Blue Stone) and *Abu Zeine* (the Father of Beauty). In the Arab village of Baradiya, identified with the Jewish village of Parod, the gravesite of *Sheikh Mantzur* was associated by the Jews with that of Rabbi Tanchum of Parod, a contemporary of Rabbi Yochanan. Near Shfaram the traditional site of Rabbi Yehuda Ben Baba's grave was identified with the burial place of *Banat Yaqub*, a name used by the Muslims for many of their holy sites.[6]

Jerusalem was the most significant place within the Holy Land's Jewish sacred space at the end of the Ottoman period and during Mandate rule. Jewish pilgrims who arrived in Jerusalem during this period were able to visit some twenty holy sites,[7] some of them of central importance, others of lesser status. Pilgrimage to these sites generally took place in accordance with the Hebrew calendar and the dates of the various Jewish holidays. Here, too, only a small number of these pilgrimage sites were under Jewish ownership. Of all the sacred places, the Western Wall received the most attention and was considered to be the most important, but it was not under Jewish control and during the nineteenth century several efforts were made to purchase it and transfer it to Jewish hands. During the Mandate period, when the Western Wall became a point of conflict between Jewish and Arab residents of the city, the site was transformed into a national Zionist symbol.[8]

In addition to the Western Wall, there were other holy sites in the Jerusalem area which served as Jewish pilgrimage destinations up until 1948,[9] but were under Muslim control. Near the summit of the Mount of Olives are two sites which Jewish tradition identifies as the Tomb of Hulda the Prophetess and the Tombs of the prophets Hagai, Malachi, and Zachariah. The Tomb of Hulda the Prophetess lies in the basement of one of the structures on the Mount, and is also identified as the burial place of Saint Pelagia and Rabi'a al-'Adawiyya; it was held as an Islamic endowment by the al-Alami family from the Ayoubi period on.[10] The burial-cave of the prophets Haggai, Malachi and Zechariah—an impressive example of a radial burial system from the Byzantine period—referred to by the Arabs as *Ghar al-Anbiyya* (the Cave of the Prophets), was purchased at the end of the nineteenth century by the Russian Monastery on the Mount of Olives, but an agreement between the monastery administration and the leaders of the Jewish community in Jerusalem ensured the Jews' right to free access to the site, while also guaranteeing that no objects of Christian symbolism would be placed there. Up from the Kidron Valley lay the Tomb of Shimon Hatzadik, one of the more important of the sacred Jewish sites in Jerusalem, which attracted pilgrims en masse, particularly Jews from Middle Eastern countries. The burial cave and the area surrounding it were purchased during the nineteenth century by the Jews of the city, and pilgrimage activity at the site reached its pinnacle each year on Lag Ba'Omer, when Jewish Jerusalemites, particularly those of Middle Eastern background, would gather near the cave and hold a kind of *hilula* or festival that included prayer services in the cave itself, first-haircut ceremonies for small boys and a mass picnic in a carnival atmosphere.[11]

A position of centrality among the Jewish holy sites in Jerusalem was held by King David's Tomb on Mount Zion, to which pilgrims would make their way primarily on the festival of Shavuot, traditionally recognized as the anniversary of King David's birth and death. Because King David's Tomb was held by the Muslim Dajani family, Jews were not permitted free access to the site. They had to content themselves with visiting a duplication of the grave that was located in the second and upper floor of the building.

To the holy places in Jerusalem proper one must add other pilgrimage destinations located in the city's environs which were also part of Jewish sacred space in Palestine. One of the most important of these sites, along with the Cave of the Patriarchs, was Rachel's Tomb, situated on the road that connected Jerusalem with Bethlehem and Hebron. The significance of these two sites lay, of course, in their traditional status as the burial sites of the Jewish people's Patriarchs and Matriarchs. Rachel's Tomb was one of the only Jewish holy places to come under Jewish control during the nineteenth century[12] During the British Mandate period it became a point of contention between Jews and Muslims.[13] The result of this dispute was the inclusion of the site in the list of holy places where the "Status Quo" was to be preserved. The Cave of the Patriarchs was also a lodestone for Jewish pilgrims, but Jews were absolutely forbidden to enter the sacred compound. Except for a few exceptional instances they were obliged to make do with praying near the Cave, usually on a secondary stairway leading to the structure.

In addition to the Cave of the Patriarchs, Hebron and its environs were home to several other holy sites which attracted at least some Jewish residents of, and visitors to, Hebron for purposes of pilgrimage and prayer. Many of these sacred burial caves were under Muslim control and the Jews were forced to seek the protection of various families who held the sites. These sites included, among others, the Tombs of *Jesse and Ruth*, the *Tomb of Otniel Ben Kenaz*, the *Tomb of Avner Ben Ner and Mefiboshet*, which attracted mainly Sephardic residents of Hebron, particularly on the day following Shavuot (*issru chag*).[14] Halhul, on the Jerusalem—Hebron road, was also home to a burial site sacred to the Jews— road contained the tombs of Gad the Seer and Nathan the Prophet. Although located in a mosque, Jews would stop here to pray while traveling between Jerusalem and Hebron.

Another central site in Palestinian Jewry's sacred space was that of the Tomb of Samuel the Prophet (referred to by the Arabs as *Nebi Samwil*), located north of Jerusalem. The most important date on the Hebrew calendar designated for pilgrimage to this site, beginning in the fifteenth century, was 28 Iyyar. This custom appears to have been maintained until the eighteenth century, while later on, during the nineteenth century and the first half of the twentieth century, pilgrimage activity at the traditional burial site dwindled and the main pilgrimage-date custom was abandoned.[15] In the case of Samuel the Prophet's Tomb, as in the case of most of the other holy sites mentioned, ownership of the site was in Muslim hands and the impressive structure served as a mosque.

Development of Jewish sacred space after 1948

Political, military, and, primarily, the broad demographic changes that took place in Israel during the years 1947–49 led to the depletion of the Arab population from various areas and to the transfer of some of the sacred places mentioned above to Israeli sovereignty.

Jewish holy sites located in the Holy Land have been classified in the past in a number of ways, mainly in accordance with their historical development or their geographic location.[16] The system of categorization that I use in this article is based on the type of ownership that applied to the Jewish sites prior to the Israeli War of Independence and to the changes that they underwent after the war. Again, only a small number of the sites appearing on the Jewish pilgrimage map after the founding of the State of Israel were previously under Jewish proprietorship. A much greater number of these holy places were under Muslim ownership prior to 1948 and underwent a rapid process of Judaization after the war. Jewish control of these sites was generally achieved through the day-to-day activity of individuals—prayer, ritual, a minor amount of construction, as well as via semi-official means, involving activity on the part of various entities that were fostered and guided by the Israeli Ministry of Religious Affairs and other governmental bodies. One of the most striking results of this process was the obliteration of the sites' Muslim past and the concomitant accentuation of the Jewish traditions connected with them—a phenomenon that shall be discussed below.

The Jewish sacred space that emerged during the years following 1948 was shaped to a great degree through creativity on the part of the Ministry of Religious Affairs and other bodies, whereby ancient written traditions were connected with places that were now recognized as sacred. The holy sites addressed by this article, including King David's Tomb on Mount Zion, Elijah's Cave in Haifa, and the array of *kivrei tzadikim* in the Galilee and the coastal plain, were all developed as part of the Ministry's plan to expand and deepen the State of Israel's map of sacredness by focusing on areas and places not necessarily associated with any long-standing Jewish tradition of sanctity. This amounted to an effort to appropriate the space and make it Jewish—and Israeli. During this period, when the newly-founded state was occupied mainly in nurturing a national cult, there was an emphasis on national elements connected with the distant and recent history of Palestine.[17] The Ministry of Religious Affairs and, first and foremost, its director general, Shmuel Zanwil Kahana, made parallel efforts to stress the region's association with the Biblical past. These semi-official efforts by Kahana and his colleagues to develop Israel's sacred space were supplemented by activity "from below," mainly on the part of new immigrants from Middle Eastern countries who were accustomed to the veneration of holy places in their former homelands and who needed holy places that were close to their new places of residence.

King David's Tomb

Within the Jewish pilgrimage map of the post-1948 period, King David's Tomb on Mount Zion occupies a place of particular distinction. During this period the Tomb became the most central and sacred of all the sites located within the State of Israel, attracting hundreds of thousands of pilgrims per year. King David's Tomb was an important component of the memorial and commemorative construction enterprise that took place on Mount Zion during these years in which Jerusalem was bisected by a border. Although the Tomb did not enjoy primary importance vis-à-vis other sacred sites prior to 1948, the new geopolitical situation for Jerusalem's residents after the 1948

War promoted Mount Zion and King David's Tomb to a unique status during the period in which the city was divided.

Since the Tomb had been held for generations before the war by the Dajani family and recognized as Muslim religious endowment or *waqf*, this new reality created a complex legal and practical problem. During the War and for some months thereafter, the Mount Zion area, including King David's Tomb, was a closed military zone to which free access was not permitted. Activity in the area was administered by the military rabbinate in increasing cooperation with the Ministry of Religious Affairs which took over the site at the end of 1949.[18] The religious public, however, showed little interest in the complex nature of the Tomb's status or in the question of ownership rights and the site began to draw visitors even before the war had ended.

Director General Kahana was obliged to contend with the problematic nature of the Tomb's status. Immediately after the war he initiated a long series of religious ceremonies that brought about a radical change in the status of King David's Tomb and served to encourage Jewish control of the Tomb structure, in the absence of any official decision by the State of Israel. This endeavor was roundly condemned by various official Israeli bodies from its earliest stages.[19]

From the point of view of the State of Israel, the process of gaining religious control over Mount Zion and King David's Tomb was a desirable one in many ways, and various parties actually promoted the process during the post-war period. The use of holy sites as a political-military tool is a familiar one in the history of the Holy Land, and the issue of Mount Zion seems to have been treated this way from Israel's inception.[20] Apparently for this reason, as early as 1949, Israeli Prime Minister David Ben-Gurion stated that in addition to conducting archeological excavations at the site, a Jewish "holy place" should be "established" there. The main reason for this was the desire to create facts on the ground and to eternalize the Jewish character of Mount Zion by developing it as a Jewish holy site, in a process that involved finding proof that King David was actually buried there.[21] "So long as the [archeological] excavations do not find the tombs of the House of David, the Muslim tradition of King David's Tomb will stand,"[22] Ben-Gurion said, stressing the urgency of investigating the nature of the sacred site and his fear that the State of Israel would be forced to retreat from the area.

And, indeed, the process of turning Mount Zion and King David's Tomb into the State of Israel's central religious site began immediately after the war, gaining momentum during the 1950s. Extensive involvement on the part of the Ministry of Religious Affairs and its Director General Kahana, in conjunction with the Society for the Holy Places and the Mount Zion Committee which the latter founded and headed, were what drove this process.[23] However, the very fact that Mount Zion was sacred to the three monotheistic religions made its administration exceptionally complex. Particularly vexing was the matter of the status and definition of King David's Tomb, an issue that was the focus of disagreements and conflicting interests even within the Ministry. On the one hand, it was Kahana himself who initiated extensive

Jewish prayer activity at the site, with the goal of eradicating the Muslim past of King David's Tomb. He saw to the placement of numerous Jewish symbols in and around the Tomb, aimed at demonstrating the political-religious change that had taken place at the site and impressing this fact upon visitors. With the concurrence of the Ministry's architectural advisor, Meir Ben Uri, the phrase "David King of Israel Lives and Endures" was painted over the niche above the tombstone, while large oil-burning candelabra were hung nearby.[24]

On the other hand, a special department within the Ministry of Religious Affairs was charged with preserving the entire array of Muslim religious endowments in Israel, and was also responsible for the existing status and maintenance of King David's Tomb. The Ministry's Muslim and Druze Department was responsible for coordinating all religious and juridical issues with regard to those faiths, including matters related to preservation of the sites sacred to them.[25]

In order to address this problematic issue, the Ministry of Religious Affairs founded, in late 1948, a Committee on the Preservation of Muslim Religious Buildings, whose members included Prof. Leon Arieh Mayer, Jacob Pinkerfeld, and Dr. Haim Zeev Hirschberg, director of the Muslim and Druze Department. As part of this Committee's activity, a number of Muslim prayer and pilgrimage sites were cleaned and restored during 1949–50. These included the Sidna-'Ali Mosque near Arsuf, the mosques of Ein Kerem, the White Mosque in Ramle, the Tomb of Abu Hurayrah in Yavne and King David's Tomb on Mount Zion.[26] Formal responsibility for King David's Tomb was transferred to the Ministry's Muslim Department and, during a tour of this site by Muslim Department members immediately after the cessation of hostilities, it became clear that urgent repair of damage to the building was in order.[27] These repairs were carried out only in the summer of 1951, with the approval of the Department of Antiquities. Jacob Pinkerfeld was charged by the Religious Affairs Ministry's Muslim and Druze Department with handling renovations in the room containing the Tomb and its adjacent area.[28]

The active measures taken by Kahana on Mount Zion served only to intensify the differences of opinion between himself and the Ministry's Muslim Department. Haim Zeev Hirschberg, the Department's director, strove valiantly to preserve the "Status Quo" within the Tomb structure, refusing to "develop and plan David's Tomb as the principal holy place of the Jewish people in the State of Israel," and demanding that nothing at the site be changed. This approach was informed both by the site's Muslim *waqf* status and the fact that various state officials, first and foremost among them Prime Minister David Ben-Gurion, were now striking a tone of great caution and sensitivity and taking a policy line of not altering the "Status Quo" at the site.[29] Kahana, however, and others of similar outlook, felt that "the tombstone is the stone that covers the opening leading to the many caves whose existence has been handed down by tradition for over two thousand years,"[30] and as such the site should be developed as a Jewish shrine. Hirschberg's efforts to maintain the physical and religious status of King David's Tomb were thus in vain. Instead, the prevailing attitude at the Ministry of Religious Affairs' attitude was that "the Tomb is not a research subject for Israeli cultural institutions, but rather a place sacred to worshipers. King David's Tomb does not belong to the Muslim Department, but rather to [the Department of] Jewish Holy Places."[31]

Pinkerfeld, in protest of the changes that Kahana was instituting at the Tomb complex, decided to cease cooperation with the Ministry of Religious Affairs. He was followed by Hirschberg, who decided to wash his hands of any responsibility for what was taking place at the Tomb.[32] In late 1951 an agreement was signed between the Muslim and Druze Department and the Mount Zion Committee providing for the leasing of "all of the houses adjacent to the courtyard of King David's Tomb and the endowments of the houses in which you have organized synagogues, on condition that you maintain the site, repair the buildings and pay a rental fee."[33]

The solution found for the problem of Jewish activity at the Tomb was similar to that achieved a year later at Elijah's Cave, to be discussed more extensively below. Elijah's Cave in Haifa, which had Muslim *waqf* status, was also rented to the Society for the Holy Places, thereby legitimizing Jewish activity at both sites. Antiquities Department director Shmuel Yeivin was opposed to the activity instituted by Kahana and the Mount Zion Committee at King David's Tomb as being "a kind of renewal of the altars and their connection with popular worship." He was of the opinion that they had no legal basis.[34] Nonetheless, his opposition proved futile and the development activity at the site continued in full force throughout the 1950s and 1960s.

The intensified activity of the Ministry of Religious Affairs on Mount Zion and at the King David's Tomb complex during the 1950s aroused interest within the Arab world as well, leading to vigorous opposition on the part of the Dajani family, which had previously controlled the Tomb structure and the many rooms surrounding it.[35] In 1954 the governments of Transjordan and Iraq submitted a formal complaint to the UN Security Council against the measures that the State of Israel was taking at the site and the changes that were being made to the Room of the Last Supper and to the Tomb. The Jordanian and Iraqi delegates claimed that these two rooms had been converted into synagogues which were now being used by Jewish pilgrims. In response, the Ministry of Foreign Affairs conducted a tour of Mount Zion and the Tomb for foreign ambassadors in an attempt to prove that the accusations were unfounded.[36] In reaction to material submitted to it by the Ministry of Religious Affairs,[37] the Foreign Ministry asserted that the Arab complaint actually related to the Room of the Last Supper, to which no changes had been made, and that the State of Israel was strictly maintaining the "Status Quo" and not permitting any changes.[38] Israel's official representatives found it convenient to ignore the fact that the lower portion of the building, the location of King David's Tomb, was supposed to be subject to the "Status Quo" dating from the Mandate period, and that this area had been used previously as a Muslim mosque. Despite the controversy and lack of clarity surrounding the issue, Israel's representatives answered the charges by stating that "in the lower room [the room housing the Tomb itself] there are no signs of a mosque. In one room there is a *mihrab*, but we are informed that this kind of symbol is found in many private Muslim homes and that it does not, in itself, point to the existence of a mosque at the site at any given time. Indeed, there are several indications that the site served as a Jewish synagogue in ancient times," based on Pinkerfeld's excavations.[39] Ultimately the Arab protests regarding Israeli activity on Mount Zion died down. Only after the Six-Day War did the Dajani family undertake to reclaim its ownership of King David's Tomb and the surrounding rooms.[40]

Elijah's Cave, Haifa

One of the three Jewish holy sites most extensively developed by the Ministry of Religious Affairs during the years 1948–67 was Elijah's Cave, on the outskirts of Haifa. The unique nature of the development process at this site during the period in question stemmed from, among other things, the fact that the Cave had historically been regarded as sacred by Jews, Christians, Muslims, and Druze.

The figure of Elijah the Prophet is closely connected with Jewish tradition regarding Mount Carmel, and Elijah's Cave, on the mountain's northern slope, figures prominently in this context. The Cave is where Elijah is traditionally thought to have stayed while fleeing Ahab, King of Israel. Over the generations Elijah's Cave also came to be venerated by Christians, who believed that Mary, the mother of Jesus, stayed there upon returning with the Holy Family from Egypt. They also call the Cave "The School of the Prophets," based on the Christian belief that Elijah and Elisha gathered there with all of their disciples.[41] The Druze and the Muslims also regard the Cave compound as holy. They identify Elijah the Prophet as *El-Khader*, the green prophet who symbolizes water and life, a miracle worker who cures the sick,[42] and the site is considered one of the most important Muslim pilgrimage destinations in the region.

As with King David's Tomb on Mount Zion, Elijah's Cave was until 1948 a Muslim religious endowment, referred to as *Waqf El-Khader*. The place was under the control of the *Haj Ibrahim* family of Haifa. At the end of the nineteenth century members of the family built a series of rooms intended as lodgings for visitors and cure-seekers wishing to stay near the holy site and avail themselves of its miraculous healing powers.[43] Both Jews and Christians had the right to visit the site and pray there.[44]

The 1948 War caused a major change in the religious environment of Haifa. The war's broad demographic consequences—the departure of a significant portion of the Arab population and Haifa's transformation into an Israeli city—led, among other things, to a Judaization of Elijah's Cave and to its development as a Jewish pilgrimage site. The site's development during the 1950s was the result of the combined activity of local parties, mainly members of the city's Sephardic Jewish community, and the Ministry of Religious Affairs which contributed greatly to shaping the physical and religious atmosphere at the site. Since Elijah's Cave was, prior to 1948, Muslim *waqf* property, it was transferred, along with many other Islamic religious endowments in Israel, to the Religious Affairs Ministry's Muslim and Druze Department, which had official responsibility for Elijah's Cave during the years following the founding of the state.[45]

Jewish appropriation of the site was carried out in an intuitive and rapid manner, as described by Kahana: "After the liberation of the state, the Carmelites [monks of the Stella Maris Monastery] and the Arabs left the area, and the official in charge of Mount Zion [i.e., Kahana himself] took an interest in the Cave and Judaized it fully."[46] Nevertheless, the rapid Judaization of the Cave—a place sacred to Muslims at which intensive Jewish activity was now taking place—posed a difficult legal and practical problem to the Religious Affairs Ministry. Only in 1953, that is, some five years after the city came under Israeli control, was an agreement providing for the leasing of the Cave and its surrounding buildings signed by the Muslim and Druze Department (to which authority over the site had been transferred) to the Society for the Holy Places.[47] The Society, which was charged mainly with the development of Mount Zion and King David's Tomb in Jerusalem, retained control of Elijah's Cave during the 1950s and 1960s via a committee called the Committee of Elijah's Cave. This committee was responsible, along with the Religious Affairs Ministry and various other bodies, such as the Haifa Municipality, for developing the Cave. The rationale that lay behind this rental arrangement at the Cave was the desire to "make it possible to address its special character and to ensure the implementation of a *specific* [sic] line and of decisions taken by the Ministry of Religious Affairs and the government where necessary."[48]

The Haifa Municipality took it upon itself to sponsor development of the area around the Cave, and during the years 1953–54 paved a path to the site and created a landscaped garden around it.[49] These areas were leased by the Muslim and Druze Department as the body responsible for the Muslim *waqf* property at the Cave site,[50] and the Municipality and the Ministry of Religious Affairs planned renovations to the buildings around the Cave and a plaza large enough to accommodate the large numbers of pilgrims visiting the site.[51] Dedicated in mid-1955, the garden attracted numerous visitors and worshipers. An article in *Hatzofe* newspaper stated: "It is most instructive that since the Cave and its surrounding area have been given a new aspect, it is being visited in infinitely greater numbers than before, despite the fact that it has lost much of its old picturesque and 'exotic' character. Jews from everywhere are coming en masse to the Cave, which has become a major attraction in Haifa."[52] A sign posted at the site by the Ministry of Religious Affairs declared the Cave to have been "an ancient place of prostration for the Jews of Haifa" and noted the traditional pilgrimage dates.[53]

The Galilee

The Upper Galilee, which prior to 1948 had a dense Arab population, was included after the war in the territory of the new state. Many local Arab villagers left the area or were driven from it, and, in line with the demographic changes that took place in the region, its holy places—including *kivrei tzadikim*—came under Israeli sovereignty. This situation afforded the Jews of the region, particularly those of Safed, the opportunity to appropriate the shrines and to develop them as Jewish pilgrimage sites, without recognition of their Muslim past.[54] The Galilee holy sites—which formerly had served the region's entire population, both Muslim and Jewish, and many of which were now located in or near the area's abandoned Arab villages[55]— underwent a process of Judaization. In this way the 1948 War's dramatic impact and demographic effects on this region led the proliferation of dozens of venerated grave sites. Beside the Tomb of Rabbi Shimon Bar Yochai in Meron—for generations the Galilee's most prominent Jewish pilgrimage destination, a site to which thousands of Jewish visitors made their way—a complex network of *kivrei tzadikim* scattered across the breathtaking Galilee landscape was developed, attracting pilgrims in large numbers. Until 1948 some of these sites had served the region's Muslim population, but now were Judaized after local private parties and organizations involved in identifying and developing holy places joined forces.[56] The Ministry of Religious Affairs took care to enclose some of the sites and to have tombstones and other structures placed upon them. In addition, mention should be made of the new Jewish immigrants that were brought into the Galilee during the 1950s and 1960s, some of whose settlements were established near the ruins of Arab villages where sacred gravesites were conspicuously visible. These immigrants, most of whom came from Islamic countries, played an important role in developing the Galilee holy sites.

Thus, for example, the gravesite of Rabbi Yishmael Ben Rabbi Yose Haglili remained among the houses of the abandoned Arab village of Dalata after 1948. When the village was razed, as part of a larger campaign to dismantle abandoned Arab villages in the Galilee, the gravesite was left as it was and the residents of the nearby Jewish village of Dalton began to visit it on a regular basis.[57] At other times a different process took place: the remains of Muslim gravesites in various parts of the Galilee were simply eradicated. This process led to an intensified sense of the importance of the Jewish sites that were now being identified. This was the case with regard to the grave of Rabbi Chananya Ben Akashia near Kfar Chananya, which was part of a Muslim burial area adjacent to the Arab village of Kafr Anan. During the latter half of the 1950s the Muslim gravesites were razed while attention was focused on the nearby Jewish sites.[58] The outcome of this process was, ultimately, a significant emphasis on the *kivrei tzadikim* of the Galilee, within the State of Israel's general map of sanctity.

Since most of the Galilee shrines were, at the beginning of the 1950s, merely landmarks of greater or lesser prominence within the overall landscape—caves, columns, heaps of stones or old gravestones, the Ministry of Religious Affairs made an effort to rebuild and redesign them. Site development frequently included the paving of a path from the main road to the site.

A sign would usually be placed along the way indicating the present distance from the gravesite. Construction activity at the burial places themselves often included enclosure of the sites, with iron gates placed at the entrances. Facilities were provided for candlelighting, and in many cases old trees, which themselves had come to be considered sacred, were incorporated into the sites. Sometimes the grave was left with no building over it and only the tombstone updated, with the original coffin covered by a concrete block and the placement of suitable stone signage.[59] In most cases buildings were constructed above the graves, generally using stones from the area or, alternatively, concrete,[60] and a small domed roof, painted white in order to draw attention to the site and to make it conspicuous for its Jewishness, was placed on top. In this way a network of white "statues" sprang up across the green Galilean landscape. The shrines' Jewishness was further emphasized by incorporating into the tomb structures of *menorahs* and "memorial horns"—"horns of the altar"—that were frequently placed at the four corners of the memorial building, serving as a kind of trademark for the tombs refurbished by the Ministry of Religious Affairs during the 1950s and 1960s. These elements coalesced into a distinct style indicative of the attempt to invent a Jewish architecture of sacred space.

Unquestionably, this process was not well received by the Muslim communities that remained after 1948 in the Galilee and in places where sites now recognized as sacred to the Jews were situated within large Arab population centers. In some cases where gravesites were developed, such as that of Rabbi Yehuda Ben Baba near Shfaram or of Rabbi Yose of Peki'in, we hear of intentional destructive activity on the part of these populations. Gravesite development during the 1950s and 1960s frequently involved the expropriation of land near the sites, which generated much discontent among the region's Arab inhabitants.[61] Conflicts between the Ministry of Religious Affairs and the Arab villagers occasionally resulted in desecration of the holy sites.[62]

The coastal plain

During the Mamluk Period (thirteenth–sixteenth centuries), burial sites of the sons of Jacob were identified in the coastal plain region. The graves of Benjamin, Judah, Gad and others were situated during this period along the main road connecting Cairo and Damascus. After Israel was founded, Jewish immigrants were settled in this area in large numbers, and many of these sacred gravesites were Judaized, becoming Jewish pilgrimage destinations. Despite the fact that these sites had a Muslim heritage and were all, until 1948, active Muslim pilgrimage sites where almost no Jewish activity took place, this earlier heritage was obliterated and the sites were incorporated into the network of Jewish pilgrimage and prayer sites visited by residents of the region and of Israel in general. This sanctification process in the coastal plain area was the result of several factors, the most significant of which was the demographic changes that characterized the region in the wake of the 1948 War—the exodus of large numbers of Muslims and their replacement with a Jewish immigrant population—had a major impact on many areas of life, including the identity of the region's shrines.

From the thirteenth century on, Jewish pilgrims refer to the tomb of Rabban Gamliel in Yavne as being located in a mausoleum associated with *Ali Abu Hurayrah*, a companion of the Prophet Muhammad and the narrator of Hadith who, according to some Muslim traditions, was buried at Yavne. This impressive structure was located on a hill to the west of the ancient Tel Yavne site, at the end of the Muslim cemetery of the late Arab settlement, and to its west. It is difficult to determine whether Jewish pilgrimage activity existed at the site during the late Ottoman era and under the Mandate. Although the gravesite of Rabban Gamliel is mentioned in several period sources,[63] it is hard to conclude from this that the site was a regular pilgrimage destination, or to determine whether ceremonies were held there on a routine basis. Clearly, the great change in status undergone by the tomb of Rabban Gamliel, and its increased importance after Israel's founding, are closely related to the presence of the new Jewish inhabitants who had immigrated from Islamic countries and settled in what was left of the Arab village of Yavne.[64] It was this population that adopted the *Abu Hurayrah* gravesite and initiated intensive pilgrimage activity there. The Muslim context and tradition regarding the site were completely eradicated during this period, while Yavne's new Jewish residents instantly Judaized the site and identified it as the burial place of Rabban Gamliel.

The tradition of Yavne as Rabban Gamliel's place of burial was not entirely unfounded, since the Jewish writings and the pilgrimage literature from the Middle Ages onward refer to the presence of his grave in this area. During this period the prevailing opinion was that the Muslim veneration for these holy sites was itself based on an older Jewish tradition. In the words of Kahana: "In most cases, the [sacred] places are based on stories of the area inhabitants, Jews and Arabs, which were generally believed if they seemed credible. It was actually speculated that the traditions had been passed down to local inhabitants, even to the Arabs, from earlier periods when Jews had resided in the area."[65] Others held an even firmer opinion that "[t]he literary sources reveal the struggle that renews itself with every generation between Jewish pilgrims to the land of their forefathers, seeking the sacred buildings [and] geographical landmarks that preserve Jewish tradition, and the Jew-haters and rivals of the Christian and Muslim faiths seeking to blur, distort and obliterate, to the fullest possible extent, anything Jewish."[66] In the case of Rabban Gamliel's tomb, the attitude was similar, and since there was no custom of active Jewish pilgrimage to the site during the pre-state period, the changes that took place at Yavne after 1948 were particularly dramatic. Visitors to the gravesite, at first area residents who had immigrated from Muslim countries and, later, visitors from more distant places, viewed this shrine as a convenient venue serving needs and customs with which many of them had become familiar in their countries of origin, particularly in North Africa.

The issue of ownership of the Abu Hurayrah/Rabban Gamliel gravesite was a complex one.[67] On the one hand, the tomb of Abu Hurayrah, as Muslim *waqf*, fell under the authority of the Ministry of Religious Affairs' Muslim and Druze Department—the body which was responsible for maintaining and preserving the site.[68] On the other hand, the Ministry of Religious Affairs was aware of the Jewish activity that had begun to take place at the site immediately after 1948, and it was thus also involved in the process of turning it into an active Jewish pilgrimage destination. Supervision and management of the Abu Hurayrah tomb was entrusted to the Ministry of Religious Affairs' Muslim and Druze Department. Jacob Pinkerfeld, the architect responsible for restoring and preserving the Yavne site, witnessed the process by which it was designed and consecrated as the burial place of Rabban Gamliel. In a report that he submitted in 1949 on his architectural and archeological activity at the site, he noted the existence of "a campaign aimed at turning this Muslim monument into a modern synagogue, for the use of the new immigrants who have settled in the area." After investigating the matter with the local residents, it turned out that a Ministry of Religious Affairs rabbi who had visited the place "told them [i.e., the Jewish immigrant residents] that 'Abu Hurayrah' was an ancient synagogue that should be restored to its original purpose."[69] Pinkerfeld added later that "[t]he legend-generating power of the place [the tomb of *Abu Hurayrah*] remains as potent as ever," and that he had heard about "a belief common among Oriental Jews that the grave of Rabban Gamliel of Yavne was located here," referring, of course, to the local residents who were currently caring for the burial site and who regarded it as sacred.

Over the last two decades, activity aimed at identifying the graves of the sons of Jacob in the coastal plain area has intensified significantly, but in contrast to the prevailing scholarly assumption that this process dates only from the 1970s and 1980s, it is clear that, as early as the immediate post-1948 period, Jewish inhabitants of the area began to take an interest in the aforementioned traditions and had a hand in converting the Muslim gravesites near their communities into Jewish pilgrimage sites. As was the case in Yavne, the graves of Benjamin and Judah were sanctified by a process driven primarily by Jewish residents of Middle Eastern origin who had settled in the region during the period following Israel's War of Independence.

The gravesite of Benjamin, son of Jacob, is located a few kilometers east of Kfar Saba, on the road to Qalqilya, and was apparently built during the Mamaluk period.[70] From the fourteenth century on Jewish pilgrims identified the site as Benjamin's burial place. They undoubtedly were moved to visit it by the Muslim tradition regarding the place, along with the other gravesites of the sons of Jacob along the region's main road. Zev Vilnay, who visited the place during the 1930s, reported that the tomb, which stood out due to its white domed roof and which was called *Nebi-Yamin* by the Arabs, was surrounded by a large yard, enclosed by a high fence, and that the site served as a place of worship mainly for the inhabitants of Arab Kfar Saba. In the middle of the yard stood a small round room containing a tombstone covered with a green cloth designating it as a grave.[71]

After the State of Israel was founded, Nebi-Yamin was also included in the list of Muslim religious endowments within Israeli territory, and was also placed under the authority of the Ministry of Religious Affairs' Muslim and Druze Department.[72] Here as well, as in the case of the grave of Rabban Gamliel in Yavne, the initiative extended to the point of sanctifying the site and turning it into a place of pilgrimage for the Jewish residents of the nearby *ma'abara* (immigrant transit camp): "Someone told the new immigrants that *Nebi-Yamin* was the burial place of Benjamin, son of Jacob ... and they began lighting candles at his grave."[73] Jews—area residents as well as visitors from elsewhere—began visiting the gravesite, despite the fact that it never became a mass pilgrimage destination, due perhaps to its peripheral location and its proximity to Israel's eastern border. During this period the neglected grave still remained under the control of the Muslim and Druze Department;[74] only in 1958 was it placed under the authority of the Ministry's Department of Holy Places.

The process that took place at the gravesite of Judah, son of Jacob, located farther to the south in the modern town of Yehud, was quite similar to the one described above at the grave of Benjamin. The first Jewish settlers in the Arab village of Yehud appear to have displayed little interest in the sacred status of the grave of Nebi Huda ibn Sa'idna Yaqub; only later, due presumably to the demographic changes taking place in the area, did a change in attitude toward the site emerge. It should be remembered that the burial place of Judah, son of Jacob, was identified over the generations with several places in Palestine. These traditions were usually based on local place names; the tradition pointing to the grave's location in the village of Yehudiya, east of Tel Aviv, was only one of them. This Arab tradition seems to have stemmed from the place-name that preserved the name of Yehud mentioned as belonging to the Tribe of Dan (Joshua 19:45). This gravesite, as Muslim *waqf*, was also placed under the authority of the Ministry of Religious Affairs' Muslim and Druze Department after Israel's founding, and during the 1960s was made the responsibility of the Custodian of Absentee Property. During this period the grave was located at the heart of the Jewish locality, however, it had been neglected over the years and its status had deteriorated. Two of the impressive Muslim building's three domed roofs collapsed, as a result of which only one of its rooms remained standing by the end of the 1950s.

Only during the early 1960s did the Ministry of Religious Affairs begin to take an interest in the site, but it is difficult to determine the source of this initiative and whether it came from "below," that is, due to the activity of local Yehud residents, or from the Ministry itself. There are some indications that a few Jewish pilgrims did visit the site and light candles there,[75] and this limited pilgrimage activity, along with the fact that the tomb ruins were located at the center of the locality, seems to have provided the local council and the Religious Affairs Ministry with their main impetus for rehabilitating the site.[76] The question of the gravesite's authenticity and sacredness to Judaism did not trouble the local residents in the least, nor was it of any concern to the Ministry employees involved in the initiative, who relied on Vilnay's reference to the Jewish tradition locating the gravesite of Judah there as proof of the site's sanctity,[77] and so embarked on their development activity there.

Correspondence found in Ministry of Religious Affairs files regarding the grave of Judah makes it possible to follow the renovation and development process that took place at the site, starting in 1962.[78] The Ministry's Department of Holy Places conducted a tour of the site to determine its physical status and the possibility of rehabilitating it. Later, the Ministry of Religious Affairs sought the assistance of the Land Registry Office and of the Yehud Local Council in determining who owned the tomb.[79] It turned out that the tomb, along with the group of rooms adjacent to it, had Muslim *waqf* status. Since it had previously been placed under the authority of the Custodian of Absentee Property, it was therefore incumbent upon the Ministry of Religious Affairs to obtain approval of the changes planned for the tomb and its environs before undertaking any activity there. The Ministry's Muslim Department, which was responsible for the adjacent Muslim cemetery, conditioned its approval on assurances that the tomb area would not be negatively effected or "Muslim sentiments" offended as a result of the renovations.[80] Only in 1964, after long preparations, did the Public Works Department begin its refurbishment activity at the site, in an atmosphere of cooperation between the Religious Affairs Ministry, which funded materials for the project, and the Yehud Local Council, which budgeted manpower.[81] The renovated structure was dedicated in 1964, at which time an impressive *parochet* (Torah ark curtain) was placed over the tomb.

Conclusion

The existing literature contains numerous explorations of the way in which war affects space, both in general and with particular attention to the Holy Land.[82] By contrast, one finds almost no discussion of how wars and hostilities affect sacred space and holy sites in particular.[83] While the history of Palestine is rife with wars and conflicts over the status of the Holy Places, political disputes and campaigns of conquest motivated by religious tensions and the struggle for control over the sacred sites, there has been almost no investigation of the geographic effects of these conflicts over time, much less with regard to the period in question—the two decades following the State of Israel's founding.

The present study offers a unique perspective on the impact that the 1948 War had on sacred space in the Holy Land. This war, and Israel's founding, had a tremendous effect on the fate of all of the holy sites in the area, and in particular, on sites that served as Jewish pilgrimage destinations. The war and the subsequent division of the land led, on the one hand, to a weakening of the practical status of those shrines that remained on the other side of the border and to which Jewish access was impossible. On the other hand, the territorial partition caused the status of other holy sites, those situated in the western part of the Holy Land, to be upgraded. Although the tradition of Jewish worship at gravesites such as those of Yehuda Ben Baba near Shfaram or Rabban Gamliel in Yavne, is rooted in the region's more distant past, the post-1948 phenomenon of pilgrimage to these sites was almost entirely unprecedented. During this period, various parties—both individuals and organizations—took advantage of the new political reality created by the territorial partition to transfer many shrines that had been under local Muslim control into Jewish hands. The Ministry of Religious Affairs has retained its authority over these sites up to the present day, even where legal rights to the properties in question have not been determined.

The process that took place during the two decades after Israel's founding may be analyzed within several different contexts, most notably that of the Jewish–Arab political conflict. The State of Israel's sovereignty over areas in which sites sacred to the other religions, in particular to Islam, were located, led to vigorous efforts to appropriate these sites after 1948. The process by which the Jewish holy places were developed was, beyond a doubt, part of a broader process by which the newly-founded state sought to create symbols and commemorative and memorial sites within its sovereign territory. But the effort to bestow consequence on the Jewish holy sites developed after 1948 was also important in terms of Israeli society's internal politics and in the context of the attempts made by certain political groups to impose their own interpretation on the space in question. Thus, the ethos of the national Jewish past, in its secular-Zionist version which tended to focus on the history of Hebrew sovereignty in the Land of Israel and on the generations-long national struggle for freedom and independence, was contrasted with Kahana's quite different interpretation of events. Kahana's historical perspective on the Holy Land was more complex, including as it did, in addition to the various locations associated with Zionist heroism, the land of the Bible and the places inhabited by the Sages of the Talmud and other key figures in Jewish history. The gravesites of *Ha'ari Hakadosh* in Safed and of *Rabbi Meir Ba'al Haness* in Tiberias were, according to this approach, an integral part of the symbolic map of the new State of Israel and an expression of renewed sovereignty over the Land of the Patriarchs, no less than Herzl's grave in Jerusalem or Bialik's in Tel Aviv.

Adding onto the map of Zionist heroism with its Tel Hai and Modi'in, the map of Zionist settlement with its Revivim and Hanita, and the map of Jewish archeology with its Beit She'arim and Massada, Kahana sought to superimpose a map of gravesites of kings, prophets, Tannaim and Amoraim, a map that reflected his own interpretation of the history of the Land of Israel and of the Jewish people. Clearly, the sacred places that I have discussed in this article were not all equal in terms of their importance and status. Some, such as King David's Tomb in Jerusalem and Elijah's Cave in Haifa, were of national-state importance. On the other hand, there were pilgrimage sites whose importance was regional and local, the grave of Rabban Gamliel in Yavne being a good example of such a site. In some cases, as we have seen, the drive to appropriate and develop a site came from "above," as part of a broader intentional policy. Other sites, by contrast, were developed from "below," reflecting the need felt by residents of peripheral parts of the country for holy places in their areas of residence.

As with the 1948 War nineteen years earlier, the Six-Day War had a tremendous influence on most aspects of life in the Holy Land, and the issue of worship at holy sites was no exception. The occupation of Judea and Samaria, as well as East Jerusalem, had far-reaching consequences that made it possible for Jews to visit their historically sacred sites in an almost unlimited manner. After nineteen years of forced separation, 1967 ushered in a period of intensive activity at the Western Wall and other places in these areas. Not only was it now possible for Jews freely to visit the Tomb of Samuel the Prophet, Joseph's Tomb, and the Cave of the Patriarchs, but the very fact that this space fell under Israeli jurisdiction as a result of the war meant that control, supervision, and development of the holy sites became Israel's responsibility and obliged the country's leaders to face the complex issues raised by them. The return to these sacred places led, of course, to a decisive change in the map of the holy sites that had been developed after the founding of the state. King David's Tomb on Mount Zion, which had been the most central and important shrine within Israel's sovereign borders, suddenly lost its uniqueness and became again just one of a long list of sites sacred to Judaism in the Jerusalem area. By contrast, the *kivrei tzadikim* in the Galilee, many of which had previously served the region's Arab population and for whose development Kahana and his associates created the physical infrastructure after 1948, enjoyed a surge in popularity, continuing, throughout the 1970s and 1980s, to be featured prominently in pilgrimage itineraries.

Notes

1 B.Z. Kedar, "Wars as Historical Turning Points," in Asher Susser (ed.) *Six Days – Thirty Years: A New Look at the Six-Day War*, Tel Aviv: Am Oved, 1999, pp. 17–28 [in Hebrew]; A. Golan, *Wartime Spatial Changes: Former Arab Territories within the State of Israel, 1948–50*, Beer Sheva: Ben-Gurion University, 2001 [in Hebrew].
2 D. Bar, "Recreating Jewish Sanctity in Jerusalem: The Case of Mount Zion and King David's Tomb Between 1948–67," *Journal of Israeli History*, 2004, vol. 23, no. 2, pp. 233–51; *ibid.*, "Reconstructing the Past: The Creation of Jewish Sacred Space in the State of Israel, 1948–67," *Israel Studies*, 2008, vol. 13, no. 3, pp. 1–21.
3 *See e.g.*, Central Zionist Archive [hereinafter: CZA], S25/2932, *The Administration of the Holy Places in Palestine*, n.d., n.a.
4 *See e.g.*, *To Know the Land*, Ein-Charod, Hakibutz Hameuchad, 1965, p. 407 [in Hebrew].
5 For further discussion, *see infra*, pp. 76–79.
6 For details about the Galilean Holy Places, *see* D. Bar, *Sanctifying a Land: The Jewish Holy Places in the State of Israel: 1948–1968*, Jerusalem, Yad Ben Zvi and Ben-Gurion Institute in the Negev, 2007, pp. 30–35 [in Hebrew].

7 For a list of these holy sites, *see* the handwritten list entitled *The Holy Places in Jerusalem and its Environs*, n.a., n.d., CZA, J1/3388. This list distinguishes between holy sites and historical sites. A separate list is devoted to the latter which includes, among other places, Zedekiah's Cave, Hezekia's Pool, Abraham's Tent near Hebron, Ein Fara in Wadi Kelt, etc.
8 On the Western Wall affair *see*, Report of the International Commission on the Western Wall, the Development of the Dispute. Investigations and Testimonies in Jerusalem. The Jewish Memorandum. The Ruling. The King's Statement. With Pictures, London: H.M.S.O, 1931 [in Hebrew].
9 On the sacred Jewish sites outside the Old City walls prior to 1948, *see* A.M. Luncz, *Guide to Eretz Israel and Syria, Jerusalem*,published by the author, 1891, pp. 87–168 [in Hebrew].
10 O. Limor, "Saint Pelagia's Tomb: Sin, Penitence and Salvation on the Mount of Olives," *Cathedra*, 2006, vol. 118, pp. 13–40 [in Hebrew].
11 For a description of Jewish Holy Sites in Jerusalem, *see* Bar, *Sanctifying a Land*, n. 6, pp. 24–28.
12 For a brief discussion of the renovations conducted at Rachel's Tomb during the nineteenth and twentieth centuries, *see* L.G.A. Cust, *The Status Quo in the Holy Places, with an Annex on the Status Quo in the Church of the Nativity, Bethlehem by Abdullah Effendi Kardus*, Harrow: His Majesty's Stationery Office, 1929, pp. 46–48.
13 *See* CZA *J1/3569*, Letter by S. Zahavi to Y. Ben-Zvi, 22 Oct.1944 [in Hebrew].
14 M. Meni, "The Harvest Festival in Hebron," in Yom-Tow Lewinsky (ed.), *The Book of Festivals: The Jewish Festivals, their Value, Customs and Influence on Jewish Life and Literature from Ancient Times to the Present*, Tel Aviv: Doron–Dvir, 1953, pp. 198–200 [in Hebrew].
15 G. Kitzis, "28 Iyyar: Pilgrimage to the Tomb of Samuel the Prophet," *Kardom* 1980, vols. 10–11, pp. 62–64 [in Hebrew].
16 *See e.g.*, Z. Vilnay, *Sepulchral Monuments in Palestine*, 3rd edn, Jerusalem: Achiever, 1986 [in Hebrew]. Vilnay distinguishes between the burial places of Biblical figures and those of figures from the Mishnaic and Talmudic periods and from the Middle Ages.
17 M. Azaryahu, "From Remains to Relics: Authentic Monuments in the Israeli Landscape," *History and Memory*, 1993, vol. 5, no. 2, pp. 82–103.
18 Israel State Archives [hereinafter, ISA] 98, GL-11/6316, Letter to the Ministry of Religious Affairs' Press Officer Y.L. Levanon, the Ministry of Religious Affairs, 28 Dec.1949 [in Hebrew].
19 *See e.g.*, the Jerusalem Municipal Archives [hereinafter: JMA], container no.1878, file no. 29/41, Letter from the Mayor of Jerusalem to the District Commander, 2 Nov.1949, in which he writes that "this matter [the formation of a committee to address the issue of King David's Tomb] should not be neglected, since in the meantime 'good Jews' may be able to gain a 'foothold' there which will be difficult to challenge afterward" [in Hebrew].
20 CZA, S21/314, Consultation regarding improvements on Mount Zion, 8 Nov. 1949. A position is expressed according to which "Mount Zion is, for us, first and foremost an issue of occupying the site" [in Hebrew].
21 IDF Archive, Section: Journals – the Complete Ben-Gurion's Diary, 28 Sept. 1949 [in Hebrew]. Later on, while Pinkerfeld was conducting excavations near the Tomb, Ben-Gurion expressed concern that the site would be found not to have been the true place of King David's burial, and he considered calling a halt to the excavations. *Ibid.*, 26 June 1951.
22 Ben Uri Archive [hereinafter: BUA], 233.00, Report by M. Ben Uri to S.Z. Kahana, 9 May 1951 [in Hebrew].

23 ISA, 98, GL/6/6261, Bylaws of the Mount Zion Society; ISA, 8, GL-12/6380 (n.d., n.a.), document describing how matters progressed during the period in which the Committee on the Holy Places was being formed. The Committee's date of registration was 27 July 1950 [in Hebrew].
24 ISA 98, GL-6/2931. Letter from M. Ben Uri to S.Z. Kahana, 16 Aug. 1951. *Major Points of the King David's Tomb Plan* (with a Schematic Illustration of the Tomb and the Rooms Adjacent to It) [in Hebrew].
25 *See* the Institute for Religious Zionism's Archive of Religious Zionism [hereinafter: ARZ], Mossad Ha-Rav Kook, Mizrahi Movement World Center (298), for a semi-annual *Report on the Department for Islamic and Druze Affairs, Aug. 1948 – Jan. 1949*, by H.Z. Hirschberg. [in Hebrew] The report provides information on the Department's establishment and its role with regard to the preservation of Muslim holy places and the administration of Muslim religious endowments.
26 *See* the Department's activity report, published as a short pamphlet: L.A. Mayer, J. Pinkerfeld, and H.Z. Hirschberg, *Some Principal Muslim Religious Buildings in Israel*, Jerusalem: Hamadpis Ha'memshalti, 1950; *See also*, ISA, 8, FL-16/44864. [in Hebrew] A document written by L.A. Mayer, Advisor for the Preservation of Sites Sacred to Islam, serves as the basis for the work cited above, where he reports on activity at the Tomb of Abu Hurayrah.
27 ISA, 98, GL-6/2932. Protocol prepared by Y. Fabritzky of the Ministry of Religious Affairs, 28 Sept. 1949 [in Hebrew]; *See also* the discussion of the neglected state of the buildings in *Pinkas ha-Har*, vol. 1, personal archive of S.Z. Kahana [in Hebrew].
28 J. Pinkerfeld, "David's Tomb," *Louis M. Rabinowitz Fund for the Exploration of Ancient Synagogues*, 1960, vol. 3, pp. 41–44. Israel Antiquities Authority Archive [hereinafter: IAAA]: Tikiyat Pikuah Mada'ei Yisrael: P/2/Jerusalem/E/11/X, Mount Zion [in Hebrew]. Of particular note is the fact that the 1950 work by Mayer, Pinkerfeld and Hirschberg included no discussion of David's Tomb even though Pinkerfeld had been involved in investigating the site. The reason for this appears to be reluctance on the part of the Religious Affairs Ministry personnel involved in publishing the book to include the Tomb in the official list of Muslim *waqf* buildings and thereby to recognize it as having been under Muslim proprietorship before the war.
29 *See* the Report on the Status of Mount Zion, submitted by M. Ben Uri to S.Z. Kahana, 5 Sept. 1951, BUA, 232.00 [in Hebrew].
30 *Ibid.*
31 These were the words of M. Ben Uri, Kahana's architectural advisor who, apparently, identified with them himself. *See*: ISA, 98, GL-6/2931, Letter from M. Ben Uri to S.Z. Kahana, 6 Sept. 1951, *King David in the Hands of the Muslim Department* [in Hebrew].
32 ISA, 98, GL-6/2931, Letter from Y. Pinkerfeld to S.Z. Kahana, 23 Nov. 1951, in which he writes that he sees no possibility of continuing to take responsibility for what was going on at King David's Tomb. *See also* H.Z. Hirschberg's letter to S.Z. Kahana, 23 Nov. 1951, ISA, 98, GL-6/2931 [in Hebrew].
33 ISA, 98, GL-6/2931, Letter from H.Z. Hirschberg to the Committee on Holy Places, the Mount Zion Committee, 3 July 1951; *see also* Hirshberg's letter to Y. Shatner, Custodian of Absentee Property, Jerusalem, 30 June 1953, ISA, 98, GL-6/2931 [in Hebrew] in which he reports that the King David complex was rented to the Society for Holy Places for a three-year period, with an option to extend the lease for an additional three years, and that the Society was interested in leasing the property for a period of twenty-five years.
34 ISA, 162, GL-13/44864, Letter from S. Yeivin to the Minister of Education and Culture, 25 May 1952 [in Hebrew].

35 ISA, 98, GL-6/2931, Letter from Y. Yehoshua, Deputy Director of the Muslim and Druze Department, Ministry of Religious Affairs, to Kahana, 25 Nov. 1953, in which he discusses an article in the newspaper *Al Dafiya*, published in Jerusalem's Old City on 20 Nov. 1953 [in Hebrew].
36 ISA, 130, HZ-4/2397, Report by M. Mendes, the Department for Christian Churches, Ministry of Religious Affairs, on the French Consul-General's visit to the site, 14 Jan. 1954 [in Hebrew].
37 ISA, 130, HZ/4/2397, 16 Nov. 1953, Letter from S.Z. Kahana to Y. Herzog, Advisor on Jerusalem Affairs, Ministry of Foreign Affairs [in Hebrew].
38 ISA, 130, HZ/4/2397, for the State of Israel's official response [in Hebrew].
39 ISA, Section 130.13, HZ/13/2588, 26 Jan. 1954, Letter from Y. Herzog, Advisor on Jerusalem Affairs, to A. Biran, Jerusalem District Officer [in Hebrew]. In the letter Herzog addresses J. Pinkerfeld's claim that the niche behind the tombstone testifies to the existence of an ancient synagogue at the site. This niche is now more commonly thought to date from the construction of the Church of Saint Mary on Mount Zion during the Crusader period. It should also be recalled that the *mihrab* found in the southern wall of the room next to the Tomb chamber mentioned by Herzog was covered several years ago by a wooden board and can no longer be seen.
40 *Yedioth Acharonot*, 1 Aug. 1967 [in Hebrew].
41 ISA, 98, G-10/5808, *Scola Prophetarum*, 1911.
42 A. Augustinović, *"El Khader" and the Prophet Elijah*, Jerusalem: Franciscan Printing Press, 1972.
43 ISA, 8, GL/5/14939, Letter from B. Fishman, Director of the Land Registration Department, to the Director of the Division for Religious Life in the State, 29 Nov. 1949; ISA, 162, GL-13/44864, n.a., 2 Sept. 1948, list of burial sites (*wallies*) sacred to the Muslims; ISA, 98, GL-6/2950, n.d., list of Muslim *waqf* properties identified in Haifa. The survey indicated the existence of 8 rooms, a hall and two restrooms in addition to Elijah's Cave [in Hebrew].
44 Fr. E. Hoade, *Guide to the Holy Land*, Jerusalem: Franciscan Printing Press, 1942, p. 358.
45 ISA, 98, GL-6/2950, Letter by Shalom Darwish, Ministry of Religious Affairs, to the Director of the Ministry's Muslim and Druze Department, 18 Nov. 1952.
46 S.Z. Kahana [signed Dr. S.Z.K.], "Elijah's Cave on Mount Carmel," *Hatzofe li-Yeladim*, 15 Aug. 1951, vol. 5, no. 49, p. 754 [in Hebrew].
47 ISA, 98, GL-2/2936, rental contract signed on 17 Feb. 1953, by Dr. H.Z. Hirschberg, Director of the Muslim and Druze Department in the Ministry of Religious Affairs, and the Society for the Holy Places, Jerusalem. [in Hebrew]. According to the contract, the Department was to lease, for a symbolic fee, the house adjacent to the Cave, which had the status of Muslim religious endowment. The contract period was for three years.
48 Archive for the Study of Religious Zionism, Bar-Ilan University [hereinafter: ASRZ], Section Dr. Z. Warhaftig, cycle 1, Report by S.Z. Kahana to M. Shapira, Ministry of Religious Affairs, 19 July 1954, about the conflict with the Carmelites at Elijah's Cave [in Hebrew].
49 ISA, 98, GL-2/2936, Letter from the Mayor of Haifa, A. Hushi, to S.Z. Kahana, 29 Apr. 1953, containing details regarding the agreement between the Haifa Municipality and the Ministry of Religious Affairs; SA 98, GL-2/2936, Response by S.Z. Kahana to A. Hushi, 11 May 1953, in which he demands that the Religious Affairs Ministry, with the assistance of the Chief Rabbinate and Haifa's Religious Council, be responsible for maintaining the Cave, the synagogue, and the surrounding area used for worship, while [proposing that] the Municipality continue to care for the adjacent garden [in Hebrew].

50 ISA, 98, GL-2/2936; ISA, 98, GL-6/2931, Contract signed 1 May 1954, between the Muslim *waqf*, represented, as it were, by the Ministry of Religious Affairs' Muslim Department, and the Haifa Municipality [in Hebrew].
51 *Yedioth Acharonot*, 18 Jan. 1954. Haifa's Muslim Council informed the Municipality that it opposed the Municipality's involvement in maintaining the garden surrounding Elijah's Cave. The Muslims asserted that Elijah's Cave was Muslim *waqf* and had automatically become absentee property after the founding of the state, and that any change at the site had to be approved by the Muslim Council; the Council vigorously opposed any change at the Cave site [in Hebrew].
52 D. Zakkai, "Visitors En Masse at Elijah's Cave," *Hatzofe*, 11 Sept. 1955 [in Hebrew].
53 ISA, 98, GL/15/14917, 28 Feb. 1957, Letter by D. Levinson, Government Tourist Office, to S.Z. Kahana [in Hebrew].
54 M. Edra'i, *Ha-Boker*, 17 Sept. 1948, on the consequences of the War of Independence for the Jewish holy sites in the Galilee [in Hebrew].
55 *See e.g.*, ISA, 98, GL-25/14917, for several documents that touch on the conflict between the Ministry of Religious Affairs and the Arab residents of the village of Gush Chalav, regarding ownership of the graves of Shemaya and Avtalyon, located within the village. *See also* ISA, GL-6/14918, 25 Jan.1959, Letter from S.Z. Kahana, Ministry of Religious Affairs, to the Military Governor, Safed. The letter contains information regarding the intention to demolish the remains of the Arab village of Dalata, the burial place of Rabbi Yishmael, son of Rabbi Yose Haglili. This gravesite was regarded as sacred by the Arabs of the area, who identified it as the burial place of *Sheikh Isma'il*.
56 Particularly conspicuous in this context was the activity of the Committee for the Preservation of the Holy Places, which was active in the Upper Galilee before and after the War of Independence. This group, headed by Rabbi A.L. Zilberman and, later, by his son, Rabbi D.B. Zilberman, was active mainly in the area of Safed, and was responsible for the registration of several sacred gravesites in the area as *heqdesh* (Jewish religious endowment). *See* ISA, 130, P-1/890, 29 Jan. 1948, Letter from Rabbi A.L. Zilberman to Chief Rabbi B.Z. Uziel containing information regarding the registration of holy sites as Jewish [in Hebrew].
57 The gravesite stood among the houses of the village of Dalata. The site was identified with Sheikh Isma'il. The gravesite was later renovated and is mentioned in a listing of abandoned Arab villages. *See* IAAA: *Tikiyat Pikuah Mada'ei Yisrael*: P/Dalata, Report of the Northern Survey Team, Y. Olami, July 1966; this document also contains several pictures of the restored tombstone, surrounded by the remains of the destroyed village [in Hebrew].
58 BUA, 222.00, Letter by M. Ben Uri to the Public Works Authority Nahariya, 28 July 1957, regarding renovation of the gravesite in Kfar Chananya. Appended to the letter is a plan of the site and its environs. *See also* BUA, 222.00, M. Ben Uri's letter to S. Hirschberg, Muslim and Druze Department, Ministry of Religious Affairs, 28 July 1957, regarding the need to remove from the vicinity of the site Muslim graves that were found next to the Jewish ones. Ben Uri proposes "designating the area adjacent to the tree as the traditional shrine of Rabbi Yose Chalafata and Rabbi Shimon ben Chalafata." *See ibid.*, response by Y. Yehoshua, Deputy Director of the Muslim and Druze Department in the Ministry of Religious Affairs, 2 Aug.1957, proposing that the area be covered "with greenery and turned into a lawn through which visitors to the site will not be allowed to pass" [in Hebrew].
59 *See e.g.*, the renovation plan for the Tomb of Rabbi Yochai in Gush Chalav, ISA, 98, GL/6/14918, Letter by M. Ben Uri to B. Kahana, 26 Mar. 1961 [in Hebrew].

60 *See e.g.*, ISA, 98, GL-13/6293, Letter by M. Ben Uri to Baruch Kahana, Ministry of Religious Affairs, 8 Feb. 1959, containing a sketch of the "re-establishment" of the gravesite at Kerem Ben Zimra [in Hebrew].
61 *See Israel State Yearbook [Shnaton ha-Medina]*, 1955 (Rosh Hashanah Eve, 1955, pp. 77–80; ISA, 98, GL-25/14917, Letter from the Minister of Religious Affairs, Moshe Shapira, to the Minister of Finance, 3 Nov. 1952; ISA, 98, GL-25/14917, Letter from M. Levin, Director of the Israel Lands Administration, to the Minister of Finance, 3 Mar. 1953, announcing the expropriation of 510 sq. m. near the gravesites of Shemaya and Avtalyon in Gush Chalav; ISA, 98, GL/2/6309, 13 July 1961, Exchange of letters between Baruch Kahana, Ministry of Religious Affairs, and the Director of the Land Arrangements Authority [*Minhal Mekarkaei Yisrael*] Haifa, containing a request to register as *heqdesh* (Jewish religious endowment) the traditional gravesites of Micha Hamorashti and of Rabbi Yehuda Halevi and Ibn Ezra, located in a cave within an old building in the village of Kabul [in Hebrew].
62 *See* letter from Baruch Kahana to Yusuf Hassan Ali, Chairman of the Peki'in Local Council, 7 Sept. 1958, ISA, 98, GL/6/14918 [in Hebrew], in which he complains about the desecration of the Cave of Rashbi in Peki'in. *See also* the mention of a similar desecration at the gravesite of R. Yose of Peki'in, ISA, 98, GL/6/14918, Letter from B. Kahana to the Peki'in Local Council, 26 Sept. 1961 [in Hebrew].
63 Z. Vilnay, "Tombs of Saints in the Arab Tradition," *Eretz Yisrael Year Book*, 1926, p. 131 [in Hebrew], where only the Muslim tradition regarding the site is mentioned.
64 By mid-1950 there was already a population of some four hundred Jewish families in the area. *See* the interesting description of settlement in the village by S. Avraham, *Haaretz*, 25 May 1950. Yavne was settled by immigrants from North Africa and central Europe.
65 S.Z. Kahana, "Stories of Pilgrimage to the Tombs of the Righteous and to the Holy Sites of the Land of Israel," *Yeda-Am*, 1981, vol. 54, pp. 44–45 [in Hebrew].
66 M. Ben Uri, "Holy Places and Tourism in Israel," *Hatzofe*, 20 May 1954 [in Hebrew].
67 IAAA, *Tikiyat Pikuah Mada'ei Yisrael*: P/Yavne X, Report from 24 Aug. 1948 on a joint tour by officials of the Ministry of Religious Affairs and members of the military unit stationed at the site. IDF soldiers removed the green Muslim covering from the grave [in Hebrew].
68 ISA, Section 162, GL-13/44864, list of sacred Muslim gravesites (*wallies*) located within the State of Israel and in the Occupied Territories, 2 Sept. 1948 [in Hebrew].
69 ISA, 98, GL-16/44864, Letter from J. Pinkerfeld, Monument Guard, to the Director of the Department for Islamic Affairs in the Ministry of Religious Affairs, 3 Apr. 1949 [in Hebrew].
70 E. Ayalon, "Nebi Yamin (Kever Binyamin, Kfar Saba)," *Archeological News*, 1982, vol. 78–79, pp. 41–42, reports on its early history in the context of excavations and survey conducted at the site. During the Middle Ages, the site was identified, including a monumental gate with thirteenth century inscriptions. His assumption is that only from this point on did an identification of the site as Benjamin's burial place coalesce [in Hebrew].
71 Vilnay, *Sepulchral Monuments in Palestine*, n. 63.
72 ISA, 162, GL-13/44864, list of sacred Muslim gravesites (*wallies*) located within the State of Israel and in the Occupied Territories, 2 Sept. 1948 [in Hebrew].
73 ISA, 162, GL-13/44864, Letter from S. Yeivin to the Minister of Education and Culture, 25 May 1952, noting his complaints about S.Z. Kahana's activity and about the holy site development process [in Hebrew].

74 ISA, 98, GL/5/14908, Letter from H.Z. Hirschberg, Muslim and Druze Department, Ministry of Religious Affairs, to S.Z. Kahana, 16 Dec. 1956, and *ibid.*, Kahana's response, 30 Jan. 1957 [in Hebrew].
75 ISA, 98, GL/6/14918, 30 Jan. 1962, Letter from B. Kahana to A. Meir, Ministry of Religious Affairs [in Hebrew].
76 ISA, 98, GL-14/6293, Letter from M. Ben Uri to Baruch Kahana, 12 Mar. 1963, accompanied by a diagram of the tomb by M. Ben Uri, 4 Mar. 1962, with a sketch of the site before the renovations; ISA, 8, GL/6/14918, letter from A. Meir, Ministry of Religious Affairs to the head of the Yehud Local Council, 10 Dec. 1962 [in Hebrew].
77 ISA, 98, GL-14/6293, Letter from A. Meir, Ministry of Religious Affairs, to M. Ben Uri, 16 Mar. 1962; ISA, 98, GL/6/14918, Letter from S.Z. Kahana to M. Ben Uri, 19 Mar. 1962, in which he notes that the tomb is not that of Biblical Yehudah *ben* Ya'akov [Judah, son of Jacob] but rather that of Yehudah *bar* Ya'akov from the Talmud [in Hebrew].
78 ISA, 8, GL-12/6380, Letter from M. Ben Uri to S.Z. Kahana, 16 Oct. 1964 [in Hebrew].
79 ISA, 98, GL/6/14918, Letter from the Legal Advisor to the Ministry of Religious Affairs to the Yehud Local Council, 16 Sept. 1962, including a plan for the development of the grave of Judah. The document provides a view of the site prior to its renovation, as well as plans for its post-renovation appearance. The tomb stands next to the Muslim cemetery [in Hebrew].
80 ISA, 98, Gl-12/6380 [in Hebrew].
81 ISA, 98, GL/5/14908, Letter from A. Meir to the Public Works Department – Tel Aviv, 12 Sept. 1963 [in Hebrew].
82 For example, Golan, Vilnay, *Sepulchral Monuments in Palestine*, n. 1; *ibid.*, "From Arab Towns to Israeli Cities: Lod and Ramle During and After the War of Independence," *Yahadut Zmanenu*, 2001, vol. 14, pp. 263–89 [in Hebrew].
83 For a few isolated instances, *see* discussion of the impact of the 1948 division of the Indian subcontinent on the fate and status of the holy places in C.E. Ernst, "India as a Sacred Islamic Land," in D.S. Lopez (ed.), *Religions of India in Practice*, Princeton, N.J.: Princeton University Press, 1995, pp. 556–63; Dimitri Pentzopoulos' description of the Turkish–Greek dispute and its effects on the region's population in *The Balkan Exchange of Minorities and its Impact upon Greece* (first published in 1962), London: Hurst, 2002, pp. 199–219.

5 The three kinds of holy places in Jewish Law

The case of Nachmanides' Cave in Jerusalem as a third kind

Michael Wygoda

Introduction: the dispute concerning Ramban's Cave

In April 2000, Palestinians clashed with Jews and Israeli police officers when the former attempted to fence in a five-dunum plot of land in Wadi Joz in East Jerusalem, owned by the Abu Jibna family, containing what Jews claimed to be a Jewish holy place, Ramban's Cave. On 14 May 2000, in resolution of this dispute, Israel's Minister of Religious Affairs, Yitzchak Cohen, declared the disputed site to be a Jewish holy place. The site in question is an area near the Tomb of Rabbi Shimon Hatzadik (Simon the Just) that Jews refer to as Ramban's Cave (in reference to Rabbi Moshe ben Nachman, known also as Nachmanides). The Arab owners of the site wished to erect a fence around the area and turn it into a car rental lot, while the Jewish parties to the dispute claimed that enclosing the area would compromise access to their holy place. The site is thought to be where the Ramban prayed and studied while he was in Jerusalem in 1267; for this reason it was accorded sacred status in Jewish tradition. The Ministry of Religious Affairs' decree led the Jerusalem Magistrates Court[1] to decide, on 22 May 2000, to cease the legal deliberations that it had been conducting on the topic. The reasons given by Judge Carmi Mossek for this decision were as follows:

> [...] when a court is asked to determine whether a place is sacred, that is, to determine the site's nature—in light of the provisions of Sections 2 and 3 of the King's Order-in-Council, the court shall refrain from ruling on this issue, but rather refer it to the Minister of Religious Affairs [...] On 14 May 2000 a decision was made by the Minister of Religious Affairs [...] according to which the Ramban's Cave is a Holy Place, relying on Section 3 of the Order-in-Council [...] Thus, it may be stated that the Minister of Religious Affairs exercised his exclusive authority and rendered a decision regarding the issue with which I was faced, that is whether the Ramban's Cave is indeed a holy site.

A petition against the Minister of Religious Affairs' decision was submitted on 13 June 2000 to the High Court of Justice by the Arab owners of the plot of land, who questioned whether it had ever been a holy place and stated that the Minister's decision was thus *ultra vires*.[2] In order to formulate a clear position on the issue, on 23 October 2000, the new Minister Yossi Beilin appointed an Advisory Committee charged with determining whether the dispute in question should be considered a dispute regarding a holy site.

Committee member Dr. Shmuel Berkowitz, on behalf of the appointed committee, concluded on 4 May 2003 that the Ramban's Cave is indeed a site sacred to Jews, albeit of "lower-level" sanctity. Nevertheless, Dr. Berkowitz concluded that Israeli courts have authority to rule in this regard since the dispute relates to the right of access to the site, a matter regulated by the Protection of Holy Places Law, 5727–1967. The King's Order-in-Council of 1924 does not apply.[3]

In the following discussion I would like to focus on the question: Who is authorized to declare a site holy, and upon what criteria should this decision be based?[4] But first a few words need to be said about the concept of holiness.

The concept of holiness

The concept of holiness is a vague and context-dependent; its ambiguous nature cannot be conveyed by a strict and laconic definition. Nevertheless, one may venture to highlight the following issues:

In Jewish tradition, God Himself is defined as holy (*kadosh*), as in Leviticus 19:2, "I am God your Lord [and] I am holy," and in Isaiah 6:3, "Holy, holy holy is the Lord of Hosts," and God is referred to in the rabbinic literature of the Talmudic era as the "Holy One, Blessed be He." This usage reflects the transcendent, distant, and incomprehensible quality of that which is "holy."[5] It is not surprising that the concept of holiness remains enshrouded in mystery.

The entities to which holiness is attributed in the Bible are exceedingly varied. Examples include: people—"The man whom God chooses shall then be the holy one" (Numbers, 16:7); time—"God blessed the seventh day, and He declared it to be holy" (Genesis 2:3); objects—"and it [the altar] will be holy of holies" (Exodus 40:10). Sanctity is also, as already noted, attributed to places. What is common to all of the entities referred to as holy is that their holiness distinguishes them from their natural surroundings—"Set a boundary around the mountain and declare it holy"—and consecrates them to the divine and spiritual sphere.[6] In other words: the world of holy entities/objects is connected in some way or other to the Most Holy, to God.

It is not my intention here to address the nature of holiness from a philosophical perspective, the issue of whether holiness is immanent or functional, that is, whether it is inherent to the material nature of the sacred entity. I shall not discuss the question of whether an entity's immanent holiness requires that one treat it in a special manner, or whether the holiness derives from the fact that the site was treated in a specific manner. This age-old dilemma, about which opinions are still divided today, is not relevant to our discussion.[7] Our focus here will be on the halakhic and legal question: How may the holiness of a place be determined?

The source of a site's holiness

The first biblical attribution of sanctity to a place occurs early in the Book of Exodus, when God appears to Moses in the burning bush and says to him, "Do not come any closer. Take your shoes off your feet. The place upon which you are standing is holy ground" (Exodus, 3:5).

The second occasion on which the holiness of a place is mentioned is also in the Book of Exodus. Prior to the giving of the Torah, God repeatedly warns Moses that the children of Israel must not be permitted to draw near to Mount Sinai during this episode of revelation: "Go back down and warn the people that they must not cross the boundary in order to see the Divine, because this will cause many to die" (Exodus, 19:21). And Moses responds: "The people cannot climb Mount Sinai. You already warned them to set a boundary around the mountain and to declare it sacred [*vekidashto*]" (Exodus 19:23).

What is interesting is that Mount Sinai was sanctified only for the occasion of the giving of the Torah; once that event had taken place it was no longer accorded any special status, as is clear from the following verse:

> Set a boundary for the people around [the mountain], and tell them to be careful not to climb the mountain, or [even] to touch its edge. Anyone touching the mountain will be put to death. You will not have to lay a hand on him for he will be stoned or cast down. Neither man nor beast will be allowed to live. But when the trumpet is sounded with a long blast, they will then be allowed to climb the mountain."
>
> (Exodus 19:12–13)

In the generations since, the list of places sacred to the Jewish people has lengthened considerably. Contemporary Israel abounds in holy sites. However, the Regulations Pertaining to the Preservation of Sites Sacred to Judaism, 5741–1981, instituted by the Minister of Religious Affairs by virtue of the authority vested in him by the Protection of Holy Places Law, 5727–1967, have up to now attributed sanctity only to sixteen sites, the best-known of these being the Western Wall and the Cave of Shimon Hatzadik in Jerusalem, Rambam's Tomb in Tiberias, and the Tomb of Rabbi Shimon Bar Yochai in Meron.

Three distinct types of sanctity appear to be attributable to places:

- Jewish law (*halakha*) distinguishes certain places and defines them as holy, with a concomitant requirement for special behavior in them. Examples of such places include: the Land of Israel, Jerusalem, the Temple Mount, and the Temple. Mount Sinai at the time of the giving of the Torah would also be included in this category.
- According to *halakha,* a place in which a certain *mitzvah* or commandment is regularly performed, such as prayer or Torah study, is regarded as

sacred, although the dedication of specific sites for the fulfillment of these mitzvoth is at the discretion of the Jewish community itself. Sites of this nature are exemplified by the *beit knesset* (synagogue) and the *beit midrash* (Torah study hall), which bear the halakhic status of *mikdash me'at* (minor Temple).[8]

- In certain instances, due to an event that occurred in a particular place—a revelation, a miracle, the burial of an important person, etc.—people attribute sanctity to the site and regard themselves as bound by the behavioral requirements pertaining to a holy site, even though *halakha* does not actually obligate them to do so. Here the source of the site's holiness is, first and foremost, people's attitude toward it—custom rather than law.

A fascinating paradox characterizes the latter two forms of sanctity: the second type of holy place is chosen from below, by people, while its holiness is assigned from above (by *halakha*); the third type of holy place is, however, determined from above (at least in terms of being recognized by those who believe in it), while its sacred status is accorded from below, based on the believing population's attitude toward it.

The first two types of holy place are characterized by the promulgation of clear *halakhot*. For instance, Jewish law has determined the precise dimensions of the Temple Mount,[9] and even distinguishes between different degrees of sanctity, as may be seen from the following *mishnayot*:[10]

> There are ten degrees of holiness. The Land of Israel is holier than all other lands [...] The walled cities [of the Land of Israel, from the period of Joshua] are still more holy [...] Inside the wall [of Jerusalem] is still holier [...] The Temple Mount is even holier [...] The Rampart is even holier [...] The Court of Women is even holier [...] The Court of the Israelites is even holier [...] The Court of the Priests is even holier [...] [The area] between the Hall and the Altar is holier than [the Court of Priests] [...] The Sanctuary is still holier [...] The Holy of Holies is holier than all of these places.

The *Mishnah* also details the laws that pertain to the various holy places, according to their degrees of sanctity:

> There are ten degrees of holiness. The Land of Israel is holier than all other lands. And what is its holiness? People bring the *omer* offering, and the *bikurim* offering (first fruits), and the two loaves from there. These cannot be brought from any other land [...] The Holy of Holies is holier than all of these places, since none may enter except the *Kohen Gadol* (High Priest) on Yom Kippur at the time of the *Avodah* Service.

This is also the case with regard to holy sites of the second kind: *halakha* describes in great detail the defining features of the *beit knesset* and how one should behave in it.[11] A few examples of the *halakhot* pertaining to the *beit knesset*: only a place in which people pray regularly[12] in a *minyan* (prayer quorum)[13] may be considered to be a *beit knesset*; a *beit knesset* may not be established near an unclean place;[14] some feel that only a building built by human hands can be considered to bear the sanctity of a *beit knesset*, while *karka olam*, the "ownerless ground" of, for example, a cave, cannot be sanctified as a *beit knesset*;[15] if the place fell under the control of alien elements, some feel that the sanctity of the *beit knesset* is nullified.[16] *Halakha* also states that a *beit midrash* is holier than a *beit knesset*, and that a *beit knesset* may therefore be turned into a *beit midrash*, but not the opposite,[17] based on the rule that "one should rise in sanctity but never descend."

In contrast, the *halakhic* sources do not define holy places of the third kind, nor, of course, do they determine how one should behave in them. The sacredness of these sites is determined by the public, based on custom as derived from religious belief and tradition. A lack of clarity thus attaches to this third-level form of holiness.

Holy places of the third kind—their nature and definition

The attribution of holiness to a place due to a special event that occurred there is an age-old practice.[18] An early *midrash* cites an *aggadah* (legend) according to which a *tzadik* (righteous person) who died is not impure, and thus the Prophet Elijah, even though he was a *kohen*, was able to touch the corpse of Rabbi Akiva. The text of the *midrash* is as follows:[19]

> Although I said to them [the *kohanim or priests*]: you should not contaminate yourself, nevertheless for the sake of an unburied dead person (*met mitzvah*) you should defile yourself, and also for the sake of [dead] *tzadikim*, because *tzadikim* are considered alive even after death. A story is told of Rabbi Akiva who was captured and put into a prison, and Rabbi Yehoshua haGarsi was serving him ... Eliyahu came and knocked on the door. [Yehoshua] said to him: Who are you? and he replied I am Eliyahu. [Yehoshua] said to him: What do you want? [Eliyahu] answered him: I came to inform you that Rabbi Akiva your master has died. ... Eliyahu got stronger and took care of the body of Rabbi Akiva. Rabbi Yehoshua said to him: Aren't you a *kohen*? [Eliyahu] said to him: my son, there is no defilement from the dead bodies of *tzadikim* and *chachamim* [sages].

Rishonim [rabbis and *poskim* (Jewish legal decisors) who preceded the compilation of the *Shulchan Aruch*] wrote of the importance of *kivrei tzadikim*, burial places of righteous persons, although they did not define them as holy places. Thus writes the Ran, Rabbi Nissim of Gerona[20] (Spain, fourteenth century):

> And thus the presence of the Prophets and the Hassidim is responsible for the flow of the *Shefa* (abundant spiritual energy) throughout the generations,

and through them it may be channeled toward all those of their generation who are properly prepared, all the more so toward those who abide with them and take part in their activities. And not only while they live, but also after their death, their burial places merit the presence of the *Shefa* on one of the sides, since their bones which already served as vessels for the Divine *Shefa* still retain something of the merit and honor associated with the *Shefa*. And it was because of this that the Rabbis of blessed memory said that one should prostrate oneself at the tombs of the righteous and pray there, since prayer in such a place is highly desired, due to the presence of bodies which have already received the Divine *Shefa*.

And some have defined the burial place of a *tzadik* as a holy place. These include Rabbi Chaim Paltiel of Magdeburg (Germany, fourteenth century), who said, "And a holy place [a place where one's fathers are buried] is conducive to the favorable reception of one's prayer."[21] This view is shared by the Maharil (Germany, fifteenth century): "The graveyard is the *tzadikim*'s resting place, and thus it is a holy and pure place, and prayers offered on holy ground are most acceptable."[22] Similar statements may be found in the writings of several of the *Acharonim*, or later *poskim*, including Rabbi Shlomo Ganzfried,[23] the nineteenth-century author of the *Kitzur Shulchan Aruch*:

> It is customary to go on Erev Rosh Hashana, after the morning service, to the cemetery and pray at the graves of *tzadikim*, give charity to the poor and say many supplications to arouse the holy *tzadikim* who are buried there to intercede on our behalf on the day of judgement. Also, since this is the burial place of *tzadikim*, the place is holy and pure, and prayers said there are received more favorably because they are said on holy ground: The Holy One, blessed be He, will deal graciously (with us) in the merit of the *tzadikim*.

Above all, popular tradition and prevailing belief affirmed the sanctity of the graves of *tzadikim* and the desirability of visiting them and praying at them.

Over the generations there have been *kohanim* who, in light of the midrashic source quoted above, have not refrained from visiting *kivrei tzadikim*; however, the sanctity of cemeteries is not firmly anchored in the world of *halakha*, and the *midrash* should be understood as an aggadic legend or parable. A clear expression of this distinction is provided by Rabbi Shlomo Ganzfried, who, while indeed recognizing the grave of the *tzadik* as a holy place which it is desirable to visit on the day before Rosh Hashana, nevertheless directs harsh words of condemnation toward those *kohanim* who visit *kivrei tzadikim* in contravention of the *halakha* that forbids them to defile themselves by coming into contact with dead bodies. He writes:

> There are uneducated *kohanim* who go to the graves of the righteous out of the belief that such graves do not have the power to defile them. They are wrong, and this practice should be opposed.

It is important to distinguish between the *halakhic* definition of a holy place and the belief that the gravesite of a particular *tzadik* or any other site where a unique event took place is sacred. According to *halakha*, a grave is impure and defiles those who come into contact with it, even if it holds the remains of the generation's most illustrious *tzadik*.[24] A belief in the special powers and sanctity of a *tzadik's* gravesite does not make the site holy from a *halakhic* point of view, and a *kohen* is forbidden to approach it.[25]

Other *poskim* were opposed in principle to the widespread custom of visiting *kivrei tzadikim* or other sites and praying there;[26] included among these *poskim* were some who recognized the "holiness" of these sites but who nevertheless were concerned about the serious theological misconception that had taken root among the masses who visited them.[27] Yet even they acknowledged that their admonishments had little effect, "as the vast majority of the people were strongly and obstinately attached to these customs."[28]

And since the holiness of sites of the third kind is based on aggadic sources or popular belief, rather than on *halakhic* sources, no litmus test in Jewish Law has been found for determining the sacred status of a site or the *halakhic* significance of such sanctity.

It appears that this form of sanctity is more factual than legal in nature. A site is holy if the relevant believer population treats it as such—making pilgrimages to it, visiting it regularly and conducting some kind of religious ritual there. This is in contradistinction to the *halakhically*-based sanctity, for example of the Temple Mount, a sanctity that bears no relation to public attitudes toward the site or to the issue of whether it is regularly visited or not.

Still, this definition itself poses certain challenges and leaves many questions unanswered. It does not, for instance, tell us how many people have to visit a particular site in order for it to be considered holy, how frequently and over how long a period of time, etc.

The Protection of Holy Places Law, 5727–1967

The Protection of Holy Places Law, 5727–1967 does not define what a holy place is.[29] To arrive at such a definition we therefore have to rely on external sources. Some say that "our first recourse should be to the religious sources," since sanctity is "a religious concept by its very nature and essence."[30]

The Jewish religious sources state unequivocally that synagogues and *batei midrash* are holy places,[31] and that their sanctity endures even after they have been destroyed or have ceased to be employed for their original purposes.[32] However, given the particular time period in which this law was passed (just after the Six-Day War), it is doubtful whether the Israeli legislator had these places in mind: the purpose of the law was to ensure freedom of access and worship at the sites recognized historically as sacred by each of the religions in question (Christianity and Islam in particular)—sites that came under Israeli control due to the war. In any case, it is clear that the legislator intended the law to cover "third kind" holy places as well, despite the vagueness of their *halakhic* definition.

Although we certainly ought to have "recourse to the religious sources" when seeking to define the concept of the "holy place" in terms of the aforementioned law, we need not necessarily refer to Jewish *halakhic* sources, but rather (and perhaps primarily) to texts on Jewish custom and to extra-*halakhic* sources (such as the kabbalistic and mystical literature), which are also manifestations of religious experience and which testify to the sensitivity of large populations of believers to the holiness of these sites. The legislator's main concern is to honor the belief in these sites shared by adherents of the religion in question, and, in the name of public order, to prevent any outrage to their sensibilities. The legislator is not necessarily concerned to abide by the dictates of the relevant faith's official legal sources—in the case of Judaism, those of the *halakhic* literature.

The holy places and property rights

Article 1 of the Protection of Holy Places Law states:

> The Holy Places shall be protected from desecration and any other violation and from anything likely to violate the freedom of access of the members of the different religions to the places sacred to them or their feelings with regard to those places.

The wording of the law appears to lend legitimacy to the violation of individual property rights, since it does not limit religious believers' freedom of access to public areas only. Israeli courts have yet to rule regarding the proper balance to be struck between the public's right to visit the places sacred to it and property rights which have in the meantime been recognized as constitutional in nature.[33]

With regard to the position taken by Jewish Law in this regard, mention should again be made of the principle that the laws pertaining to the sanctity of a *beit knesset* do not apply to a *beit knesset* built on private premises, since the owner may at any time force the worshipers to leave.[34] And it goes without saying that one may not take over a private property by force and establish a synagogue there, since this would be considered a *mitzvah haba'a be-avera* (a *mitzvah* performed by means of a transgression).[35]

Moreover, even if the area that is privately owned is defined as a holy place, this in itself is insufficient to justify violating property rights and to confer on others freedom of access to it.[36] If, indeed, prevailing custom dictates that the site is open to all, as is the case with regard to most "third kind" holy sites, the custom must not be violated. This however, is not due to the sanctity attached to the site, but rather to the rule *metzer she hecheziku bo rabim assur lekalkelo* (an area that has been used by the public may not be withdrawn from public use);[37] in this regard, a holy place is no different from any other place that has customarily been used by the public, even for secular purposes.

Conclusion

Ultimately, despite the conclusion reached by the Advisory Committee, the Minister of Religious Affairs rescinded his decision to declare Ramban's Cave a holy place, and the petition was not subjected to exhaustive deliberation. The matter was again placed before the Jerusalem Magistrates Court,[38] which ruled as follows:

> It appears to me that we have no choice but to consider [all] of the evidence and to decide whether the site is indeed sacred, or whether the defendants raised this claim only after the plaintiffs began preparing the site [for their intended use of it], and in order to prevent the defendants from doing so.

As of this writing, the dispute regarding the sanctity of Ramban's Cave has yet to be resolved.

Notes

1 Civil File 7623/00 *Ishak Khalil Jibna et al. v. the National Center for the Development of the Holy Sites et al.* (unpublished).
2 *HCJ 4238/00 Mutawalli Abu Jibna et al. v. the Minister of Religious Affairs et al., Takdin* 2003(3) at 1350. [in Hebrew].
3 *See also*, HCJ 222/68 *Nationalist Circles, et al., v. the Minister of Police*, PD 24(2) 141, and in HCJ 267/88 *Reshet Kollelei Ha Idra, v. The Local Administrative Court*, PD 43(3) 728 [in Hebrew]. *Cf.* Civil File 2085/97 *Sheikh Raid Salah v. Israel Development Authority* (unpublished) [in Hebrew].
4 The issue of the holy sites is discussed extensively by my colleague and friend A. Hacohen, "'What Does Sanctity Have to Do with Law?' The Holy Sites and the Legal System", *Parashat HaShavua, Teruma-Tetzaveh*, 5763–2003, no. 110. [in Hebrew]; *ibid.*, "How Awesome is the Place," Holy Sites: Court, Law and Sanctity," 5764–2004, vol. 3, *Sha'arei Mishpat*, pp. 341–73 [in Hebrew]. *See also* the myriad sources and references listed in the article. My more limited discussion focuses on the issue of how a site's sanctity may be determined, approaching the question from other vantage points.
5 *See* Rabbi J.D. Soloveitchik, *The Lonely Man of Faith*, Jerusalem, Mossad Harav Kook, 5735–1975, pp. 30–31. [in Hebrew]. English version: New York: Doubleday, 1992.
6 Thus Rashi, commenting on Leviticus, 19:2 ("You must be holy, since I am God your Lord [and] I am holy") – "Keep aloof from forbidden sexual relations and from sinful thoughts." *See also* Rabbi S. Goren, "The Holy Places in Light of Halakha," *Machanayim* 5728–1968, vol. 116, p. 7 [in Hebrew]. One may, in any case, point out that the concept of holiness is capable of reflecting a negative distinction and separation, as in "[If you do so] the yield [...] will be forfeit." (Deuteronomy 22:9). Rashi's comment here is of interest to our discussion: "[...] to anything for which a man has repugnance, be it on account of its sublimity as, for instance, holy things, or be it on account of some bad quality, as, for instance, something that is forbidden, the term "holy" (*kadosh*) is appropriate, as, for instance, "Come not near me for I make thee holy (*kadosh*)" (Isaiah 65:5)." Another example: "There shall be no prostitute (*kadesha*) of the daughters of Israel, nor a man prostituting *(kadesh)* himself of the sons of Israel."

(Deuteronomy, 23:18). It is a well-known phenomenon of the Hebrew language that the same word can sometimes express opposite meanings, but this goes beyond the parameters of our discussion.

7 For a review of some of the relevant sources, *see* Hacohen, "What Does Sanctity Have to Do with Law?" n. 4.
8 *See Megilla* 29a.
9 *See Mishnah Midot*, Ch. 2.
10 *Kelim* 1:6–9.
11 *See Shulchan Aruch*, Orach Chayim, 153.
12 A temporary place of prayer does not bear the sanctity of a *beit knesset*. *See Shulchan Aruch*, Orach Chayim, 154:1: "The public square of a city, even though people pray in it on fast days, is not holy inasmuch as it is temporary; nor do houses and courtyards in which people gather to pray in a temporary fashion (that is, occasionally and as circumstances dictate, rather than regularly) bear a character of holiness." The *Mishnah Berurah*, 154:2, states: "It goes without saying that if people gather to pray in a house where people live and carry out their daily functions, it may certainly not be considered to be a *beit knesset*, even if prayer services are conducted there regularly, since it is not designated solely for prayer" (my translation).
13 The prayer of individuals does not confer on a place the status of *beit knesset*, even if the individuals in question pray there on a regular basis. *See Chidushei haRamban, Megilla* 27b, s.v. *veod*; *Resp. Mahari Ben Habib* cited in the *Beit Yosef* and the *Shulchan Aruch*, Orach Chayim, 151:2, states that a *beit midrash* is holy only if it is used for study by a sizeable group "as with a *beit knesset*."
14 *See Mishnah Berurah*, 151:41, which has harsh things to say about uncleanness in the vicinity of a *beit knesset*: "And in any case to use it for purposes that are highly offensive, such as uncleanness and the like would appear to forbidden in every light. And so a synagogue may not be established if the property above it is used for this offensive purpose (*taz*)." And if a synagogue may not be established in a place that is adjacent to an unclean area, then it is all the more clear that it may not be established in the unclean place itself.
15 *See Resp. Yabia Omer*, part 8, Orach Chayim, no. 16 s.v. *veaikara im*.
16 *See Resp. Yabia Omer, ibid*. On the differences of opinion between the *poskim*, or Jewish legal decisors, regarding this issue, *see* Rabbi Y.Y. Wachtfogel, "The Synagogue that was Destroyed," *Noam*, 5728–1968, vol. 11, pp. 15–20 [in Hebrew].
17 *Shulchan Aruch, 151:1*. See also *Mishnah Berurah*, 151:1 [in Hebrew].
18 *See e.g.*, E. Reiner, "Destruction, Temple and Holy Place: on Issues of Time and Place during the Middle Ages," *Kathedra*, 5761–2001, vol. 97, pp. 47–64 [in Hebrew].
19 *See Midrash Aggadah* (Buber), *Vayikra*, Ch. 21, s.v. *emor el* [in Hebrew].
20 *Drashot HaRan*, HaDarush haShmini. *See also Sefer haChinuch*, Mitzva 263 [in Hebrew].
21 Cited in the *Responsa* of the Maharam, Rabbi Meir ben Baruch of Rottenberg, Lvov edn. no. 164 [in Hebrew].
22 Maharil, *Minhagim* (Book of Customs), *Hilkhot Ta'anit*, 18 [in Hebrew].
23 *Kitzur Shulchan Aruch*, 128:13 [in Hebrew].
24 In evidence of this, the *poskim* cite a *midrash* in which the impure ones who complained to Moses about being unable to bring the Passover sacrifice were the bearers of Joseph's coffin. *See Pe'at HaShulchan* (Israel ben Samuel Ashkenazi of Shklov, a student of the Vilna Gaon), 2:16 [in Hebrew].
25 On this issue *see also Piskei HaRosh*, Baba Metziya, 9:47; *Tosafot*, Baba Metziya 114b s.v.*Mahu sheyesadru*; *Chiddushei HaRamban*, Yebamot 61a, s.v. *Ha d'amar*; *Chiddushei HaRitba*, Megilla 3b, s.v. *Ve-din met*; *Resp. Yabia Omer*, part 4, Yore De'ah, no. 35 [in Hebrew].

26 Based on the *midrash*: R. Shimon ben Gamliel said: "Do not erect headstones for the righteous. They are remembered by their words,"*Bereishit Raba* (Vilna) Parasha 82, 10. And Maimonides ruled: "The entire cemetery should be marked, and headstones should be made to mark the graves. But headstones should not be made for the graves of *tzadikim*, as they are remembered by their words, and people should not be encouraged to visit [the] graves [of *tzadikim*]." Maimonides, *Hilchot Evel* (Laws of Mourning), Ch. 4, *Halakha* 4 [in Hebrew]. A. Hacohen has pointed out the irony of the fact that Maimonides' Tomb is one of the few sites recognized as sacred by Israeli law. *But see Resp. Iggerot Moshe*, Yore De'ah, part 4, 57:5, for a justification of the custom of erecting headstones on the graves of prominent scholars, which would seem to violate this *halakha*.

27 *See e.g.*, Paltiel, *Responsa* of the Maharam *supra* note 21. *See also* the *Responsa* of Maharam Mintz, no. 79; *Chochmat Adam*, 89:7, and M. Hildesheimer, "A Portrait of Rabbi Azriel Hildesheimer," *Sinai*, 5724–1964, vol. 54, p. 67—at p. 94, n. 166; Y. Lichtenstein, "Visiting and Praying at Gravesites – Supplicating the Dead?" *Techumin*, 5760–2000, vol. 20, p. 188 [in Hebrew].

28 So writes Rabbi Chaim Mashash, Chief Rabbi of Morocco during the early twentieth century, in a responsum in *Mayim Chayim*, no. 207 (quoted in *Techumin, ibid.*) [in Hebrew]. *See also Bait Hadash, Yoreh De'ah*, 217. It should, however, be noted that the custom of praying at *kivrei tzadikim* and at holy places has been generally authorized by the halakhic sages, some of whom have even accorded this practice the status of a *mitzvah*.

29 Published in *Sefer HaChukim*, no. 499, 28 June 1967, p. 75. For the official translation of the law: Online. Available: http://www.mfa.gov.il/MFA/Peace%20Process/Guide%20to%20the%20Peace%20Process/Protection%20of%20Holy%20Places%20Law (accessed 23 July 2008).

30 *See* S. Berkowitz, *The Legal Status of the Holy Places in Jerusalem* (Jerusalem, publisher not specified, 1997), p. 65 [in Hebrew]. Justice England takes this stance in HCJ 4128/00 *The Director General of the Prime Minister's Office, et al. v. Anat Hoffman et al.*, PD 57(3) 289, para. 7. This position was not shared by the other justices; *see also*, Hacohen, "What Does Sanctity Have to Do with Law?" n. 4, p. 362. These latter justices raise the concern of holy site "inflation." Regarding this it must be stated that, even according to Berkowitz, the legal authority to declare a place sacred always lies with the Minister, who is under no obligation to sanctify every site that the followers of the relevant religion treat as holy. If he declares a site to be holy, it would only be after having been persuaded that the religion regards it as such. This is a necessary, though insufficient, condition.

31 *See Shulchan Aruch*, Orach Chayim, no.151 ff., and the aforegoing.

32 *See Shulchan Aruch*, Orach Chayim, 151:10: "Even after they have been destroyed, they remain sacred." The Talmud derives this *halakha* from Leviticus 26:31, "[I will] make your sanctuaries desolate" – they are sacred even when desolate" (*Megilla* 28b).

33 This issue could conceivably have been the focus of HCJ 4238/00 *supra* note 2, regarding Ramban's Cave, since the cave is situated on private property. However, based on the discussion below, the Minister appears to have changed his original intention, and the petition was therefore canceled.

34 *See Shulchan Aruch*, Orach Chayim, 154: 2: "A house that is rented for the purpose of prayer does not fall into the category of a *beit knesset*." The reasoning behind this is as follows: "Inasmuch as, once the rental period has ended, the owner has the right to refuse to renew the arrangement, the place of worship must therefore be regarded as temporary and is not considered sacred" (*Mishnah Berurah*, 154:4).

35 *See Encyclopedia Talmudica*, vol. 3, s.v. *beit knesset*, p. 191: "The Temple Mount, the place of the Holy temple, was properly purchased by King David from Meorna the Yevusi", referring to *Sefer haEshkol*.

36 *See* the *Resp. Maharam of Padova*, no. 85. *See also Resp. Chavot Ya'ir*, no. 59 [in Hebrew]. Of interest in this context is a ruling issued by Rabeinu Gershom Me'Or Hagolah, according to which, "If a person permits a synagogue on his property to be used by a congregation for prayer, and he quarrels with one of the members of the congregation, he may not forbid his adversary from praying there if he is not prepared to forbid the entire congregation from doing so." Cited in the *Responsa* of the Maharam, Rabbi Meir ben Baruch of Rottenberg, Prague edn, no. 1022 [in Hebrew].
37 Maimonides, *Hilchot Nizkei Mamon*, 13:24 [in Hebrew].
38 Civil File 7623/00 *Ishak Khalil Jibna et al., v. the National Center for the Development of the Holy Sites, et al.* 2005(2), *Takdin*, 9137, decision of 22 May 2005 [in Hebrew].

6 The *waqf* in Israel since 1965
The case of Acre reconsidered

Yitzhak Reiter

In 1989 I published an article in Hebrew in which I reviewed the implementation of the 1965 amendment[1] to the 1950 Absentees Property Law[2] as an expression of the Israeli Government's policy regarding the *waqf* properties in the country.[3] In this present essay I intend to revisit the case study some twenty years later in order to reevaluate the findings in light of developments since the second half of the 1980s and to reconsider my former conclusions. I will also look at the *waqf* issue in a broader political perspective in an attempt to reexamine the conceptual framework in light of the scholarly work done by Michael Dumper, Alisa Rubin-Peled,[4] and Laurence Louër.[5]

This article considers the *waqf* in Israel as a political issue between the state and its Arab, mostly Muslim, minority. My main purpose here is to examine implementation of the 1965 law, and to assess its degree of success in achieving its political and economic goals. Major sources for the study include the record (*sijill*) of the Acre Shari'a court for the years 1962–85, minutes of the Acre *waqf* Board of Trustees, archives of the Muslim Department of the Ministry of Religious Affairs [hereinafter: MRA], and the archives of the Bureau of the Advisor for Arab Affairs in the Prime Minister's office [hereinafter: AAA]. Additional information was obtained through personal interviews with the Qadi of Acre, *waqf* administrators (*mutawalli*s), and trustees.

I chose Acre as a case study because a relatively large part of the Old City of Acre was under the Muslim *waqf*. In 1965 there were 7,500 Muslims living in Acre, out of a population of 33,000 (including 2,000 Christian Arabs). In 2006 there were 11,000 Muslims and 1,000 Christian Arabs out of the city's population of 46,000. Most of the Muslims reside in the old part of the city, where the urban *waqf* properties are located. That part of the city has been slated for development as a tourist center since the 1960s because of its *waqf* public monuments such as the Khan al-'Umdan and Al-Jazzar's Mosque. However, the residential area turned into a slum and the state authorities planned to relocate its inhabitants to the new section of the city or to the nearby village of al-Makr. Generally speaking, Jews and Arabs coexist in Acre. The Arabs are represented in the municipality by a deputy mayor and other members of the local government.

Before delving into details of the Israeli legislation and the particular case of Acre, let us first look at the historical development of the *waqf* institution in Palestine. Throughout the years of Muslim rule in Palestine, thousands of private individuals as well as high-ranking officials, on their own behalf or on behalf of the state, endowed urban and rural properties as a religious endowment called *waqf*. *waqf* is an institution of charitable trust in Islam, considered to be an act of pious charity for the public benefit or for the benefit of the endower's family and descendents for eternity. It is estimated that up to the twentieth century, between 80,000 and 100,000 dunams (20,000–25,000 acres) of rural land were dedicated in Palestine and registered as *waqf*, while between 600,000–1,000,000 dunams were registered as land regarding which some of its taxes and agricultural products were dedicated for *waqf*s (*ghayr sahih*), all in addition to hundreds of urban buildings which enjoy *waqf* status.[6] Most of the donated *waqf* assets were dedicated for public purposes, such as for the establishment and upkeep of mosques, Islamic seminaries (*madrasa*s), cemeteries, and the like. Once endowed, the *waqf* property was regarded inalienable and its assets could not be easily traded in the free market as private properties; the reason for this was to safeguard the charitable act as eternal. This conceptual and legal principle has led many scholars and Muslim politicians in the twentieth century to claim that the *waqf* is an economically stagnant institution, and should be abolished and replaced by a modern system.[7]

As I will discuss in the 'Transactions' section below, the above claims overlooked the fact that Islamic law permitted the exchange (and even sale) of original *waqf* properties in cases of both necessity and benefit, on condition that the substitute property would serve for the original purpose (beneficiary) of the charity as stipulated by its founder in the endowment deed.[8] During the Ottoman period many *waqf* endowments suffered from neglect, poor administration and even embezzlement. In the nineteenth century the Ottomans reformed the system by putting most *waqf*s dedicated for public purposes under a central ministerial administration for funding religious, educational, and other welfare ends of the state. Privately administered *waqf*s for public purposes—which constituted only a small number of endowments—and family *waqf*s—which were large in number but small in terms of their physical properties and value—were outside the jurisdiction of the Ministry but under the (inefficient) supervision of the local *shari'a* court *qadi* (judge).

In Palestine the British Mandate government formed the Supreme Muslim Council, which was headed until 1937 by the Grand Mufti Hajj Amin al-Husayni. As President of the Council, he was entitled to administer *waqf* properties which had been in the jurisdiction of the Ottoman *waqf* Ministry. In October 1937, after al-Husayni escaped abroad following his involvement in the 1936 Arab riots, the government appointed a three-body committee to strictly supervise *waqf* administration by the Supreme Muslim Council. Prior to the 1948 War, all three members of this supervisory committee were civil servant Muslims. During the war, the Council's members fled the territory that in 1948 became Israel, and thus were declared as "absentees" in the 1950 Absentees Properties Law as were other Palestinian refugees who owned land and other properties in the area that became the State of Israel.

One of the debated issues regarding Israel's policy of the *waqf* as both an Islamic institution and as an issue of real estate properties centers on the moral justification of this policy in light of the Arab–Jewish conflict. Aharon Layish, a prominent Israeli professor of Islamic law, who also was the initiator and principal drafter of the above mentioned 1965 enactment when he was the Prime Minister's Deputy Advisor on Arab Affairs, described Israel's policy as consistent with reforms of the *waqf* institution enacted in the Arab–Muslim world. He also described one of the main purposes of the "reform" as adapting a traditional institution to modern public life.[9] Alisa Rubin-Peled criticized his approach, since Arab states did not expropriate public *waqf* assets for other purposes (such as settlement) but handed it over to a ministry which used the revenues for funding the operation and upkeep of mosques, cemeteries, and so on, as was the situation before the reform. Whereas Arab states handed the public *waqf*s over to a *waqf* ministry mostly headed by a high-ranking Muslim religious figure, in Israel the government abolished the higher Islamic body—the Supreme Muslim Council—and transferred some of its functions to a Jewish-administered Ministry of Religious Affairs.[10] In my 1989 article I adopted the "reform" terminology, but criticized the policy and concluded that the 1965 amendment did not achieve its official "reformist" ends. In describing the development of the Israeli policy regarding the *waqf* in the present article, I add the main and hidden purpose of the 1965 amendment and assess its success in light of developments since the 1980s.

Dumper also criticized Layish's approach (although he himself used the word "reform" to describe the law) and presented Israel's policy as a mode of political cooptation.[11] Rubin-Peled challenged Dumper's approach as well. She claimed that Israel's policy towards the Islamic institutions was as multi-faceted and contradictory as its overall policy towards the Arab minority. Based on Israel's National Archive, she concluded that the government policy was motivated by a combination of three elements: a genuine desire to grant a degree of cultural and religious autonomy, a security-minded quest for control, and a desire to mobilize the economic resources of the Muslim community for state purposes.[12] I will argue that the last of Rubin-Peled's points was the main motivation for the 1965 enactment and that the first two elements were secondary. In addition, I claim that the assumption of the drafters of the 1965 bill, namely that the Muslim-administered *waqf* institution is economically stagnant and that only its release from the *shari'a* jurisdiction would boost its economic development, was completely wrong.

The post-1948 policy and the 1965 amendment to the Absentees' Property Law

Soon after the State of Israel was established, an intra-ministerial struggle over the control of *waqf* land ended with a decision to declare public *waqf* land as "absentee property" and nationalize them via transfer to a government custodian according to the 1950 Absentee Property Law. The 1950 law defined "absentee property" as property regarding which "an absentee was its legal owner, or its beneficiary, or its holder ... " This sweeping definition was aimed at capturing *waqf* assets, regardless of the fact that beneficiaries of the endowments, at least those for public ends, still resided within the State of Israel. Since the Palestinian refugees who mostly used the *waqf* properties and the waqf administration (Supreme Muslim Council members) fled from the territory that became Israel in 1948, the government of Israel decided to take control over *waqf* properties by declaring them properties of "absentees," despite the fact that some 120,000 Muslims remained in Israel and were in need of these *waqf*s. In late 1951 the Custodian of Absentee Property reached an agreement with the Ministry of Religious Affairs, according to which the latter would act as its agent for administering urban *waqf* property. The arrangement determined that income from *waqf* property would be channeled to fund religious services for the Muslim community.[13] The Ministry of Religious Affairs nominated committees of Muslim notables to administer the property in the cities, and made recommendations regarding the use of the funds which accrued from the property.[14] As a result, religious properties such as mosques and Muslim cemeteries were handed over to be administered by Muslim clerics as employees of the Ministry of Religious Affairs, while the main property, both urban and agriculture, was controlled by the Custodian. This arrangement was considered temporary, and the Muslims continued to demand that the government restore the *waqf* property to their direct administration by autonomous institutions.

Two legal problems emerged from this policy. The first was that custody meant administration rather than ownership. In 1953, however, the Custodian interpreted his jurisdiction as an owner and hence sold most of the *waqf* land with most of other absentee properties land to a governmental Development Authority. It appears that this action was part of the policy of Prime Minister David Ben-Gurion, to prevent the return of Palestinian refugees to their lands and homes. A large share of absentee properties was sold to the Jewish National Fund (JNF—Keren Kayemeth LeIsrael) which, according to its regulations, can transfer land only to Jews.[15] It is still unknown if the government officials were aware of the fact that this action was actually illegal or if they genuinely believed that the Custodian had the right to sell properties under his jurisdiction. From 1955 on, the Supreme Court discussed the exact jurisdiction of the Custodian[16] and government officials realized that they would have to find a way to retroactively legalize the Custodian's land sales. This matter was resolved in the 1965 amendment to the Absentee Properties Law.

The second legal problem was that since Israel did not abolish the *shari'a* court's jurisdiction over the *waqf*, according to the *shari'a* and to long-standing practice, a *qadi* could dismiss a *waqf* administrator—in this case the government Custodian—and appoint a Muslim administrator in the Custodian's place. The government policy of maintaining a certain scope of autonomy to non-Jewish denominations by incorporating their religious courts in the

Israeli legal system contradicted its land-ownership strategy regarding *waqf* assets. In fact, already in 1952, Muslim activists were successful in being appointed by the *shari'a* court as administrators of certain *waqf*s and they submitted a file to the Israeli High Court of Justice claiming the transfer of *waqf* properties (which were in the hands of the government Custodian) to their possession. As an example, the *Qadi* of Acre—Sheikh Musa al-Tabari—initiated a test case in court. He appointed a businessman from the nearby village of Dir al-Asad, Bulus Hanna Bulus, as an administrator (*mutawalli*) of the Dir al-Asad *waqf*, and later approached the High Court.[17] Another "*waqf*-release entrepreneur" was Sa'id Habbab from Jaffa, who served as the chair of a Muslim Committee advising the Ministry of Religious Affairs regarding the administration of *waqf*s in Jaffa, to whom I shall refer below. This trend of Muslim activists seeking legal recourse against the Custodian and demanding the release of *waqf* property under his possession was of concern to the government, which first exerted pressure on *qadis* ordering them not to appoint *mutawalli*s. Later, when the pressure proved ineffective, the government initiated legislation.

The government initiative to amend the 1950 Absentees' Properties Law was motivated by three factors: first, Israel's policy of handing the *waqf* assets over to the administration of a (Jewish) Government Custodian raised grievances among the local Muslim community and led to political protest, and the leading party—Mapai—was interested in appeasing the Muslim community, particularly before general elections took place.[18] Second, neglect, misadministration, and even embezzlement of *waqf* properties during the 1950s, in which local Muslims close to the government echelons and government agencies were involved, also outraged the Muslim community as well as general Jewish public opinion.[19] Finally, the most urgent factor leading to the 1965 bill amending the 1950 law was a legal loophole enabling the *shari'a* courts to appoint Muslim administrators to replace the Government Custodian. The government was afraid that not only urban *waqf* buildings would fall in the hands of smart Muslim "*waqf*-release entrepreneurs" but also that the sale of the large quantity of rural *waqf* by the Custodian to the government would be declared void. A few Muslims newly appointed by the *shari'a* court sued the Custodian in civil court to demand the release of *waqf* assets to their possession. The Government Custodian hired a special advocate whose task was to delay the court hearing until the Knesset could amend the law and solidify the Custodian's position as an owner of the *waqf* assets. The following example indicates the urgency in amending the law. Sa'id Habab from Jaffa, who acquired an appointment as *waqf mutawalli,* had already sold a few assets to real estate developers and received the money believing that as an appointed administrator he would take over *waqf* properties from the Custodian and could behave as their owner. When the law was finally enacted in February 1965, it retroactively legalized the Government Custodian's actions of *waqf* sales and preempted the release of public *waqf* assets to *mutawallis*. Thus, Habab could not deliver the goods to the real estate developers who gave him an advanced payment, and so he fled the country with their money. The embezzlement by some Muslim "*waqf*-release entrepreneurs" appointed by the *shari'a* courts was one of the justifications for the Israeli policy of nationalizing the *waqf*.

The principal idea behind the 1965 amendment was to release a handful of urban *waqf* assets to Muslim bodies whose members would be appointed and supervised by the government, on the one hand, while setting a legal device for retroactively legalizing the sale of rural *waqf* land by the Custodian to the State, on the other hand. The former reflected the political aim of the 1965 law—to appease the Muslim community on this issue and to downplay the gravity of the problem. However, the law's explanatory note did not hide the fact that one of the main purposes of this legislation was to strengthen the government's position regarding some of the *waqf* properties.[20] However, when the bill was discussed in the Knesset Finance Committee the Muslim Knesset Members and attendants were told that the Custodian should acquire full ownership according to the amendment "in order to enable him to transfer it back to the Muslim Trusteeships."[21] It should be noted that the Muslim public in the 1950s and 1960s had no idea of the fact that the Custodian sold most of the *waqf* properties to the government. Since the main opposition to the government policy on the *waqf* came from the Muslim communities in the cities, the government hoped that if urban *waqf* properties would be administered directly by Muslims, it would appease the Muslim community and at the same time strengthen the state's ownership of the vast plots of rural *waqf* land.

According to the 1965 law, boards of (Muslim) trustees were nominated for *waqf* administration in five cities: Acre, Haifa, Ramla, Lod, and Tel Aviv-Yaffo (Jaffa).[22] These boards are corporate bodies, competent to acquire rights and assume legal obligations. Their task is to administer the *waqf* properties which the Custodian releases to their administration, and to utilize the revenues for the benefit of Muslim residents in their jurisdiction. Revenues from properties that were excluded from their administration (i.e., properties that were used for development and cannot be released to them) may be used for the construction of educational, religious, health, social, and welfare facilities intended to serve all Israel's Muslim citizens. The trustees are public servants who work as volunteers. Their yearly budget must be confirmed by the government, and their actions are subject to inspection by the State Comptroller. By law, family *waqf* properties are to be released to the beneficiaries of the endower's family.

The basic principles of the 1965 law were as follows: First, the major tenet of the *waqf*—the *shari'a* interdiction on transferring property in any way (sale, lease, mortgage, etc.)—was canceled. The language of the law blurred the abolishment of a *shari'a* law by using general wording: "under any law."[23] Thus, according to the law, full ownership of the property was vested in the Custodian, permitting him to transfer it to the beneficiaries in the family *waqf*, or to a board of trustees, in the case of a public *waqf* (but not to *shari'a* court-appointed *mutawallis*). The board of trustees was allowed to conduct transactions and to transfer the property (to sell, to lease, etc.) with no restrictions, except for land on which a mosque is built. This principal of the law was aimed at overcoming what the law drafters viewed as the economic hindrance of the *waqf* according to the *shari'a* in which any transaction is bound by legal justifications and a procedure in court. This reflected the economic purpose of the law, namely to enable the Muslim trustees to sell real estate in urban development areas. Second, revenues from *waqf* properties could now be legally used for purposes other than those stipulated by the founder in the endowment deed (*waqfiyya*) as long as the general purpose of the well-being of the Muslim community (including religious and welfare services and facilities) is guaranteed. Third, the boards of trustees administering the *waqf* were to be nominated and supervised by the government, instead of by the *shari'a* courts.[24]

The main question to be addressed in the following sections is: did the government achieve the political and economical purposes behind the 1965 law. I used Acre (Arabic: 'Akka, Hebrew: 'Akko) *waqf* affairs as a case study. In the following section I will survey the history of *waqf* in the city of Acre. Then I will elaborate on the implementation of the 1965 law in Acre in three main fields: appointment of administrators, ongoing management of the properties and transactions of *waqf* assets comparing the Acre case study to other cases and concluding by addressing the political issue of Israel's policy.

Waqf in Acre

In 1922 a British officer estimated that 90 percent of Acre's urban area was *waqf* at the end of the Ottoman period.[25] His estimation was wrong. A recent study by Moshe Meiri shows that between 20 to 25 percent of the 300 dunams of the Old City of Acre belonged to the *waqf*. Original registers recently found at the al-Jazzar Mosque listed in the late 1930s, 310 rented *waqf* assets out of 1,651 buildings, mostly residential houses in addition to other non-rented properties.[26] The exact space and real estate quantity of the *waqf* in Acre as well as in Palestine as a whole is very problematic to trace. However, there is no doubt that the endowments established in eighteenth-century Acre contributed greatly to the city's development as a major port. Acre's location at the northern tip of a bay, surrounded by the fertile lands of the Western Galilee, turned the village into a port city that could compete with Beirut and Sidon. In the mid-nineteenth century *waqf* holdings in Acre included all public institutions (places of worship, Islamic college (*madrasa*), library, public baths and water system) and a significant part of the commercial facilities (markets, khans and stores). The activities of these institutions were maintained by revenues from agricultural lands and orchards in the rural areas north and east of the city.

Al-Jazzar's *waqf* is the largest endowment in Acre, and the only *waqf* in this city which was publicly administered under the Ottoman Ministry of *waqf* and later by the Supreme Muslim Council during the British Mandate rule in

Palestine.[27] The *waqf* was created in May 1786 by Ahmad al-Jazzar, governor (*pasha*) of the provinces of Sidon and Damascus. The endowment included: a mosque, an Islamic college with fifty rooms for the lodgings of forty students from the four schools of Islamic law, a large religious library, a public fountain, an underground water reservoir, a ritual bath, a sundial, a garden, and twenty-nine stores surrounding the mosque courtyard. The endowment also included properties both in Acre itself and in the surrounding area: three large markets, and dozens of stores at different locations throughout the city, two khans, two bathhouses, a newly-constructed water system for the city and an additional public fountain, numerous residences, and many orchards with a network of irrigation canals.

Unlike Al-Jazzar's *waqf*, the other four public *waqf*s extant in current day Acre were administered privately by a *mutawalli* who was appointed and supervised by the local *qadi* of the *Shari'a* Court. The earliest of them was created by Hajj Muhammad ibn Shaykh Khalil al-Sha'bi in 1703. The dedicated holdings included: a mosque built by the founder (at the time, this was the only active mosque in Acre), a bathhouse (the first in Acre), 13 stores/warehouses in the vicinity of the port, 15 stores in the city, a bakery, a coffeehouse, and two dwellings.[28] Fifty years later (1170/1755) another endowment (named *al-Sadiqi*) was created, during the rule of Zahir al-'Umar al-Zaydani (1730–71). The founding deed (*waqfiyya*) was not preserved, but as in the case of the *Al-Sha'bi waqf*, the revenues were dedicated to the upkeep of a neighborhood mosque. In addition to the mosque, the endowment apparently included stores, apartments and agricultural lands east of the city. In the course of time the two *waqf*s were administered together by a *mutawalli* who was the founder's descendant.

'Ali Pasha, the district governor (*qaimaqam*) of Acre, also created an endowment in 1813.[29] The properties dedicated included a complex built on some 1.6 acres in the al-Majadala neighborhood in Acre, including a mosque, halls, a private bathhouse, water reservoirs, residential rooms, a public fountain, a large courtyard, and an orchard. In addition, the endower gave a large khan, and orchards and agricultural lands in the villages north of Acre (about 590 acres).

Another important *waqf* was established in Acre in 1862 by a sufi sheikh named 'Ali Nur al-Din al-Yashruti.[30] The endowment properties, which apparently were donations of his followers, included a sufi lodge (*zawiyya*), a nearby complex with a hall for prayer and festivities (*takiyya*), a public kitchen, an inn for travelers and the needy, and a number of stores. In addition, this *waqf* included some 613 acres of agricultural land in four villages near Acre. Like other sufi endowments, this was a family endowment for the upkeep of the *zawiyya*, at the center of which were the order's institutions. The posts of sheikh and administrator of the *waqf* and the lodge are passed down from the sheikh of the order to his eldest son. The *waqf* properties were administered as a common economic and social unit for the order's members, and they tended the fields and received the revenues as a group.[31] The social welfare institutions and the economic resources apparently attracted the poor and needy to join the order.

All five endowments described above have the following in common: a) they are relatively large; b) their first beneficiary is a religious institution; c) the revenues, after deductions for the maintenance of the religious and public institutions, are meant for the founder and his family; d) the position of *waqf* administrator was given to the most talented of the endower's descendants. The 1965 amendment of the Absentees' Properties Law at least prevented family administrators of public *waqf*s from employing *waqf* revenues for their own benefit at the expense of the public. Of the five large Acre *waqf*s, the Al-Jazzar endowment is exceptional in its imperial (sultanic) form and its impressive size.[32]

Implementing the 1965 amendment in Acre

Since the 1965 law only affected *waqf*s determined as "absentee property," of the five *waqf*s in Acre only the Al-Jazzar *waqf*—the largest of them—fell under this category. Its properties were administered by a board of Muslim trustees appointed by the government. The other four *waqf*s were never classified as absentee property because their administrator prior to 1948 did not leave the territory that in 1948 became Israel. Their administrators (*mutawallis*) were appointed and supervised by the *Shari'a* Court.

The following sections are based on a comparison between the administrations of the two kinds of *waqf*: the al-Jazzar *waqf* which was under the jurisdiction of the Absentees' Property Law and the remaining four *waqf*s under the jurisdiction of the *Shari'a* Court. The comparison will relate to the following topics: appointment of administrators (*mutawallis vis-à-vis* trustees) as a source of achieving political ends, ongoing administration of the properties and transactions of *waqf* assets—the last two refer to the economic purposes of the law. An attempt will be made to prove two hypotheses: first, that because the government implemented its policy in an inconsistent fashion, the law's social and economic aims were not realized; second, that the traditional administration of the *waqf* properties by the *Shari'a* Court, even in the twentieth century, does not necessarily signify economic stagnation. Overall, I will argue that the misuse of the 1965 amendment thwarted the achievement of the law's political end—appeasing the Muslim community and playing down the *waqf* issue in its political agenda. Put differently, although the amendment retroactively legalized the nationalization of *waqf* assets including significant rural *waqf* land, impaired implementation of the law in the five cities created ongoing anger among the Arab Muslim minority regarding the government policy and hence, an increasing political outcry to change the law.

Appointing administrators

The 1965 law was aimed at enabling the *waqf* administrators—the trustees—to institute policies of modern business management of the properties, regardless of the *shariʻa*'s restrictions. One would expect that the government appointing the trustees would consider their administrative skills and ability to handle *waqf* affairs according to the rules of modern economics. On the other hand, one would assume that *mutawalli*s appointed by the *qadi* would be chosen because of their descent from the endowment's founder and not necessarily for their administrative skills. This study refutes both these assumptions.

From 1965 to 2007 the government appointed four different boards of trustees in Acre to administer the Al-Jazzar *waqf* properties handed over to them by the Custodian. Three of the five trustees on the first board, which began its activities at the end of 1967, had been members of the advisory committee administering the endowments for the Ministry for Religious Affairs before 1965.[33] The first board included representatives of notable local families; the resources it wielded won it a standing in the public eye which extended beyond its official role. However, this was followed by a failed attempt to appoint a heterogeneous board of trustees which would provide a system of checks and balances and act according to the norms of modern public administration. In Acre, as well as in the other four boards of trustees in Jaffa, Lod, Ramla, and Haifa, the most important criteria for becoming a trustee was one's political affiliation (personally or through his extended family) to one of the Israeli coalition parties.[34] In addition, personal conflicts interfered in the work of most of the boards of trustees. The second and third boards of Acre included members of notable families, and the rivalry between them caused more conflicts than cooperation. The solution to this situation was found in 1982 by appointing to the fourth board seven public servants who exhibited higher abilities of public administration. The new appointees were university graduates or individuals with experience in public administration. Following these new appointments, the situation stabilized.

When I revisited the boards of trustees some twenty years after my previous study, I was astonished to see that in four out of the five of them the same figures who were appointed during the 1970s were still in office. Of them, the Acre board was the most successful due to the more skilful personalities of the trustees. This was the only place where the trustees had demanded since the 1990s that the government replace them, but the government and many among the Muslim community asked them to stay in office, fearing that if other people would be appointed they would be corrupt.[35] This explains why opposition of Islamic Movement activists against the trustees was contained.[36] An exception was the *waqf* board in Tel Aviv–Jaffa. Here, the first three chairmen of the board were tried in criminal court for corrupt administration of the *waqf* sources. Such affairs harmed both the image of all the boards of trustees and the entire system created by the 1965 law. Many Muslim public figures refused appointments as trustees, fearing the stigma,[37] and the government had to appoint Jewish civil servants to serve as the board of trustees in Tel Aviv-Jaffa. This reflected the failure of the 1965 amendment due to the awkward way the government implemented it. The exceptional case of the current (fourth) Acre board of trustees attests to the fact that had the government appointed skilful and non-corrupt personalities, the policy would have had more chance of success.

As for the *waqf*s which remained under *shari'a* court jurisdiction, which were not considered to be absentee property, traditionally the court respected the endowment deed's stipulation according to which the *mutawalli* should be the most talented (*al-arshad*) among the endower's descendants. The practice is that any of the descendants who consider himself *arshad* must produce a petition signed by the beneficiaries and local notable personages or file a lawsuit and have witnesses prove that he is indeed the most suitable of the descendants. In any case, according to Islamic law, the *qadi* must prefer a *mutawalli* from the founder's family to a stranger, as long as he possesses the necessary qualifications for the position.[38] More than one *mutawalli* may be appointed in situations when this is so stated by the founder or when the *mutawalli* neglects *waqf* affairs to such an extent that he may be dismissed. In such a case, the board of *mutawalli*s must act unanimously.[39]

Reviewing the *Shari'a* Court records, I found minimal involvement by the *Shari'a* Court in the internal administration of the *waqf* under its jurisdiction and supervision. The court related differently to endowments whose major beneficiaries are the endower's descendants than to *waqf*s for public purposes. In the family *waqf* there is a tendency to respect the wish of the founder and to appoint one of his descendants, even though he may not always fulfill the requirements set by Islamic law, and may not be qualified to administer the *waqf* according to modern financial principles. Such was the case in the *al-Sha'bi* and *al-Sadiqi* endowments of Acre: the *mutawalli* appointed in 1964 was old and incompetent, as is seen in a special decree of the *qadi* requesting a quarterly financial statement.[40] However, in the case of a public endowment like the *al-Yashruti waqf* or a family endowment about to acquire public status (*mundaras*) due to the endower's advanced age and childless state, the *qadi* appointed a board of *mutawalli*s. This approach on the part of the Muslim courts may be an attempt to compensate for the limited powers of supervision the *qadi*s wield over the administration of the *mutawalli*s.[41]

An effort was made by the *qadi* to adapt the administration of the *Al-Yashruti waqf* of Acre to changing social conditions. This was borne out by acts such as replacing the chief *mutawalli*, who was a farmer, with his son, a public figure and prominent businessman.[42] This appointment reflects a tendency to adapt the administration to the conditions of the modern economy, in which successful financial administration demands influential contacts and knowledge of the modern business world. The change in policy stems from an internal decision on the part of the members of the *sufi* order, who appoint the *mutawalli*s from their cohorts, as needed. In this situation, the *qadi* filled no more than a formal role. His decision that the *mutawalli*s will act upon the vote of the majority, is foreign to the *shari'a*, and was undoubtedly influenced by modern norms of public administration.

In conclusion, in comparison, the nominations of trustees and *mutawallis* by *shari'a* court *qadis* were by and large more successful than appointments by the government.

Release of waqf properties to the Acre board of trustees

The members of Acre's first board of trustees expected the 1965 law to establish their direct control as an independent corporate body over the properties formerly administered by the advisory committee for the Ministry for Religious Affairs. They were especially interested in the extensive property of the *Al-Jazzar waqf* and several additional mosques and cemeteries. Much chagrin was felt by the board of trustees when this expectation was only partially fulfilled. Even those properties transferred by the Custodian to the board of trustees were released in a slow, tedious process; more than once tiresome haggling brought the trustees to the brink of resignation.[43]

After years of negotiations between the board and the government representatives, the board received twenty-one properties, some of great value. However, those properties were subject to long-term lease, for low rent, to the Authority for the Development of Old Acre—a government company created to develop Acre as a tourist site while preserving its special architecture and history.[44] These agreements prompted a rumor that the board of trustees had sold the properties to the government, causing agitation against the board within the Muslim community.[45] The board also received 60 additional properties for direct administration, mostly stores (in addition to the mosques and cemeteries) whose rent constituted one-third of the board's entire income during the period covered by this study. The revenues of the board of trustees were not enough to fund renovations of the Al-Jazzar Mosque, and when emergency repair was needed, the trustees applied to the government demanding special financial support.

The situation in the other four cities was worse.[46] In Ramla, Lod, and Haifa the Custodian released far less property than in Acre although he was expected to hand the *waqf* properties over to the Muslim trustees as the 1965 amendment was understood by the public.[47] In Tel Aviv–Jaffa discharged property was located in metropolitan development areas of Tel Aviv, raising its value. The board repeatedly demanded the release of additional property. The number of the released assets was lower and less income-producing, as long as they are not sold for development purposes. The lack of revenues impelled the trustees to sell *waqf* properties or to initiate the construction of buildings on old Muslim cemeteries, and an attempt was made to lease for a long term the Hassan Bey Mosque in Tel Aviv and to sell two cemeteries, Tasso and Abu Kabir—all failed.

Ongoing administration

The revenues of the Acre board of trustees are derived from the following sources: 20 percent from rental payments of *waqf* assets to private tenants; 14

percent of rental payments from assets possessed by the Authority for the Development of Old Acre; 20 percent from entrance fees to the Al-Jazzar Mosque; 20 percent from the government funding of religious services; and the rest (some 26 percent) from advance payment that new tenants pay. The board's budget until 1985 was about US $50,000 a year, and this was gradually raised to US $175,000 in 2007 due to the increase in rental payments, the number of tourists who visited the mosque and the introduction of government funding in the late 1990s.

In the past, the board was responsible for the upkeep of six mosques and two Muslim cemeteries in Acre, and today it is in charge of two mosques only, while three mosques are operated by the two factions of the Islamic Movement and one by the Israeli Government.[48] It employs a dozen workers—maintenance staff, guards and clerks—and pays them salaries amounting to about half its budget.[49] Another one-third of its budget is spent on the maintenance and upkeep of the properties; the remainder goes to social welfare services (grants and loans to the needy and a special loan for students) and to funding religious sermons on Muslim holidays.

The State Comptroller's report found in 1984 that the Acre board administers its property more competently than boards in other cities.[50] There were few cases of neglect in collecting rent, failure to update rent or transferring properties free of rent for reasons of social welfare.[51] The board claimed that it does not collect interest on tardy rent payments due to the *shari'a* law forbidding interest.[52] Thus, ongoing administration of the property by the board of trustees follows the traditional path. At times, low rents or non-updated rents are considered as social assistance to members of the Muslim community. Social welfare stipends as well as low rent arrangements are the traditional way *waqf* administrators have gained the political support of the Muslim public. In other words, although the *shari'a* stipulations were replaced by a civil law, the Islamic pious and communal concept of the *waqf* was voluntarily implemented by the trustees.

The ongoing administration by the private *mutawalli*s, however, was quite different. The *Al-Sha'bi and Al-Sadiqi waqfs* yield only a tiny income from rentals. The *waqf* income from 1985 came to about US $1,500. Since the income was not enough to fund all the mosque expenses, the *mutawalli*s decided to house the Imam and the cleaning woman for free in the *waqf* rooms adjoining the mosque, in exchange for their work. This was a significant change from ten years earlier, when the *waqf* had a positive balance and used its funds for scholarships for needy Muslim students from Acre studying at universities—an allocation of *waqf* funds not even stated in the *waqfiyya*.[53]

The administration of the *Al-Yashruti waqf* is different. The *waqf* properties in Acre are indeed administered by the *mutawalli*s, but the lands in the rural periphery were employed for development purposes by the Custodian. Until late 1980, the *waqf* income totaled about US $20,000 a year, insufficient even to fund regular maintenance, religious ceremonies and social welfare activities of the *sufi* order. Some 15 *waqf* houses in Acre were rented in the past, on a nonprofit basis, to needy *tariqa* followers.[54] But due to contributions from wealthy order members, from the 1990 on the *waqf* administration decided to evacuate the tenants and to construct a new complex of the shrine and adjacent facilities. The *Yashruti waqf* properties are run today on a commercial basis integrating modern planning methods.[55] This is definitely an innovation of the *sufi* community *waqf*s in Israel and as far as I know has no equivalent anywhere else.

In the mid-1980s the State Comptroller and the Knesset Committee of Interior Affairs found that the boards of trustees in the five cties did not hold regular sessions, neglected the upkeep of the cemeteries and delayed submission of the annual budget for approval by the government. However, it also found that concerning its ongoing administration, the Acre board was in a better situation than other boards of trustees; the Acre board was the only one to have a balanced budget.[56]

Transactions

As stated, the law drafters viewed the *waqf* as an economic hindrance, as concluded by Prof. Gabriel Baer who wrote that this was the incentive that led modern Islamic states to reform the *waqf* institution.[57] This perception stems from one of the main principles of the *shari'a*, which prevents transactions of *waqf* properties. Indeed, *waqf* properties were regarded as inalienable. Their eternal nature stems from the notion of *waqf* endowment as a charitable act for which the endower will be eternally remunerated in the afterworld.[58]

As I have demonstrated in my previous studies, in spite of this principle, Islamic jurists have ruled that a *qadi* is empowered to overrule the founder's stipulation if the property in question becomes valueless and unproductive. Their opinions developed not as an abstract theory, but in response to actual challenges. Thus, their rulings reflect practical problems regarding the administration of *waqf* properties and solutions that they grounded in the principles of Islamic law.[59] They endorsed two major justifications to legitimize transactions in *waqf* assets: on the one hand, *maslaha* or *manfa'a*, benefit for the endowment, and on the other hand, *darura*, duress regarding the physical or economic condition of the estates.[60] Two major methods of alienating *waqf* assets were legalized by the jurists under the above-mentioned circumstances. The first allowed for the leasing of *waqf* properties for long periods in a variety of forms.[61] The second method abandoned the interpretation of viewing the asset as an absolute perpetual element and allowed, under certain conditions, the exchange or even the sale of properties as a means of ensuring the charitable purpose of the *waqf*. Thus, the *waqf*'s income could fund the charity and perpetuate the charitable nature of the endowment and satisfy its eternal nature (as opposed to the eternal nature of the properties originally endowed). The method was *istibdal*, the exchange of a *waqf* property for a substitute property that would become *waqf*. This method was developed to an exchange for money—*istibdal bil-darahim*, which should be invested in the purchase of a substitute property for the *waqf*. Only the *qadi* can authorize these measures and he must examine the conditions of each transaction separately.

A study of Muslim court records in Israel from the end of the Ottoman period and the Mandate shows that in fact the *qadis* introduced a series of measures in order to ensure *waqf* benefit from the exchange and to fix the appropriate amount.[62] The *qadis* engaged expert appraisers, heard testimony from witnesses, investigated the buyer, and at times visited the property.

The 1965 law gave the board of trustees free rein as owners of the properties. It might be assumed that the board would be released from the traditional *shari'a* restrictions and would administer the properties according to purely economic considerations as, in fact, the 1965 law enabled it to do. Surprisingly, the Acre board did not carry out even one property transaction, not even transfers permitted by the *shari'a* under certain conditions, despite the tempting offers they received. For example, in 1965, a group of entrepreneurs offered to buy Khan al-'Umdan from the board. They proposed to turn this historic and architectural site into a hostel for tourists and build a Jewish–Arab cultural center, which would serve the Muslim population in the city. According to one of the board members, the entrepreneurs offered a vast sum. The board, aware of the legal possibilities open to it, preferred nonetheless to seek the *qadi*'s advice. They turned down the offer not for religious reasons, since the sale was justified and economically necessary and could have been supported by the *shari'a* mechanism of *istibdal*. The board members explained that "Muslim public opinion does not condone deals of this sort, since the Muslim public views the Khan al-'Umdan as a vestige of our forefather's culture *(athar ajdaduna)* and no rational justification would persuade it to let the khan out of Muslim control.[63] One should view this attitude in the framework of politics of identity. Israeli Muslims who suffered from the obliteration of their past by the Jewish state are striving to preserve their cultural and architectural landmarks.[64] The public factor, then, had greater weight for the board of trustees than rational economic considerations.

However, *mutawallis* carried out economically motivated transactions of endowments not affected by the law, contradicting the "stagnation image" of the *waqf*. Between 1965 and 1990, the *Shari'a* Court records of Acre registered six special dispensations permitting transfers of *waqf* property. All six were granted to the *mutawalli* acting on behalf of the 'Ali Pasha *waqf*.[65] All of the many *waqf* properties of 'Ali Pasha, except for the neighborhood mosque, were sold within the framework of these dispensations. In two cases, the *qadi* allowed the *waqf* administration to carry out an exchange of *waqf* properties for a sum of money which was used to acquire another property (*istibdal bil-darahim*). In both cases, the *mutawalli's* advocate was not interested in linking the sale to the acquisition. In other words, he wanted to sell without necessarily buying a specific property.[66] The *Shari'a* court found a way to assist him through a technical separation of the two actions: he was granted general permission to sell and specific permission to buy. By doing this, the court laid the foundation for circumventing the traditional *shari'a* restrictions and permitted the sale of *waqf* property. Similarly, the lease of a large house in the village of Mazra'a near Acre, for a period of forty-eight years, was registered as long-term lease, though the conditions differed from those of *ijaratayn*.[67] Three years after being leased, the property was sold outright to the lessees.[68]

One interesting document in the court's records is a dispensation dated from 1974 given by the *Shari'a* court at the request of the 'Ali Pasha *waqf* administrator, to sell the main property of the *waqf*—the complex built on some 1.6 acres in the al-Majadala neighborhood (except for the mosque). The document said that the buildings were old, deteriorating, and in a location inside the Old City with no economic future. The document does not state the identity of the buyer, which happened to be a non-Muslim—the Baha'i Association—nor the price of the property. The advantage (*hazz wa-manfa'a*) to the *mutawalli* and the beneficiaries—the endower's descendants—is noted.[69] The court was not motivated by the profit to the *waqf* itself, but by the advantage to the *mutawalli*, in this case a woman who was the sole beneficiary. At the court's demand, the *mutawalli's* agent created a special bank fund for the maintenance of the mosque.[70] This was not noted in the *sijill*. In this way the *qadi*, whose function is to execute the *shari'a*, managed to find a legitimate way (ostensibly according to the *shari'a*) not only to bypass the *shari'a* limitations, but also to replace the *waqf* institution (in the past the sole agent for carrying out public welfare activities) with a modern-day economic institution, the trust fund. It is possible that the fact that the *mutawalli* of the 'Ali Pasha *waqf*, a Turkish woman, was the sole beneficiary and that she did not live in Israel made it easier for her agent in Israel to obtain the *Shari'a* Court's authorization for all of the above transactions. In any case, the dispensations granted by several *qadis* indicate much leniency on their part on the issue of adapting the management of the properties to modern economic norms.

Conclusion

The 1965 amendment to the Absentees' Property Law had two major goals: one, to mollify Muslim opposition to the government policy of determining Islamic *waqf* assets as absentee property and handing most of them over to the government; two, to release urban *waqf* assets from the restrictions of the *shari'a* with the expectation that the board of trustees would sell many of them in the free market. The economic intent of the 1965 law in Israel was based, *inter alia*, on the assumption that the legal limitations of the *waqf* institution and its traditional administration, which is not based on economic considerations, lead necessarily to financial stagnation. Transferring full ownership of *waqf* properties to the boards of trustees and releasing the trustees from the bonds of Islamic law were intended to resolve this problem.

The findings of this study indicate, however, that the Acre board of trustees has not fulfilled the expectations of the lawmakers on this issue. The board tended to administer the *waqf* according to traditional methods. In its ongoing management, it continued to rent properties in protected rental plans instead of for profit, and did not charge interest for tardy rent payments. The board was reluctant to transfer properties and failed to develop and improve properties, even though the *waqf* could have profited greatly from such actions. The reason for this lack of progress is found in the way the government implemented the 1965 law. The long and tedious process of releasing *waqf* properties to the administration of the board of trustees caused the board to lose control of the most valuable properties. This put the trustees, identified publicly with the authorities, continuously on the defensive. They had to prove over and over again that they were not participating in what the Arab Muslim population viewed as government policy to maintain control of *waqf* property. As a result, the trustees concentrated on apologetics and seeking public support, while demanding that the government release more *waqf* properties to their control or, alternatively, that it provide funds for religious and welfare services.

As in Acre, the Ramla, Lod, and Haifa boards of trustees did not transfer ownership of property. Tel Aviv–Jaffa is the exception to this situation. The board of trustees there sold and leased a number of valuable *waqf* properties, including mosques and ancient cemeteries.[71] The terms of these transactions clearly show that profit to the *waqf* was not the main motive. Suffice it to say that the first three chairmen of the board were tried in criminal court in connection with the fulfillment of their duties and were dismissed from the board. Thus, the economic intention of the reforms, to enable economically profitable administration of *waqf* property free from the limitations of the *shari'a*, was not achieved. The public atmosphere of disputes and insinuations prevented the trustees from exploiting the possibilities given them by the law to the fullest advantage.

Unexpectedly, it was precisely those endowments that were not affected by the 1965 law, and continued to be administered by the *mutawalli*s under the supervision of the *Shari'a* Court, which underwent a radical change. The *qadi*, representing the *Shari'a* Court, brought the administration of these properties closer to modern social and economic conditions than the board of trustees. Clearly, the basic assumption that Islamic legal impediments caused economic stagnation to *waqf* property was wrong. The *qadis* did continue to administer family endowments in the traditional manner, as regards internal administration, but their attitude toward the appointment of *mutawalli*s as administrators of public endowments was influenced by norms of modern administration. This is demonstrated by the appointment of a board of directors that was authorized to make decisions by majority vote, as in the case of the *Al-Yashruti sufi waqf*. In the ongoing administration as well there were signs of modern influence; for instance, scholarships were given to students who did not study religious subjects, and long-term plans were devised to change the property designation. Modern influences can be seen in the permits granted by the *Shari'a* Court to transfer *waqf* properties. The traditional *istibdal* was used as a device enabling the sale of *waqf* properties when there was financial justification to do so, despite the law forbidding transfer of ownership. Indeed, the application of this device was hindered by substantive and procedural limitations, but the *qadis* have demonstrated that almost everything could be included under the principle of *maslaha*—advantage to the *waqf*. This justified the sale of *waqf* properties by a general permit, without even taking the trouble to justify the sale by the legal *istibdal* device. The *qadis* contented themselves with noting the advantage to the beneficiaries, the descendants of the founder.

What was the fate of a public institution (such as the Al-Majadala Mosque at the heart of the 'Ali Pasha *waqf*), which until modern times was maintained and funded solely by the *waqf*? Here, too, it was the *qadi* who provided the modern alternative to the *waqf* institution: a trust fund in the bank, the revenues of which go toward the upkeep of the mosque.

The attitude of the *qadis*, who supervised the implementation of the *shari'a* laws, to the possibilities of adapting the *waqf* institution to modern social and economic conditions is especially interesting. The *qadis* in Israel reiterate, on almost every public occasion, the religious character of the *waqf* institution, emphasizing that the abstract ownership (*raqaba*) of the property belongs to God according to the *shari'a* and that "Allah is not absentee."[72] In light of this they demand that the *waqf* properties be restored to the Muslim community. However, the *qadis* have for the most part accepted the 1965 law as the lesser of evils, on the condition that the government does in fact release more *waqf* properties to the boards of trustees. In addition, they demand the appointment of trustees who will justify the trust invested in them. According to Sheikh Hubayshi, the *qadi* of Acre during the 1970s and 1980s, there is no contradiction between the *shari'a* and modern economic considerations. In his view, the *istibdal* and long-term lease devices satisfy all modern economic requirements.[73] Indeed, the decrees of the Acre *qadis* prove that they were able to adapt and modernize the *waqf*, basing themselves on the principle of *maslaha* (public welfare), even at the cost of overriding substantive instructions in the *shari'a*. The *waqf* institution today falls short of fulfilling its traditional goals despite the fact that the *Shari'a* court found a way to adapt the *waqf* to modern economic conditions because of the limited supervision the *qadi* has over the administrators of the endowments. The supervision system established by the 1965 law of the boards of trustees is more efficient. Replacing representatives of notable families on the board of trustees in Acre with public servants who have an academic and professional education ensures a proper administrative approach in tune with modern needs.

Overall, implementation of the law by the government was inconsistent and incompatible with the intention of the legislators and the express wording of the law, and thus prevented the realization of two important goals of the reform. As for the political purpose of the 1965 law—to appease the Muslim community and remove the *waqf* as a political issue from the public agenda—the government's policy in implementing the reform perpetuated the confrontations between government representatives and the Muslim community and caused various conflicts which are still unresolved on the public agenda today. The government never planned to give up control of *waqf* affairs (and assets), but the 1965 amendment drafters actually intended to grant the Muslim community relatively autonomous administration of their public property; nevertheless, government officers fell short of actualizing this policy.

Owing to the limitations on the board of trustees in Acre and elsewhere, in the late 1970s the newly established Islamic Movement began to assume responsibilities in the realm of religious services and other public affairs. In Acre, the Movement took over three of the six mosques under the board's possession. It marked all streets of the Old City with green signs containing Islamic obligations and traditions in an attempt to dominate the open space. However, relations between the board members and the Islamic Movements are good. They cooperated in fixing a unified loudspeaker system for a simultaneous call to pray (*adhan*) in all six mosques and the board purchased six electronic clocks showing the exact time of prayers and donated one to each mosque.[74]

Another issue stemming from the 1965 amendment was reparation money (Hebrew: *kaspei ha-tmurah*). According to Article 29 of that amendment, the Custodian was to allocate money from absentees' properties under his administration as reparations targeted for the public purposes of the Muslim community. This article gave additional legal validity to the transfer of ownership of the mostly rural *waqf* land to the government, while the Muslim community was entitled to reparation money. Put differently, if the Muslim community were to benefit from reparations, the Muslim minority would have no legal or moral basis to reclaim *waqf* land. Here again, the government failed to use this principle as leverage for providing equal services and facilities to the Arab Muslim population. The reparation was arbitrarily determined by the Finance Ministry regardless of any real account of the *waqf* estates' revenue and was a relatively a small fund of some US $100,000–250,000 annually. The Prime Minister's Advisor on Arab Affairs headed a public committee which used these funds in its policy of cooptation. The Custodian and Israel Lands Administration officials used to claim that they were unable to produce solid accounting of the assets and their revenues–expenditure balance, although a survey of all absentee properties was carried out in 1965. Muslim politicians never applied to the Supreme Court in order to demand a professional accounting of the reparation money, because by so doing they would legitimize the 1965 law and the government policy of nationalizing their religious endowments.

In summation, compared to my previous study of the late 1980s, in this revised study, I found that the government's implementation of the law had in fact deteriorated. This is obvious from the fact that today there are no Muslims who agree to serve as trustees subject to the Absentees' Property Law, because they do not want to be regarded as corrupt personalities or as those who betray their communal/national interest. Hence, the government appointed a Jewish board of civil servants as trustees of the Tel Aviv-Jaffa *waqf*. As for the rest of the boards (Ramla, Lod, Haifa) the same personalities have been serving as trustees for over thirty years. Regarding the budget, the Acre case was much improved, due to an allocation of funds from the government ministries (and not from the government Custodian who holds a conservative approach towards the Muslim community). Here it should be noted, following Alisa Peled-Rubin, that different government agencies applied diverse policies regarding the religious needs and services of the Muslim community.[75] The less liberal was always the Israel Lands Administration, of which the government Custodian served as an organ. But the political dimension of the *waqf* issue remained the same and it is manifested in conflicts over *waqf* buildings and cemeteries in Jaffa and elsewhere in the country.

Finally, the moral justification of the government's policy should also be discussed. As Dumper puts it, in order to establish a viable and credible state, newborn Israel had to gain ownership of the land under its control.[76] I would add what I heard numerous times from Israeli officials: in order to absorb and settle a great deal of Jewish newcomers to Israel after 1948, in a state of emergency the government found no choice but to expropriate abandoned land, i.e., land that was formerly owned by those who left the country that became Israel and who themselves became refugees, including *waqf* land which was owned by the Supreme Muslim Council representing anti-Zionist politics. Another justification for Israel's policy was that the *waqf* institution is an archaic system not compatible with modern life, particularly since unlike pre-twentieth century times the modern state is responsible for delivering religious and welfare services and facilities directly to the people. Hence, there is no need for an intermediary institution such as a *waqf,* which is known for its economic stagnation and poor administration. Indeed, the *waqf* institution has lost some of its importance in modern times. The modern state fulfills many of the functions previously discharged solely by the *waqf*, and the state provides alternative institutions for charity that are better suited to the needs of a developing society (for example, scholarship funds). The dwindling rate of endowments dedicated in Israel was apparent by the close of the Ottoman period, and has come to a near halt in the modern State of Israel. The *waqf* is not viewed by the Muslim community in Israel as a means to realize social and religious goals. The same is true for other Arab Muslim countries.

Given the special circumstances of the Arab–Israeli conflict and the fact that Israel as a modern state decided to provide religious services via a government ministry, one could justify the government's policy under two conditions: first, that the government would deliver all necessary services to the Muslim community on an equal footing to the Jewish one; and that Muslim figures would be genuinely involved in the administration and decision-making regarding the allocation of funds and other benefits. Unfortunately, as this study shows, the government has failed so far to address properly these two methods[77] and thus, the *waqf* continues to pose a political problem and to arouse religious and national feeling in Israel's Muslim community. In my view the government should choose one of the two following policies: a) to continue the British Mandate model prior to 1948 according which a Muslim body administers the *waqf* properties but is subject to a three-member supervisory committee of high-ranking Muslim government officers; b) the boards of trustees should be abolished and its place should be taken by a newly established Authority for the Upkeep and Development of Muslim Holy Sites and Religious Buildings similar to the existing authority which handles Jewish holy places. The new body should be formed by both government officers and Muslim public figures and headed by a chief *qadi*. The Custodian should transfer to this authority reparation money for all assets that he sold to the government after a real economic evaluation and its budget should be an endowment that safeguards the expenses for Muslim holy places and other religious services.

Notes

1 Absentee Property Law (Amendment No. 3) (Release and Use of Endowment Property), passed in the Knesset, 2 Feb., 1965 *Sefer Chukim*, vol. 445, p.58 [in Hebrew]. For the bill and the explanatory note, see *Divrei HaKnesset* 1965, vol. 48, (The Knesset's records), pp. 1143–46 [in Hebrew].
2 Absentees' Property Law, 1950 (passed in the Knesset on 29 Mar. 1950) [in Hebrew].
3 Y. Reiter, "Ha'arachat HaReforma BeMossad HaHeqdesh HaMuslemi BeIsrael: Ha*Waqf* Be'Akko" (An Assessment of the Reform in the Muslim *Waqf* Institution in Israel – The *Waqf* in Acre) 1989, vol. 32, *HaMizrah HeHadash*, pp. 21–45 [in Hebrew].
4 M. Dumper, *Islam and Israel, Muslim Religious Endowments and the Jewish State* (Washington, D.C.: Inst.for Pales. Studies, 1994); Alisa Rubin-Peled, *Debating Islam in the Jewish State: The Development of Policy Toward Islamic Institutions in Israel*, Albany, N.Y.: SUNY, 2001.
5 L. Louër, *To Be an Arab in Israel*, London: Hurst, 2007, p. 146.
6 A. Layish, "The Muslim *Waqf* in Israel," *Asian and African Studies*, 1966, vol. 2, p. 59, at 45.
7 G. Baer, *A History of Land Ownership in Modern Egypt: 1800–1950*, London: Oxford University Press, 1962, p. 165.
8 Muhammad Abu Zahra, *Muhadarat fi al-waqf*, 2nd edn, Cairo: Dar al-Fikr al-'Arabi, 1971, p. 6 [in Arabic].
9 For the nineteenth-century reforms, see J.R. Barnes, *An Introduction to Religious Foundations in the Ottoman Empire*, Leiden: E.J. Brill, 1987.
10 Rubin-Peled, *Debating Islam in the Jewish State*, n. 4, at p. 11.
11 Dumper, *Islam and Israel*, n. 4, Chs 2–3.
12 Rubin-Peled, *Debating Islam in the Jewish State*, n. 4, at p. 13.
13 According to the agreement of 19 Nov. 1950, between the Deputy Minister for Religious Affairs and the Custodian. *Ministry of Religious Affairs* [MRA], file H"M 2.
14 *Prime Minister's Office – Department of the Advisor for Arab Affairs* [AAA Dept.], file 67.5.
15 *See* O. Yiftachel, *Ethnocracy: Land and Identity: Politics in Israel/Palestine* (Philadelphia, Penn.: University of Pennsylvania. Press, 2006), pp. 136–42; *ibid.* and A. Kedar, "On Power and Land: Israel's Land Regime," 2000, vol. 16, *Teoria VeBikoret*, pp. 67–100 [in Hebrew].
16 High Court of Justice, Bagatz Bulus 69/55, *Piskei Din*, 1956, vol. 10, p. 681 [in Hebrew].

17 *Ibid.*
18 *Supra* note 3.
19 *Ibid.*
20 "To remove doubts that had arisen following the judgment in the High Court of Justice 55/65." For the significance of this ruling, *see* Layish, "The Muslim *Waqf* in Israel," n. 6.
21 Discussion with Layish, 1989.
22 The law stated also Nazareth and Shfaram, but the government avoided appointing trustees in these two cities under the claim that there were no significant *waqf* properties in their municipal boundaries.
23 Article 29 ff.
24 On the analysis of the new stipulations of the law, *cf.* Layish, "The Muslim *Waqf* in Israel," n. 6, pp. 61ff.
25 J.B. Barron, *Mohammedan Waqfs in Palestine*, Jerusalem: n.p.,1922, p. 63.
26 Draft of M.A. thesis by M. Meiri, my student at the Dept of Islamic and Middle East Studies, Hebrew University of Jerusalem. Of the 310 rented units 128 are shops, 82 stores, 93 residential apartments, four offices, three baths (*hamam*), one coffee shop, and one khan.
27 For a photocopy of the *waqfiyya*, *see supra* note 3, pp. 143–47.
28 For a photocopy of the *waqfiyya*, see *ibid.*, p. 142.
29 For copies of the *waqfiyya*, *see Israel State Archives*, 'Awni 'Abd al-Hadi files, 34/153. For another version, see MRA file H"M/3/a39 and file H"M 3/317. For the historical background *see* Ibrahim al-'Awra, *Ta'rikh Wilayat Sulayman Basha al-'Adil*, Sidon, n.p., 1931, p. 191 [in Arabic].
30 The manuscript of the *waqfiyya* is in the library at Leiden no. 681/4–1 F. *See also* A. De Jong, "The *Sufi* Orders in Palestine," *Studia Islamica,* 1983, vol. 58, p. 159.
31 Y. Vashitz, *The Arabs in Palestine*, Merhavia, 1947, p. 50 [in Hebrew].
32 For the "sultanic" *waqf see* Barnes, *An Introduction to Religious Foundations in the Ottoman Empire*, n. 9, *passim*.
33 The appointment was published in 7 Apr. 1966, vol. 1269, *Yalkut HaPirsumim* (Israel's Official Gazette) [in Hebrew].
34 *See e.g.*, the criticism leveled by members of Knesset at the board of trustees appointed by the government, *Divrei HaKnesset*, 1966, vol. 47, pp. 245–47 and vol. 65, p. 508; *AAA Dept.*, 67.5/Acre on the appointment of trustees.
35 Interview with Hasan Sarawan, 26 Apr. 2007.
36 *See* Louër, *To Be an Arab in Israel*, n. 5, p. 146.
37 *Al-Yawm* (daily newspaper in Arabic), 30 Sept. 1975; *Ha'aretz* (daily newspaper in Hebrew), 26 Dec.1972; *Davar* (daily newspaper in Hebrew), 20 Dec.1972; *Divrei HaKnesset*, 1973, vol. 65, pp. 666, 811; *ibid.*, vol. 75, question from 18 June 1975, p. 1255; *ibid.*, vol. 76, pp. 863, 1856; *ibid.*, vol. 77, p. 3665.
38 *See e.g.*, O. Hilmi Efendi. *A Treatise on the Laws of Evqaf*, trans. by Tyser and D. G. Demetriades, Nicosia: n.p., 1899, p. 293; M. Qadri Pasha, *Qanun al-'Adl wa'l-Insaf fi'l-Awqaf*, Cairo: n.p., 1902, p. 145 ff. [in Arabic].
39 Hilmi, *ibid.*, s. 327; Qadri Pasha, *Qanun al-'Adl wa'l-Insaf fi'l-Awqaf*, s. 158.
40 *Acre sijill, qararat* 6, no. 40/64. The *qadi* warned the *mutawalli* in conversation several times against neglecting *waqf* properties as he could be dismissed. (An interview from 27 Feb. 1986 with Sheikh Muhammad Hubayshi, then secretary of the *Shari'a* Court.) Later, when the *mutawalli's* health deteriorated, the *qadi* appointed two additional *mutawallis* for the endowment: the *Shari'a* court secretary and his relative, people the *qadi* trusted. *Acre sijill, qararat* 7, no. 23/67. The *mutawalli* from the endower's family passed away and since then the revenues from the two endowments have been used for public purposes.
41 On the supervision over *waqf* administration, *see* Reiter, *Islamic Endowments in Jerusalem*, pp. 209 ff.

42 *Acre sijill, qararat 20*, no. 2/85. The *mutawalli* is Dr. Mahmud 'Abassi, then active in the Labor Party and candidate for the Knesset as leader of an Arab party.
43 *AAA Dept.*, 61.1.
44 For the activities of the Authority for the Development of Old Acre, *see Yediot 'Iriat Akko* (Newsletter of Acre municipality), Sept. 1965. For releasing the properties, see *AAA Dept.,* 61.1 [in Hebrew].
45 *AAA Dept.*, 61.1.
46 *State Comptroller's Report*, no. 24, 1974 [in Hebrew].
47 The information relating to releasing properties is taken from the *AAA Dept.*, 67.0.
48 Al-Jazzar and Sinan Pasha Mosques are operated by the board; upkeep of the Zaytuni Mosque is handled by the government; Al-Raml Mosque is operated by the Northern Islamic Movement and Zahir al-'Umar and Majadala Mosques by the Southern Islamic Movement.
49 *State Comptroller's Report*, no. 24, 1974 [in Hebrew].
50 *Ibid.*
51 *State Comptroller's Report*, no. 34, 1984; Accountant's report for the Ministry for Religious Affairs, 1984/5, *AAA Dept.*, 67.5.
52 Letter from 17 Dec.1987 to the Advisor for Arab Affairs. *AAA Dept.* 67.5.
53 Interview of 28 Oct.1985 with the *mutawalli* Hassan Sarawan.
54 Interview of 5 Mar.1986 with the *mutawalli* Dr. Mahmud 'Abbasi.
55 It is interesting to compare those administrative measures with the current administration of another *tariqa waqf* in Israel, the Husni al-Qawasma *waqf* of the Khilwatiyya Order. The order and *waqf* properties are in the villages of Baqa al-Gharbiyya and Jat in the eastern central part of Israel (near the pre-1967 border), and in the village of Zayta and other settlements on the West Bank. This *waqf* was registered in 1966 as a public association, and is run as a cooperative according to modern financial principles including investment in property, in equipment and in vehicles. Some sixty-eight acres of agricultural lands are leased to *tariqa* followers, and the shops and warehouses are rented to them at low rates as a privilege to *tariqa* followers who have attained a certain status and rank. See Y. Rosman, *Leadership in the al-Khilwatiyya Sufi Organization* (MA thesis, Tel Aviv University, 1984, pp. 30–35 [in Hebrew].
56 *State Comptroller's Report*, no. 24, 1974.
57 Baer, *A History of Land Ownership in Modern* Egypt, n. 7, p. 165.; S.D. Goitein and A. Ben-Shemesh, *Muslim Law in the State of Israel*, Jerusalem, n.p.,1957, pp. 169–71 [in Hebrew]; Layish, "The Muslim *Waqf* in Israel," n. 6, p. 53.
58 J.N.D. Anderson, "The Religious Element in *Waqf* Endowments," 1951, vol. 38, *Journal of the Royal Central Asian Society*, pp. 292–99.
59 Reiter, *Islamic Endowments*, n. 41, p. 171; *ibid.*, *Islamic Endowments in Jerusalem under the British Mandate*, p. 65; *ibid.* "'All of Palestine is Holy Muslim *Waqf* Land' – A Myth and Its Roots," in R. Shaham (ed.) Law, Custom, and Statute in the Muslim World, Studies in Honor of Aharon Layish. Leiden and Boston, Mass.: E.J. Brill, 2007, pp. 172–97.
60 Qadri Pasha, *Qanun al-'Adl wa'l-Insaf fi'l-Awqaf*, n. 38, Article 133; Abu Zahra, *Muhadarat fi al-waqf*, n. 8, p. 6.
61 Miriam Hoexter, "Le contrat de quasi-alienation des awqaf a Alger a la fin de la domination turque: étude de deux documents d'ana'," *Bulletin of the School of Oriental and African Studies*, 1984, vol. 47, pp. 243–59; *ibid.*," Adaptation to Changing Circumstances: Perpetual Leases and Exchange Transactions in *Waqf* Property in Ottoman Algiers," *Islamic Law and Society*, 1997, vol. 4, no. 3, pp. 319–33.
62 Reiter, *Islamic Endowments*, n. 41; *ibid.*, *Islamic Institutions*, n. 59.
63 Interview of 27 Feb. 1986 with Sheikh Muhammad Hubayshi and Hasan Sarawan.
64 *See* Chapter 13 by Nimrod Luz in this volume.

The waqf in Israel since 1965   127

65 *Acre sijill, qararat* 5, nos. 18/62; 22/69; 23/68; 7, no. 18/68; 8, no. 36/71; 11, no. 83/74.
66 *Ibid., qararat* 5, nos. 22/68; 23/68; 7, no. 18/68.
67 *Ibid., qararat* 8, no. 36/71.
68 Interview of 14 Apr.1985 with Mr. Donald Barrett.
69 *Acre sijill, qararat* 11, no. 83/74.
70 Interview with Mr. Gagin, the *mutawalli's* lawyer.
71 *AAA Dept.* 67.5.
72 *See e.g.*, the letter of the *qadi* for the central region of 17 Dec.1985 and the Acre *qadi's* letter of 30 Dec.1985. *AAA Dept.*, 61.1.
73 Interview with Sheikh Hubayshi, 27 Feb. 1986.
74 Interview with Hasan Sarawan 26 Apr. 2007.
75 Rubin-Peled, *Debating Islam in the Jewish State*, n. 4, p. 13.
76 *Ibid.*, p. 29.
77 For the budgetary inequality for religious services, *see also* Supreme Court ruling Bagatz 240/98 and Bagatz 1113/99 *Adalah et al. vs. the Minister for Religious Affairs et al.*, *Piskei Din* 54(2), 164; Moshe Reinfeld, "Supreme Court: Ministry of Religious Affairs Discriminated Against Arab Cemeteries," *Haaretz*, 19 Apr. 2000 [in Hebrew].

7 Holy places in urban spaces
Foci of confrontation or catalyst for development?

Rassem Khamaisi

Introduction

Holy places in cities have played various roles. Besides their spiritual and religious aspects, they also constitute a physical monument, which crystallizes the images, features, and fabric of a city's structure. Today, some cities use holy places as a main catalyst for development; in others the holy places present a deterrent to such development. Conflict over holy places between different national, ethnic, and cultural groups is the main explanatory factor for this obstacle, which eventually leads to economic hardship in the city. The question addressed in this essay concerns when, how, and in what situations does a holy place change from being a city's main selling point to being its main hindrance. For example, there might be a case of a holy site that presented a deterrent to development and later was transformed into a catalyst after changes occurred in the geo-political, functional, and structural, and eventually, in the socio-cultural situation. Or, in some cases holy places can function as a neutral monument, in the middle ground between obstacle and catalyst. Both internal and external factors can change the nature of holy places in this way.

First, I will discuss the role of holy places in shaping the image, structure and function of cities and will focus on the following points:

1. The contribution of holy places to the economic development of cities in situations of peace, stability, and conciliation.
2. In situations of conflict, disputes often focus on holy sites and their surroundings, contributing to deterioration in the city, promoting segregation and division of the urban social and community structure and the city's spatial fabric. Holy places exacerbate conflict.
3. Methods of dealing with the development of cities based on holy places as catalysts rather than as obstacles. Examples include Jerusalem and Nazareth, taking into consideration the differences between the two.

This essay is based on research conducted in the course of preparing a strategic plan for Jerusalem and a renovation plan for its Old City, as well as preparing a development plan for Nazareth, for which I was a staff planning leader. In addition, it includes data from the literature on city development and resources such as the municipalities of the two cities, the Israel Central Bureau of Statistics, as well as various open interviews conducted by the author during preparation of the plans.

The chapter consists of four parts. Part one presents a theoretical and general background, and discusses the meaning and role of holy places in cities, as well as how cultural and sacred sites constitute economic generators. Part two deals with the conflict over holy places in the Holy Land and its role in the economic development of cities on one hand, and its function as an obstacle on the other. Part three presents two case studies: Jerusalem and Nazareth. Part four summarizes and addresses the question of how to forecast the impact of holy places.

General background

A holy place is defined in this essay as a place where a religious, ethno-cultural community practices its religion and spiritual beliefs and faith. Among holy places there is a hierarchy of importance. Some of these sites constitute the core of the city and in other cities holy places are located on its periphery. Core holy places exist and develop within ethno-national, cultural-religious cities. In these cities, in particular, and in general, holy places form and represent community symbols, existing within a landscape and wielding power and spatial and resource control.[1]

Sacred places also embody a city's present significance, its citizens' identity, their myths, and cultural domination.[2] As a result of the importance of holy places, national and ethno-regional conflicts take the form of both attacking, destroying and displacing these sites by minority subordinate ethno-national religious group, and changing their symbols and function.[3]

A holy place contributes to a city's development by attracting people to visit or reside there. However, cities which are symbolic religiously and ethno-culturally are more likely to suffer from foreign attacks, such as Karbala in Iraq. In addition to such attacks, which try to change the role and function of the holy place's identity and affiliations, there are also demographic, socio-cultural, and socio-political internal changes within a city's population and these can change the role, function, and symbolism of the city's holy places. These internal changes also lead to conflict between ethno-national groups within the city. Throughout the span of history, we have observed that the affiliation of sacred places is not fixed, but is dynamic and changing. Every community has its own narrative and memories related to holy sites, to which the members of that community feel that they belong. When they gain power, they try to take control and dominate the holy place and the surrounding territory, including the city where the holy place exists.[4]

In this respect, then, holy sites can be the focal point of tensions within a city in some circumstances, while the same places in different situations can provide a source of attraction and stability. Holy places also perform an important symbolic function, providing feelings of affiliation or domination. The majority ethno-national and religious group often exercises power and attempts to impose this power through religious images that affiliate the city with one religion/culture, while ignoring others. In addition, holy places function as landmarks of space and time, and orient us regarding our position within the physical urban structure. Furthermore, sacred sites are often bound up with history. A holy place is a landmark in space; an historical event is a landmark in time.

Holy places are often located "in the middle" of cities, and other governmental and public institutions are situated close to them. Some cities have historically developed around sacred places, which function as central sites where people practice their faith, including both prayer and pilgrimage. Typical ancient Greek cities developed around the Agora and the temples, while in ancient Roman cities this occurred around the Forum and temples. A number of European cities grew around a church or cathedral.[5] The traditional Islamic city was built around the main mosque, al-Goma'a Mosque,[6] such as Mecca, al-Madina al-Munawwara. In fact, in different parts of the world up until the Industrial Revolution, most cities were built around a main holy place, such as a mosque, church or temple, which was the main component of the urban form and fabric of cities at that time.

Changes in a political and socio-economic ideological regime can signal a change in the function of a holy place. In traditional religious communities, this function differs from its role in modern secular communities. Holy places can serve as economic generators in cities. Traditionally, they create a multiplicity of economic activities by attracting visitors and pilgrims. Ranking the importance of holy places in different cities and within cities has a direct impact on their roles in development. They constitute a main target for cultural tourism, in addition to pilgrims and visitors who generate economic development and create additional economic tourism-based activities.[7]

In modern western capitals or regional cities around the world, the role of holy places as economic generators decreases. Urbanization, population and urban growth, and economic and structural change lead to urban sprawl and a city's physical expansion. Many large urban areas consist of different parts, some old, traditional, and density populated, built and developed around an organic core, and at its center the sacred site. The organic core was developed according to traditional rules and building technology, without central planning. The vast part of the city may be modern, developed according to planning rules. In new areas, the holy place is used for performing religious obligations, but does not have the same importance as it did in old, traditional cities which were built and developed around it, and which present the narrative, faith, affiliation, and identity of the local religious groups. In global cities, holy places do not function as holy entities, but as unique monuments in the city fabric. Thus, the changing role of cities and their ethno-demographic structures along with the transformation of socio-political powers have had a direct impact on the role and function of sacred sites. In some cities where there is a consensus of affiliation surrounding the holy places, these sites can serve as leverage for city development. On the other hand, when there is conflict over the sites, they become foci of confrontation and can lead to instability and fear, which in turn discourages visitors and decreases economic development in the city. In addition to the physical, functional, and economic changes in cities, there are also social and cultural changes at play.

Today, most cities are segregated, and some of them are divided according to ethno-national and cultural affiliation.[8] In these types of urban areas there are social problems and tensions. In urban centers where there are holy sites in addition to various ethnic and religious groups, the tension is even greater and serves to threaten the city's stability.

Today, in cities that are recognized as belonging to one ethnic or religious group, such as Mecca, Medina or Rome, holy places constitute economic leverage and serve as catalysts for attracting pilgrims, visitors, and developing a cultural economy.[9] There are cities that feature sacred places belonging to different religious groups, such as Jerusalem,[10] or during whose long history changes in religion and cultural domination took place, or in which changes in the sites themselves took place, such as an ancient church changed into a mosque. In these cases, the holy place cannot contribute to a city's stability in the long term. So while the holy places are constant, the surrounding population, political regime, and ethnic and cultural landscape have changed. These transformations lead to conflict over the city's symbols, and the holy places that are landmarks within the physical landscape and the urban fabric, could either accelerate the conflict or lead to multiculturalism and coexistence.

Changing the role of holy places in cities

In the aftermath of the Industrial Revolution, the role of holy places in western cities declined but did not disappear. This situation differed between countries in Western Europe and those in North America and Australia. Nevertheless, despite these differences, which we will not address here, a major change was that the focus shifted to a new center of the city, the central business district (CBD)—referred to in North America as downtown. Churches, cathedrals, and in some places small mosques, synagogues, and temples were built elsewhere. In the modern city, these sacred places function as part of the landscape, for practicing the religious obligations of the different local ethnic, religious, and cultural groups. There may be implicit tension and conflict surrounding these holy places in some cities. These tensions tend to grow and become explicit after the occurrence of particular events, such as the terrorist attack of September 11 in New York City, which cast its shadow on other cities. But the power and domination of the central government, led by one ethno-national and religious group, liberal democratic, and multicultural systems on the one hand, and a weakness of the minority groups on the other hand, led to greater stability in these cities. Nevertheless, there are religious or ethnic groups that do carry out riot activities against municipal and national discrimination policies and class disparities within the city, such as occurred in Paris and other cities in France in October 2005. In the process of globalization, which is based on a global economy and has a direct impact on a city's fabric and structure,[11] holy places play a minor role, and function as yet another historical site that people can visit along with other museums and other landmarks. For instance, the cathedral in East Berlin was transformed into a municipal museum in which the Berlin municipality placed urban architectural models of Berlin's development in the period of division until 1989, and thereafter.

In conjunction with the decreasing role of holy places in traditional cities, new cities and urban centers have grown and developed based on a modern and global economy, culture, and services. Today, in a period of globalization, such cities have created a network that leave behind traditional cities and their central holy places. Within those traditional cities that have developed new sectors, these areas tend to follow the global economy and culture,[12] while the ancient areas surrounding the holy places continue to be traditional and organic. A city's old sections, including the holy places, undergo processes of renovation and rehabilitation, including the organic and ancient holy places which now function as tourist and cultural monuments along with their religious, spiritual, identity, and symbolic roles.[13] The gaps between traditional and global cities are increasing, particularly with the growth of secular culture in some cities or parts of them. The differences between communities in terms of global, regional, and local domination create tension. In some cases this tension grows into conflicts of culture and civilization,[14] especially where the holy places represent a physical landmark that are either protected or attacked, similar to what is occurring today in Iraq in cities such as Najaf and Kuffa.

Holy places versus the urban secular

Urban communities are divided according to various categories: one is according to ethno-national affiliation, a second according to socio-economic class, a third according to socio-cultural parameters, including religious and secular groups. In many cases the division among different groups is not so sharp and dichotomous. The secular cultural community is more materialistic and modern, and does not make use of holy places for religious or spiritual purposes. Traditional religious and cultural groups, however, continue to use sacred places as part of their daily behavior in order to practice their faith. This is in addition to the role of these sites as identifiers symbolic of an ethno-national cultural group.

In secular and modern culture, holy objects and sites are often disguised as sentimental landmarks, cultural monuments or tourist attractions, which contribute to the city's economic development. Like the more institutionalized shrines of organized religion, these objects and places fill our need for physical, psychological, and cosmic orientation and mediate our contact with the larger universe. They provide a center for our identity and offer us a place in which, momentarily transcending our usual selves, we merge with past, with future and with eternal being.

Holy places as limiting development

As previously noted, holy places constitute one of the economic generators in a city in addition to other economic activities. However, in modern global cities, holy sites and the traditional religious communities living around these sites can function in the opposite manner, and can reduce economic activities when the sacred place plays a major role. For example, the level of development in Jedda or Riyad in Saudi Arabia is greater than in Mecca or Medina. Cities which developed around and are based on sacred sites continue to be traditional in nature and limit the attraction of modern and global activities and functions. Conversely, unique holy places add special status to the city, which attract people to visit, stay, and consume. In the urban fabric around ancient or holy places, we often see activities aimed at demolishing the surrounding traditional buildings, which are actually part of the heritage. This activity is taking place in the area around the main mosque in Mecca and Medina, in order to expand the area used for practicing religious rites. In these cities, there is no preservation of the historical nature of the holy sites, and the decision makers have ignored the value of the traditional urban fabric around these places.

In the global world and economy, where secular culture is dominant, traditional cities with their holy places tend to hinder the quality of economic activities. Many material activities are prohibited by religion and thus cannot develop in holy cities or within traditional religious communities. In the absence of this kind of secular and material cultural economy, it is impossible to create multiple economic activities in such areas.

On the other hand, sacred sites that create services for pilgrims cannot compete with the modern global economy. Pilgrims are often characterized by limited resources to invest or to spend on their visits. So, notwithstanding the large numbers of visitors and pilgrims, their economic contribution to the city's local economy is limited compared to global cities that attract more wealthy tourists.

Holy sites in general are related to static affiliation, while society is characterized by dynamic change. Some of this change is the result of war and conflict. In cities where religion is deeply rooted and there is a clash over the sacred places, a general conflict is launched which creates a burden on city development. In such cases, holy places turn into an obstacle to development.

Holy places in the cities of the Holy Land

The Holy Land is a unique case for examining cultural conflict. Over the generations, the three monotheistic religions—Judaism, Christianity, and

Islam—have played a central role in shaping the character of the country, having turned it into a sacred space and focus of pilgrimage, and imbuing it with diverse cultural and value-oriented significance. Some holy places in the Holy Land are sacred to more than one religion, thereby creating tension between them. Through the course of history various civilizations and armies have tried to occupy the land and to build holy places; towns and cities grew up around those holy places. Cities such as Jerusalem, Bethlehem, Al-Khalel, and Nazareth are traditional religious centers for Muslims, Jews, and Christians. In addition to these centers, there are numerous other towns and villages with sacred sites, and the history, identity, and affiliation of those sites are also conflict-ridden. The holy shrines in Jerusalem, Bethlehem, and Nazareth attract pilgrims, visitors, and tourists and generate a traditional economy based on services connected with cultural and religious needs. A short visit and walk through the urban core surrounding the sacred sites show the concentration of traditional merchants and handcrafts connected to the communities. In the periphery of these cities, however, new shopping centers are forming part of a global economy.

The Holy Land has been the site of extensive religious-national conflict, some of which—the Crusades, for example—was directed at dominating the holy places. Geopolitical and ethno-national power changes have had a direct impact on the transformational use of these sites. The fundamental motive underlying the struggle for their control and access is rooted in the need to dominate the holy place and, by extension, the rest of the city and country. Inter-religious conflicts surrounding certain sacred sites have to do with their identity, affiliation and sources, and the possible displacement by another religion. For example, Al-haram al-Sharif (Al-Aqsa Mosque and the Dome of the Rock) is clamed by Orthodox Jews as the Temple Mount. The Western Wall is known by Muslims as Al-Buraq. Other conflicts exist over the Al-Haram al-Khalily in Hebron, or the Mosque of Nebi Samwil in northwest Jerusalem. So, too, in the very name of the land, which Christians call the Holy Land, the Jews call the Land of Israel, and Muslims name *al-Sham* (Greater Syria), or *Mubarak* (the blessed) land, or Palestine. Most of these names come from religious narratives, and evoke different associations and images which create the potential for conflict.

The geo-political conflict and the holy places

The national conflicts in the Holy Land have resulted in direct conflicts at the local level. The nature of the national conflict is merged with the religious dimension, as part of the identity of the parties to the conflict—Jewish, Muslim, and Christian. All parties avoid describing the conflict as a religious one, even though it includes conflict over the sacred places. An awareness of the importance of the holy places in the conflict led the United Nations to include a section in its 1947 Partition Plan for Palestine, UN GA Res.181, 29 November 1947, which assures free access to the holy sites despite the national conflict. In addition, most proposals for a resolution, settlement or conciliation in Jerusalem include a main chapter on how to secure accessibility to the holy places in the city.[15] Thus, the national and geopolitical conflict over the Holy Land casts its shadow on the local level, while the local discord over the holy places is part of a greater ethno-national conflict.

In examining and analyzing the conflict over holy places in the cities of the Holy Land, it emerges that there are in fact two kinds of conflict. One is the geopolitical and national conflict, which we find in Jerusalem and other places where Muslims and Jews claim the same sacred sites, and each ethno-religious group has its own arguments, myths, and narrative. This kind of conflict is explicit, strong, and intertwined with the national conflict. The second conflict, while still ethno-religious, is silent and implicit, where some groups use narratives, history and images in order to secure domination. This conflict can be seen between ethnic-cultural groups such as the Jewish Orthodox, Hassidic, and secular Jewish sectors in Jerusalem,[16] or between Muslim Arabs and Christian Arabs in Ramallah, Bethlehem, and Nazareth,[17] where Muslims initiated the building of a mosque close to a church in the city core. We will examine both of these types of conflict in the cities of Jerusalem and Nazareth, each on a different scale.

Jerusalem: marginal city

Jerusalem's unique status derives from its being holy to the three monotheistic religions. The city's long history is marked by a protracted conflict for control and domination between Christianity and Islam, and since the beginning of the twentieth century, between the Jewish state, Israel and the Arab country, Palestine.[18]

In addition to the external conflict between the three monotheistic religions, there is an internal conflict and dispute over the holy places between Christian ethnic groups, making Jerusalem a highly complicated city.[19] Most of Jerusalem's holy places are concentrated in the Old City and environs. According to the definition and classification of Ramon,[20] in Jerusalem there are about 90 synagogues and Jewish religious-educational institutions, some 133 churches and religious-educational institutions for the various Christian ethnic groups and about 157 mosques and Islamic religious-educational institutions.

The multi-level conflict (geopolitical, national, cultural, and symbolic) over the city has led to spatial division and segregation between the ethno-national and religious cultural groups within the Old City and surrounding area. The Old City is divided into four quarters (Muslim, Jewish, Christian, and Armenian quarters), each one having an informal boundary. The ethno-national groups refuse to change this arrangement by creating mixed quarters or allowing individuals or groups from one quarter move to another. This preservation of the status quo is part of the conflict over Jerusalem between Palestinians and Israelis on the internal level, and between the three monotheistic religions on the external level.

The existing national conflict that is characterized by violence, the communities' traditionalism that renders them segregated and closed, competition over land use and Israel's hegemony and control of Palestinians in the city, the freeze in development in and around the Old City, and limited accessibility (including to the holy sites) by Palestinian Muslims and Christians has limited the city's development possibilities. Jerusalem's closure since 1993 to Palestinians from the occupied territories, and the rejection by most Arab and Muslim countries and the international community of the occupation of East Jerusalem and its annexation to West Jerusalem in 1967, had the effect of limiting the number of visitors and pilgrims. The situation of war and violence between Palestinians and Israelis, particularly in Jerusalem, has deterred local, national, and international investors and developers from initiating economic investment in the city. Furthermore, Jerusalem's religious and traditional character also discourages investors from investing and developing modern economic activity, which is viewed by the religious institutions as inappropriate to the city. The combination of these two factors has resulted in a process of declining economic activity in Jerusalem as a whole, and particularly in East Jerusalem. Today Jerusalem is the second poorest city in Israel, despite its being the country's largest and benefiting from governmental incentives and subsidies as a National Priority Zone.[21]

The recently constructed separation wall from the Palestinian hinterland creates a siege over Jerusalem including its holy places, and further decreases local economic and development activity.[22] Jerusalem's separation from its surrounding area is contrary to international law which prevents an occupying regime from prohibiting religious groups free access for prayer. Because of this situation, economic activity has been leaving the city for other secular and modern global cities such as Tel Aviv in Israel and Ramallah in the Palestinian Authority. This further decreases the economic institutions and reduces the multiplier component for development such as creating jobs opportunities, establishing services institutions to reduce unemployment and improve the standard of living of the community.[23]

One of the economic sectors which is connected to holy places is tourism. Conflict in and around Jerusalem, between Israelis and Palestinians, has led to a sharp decline in the tourism industry. This is illustrated in Table 7.1.

The tourism industry continued to decline as a direct result of the conflict over Jerusalem particularly after the second Intifada began in September 2000, when Israel tightened the closure on Jerusalem which began in 1993 and started construction of the Separation Wall around Jerusalem. These measures prohibit the accessibility of Palestinians to the city's Holy Places. Table 7.2 shows the decline of tourism activity in Jerusalem between 2000 and 2005.

Existing development activities (handicrafts, commercial services) in and around the Old City of Jerusalem have declined since the emergence of violence in the Jerusalem area.[24]

Holy places in urban spaces 137

The result is an additional burden on the city's economic situation, whose main factors are as follows:

1. Migration of commercial and handicraft activities out of Jerusalem. Limited numbers of visitors and pilgrims and limited accessibility of Palestinians to the holy places creates economic hardship in the Old City, whose economy is driven by visitors and pilgrims.
2. Limited land available for future development. Desire to dominate holy sites has led the municipality and Israeli government and public institutions to impose planning and development policies which concentrate and emphasize renovation in order to control Palestinian development.
3. The nature of the city as religious, traditional, and holy has effectively limited the range of economic activities, which seeks to attract the religious, traditional, and less materialistic, with a tendency to local and regional consumption, and not for global or international economic activities such as those located in Tel Aviv.
4. The city has major unemployment and lacks of infrastructure. The demographic structure, which is influenced by religious and traditional behavior, reduces the economic ability of households to consume and to produce.
5. The existence of conflict and violence creates a threat over the holy places, and increases the sense of fear. This mitigates against developers from investing in the city. Various ethno-national groups do not accept any change to the status quo of the holy places.

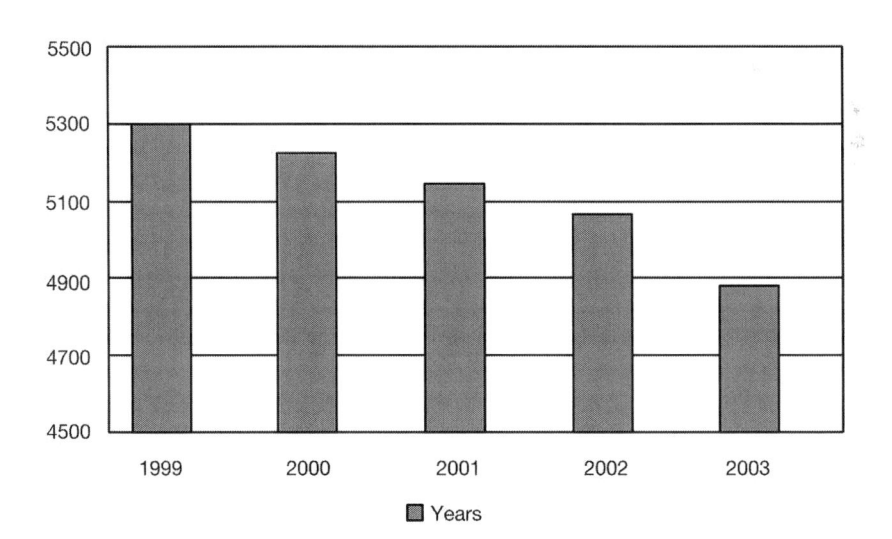

Figure 7.1 Decreasing the number of economic institutions in East Jerusalem as a result of ethno-national conflict, closure and the separation in the Jerusalem area.
Source: R. Khamaisi and R. Nasrallah, *Jerusalem in the Map II*, Jerusalem: IPCC, 2005, p. 32.

138 *Rassem Khamaisi*

Despite these characteristics, Jerusalem's Old City and the Holy Places are located at its heart. These sites constitute a departure point for Jerusalem local planning schemes and future development. Planning assumptions look to the Holy Places as a cultural economic generator. In some cases, though, there is a disparity between the holy places and their nature as symbol, identity, affiliation, and image, and possible economic development. In a situation of continuing ethno-national and religious conflict, the city's sacred sites constitute a burden on economic development.

The case of Nazareth

While in Jerusalem there is a national and ethno-cultural conflict which merged the external and internal disputes over the holy places and domination over the city, the case of Nazareth concentrates on the internal conflict over the sacred sites, which has led to outsider involvement (such as the Israeli Government, the chairman, and representatives of the Palestinian Authority, the Kingdom of Saudi Arabia, the Vatican, and other European countries) in the internal clash. This kind of explicit and implicit involvement to find a solution to the conflict is reflected in the problem that emerged in Nazareth around the Shehab el-Din *Maqqam*. Disagreement over the holy places grew as the city of Nazareth prepared for the third millennium, and the

Table 7.1 Decrease in tourism to East and West Jerusalem before construction of the Separation Wall and after the violence in 2000.

Indicators	1997	1998	1999	2000	2001
East Jerusalem					
Visitors (1000)	140	129.5	180.8	170.8	31.0
Tourists (1000)	129.4	116.3	166.6	160.5	27.3
Occupancy rooms (%)	42	36.7	46.5	46.9	14.2
Employment	934	848	939	1008	507
West Jerusalem					
Visitors (1000)	770.6	840.1	1019.5	1040.8	614.2
Tourists (1000)	491.3	515.0	675.0	735.1	244.1
Occupancy rooms (%)	55.6	55.9	63.9	60.7	28.3
Employment	4871	5105	5225	5313	3316

Table 7.2 Hotel activity among Palestinians in East Jerusalem, 2000 and 2005.

Indicator	2000	2005	Decline	% decline
No. of hotels	33	18	15	54
No. of beds	4345	1967	2378	54
Room occupancy rate (%)	44.4	36.5	7.9	17.8
No. of guests	206,583	64,784	141,799	72

city's internal conflict has created external implications and consequences. One of these direct consequences was a reduction in the number of visitors and pilgrims to Nazareth. According to estimates of the Nazareth master planners, about 850,000 tourists (visitors and pilgrims) visited Nazareth in 1995 (before the emerging Shehab el-Din conflict). The planners estimated the number of tourists in 2000 would increase to about 2.1 million.[25]

According to the Ministry of Tourism, the number of tourists visiting Nazareth in the period between January and April 2001 decreased to less then 100,000 visitors, and most of the city's hotels were closed. This situation is not just the outcome of the conflict over the city's holy places, but of other factors as well, such as the 2000 events among the Arabs in Israel, the second Intifada, and violence that reduced the number of tourists to Israel in general.[26]

Nazareth is the largest Arab city in Israel with about 65,000 inhabitants, and it functions as the regional center and ethno-national capital of the Arab minority in Israel. This minority comprises approximately 18 percent of the Israeli population and is divided between three groups—Muslim (around 78 percent), Christian (about 12 percent), and Druze (about 10 percent).[27] Until the mid-twentieth century, the majority of Nazareth's population was Christian and they controlled the resources in the city.[28]

In 2006, the city's Muslims comprised a demographic majority, about 69 percent, and the rest are Christians who belong to various ethnic-religious groups.[29] This demographic change came about from high natural population growth among the Muslims, and positive internal migration, including internal refugees who came to Nazareth after the war of 1948 and in the aftermath of establishing the Israeli state.[30]

Notwithstanding the changing ethno-religious demographic structure, most of the city leaders are Christian, and they wish to preserve the Christian features and character of the city. Nazareth is historically connected to the Christian religion and most of its traditional holy places as well. According to Christian narrative and tradition Nazareth is the place where Joseph and Mary resided and where Jesus grew up. The Franciscan Church of the Annunciation, one of the most sacred places in the Christian world, was built in the heart of Nazareth on the site of the house where Mary lived and where the angel Gabriel appeared and informed her that she would give birth to Jesus (Luke, 1).

The first mosque built in Nazareth was in 1812, the White Mosque near the Church of the Annunciation. Some say it was built between 1804 and 1808. It is located in *Harat Alghama* or the "Mosque Quarter" in the center of Nazareth's Old Market.[31] According to Muslim narrative and tradition, the Tomb of Shehab el-Din, nephew of Salah el-Din Al Ayoubi, who freed Jerusalem from the Crusaders, is located in the center of Nazareth. This is a strategic point in the city—between the main streets of the historic city, Paulus VI Street and Casanova Street, which lead to the markets, the churches and the mosque in the Old City. The *maqqam* (Tomb) is situated in close proximity to and just southwest of the Church of the Annunciation, beside a school that was built during the Ottoman period. It is surrounded by several historic important buildings such as Khan el-Basha (the Pasha cararvansary), which is part of the White Mosque trust. The structure, which includes buildings built over a period of several centuries, was renovated in 1812.[32]

According to local municipality policy as defined by Mayor Tawfiq Zayyad in 1991, Nazareth was changed from a tourism site to a tourism city, and the government formulated a policy to take steps to prepare the town for the year 2000, when millions of Christian pilgrims were expected to visit their holy sites in Israel and the occupied Palestine territories such as Bethlehem, Jerusalem, and Nazareth. In 1994, the Israeli Government decided to grant Nazareth Development Zone "A" status, which meant an extra injection of funds. At the end of May 1995, a steering committee was established to oversee implementation of the Nazareth 2000 project, and in 1996 the government approved the project as a national program.

In the mid-1990s, the Nazareth 2000 plan was initiated by the municipality of Nazareth, the Ministry of Tourism, and the Israeli Government Tourism Corporation. The purpose of the plan was to promote a significant upgrading of the city prior to the year 2000 and the third millennium. This upgrading encompassed infrastructure, transportation and pedestrianization of the Old City, including the City Square (the location of the Shihab al-Din *maqqam*), Spring Square, public markets, alleys, and historic buildings.

The Nazareth 2000 Plan was followed by another comprehensive plan—the Nazareth Master Plan 2020. This master plan and outline plans for the city were initiated by the Nazareth Municipality. A governmental committee began preparing the plans in 1995, completing them in 1999. These plans focused on tourism as a lever for the city's development. On the ground, from the mid-1990s, a great deal of infrastructural development took place in the city's historic center, including the old market, the rehabilitation of the Paulus VI main street, the construction of three new hotels, the renovation of old ones and production of national and international media programs to raise awareness of Nazareth as one of the most important tourism destinations in Israel in the year 2000. These latter programs emphasized Nazareth as one of the Christian world's holiest sites.

The conflict over the Shihab al-Din site stems from the Nazareth 2000 project. The aims of the project can be summarized as follows (based on the Nazareth municipality website):[33]

- to build a proper infrastructure for visits by tourists and pilgrims;
- to ensure comfort for the visitor today and during the expected wave of visitors in the year 2000;
- to enable all Christian communities to have access to the holy places;
- to highlight the charm of Nazareth, and to develop points of interest and long, varied touring routes.

Holy places in urban spaces 141

The project is also meant to raise the standard of living of the residents of Nazareth, develop sources of employment, increase options for tourist accommodations and services in the city, and create conditions for investment in the local tourism industry.

The Nazareth 2000 project called for construction of a large city square at the front of the Church of the Annunciation, to accommodate the vast number of pilgrims visiting the holy sites. This proposal was named "the Piazza San Marco of Nazareth." In order to create this square it was necessary to demolish the school located in the area, along with other private and semi-public commercial buildings. Situated behind the school was the Tomb of Shehab el-Din, including a small mosque. On 21 December 1997, a number of Muslims congregated in the area of the planned square and claimed that this was a *waqf* area—a Muslim holy area and site—and that they intended to build a large mosque to counter the municipality and government plans authorized by the Nazareth 2000 project. Since that time, tension between local Muslims and Christians has grown, in some cases marked by rioting and physical violence.[34]

The conflict over the Shehab el-Din site was the result of a contradiction between two planning concepts. The Muslim *Waqf* representatives asked to expand the *maqqam* and build a mosque, saying that this area was *waqf* land confiscated by the Israeli Government. On the other hand, representatives of the Nazareth municipality and the Israeli Government claimed that this area was state land, and was planned as a central city square in front of the main church. This tangible conflict comes in the shadow of the latent political, ethnic-religious competition and conflict over the city's image and allocation of resources including land use resources. As a direct result of this conflict, the economic situation in the city has deteriorated. A number of economic institutions and activities left Nazareth for other localities such as Upper-Nazareth, the Jewish twin city to Nazareth.[35] Local political parties and movements such as the Islamic Movement and the Communist Party focused on the conflict surrounding the Shehab el-Din Tomb and Mosque in the local elections, which revealed deep cultural tensions and alienation between the city's Muslims and Christians. The election results led to equal municipal members for the two sides, thus further exacerbating the situation. From that time on, the city council has not been able to create a stable coalition to govern and manage the city.

Needless to say, the Nazareth 2000 project, which was intended as a catalyst for city development, instead became an obstacle to that development as a result of the conflict over the holy places. The number of tourists has not increased, despite construction of the plaza, which continues to be used by Muslims for Friday prayers around the Shehab el-Din *maqqam*. These external and internal factors have created a situation of (semi-silent) conflict which has a direct impact on the city's development. The clash over the image of the city and control of its resources involves local politics up through the mayor of the municipality, where Muslims comprise about two-thirds of the population. The Nazareth 2000 project did not contribute to expanding the number of pilgrims and visitors to the city. Prior to the outbreak of the Al Aqsa Intifada in 2000, the number of tourists who visited Nazareth reached about 850,000, out of the 2.5 million tourists who visited Israel that year. Data from 2005 show that despite the positive national trend of growth in the number of tourists visiting Israel, tourism patterns in Nazareth did not change from what they were prior to Nazareth 2000.[36] In fact Nazareth wants to prepare itself for the new era of global development, but the continuing conflict surrounding the city's holy places has led to deterioration in the city's development.

Summary and recommendations

Holy sites which were expected to facilitate development and provide leverage in situations of religious and cultural conflict have in fact constituted obstacles. While holy places traditionally contributed to creating multiple mechanisms for development activity, in the period of globalization development takes place today in cites having a less traditional and religious image or cities having no sacred sites at all. This paper presents two cases where internal and external changes to a city's demographic and ethno-national cultural structure, power balance and resource domination have turned its holy sites into a physical monument connected deeply to emotional and spiritual feeling but articulated as well by interest groups. Notwithstanding the differences between the two cases as regards motives and size, in both cities the conflict around the holy site is articulated as a struggle for domination of the city's image and shape. The control and development of holy places is part of a greater domination of the landscape and spatial urban fabric.

Based on the notion of the rights of citizens in a city[37] and the idea of liberal democracy and multiculturalism, along with the call for greater dialogue between religions as opposed to a clash of civilizations, there is a tremendous need to develop a new approach for dealing with holy sites in urban centers. From the point of view of urban development, a new notion is needed to merge issues of global and traditional cultural development. The daily encounter between the different cultures of ethno-national groups in cities calls for greater effort towards creating and developing the idea of discovering the other as opposed to ignoring the other, which leads to a clash of religion and culture and presents obstacles to urban life. This notion must take into account the need to avoid politicization of holy places as well as their use as instruments to launch social and political conflicts. Ways to achieve conciliation and coexistence in "holy" cities are necessary in order to secure development. Ethno-national or socio-economic disparity and conflict in urban centers create a burden on cities and lead to division among diverse groups, such as in Nicosia, Beirut, Belfast or Berlin. This essay has attempted to demonstrate how the conflict over holy places could serve as a generator of cultural economy and leverage for development as opposed to serving as a burden on development in situations of conflict and violence.

Notes

1 N. Luz, *The Arab Community of Jaffa and the Hassan Bey Mosque: Collective Identity and Empowerment of the Arabs in Israel*, Jerusalem: Floershimer Inst. for Policy Studies, 2005; D.E. Cosgrove, *Social Formation and Symbolic Landscape*, London: Croom Helm, 1984.
2 D. Harvey, "Monument and Myth," *Annals of the Association of the American Geographers*, 1979, vol. 69, pp. 362–81; L. Kong, "Ideological Hegemony and the Political Symbolism of Religious Building in Singapore," *Environmental and Planning D: Society and Space*, 1993, vol. 11, pp. 23–45.
3 S. Pile, "Political Identities and Spaces of Resistance," in S. Pile and M. Keith (eds), *Geography of Resistance*, London: Routledge, 1997, pp. 1–32.
4 J.Z. Smith, *To Take Place: Toward a Theory in Ritual*, Chicago, Ill.: University of Chicago Press, 1978.
5 P. Knox and L. McCarthy, *Urbanization: An Introduction to Urban Geography*, Englewood Cliffs, N.J.: Prentice Hall, 2005.
6 A.M. Otman, *The Islamic City*, Cairo: Dar al-Afaq al-Arabia, 1999 [in Arabic].
7 Z.W. Ebrahem, *The Role of Tourists in Social Development: Evaluation Research of Tourist Villages*, Alexandria: Modern University Office, 2006 [in Arabic].
8 R. Khamaisi and R. Nasrallah, *Jerusalem: The City of Lost Peace* Jerusalem: International Peace and Cooperation Center IPCC, 2006.
9 A.J. Scott, *The Cultural Economy of Cities*, London: Sage, 2000.
10 M. Benvenisti, *City of Stone: The Hidden History of Jerusalem*, Berkeley, Calif.: University of California Press, 1996.
11 N. Brenner, and R. Kell (eds) *The Global Cities Reader*, London: Routledge, 2005.
12 S. Sassen, "Cities in a World Economy," in S.S. Fainstein, and S. Campbell (eds), *Reading in Urban* Theory, 2nd edn, Oxford: Blackwell, 2002, pp. 32–56.
13 W. Liangyung, *Rehabilitating the Old City of Beijing*, Vancouver: UBC Press, 1999.
14 S. P. Huntington, *The Clash of Civilizations and the Remaking of World Order*, New York: Simon and Schuster, 1996.
15 Khamaisi and Nasrallah, *Jerusalem*, n. 8, pp. 19–26.
16 S. Hasson, *The Cultural Struggle Over Jerusalem*, Jerusalem: Floersheimer Institute for Policy Studies, 1996.
17 D. Rabinowitz, "Strife in Nazareth: Struggles over the Religious Meaning of Place," *Ethnography*, 2001, vol. 2, no.1, pp. 93–113.
18 S.B. Cohen, *Jerusalem; Bridging the Four Walls*, New York: Herzl Press, 1977, pp. 11–29; Benvenisti, *City of* Stone, pp. 1–49.
19 T. Fenster, *The Global City and the Holy City: Narratives on Knowledge, Planning and Diversity*, London: Pearson Prentice Hall, 2004.
20 A. Ramon (ed.) *The Jerusalem Lexicon,* Jerusalem: The Jerusalem Institute for Israel Studies and the Jerusalem Foundation, 2003, pp. 279–347.
21 R. Khamaisi *et al.* (ed.) *Jerusalem on the Map 111,* Jerusalem: IPCC, 2007.
22 R.Brooks, R.Khamaisi, R.Nasrallah, and R.Abu Ghazaleh, *The Wall of Annexation and Expansion: Its Impact on the Jerusalem Area*, Jerusalem: International Peace and Cooperation Center IPCC, 2005.
23 R. Brooks (ed.) *The Wall: Fragmenting the Palestinian Fabric in Jerusalem*, Jerusalem: IPCC, 2007.
24 R. Khamaisi and R. Nasrallah, *Jerusalem in the Map II*, Jerusalem: IPCC, 2005, p. 32.
25 R. Khamaisi, *The Nazareth Area: A Metropolitan Outline for Governance Planning and Development*, Jerusalem: Floersheimer Institute for Policy Studies, 2003.
26 A. Rahamimoff, *Outline Plan for Nazareth, 2020: Final Report*, Nazareth, published by Ministry of Interior and Municipality of Nazareth, 2002, p. 118.
27 Online. Available: www.cbs.gov.il/hodat2001/22-01-121.doc (accessed 18 Aug. 2008).

28 Central Bureau of Statistics *Statistical Abstract of Israel*, no. 56, Jerusalem: 2005.
29 E.F. Chad, *Beyond the Basilica: Christians and Muslims in Nazareth,* Chicago, Ill.: University of Chicago Press, 1995.
30 Online. Available: ww.cbs.gov.il/publications/local_authorities2006/pdf/168_7300.pdf (accessed 4 Aug. 2008).
31 Khamaisi, *The Nazareth Area*, n. 25, pp 14–19.
32 Online. Available: Wikipedia http://ar.wikipedia.org/wiki (accessed 30 Aug. 2008). See also Z.N. Keawar, *History of Nazareth*, Nazareth: Venues Publishing, 2000, p. 314.
33 E. Oren and A. Rahamimoff, *Shehab el-Din Mosque, Nazareth, Progress Report*, Nazareth, unpublished report, 2002, p. 2.
34 Online. Available: www.nazareth2000.gov.il/investor.htm (accessed 15 Aug. 2008).
35 J. Jabarin, "The Right of City: The Crisis of Shehab a-Din in Nazareth," *Makan*, 2006, vol.1, pp. 7–20 [in Arabic].
36 Khamaisi, *The Nazareth Area*, n. 25, pp. 26–27.
37 K. Cohen-Hattab and N. Shoval, "Tourism Development in a Condition of a Cultural Conflict: the case of 'Nazareth 2000,'" *Social and Cultural Geography*, vol. 8, no. 5 October, 2007, pp. 701–17.
38 H. Lefebvre, *Writing on Cities*, Cambridge, Mass.: Blackwell, 1996; D. Harvey "The Right to the City," *International Journal of Urban and Regional Research*, 2003, vol. 27, no. 4, pp. 939–41.

8 The pessimist's guide to religious coexistence

Ron E. Hassner

Introduction

The Church of the Holy Sepulcher in Jerusalem is revered as the site of the crucifixion and resurrection of Jesus Christ by several Christian sects who vie zealously for control over different parts of the structure. These sects attempt to encroach on their rivals' space while continuing to defend their exclusive rights to sections that have traditionally been under their control. In May 1997, a sewer cover in the church interior broke. Concerned that the exposed sewer hole might endanger worshipers, Metropolitan Daniel, the senior Greek Orthodox priest in the church, tried to replace the cover.[1] A group of Armenian monks happened to see his activities, attacked the eighty year-old metropolitan and beat him within an inch of his life. The sewer hole, they later explained, was located in the Armenian, and not the Greek Orthodox, part of the church. A special committee convened by the Greek Orthodox, Armenian, and Latin Patriarchates in response to this incident could not resolve the question of jurisdiction over the sewer cover. For several years after this incident, it remained broken, covered with a rickety board.[2]

Despite agreements on a wide range of issues, violent incidents such as these are common at the Church of the Holy Sepulcher, where Coptic, Syrian, Ethiopian, Latin, Armenian, and Greek Orthodox worshipers struggle over the right to access, maintain or decorate every square inch of space. Tussles, fist fights, and an atmosphere of tense suspicion between the religious groups that must share this space have led to deadlock on crucial matters relating to the integrity of the church and the safety of worshipers, such as disagreement on repairing parts of the structure and an impasse on constructing an additional entrance to accommodate the surge of pilgrims for the year 2000.[3]

The tense conditions at this site are all the more astounding because several key conditions for peaceful religious coexistence have already been put in place. The "Status Quo," legal system with regard to the Christian Holy Places, established in 1757 and confirmed in 1852, is rigorously enforced by the State of Israel. The government has tried to bridge differences between the rival sects and, more often than not, has undertaken to cover the expense of critical maintenance projects itself. As a neutral party enjoying power predominance, the Israeli Government should be expected to be able to compel the parties to coexist peacefully. Additional efforts to reduce friction between the parties have included mapping out spheres of jurisdiction to the minutest of details, and the handing over the keys of the entire shrine to Muslim custodians. Yet the conflict continues unabated.

The pervasive discord at the Church of the Holy Sepulcher is particularly remarkable because it is not a typical case of inter-religious conflict over sacred space, like Jewish–Muslim disputes in Israel or Hindu–Muslim disputes in India, where contradictory religious narratives lead different groups to compete over one and the same site. Atypically, this conflict is intra-religious, occurring among various Christian sects that are driven by the same sacred texts to worship at a communal site. Any common ground that might have united these groups has been overshadowed by the competitive desire to control a space, restrict access to that space and enforce rules within it. Far more costly outcomes characterize competition over sacred places by distinct religions, as occurs frequently in South Asia, the Middle East, the Balkans, and elsewhere. The costs of these conflicts can be measured in tens of thousands of lives, particularly when sectarian violence spills over into local and regional conflicts and hampers the resolution of intractable military disputes.

Given this empirical record, the optimistic attitude that characterizes current research on inter-religious strife, including contributions in this volume, is nothing short of baffling. Scholars studying sacred sites in Israel and the West Bank have enthusiastically pointed to inter-faith harmony at the Cave of Elijah in Haifa, the Tomb of Samuel north of Jerusalem and, in the nineteenth century, the Cave of Simon the Just in Jerusalem.[4] An expert on the sharing of Sufi shrines by Hindus and Muslims in the Punjab, India, has noted "the reality of peaceful interaction that counters the stereotype of perennial Hindu-Muslim antagonism."[5] Another author, writing about shared sacred sites in the Middle East, argued that although religion is antagonistic to pluralism, "it would be misleading to conclude that for this reason there cannot be sharing among distinct religions."[6]

Hopeful outlooks such as these are part of a larger backlash against the pessimistic stance that has dominated the study of religion and politics since the publication of Samuel Huntington's *Clash of Civilizations* and the disproportionate focus on fundamentalism and extremism in the wake of September 11.[7] Authors who counter the tragic implications of Huntington's deterministic view have taken pains to point to the benevolent message at the core of all religious traditions, citing it as evidence for religious coexistence. Others have gone so far as to laud the peacemaking capabilities of religious actors and have suggested that a greater dose of religion in politics would provide the means for resolving many interstate rivalries.[8] Religious conflicts, these scholars argue, are not inevitable but rather the result of misunderstandings, mismanagement and failure to implement widely available conflict resolution measures.

If applied to religious coexistence at sacred sites, I believe this optimism is dangerously misguided. In the following pages, I will argue that the very same motivations that lead religious groups to attribute importance to sacred sites also lead these groups into conflict with religious rivals at these sites. This is why attempts to divide sacred space between religious groups, arrangements in which groups alternate in their use of the space or exclusion of all groups from a space have consistently failed to lead to harmony at sacred sites. The only exceptions to this rule occur at less pivotal "folk" sites that occupy a marginal role in the religious landscape. To illustrate the weakness of these measures, I present a brief case study of the Muslim–Hindu dispute in Ayodhya, India, in which a variety of conflict-resolution techniques failed to prevent a disastrous outcome.

I conclude by arguing that the key to resolving religious conflict at sacred sites lies not in managing tensions between rival groups but in separating those groups from one another. The difficulty lies in the fact that such separation cannot be imposed on religious groups from without. The decision to abandon a sacred site for another must arise from within the leadership of a group, a scenario that is only feasible at unique junctures in the development of a religious movement.

The root of the problem

Religious movements value sacred sites for four primary reasons: Sacred sites provide access, legitimacy, meaning, and a sense of community. Inevitably, those same reasons lead religious groups into conflict with competitors who wish to implement conflicting rules regarding access, compete for rightful title, provoke their rivals, and target its population.[9]

First and foremost, sacred sites provide access to the divine by permitting worshipers to come in contact with the sacred. Sacred sites represent earthly locations at which the divine has manifested itself through vision or miracle, where humans have communicated with the gods and to which they come in expectation of blessing, healing or forgiveness. Because these sites constitute ruptures in the ordinary realm, worshipers must abide by specific rules regarding access and behavior. These rules are designed to protect the divine presence from desecration and protect humans from overstepping dangerous limits as they approach the divine, as well as to distinguish the sacred space from the surrounding secular space. Transgressing these rules is tantamount to sacrilege.

One of a religious group's most important tasks, therefore, is to enforce these rules on access and conduct. Although driven by religious principles, this is essentially a political enforcement. It involves monitoring the boundaries of the sacred space and policing behavior within it. In the secular realm, this degree of control over space is associated with sovereignty, i.e., with the exclusive domination by a social group over a defined space. In the religious realm, protection of a sacred space from sacrilege requires similar exclusivity. It is when the sacred spaces of two or more religious groups overlap that difficulties arise, due to contradictions between what is permitted by one group and prohibited by the other. One group bans the consumption of alcohol, another employs wine in the performance of crucial rites. One religious movement requires covering the head, another demands its exposure. One sect practices a solemn ritual while the other wishes to celebrate an exuberant feast. One religion espouses inclusive services while the other bars women from its sanctuaries. Jewish–Muslim friction at the Tomb of the Patriarchs/Ibrahimi Mosque in Hebron exemplifies this type of conflict.

A second cause for the centrality of sacred sites in religious belief lies in their ability to confer an aura of legitimacy on the movements that control them. This is particularly important when several competing sects claim the right of true succession from a common religion of origin, as do the multiple Christian sects struggling over the Holy Sepulcher. Exclusive access to the divine is one important way for a religious tradition to demonstrate that it is the most authentic inheritor to the "one true faith." The group exerting exclusive control over a sacred space can bar others from access at whim, extract concessions or exert control over pilgrims entering into its domain. Saudi control over the sacred mosques in Mecca and Medina and its implications for its rivalry with Shi'ite Iran offers a prominent example for this type of conflict.

Third, sacred sites are valued because they embody the very essence of a particular religious movement, both to its members and to members of other faiths. The shrines erected at these sites often represent the religious movement at its most splendorous, displaying a religious community's power and wealth even to those barred from access. Their design and ornamentation capture key elements of the religious tradition in a symbolic form that is immediately recognizable to worshipers and outsiders alike. Many of the world's great religious shrines, such as the Grand Mosque in Mecca, the Western Wall in Jerusalem, the Church of Saint Peter in Rome or the Shinto Shrine in Ise, have become synonymous in popular perception with the religions they represent.

Given this parallelism between the religious group and its sacred space, the space itself becomes vulnerable to attack from those seeking to harm the group. Hindu, Muslim, and Sikh shrines in India are routinely targeted during riots against these communities. Similarly, mosques and synagogues throughout Israel and the West Bank suffered the brunt of sectarian violence in the early days of the Al-Aqsa Intifada, as did churches and mosques over the course of the armed conflicts in the former Yugoslavia.[10] By targeting or damaging the shrine most sacred to a group, its rivals hope to strike at the heart of the group's values, heritage, and pride. This type of attack bears unmistakable meaning. It is not merely an act of violence but a challenge to the core of the religious group and all it represent. Assaults on sacred sites are thus attempts by one group to undermine the foundations upon which their opponent's identity and faith rest.

Sacred places make tempting targets for another reason: they tend to teem with religious adherents. Believers are drawn to sacred places not only because of the religious functions these sites perform but also because these places perform specific social roles. In their function as legal, political or financial centers, sacred places draw powerful actors from all walks of life into their orbit. Temples and shrines have doubled as royal residences, courts of law, financial exchanges, and markets. Often the largest public structure at the center of a village or town, they become the primary locus of societal interaction. Rivals striking at these structures can therefore expect to exact substantial casualties from the target community. This notorious tactic is evident in the Sunni-Shi'ite conflict developing in Iraq today, in which attacks on crowded mosques have cost thousands of believers their lives.[11]

To summarize, insofar as sacred places provide believers with access to the divine, legitimacy, meaning, and community, they invite conflict with rival groups who strive to compete for access or legitimacy or who simply wish to inflict harm on their opponents. The more important a sacred site the more likely it will provide crucial functions, the more likely the friction with other groups and the greater the odds of large-scale violence.

This explains, in part, why students of religion and politics have observed peaceful coexistence at minor shrines that are not fully institutionalized into the formal framework of a religious movement. Muslim-Jewish coexistence is possible at a site like the Cave of Elijah because it is neither an official mosque nor an official synagogue. Restrictive rules that delimit access and behavior have not been implemented, and possession of such sites confers little or no legitimacy on one religious community or the other. Because they are marginal to the religious landscape of both Judaism and Islam, they make for poor symbols of the religious movement to outsiders and for poor targets of mass attack by adversaries. Should sites like these grow in importance, due to a sudden rise in their popularity or increased sectarian tension in the region, their vulnerability to conflict is certain to increase as well. At important sacred sites, conflict is inevitable. Peaceful coexistence is only possible where it matters least.

Recipes for disaster

In facing these seemingly intractable challenges, peacemakers have suggested a variety of approaches for managing coexistence at sacred sites. Their tools tend to fall into three broad categories: partition, scheduling, and exclusion. In the Jewish-Muslim and Hindu-Muslim disputes that I examine below, these strategies provide temporary solutions, at best. Instead of resolving disputes, they provide provisional accommodation in the hope that gradual understanding between the rival groups will displace tensions. Instead, such provisions merely serve to frustrate religious movements which find their access to a sacred site restricted by the presence of rivals. This frustration is made all the more acute by each group's perception that divine decree has granted it, and only it, exclusive rights to the site. As the rivals face off in a zero-sum conflict, their resentment tends to manifest itself, sooner or later, in a violent outburst.[12]

In the first conflict resolution approach, the sacred space is divided so as to permit two or more religious groups to worship at a sacred site at the same time. This can take the form of establishing restrictions on access to specific parts of a shrine or indicating spheres of jurisdiction without restricting access. The former is the approach adopted in several Indian mosques that have been constructed on top of, and with materials recycled from, destroyed Hindu temples. At the Krishna Janmasthan in Mathura, the Kashi Vishwanath Temple/Gyanvapi Mosque in Varanasi and the Quwwat-ul-Islam Mosque in Delhi, Hindu and Muslim worshipers pray in distinct areas, separated by barriers and guarded by Indian military troops.[13] The latter approach, jurisdictional division, was implemented in the Church of the Holy Sepulcher in Jerusalem and the Church of the Nativity in Bethlehem, where members of the different Christian sects are free to move about the shrine but are limited in their right to clean, maintain or decorate sectors other than their own.

In the second scenario, a detailed agreement establishes the times at which different groups have access to a site. Such an agreement might permit only one group to access the site at one time or establish periods of common versus separate worship. In most cases, division and scheduling are combined. In the Church of the Holy Sepulcher, for example, parts that are in the public domain most of the year are reserved for the exclusive use of one sect or another at dates of particular significance to that sect. Scheduling need not provide equal access to all parties involved. Only Muslims are permitted to access the Temple Mount platform in Jerusalem on Fridays and Muslim holy days; non-Muslims are permitted there at other times but may not pray there.

Finally, the strategy of exclusion seeks to resolve conflict over a sacred site by barring all religious groups from worshiping there. This can be achieved by secularizing the sacred place, conferring historical or archeological status on the site or simply locking its gates to worshipers. For example, the Hagia Sophia in Istanbul, a church converted into a mosque, could have formed the backdrop for significant Christian–Muslim tension had the Turkish government not declared the shrine a national museum in which neither Muslim nor Christian worship is permitted.

Although strategies of partition, scheduling and exclusion are routinely practiced at controversial sacred sites worldwide, their record of success is disappointing, at best, and disastrous, at worst. Before 1967, for example, Muslim authorities ruling over Hebron had barred Jews from praying at the Tomb of the Patriarchs. Upon conquering Hebron in the Six-Day War of 1967, Israel forced a division of the large prayer hall and instituted an elaborate prayer schedule designed to enable Muslim as well as Jewish prayer while keeping the parties apart.[14] Nevertheless, conflicting practices at the site soon led to violence between Jews and Muslims. Overwhelming Israeli military presence converted the shrine into an army stronghold.[15] Congregations pray under 24-hour camera surveillance, separated by head-high aluminum barricades, and keep their sacred texts in fire-proof safes for fear of desecration. These measures have all proven futile, as demonstrated by a series of attacks involving stabbings, shootings and Molotov cocktails, culminating in the brutal attack of February 1994. Thirty-nine Palestinians were gunned down by a Jewish extremist during prayer in the Tomb and an additional sixteen died in subsequent violence.[16]

The reason why accepted conflict resolution methods prove unsuccessful lies in their failure to address the root causes of violence at sacred sites, as discussed above. Neither partition nor scheduling obviate the desire by multiple parties to control access and behavior over an entire sacred space. Indeed, they deprive each party to the dispute of the ability to prevent what it considers sacrilege in half of the sacred place all the time, or in the entire sacred space half of the time. Moreover, partition and scheduling fail to resolve or even address the looming question of legitimacy. The outcome, in fact, is that sharing space and time among rival groups establishes the basis for increased competition, as each group attempts to control more space and more time to establish its authority and authenticity. The division of sacred space by fiat merely represses the conflict, creating tensions that seethe under the surface, threatening to erupt as soon as one party perceives changes in the balance of power.

The third approach, exclusion, does address the problems posed by a sacred place's vulnerability as social symbol and community center, by barring worshipers from the site altogether. However, this is a harsh measure and is likely to antagonize all religious groups involved. Only the strongest of states can afford to adopt a unilateral strategy of this sort. Moreover, only a government neutral to the interests of all religious rivals involved would be likely to desire exclusion as an outcome. The secular Turkish regime's handling of the Hagia Sophia constitutes a rare exception to this pattern.

The Indian government's failure to manage the Ayodhya crisis, on the other hand, demonstrates the dangers of attempting conflict resolution at sacred sites in the absence of strict neutrality and overwhelming power dominance. This case is worth examining because in the course of the dispute there, all of the strategies discussed above were implemented at some point or another, yet all failed to prevent conflict. The Ayodhya dispute should also be of particular interest to students of religious coexistence in the Middle East, given its similarities with the conflict over Jerusalem.[17]

The dispute over the Babri Masjid (Mosque of Babur) in Ayodhya is rooted in the belief that the Muslim Emperor Babur constructed this mosque on the site of the Ramjanmabhumi, an earlier Hindu temple marking the birthplace of the god Rama. Although this religious-historical claim is highly unlikely, it is not unreasonable given the frequency of mosque constructions on the sites of Hindu shrines by Mughal rulers, who often incorporated building materials from destroyed shrines to construct the mosques.[18]

The mosque was constructed by the Mughal emperor in the early sixteenth century. Until the mid-nineteenth century, the site was a popular folk shrine, revered for its miraculous drinking water. Muslims and Hindus shared access to the well in the central courtyard whereas the rest of the shrine was divided into Muslim and Hindu sectors.[19] This state of harmonious coexistence was interrupted in the mid-nineteenth century. The onset of direct British rule over India in 1857 was accompanied by a rise in sectarian tensions that in turn increased discord between Hindus and Muslims in Ayodhya as well.

Consequently, a low barrier was installed to keep Hindu worshipers out of the inner courtyard of the mosque. Hindu believers constructed a *chabootra*, a prayer platform, in the outer courtyard and made their offerings there. This separation, while convenient for Muslim worshipers, was unacceptable to Hindus, who appealed to the courts on several occasions. The tenuous nature of the arrangement was further underscored in Hindu attacks on the mosque during communal riots in the 1930s.[20]

In 1949, Hindu worshipers escalated the situation further when they demanded the right to worship idols of the gods Rama, Sita, and Hanuman that had "mysteriously" appeared inside the mosque. When a violent crowd attempted to storm the mosque, Prime Minister Jawaharlal Nehru instructed that the idols be removed, an order disobeyed by local police who feared mob retaliation. Instead, the mosque was placed under lock and key, barring worshipers of all faiths.[21] This second attempt to resolve the situation in Ayodhya led to further court appeals by Hindu worshipers and the founding of the Ramjanmabhumi Mukti Yajna Samiti, the Organization for Sacrifice to Liberate the Birthplace of the God Rama. Its efforts were ultimately successful. In 1986 the locks were removed and exclusive Hindu worship began in the mosque courtyard. Muslims responded by founding the All India Babri Masjid Action Committee, a movement that led their protests in the ensuing decades.

As far as extremist Hindu worshipers were concerned, Hindu prayer in the courtyard was merely the first step towards construction of a Hindu temple on the mosque ruins. In 1989 the foundations for this temple were laid, prompting widescale anti-Hindu riots and the destruction of over 400 temples in Pakistan and Bangladesh. Nevertheless, the World Hindu Council (VHP), and the Indian People's Party (BJP) continued in their campaign to construct a temple for Rama in Ayodhya. In 1990, dozens of Hindu devotees died in clashes with the police in Ayodhya. Two years later, tens of thousands of activists, using their bare hands, pick hammers, and sticks, attacked and demolished the Babri Masjid in under fourteen hours and constructed a shrine for Rama among the ruins.[22] This incident, instigated by the VHP and BJP, provoked riots across India in which an estimated 20,000 Hindus and Muslims met their deaths. The backlash was felt as far as England, where Hindus and Muslims attacked one another's sacred shrines.[23] Hundreds more died the next year in a series of bombings in Mumbai, said to have occurred in retaliation for the destruction of the Babri Masjid.

Since 1992, the ruins of the mosque have once again been placed under lock and key. Visitors wishing to approach the site must pass a steel barricade located half a kilometer from the shrine, then go through a metal detector, discard all personal items, and pass through a second metal detector.[24] The area is protected by closed-circuit cameras and a force of 3,000 policemen bearing automatic weapons. Not surprisingly, none of these measures has reduced violence at the site. Hindu extremists continue planning in earnest towards construction of a temple, with blueprints and materials already assembled and consecrated. Muslim radicals, in turn, attacked Hindu worshipers returning from Ayodhya in 2002, and staged an assault on the mosque site itself in 2005.

Good fences for bad neighbors

The consequences of the Ayodhya affair should serve as a warning to peacemakers who consider partition, scheduling or exclusion to be workable options for the resolution of conflicts over sacred places. Even when all available conflict-resolution strategies are adopted in turn, violence at sacred sites is likely to prevail and ultimately escalate. Rather than seek examples for successful conflict management where none exist, students of religious coexistence should focus their efforts on analyzing cases in which groups have avoided conflict altogether by worshiping at separate sites. This, as Arthur Conan Doyle would have put it, shifts the attention to "the dog that did not bark." For example, researchers should ask why, despite mutual Muslim and Jewish reverence toward Moses and Abraham, is there Muslim–Jewish conflict over the Tomb of Abraham in Hebron but not over the Tomb of Moses in the Judean Desert? Why, despite common Muslim and Christian veneration towards John the Baptist or Christian and Jewish reverence towards Adam and Eve, is there no Muslim–Christian or Jewish–Christian conflict over the tombs of these biblical figures? The answer, in all these cases, is related to the conscious decision by one party to a potential dispute to identify its sacred site elsewhere. Jews and Muslims identify the same site as the Tomb of Abraham, leading to major violent conflict at the tomb. There is disagreement, however, as to the location of the Tomb of Moses. Muslims worship at Nebi Mousa in the Judean desert whereas Jews believe that the location of Moses' tomb, somewhere near Mount Nebo east of the Jordan, is unknown. Muslims pray at the Tomb of John the Baptist in Damascus, but Christians worship his tomb in Ephesus, Turkey. Christians revere the Church of the Holy Sepulcher as the location of the bones of Adam while Jews place his tomb in Hebron.

The decision to place a space or event common to multiple religions at different sites can have profound implications for religious coexistence. The Jewish–Muslim clash over the Temple Mount/Haram es Sharif, for example, has been pivotal in aggravating Israeli–Palestinian relations, contributing to the failure of the Camp David negotiations in July 2000 and provoking the Al-Aqsa Intifada two months later.[25] Christians, on the other hand, have expressed their opinions regarding the resolution of the Jerusalem question in general but have not made claims to the Temple Mount

The Christian disinterest in the site so central to Jews and Muslims stems from an early Christian understanding of the Gospels as marginalizing the

Temple. Christian interpreters believed that the New Testament site of Jesus Christ's sacrifice and resurrection, the Church of the Holy Sepulcher, supplanted the Old Testament site of Jewish animal sacrifice, the Temple Mount. It was with this interpretation in mind that the Emperor Constantine decided in the fourth century to disregard the Temple Mount and build Christianity's most sacred shrine on the opposite side of the city of Jerusalem. His biographer and then bishop of Caesarea, Eusebius, described the new church, underscoring its opposition to the sacred Jewish site:

> On the monument of salvation itself was the new Jerusalem built, over against the one so famous of old which, after the pollution caused by the murder of the Lord, experienced the last extremity of desolation and paid the penalty for the crime of its inhabitants. Opposite this the emperor raised, at great and lavish expense, the trophy of the Savior's victory over death ... [26]

This decision of Constantine's explains why the conflict over the Temple Mount today involves two and not three religious groups. It was a remarkable shift, given the place occupied by the Jewish Temple in seminal events in the lives of Jesus Christ, John the Baptist, and other Christian figures. But it was not a decision without parallel.

Similar reasoning serves to explain why Islam is not a party to the dispute over the Church of the Holy Sepulcher, despite the importance of the crucifixion in Muslim accounts of the life of Jesus Christ. According to one tradition, when the Caliph Umar ibn al-Khattab conquered Jerusalem for Islam in the seventh century, he was taken on a tour of Jerusalem that included a visit to the Church of the Holy Sepulcher. Halfway through the visit, the call for prayer resounded through the city so Sophornius, the patriarch of Jerusalem and guide to Umar, invited the Caliph to conduct his prayers inside the church. Karen Armstrong, citing the ninth-century *Annals* of Eutychius, recounts what happened next:

> Umar courteously refused; neither would he pray in Constantine's Martyrium. Instead he went outside and prayed on the steps beside the busy thoroughfare of the Cardo Maximus. He explained to the patriarch that had he prayed inside the Christian shrines, the Muslims would have confiscated them and converted them into an Islamic place of worship to commemorate the caliph's prayer ... [27]

If this account is to be believed, the lack of Muslim–Christian conflict over the Church of the Holy Sepulcher, like the absence of Muslim–Christian and Jewish–Christian conflict over the Temple Mount, has its roots in a conscious decision made by a charismatic leader at a critical time in the history of a religious-political movement. Constantine, first Roman-Christian emperor, chose to position Christianity's sacred center in Jerusalem away from the city's sacred site for Jews. Umar ibn al-Khattab, successor to the Prophet Muhammad, placed the Muslim sacred site in Jerusalem apart from the Christian site but on top of the Jewish site, thus dooming Islam to conflict with Judaism but not with Christianity in the city.

Along similar lines, a more pertinent question to ask about the Church of the Holy Sepulcher is not how conflict between the Greek Orthodox, Latin, Armenian, Coptic, Syrian, and Ethiopian parties could be prevented but rather why it is that Protestant Christian movements are not party to this dispute. The answer has to do with Protestant dissatisfaction with the Church of the Holy Sepulcher as the location of the crucifixion and resurrection. In the nineteenth century Protestant biblical scholars – most famous among them General Charles Gordon – raised doubts regarding the authenticity of the Holy Sepulcher as the actual crucifixion site. Instead, they chose to focus their attention on an alternative location, a garden just outside the walls of Jerusalem that contained a tomb as well as a rock resembling a skull, identified as Golgotha.[28] The Garden Tomb, as it has come to be called, is one of the most popular Protestant sites in the Holy Land today, with some 50,000 pilgrims visiting every year. For these pilgrims, this is the true location of the crucifixion and resurrection. The struggles between their co-religionists taking place inside the Church of the Holy Sepulcher is of no interest to them.

There is, then, an alternative to conflicts at sacred places. At critical historical junctures, religious and political leaders have proven capable of focusing the attention of their constituents on sites not already "taken" by competing religious movements. However, this alternative provides no reasons for optimism regarding coexistence at sacred places for four reasons.

First, the key to peace in this account is *separation,* not coexistence. As long as rival movements continue to worship at one and the same site, accord will always remain elusive. Second, separation cannot be forced on a religious movement from without. The initiative for relocation must come from within the group itself. Tragically or not, in most cases rival religious groups have chosen competition at sacred sites over separation. Conflict is thus the norm and separation is the exception. Third, even if religious leaders would prefer separation over conflict, the constraints of tradition hamper their ability to divert worship to a new site. Change of this nature is only possible when dramatic shifts in political circumstances open up possibilities for initiative. Finally, even if separation succeeds, it may prove insufficient in preventing strife in the long run. For ultimately, Umar's refusal to pray at the Church of the Holy Sepulcher did little to prevent Jewish–Muslim conflict on the Temple Mount or intra-Christian antagonism at the Church of the Holy Sepulcher. In the end, the wisest stance for students of religious coexistence to adopt is one of sober pessimism.

Notes

1 S. Berkovits, *The Battle for the Holy Places: The Struggle over Jerusalem and the Holy Sites in Israel, Judea, Samaria and the Gaza District, Or Yehuda,* Israel: Hed Arzi, 2000, p. 236 [in Hebrew].

2 D. Sontag, "At Riven Holy Sepulcher, Anxiety as Crowds Loom," *New York Times*, 1 Dec. 1999, p. A1.
3 R. Cohen, *Saving the Holy Sepulchre: How Rival Christians Came Together to Rescue their Holiest Shrine*, Oxford: Oxford University Press, 2008.
4 I. Zilberman, *Jerusalem and Ayodhya – A Profile of Religious and Political Radicalism*, Jerusalem: Jerusalem Institute for Israel Studies, 1997; E.K. Fowden, "Sharing Holy Places," *Common Knowledge*, vol. 8, no. 1, 2002, pp. 124–46.
5 A. Bigelow, "Practicing Pluralism in Malerkotla, Punjab," Items and Issues, vol. 3, no. 1–2, 2002, p. 10. See also A. Bigelow, *Sharing Saints, Shrines, and Stories: Practicing Pluralism in North India*, Doctoral Dissertation, Dept of Religious Studies, University of California, Santa Barbara, 2004.
6 Fowden, "Sharing Holy Places," n. 4, p. 146.
7 *See e.g.*, S. Huntington, *The Clash of Civilizations and the Remaking of World Order*, New York: Touchstone Books, 1998; M. Juergensmeyer, *Terror in the Mind of God: The Global Rise of Religious Violence*, Berkeley, Calif.: University of California Press, 2000, Chs 1 and 8; J.L. Esposito, *Unholy War: Terror in the Name of Islam*, New York: Oxford University Press, 2002; B. Lincoln, *Holy Terrors: Thinking About Religion After September 11*, Chicago, Ill.: University of Chicago Press, 2003; Martin E. Marty and R. Scott Appleby (eds) *The Fundamentalism Project*, vols. 1–4, Chicago, Ill.: University of Chicago Press.
8 *See e.g.*, R.S. Appleby, *The Ambivalence of the Sacred*, Lanham, Md.: Rowman and Littlefield, 2000; D. Johnston and C. Sampson, *Religion, the Missing Dimension of Statecraft*, New York: Oxford University Press, 1994; M. Albright, *The Mighty and the Almighty: Reflections on America, God and World Affairs*, New York: HarperCollins, 2006.
9 *See* R.E. Hassner *War on Sacred Grounds* Ithaca, N.Y.: Cornell University Press, 2009.
10 S. Waxman, "Shrine to Hatred: At Joseph's Tomb, Centuries-Old Disputes Cannot be Laid to Rest," *Washington Post*, 28 Oct. 2000, p. C01; M. Dudkevich, "IAF Attacks Jericho After Synagogue Burned," *Jerusalem Post*, 13 Oct. 2000, p. 1A; L. Hockstader, "On Both Sides, Toll is Personal," *Washington Post*, 14 Oct. 2000, p. A01; M. Dudkevich, "Efrat Preparing 'Zionist Response' to Synagogue Desecration," *Jerusalem Post*, 29 Oct. 2000, p. 1; "Violence Flares in Bosnia Ceremony," *CNN International*, 18 June 2001, Online. Available: www.cnn.com/WORLD (accessed 29 Aug. 2003).
11 *See e.g.*, N. MacFarquhar and R. A. Oppel, Jr., "Car Bomb in Iraq Kills 95 at Shi'ite Mosque," *New York Times*, 30 Aug. 2003, sec. A5, p. 1; J. F. Burns, "At Least 143 Die in Attacks at Two Sacred Sites in Iraq," *New York Times*, 3 Mar. 2004, sec. A1, p. 1; R.F. Worth and R.A. Oppel, Jr., "Attacks Kill 27 Iraqi Civilians and Policemen and Many Rebels," *New York Times*, 4 Dec. 2004, sec. A3, p. 10; R.F. Worth, "Wave of Violence by Rebels in Iraq Kills 80 in 3 Days," *New York Times*, 6 Dec. 2004, sec. A6, p. 1.
12 I thank Leonard Hammer for proposing this conceptualization of the problem. On the indivisibility of sacred space, *see also*, Hassner, *War on Sacred Grounds*.
13 R.M. Eaton, "Temple Desecration in Pre-Modern India," *Frontline*. vol. 17, no. 25, 22 Dec. 2000, and vol. 17, no. 26, 5 Jan. 2000; "VHP Body Threatens Stir over Prayer Ban at Mosque," *The Hindustan Times*, 14 Dec. 2000, Online. Available: www.hindustantimes.com/nonfram/151200/detCIT12.asp (accessed 19 Feb. 2003); "Ominous Rumblings," *The Hindu*, 17 Nov. 2000; "VIIP Bid for Puja in Delhi Mosque," *The Statesman*, 14 Nov. 2000.
14 *See e.g.*, W. Claiborne, "Five Israelis Die in Arab Raid, Worst Ever in West Bank," *Washington Post*, 3 May 1980, p. A1; W. B. Ries, "Palestinian Protests Erupt after Moslem Prayers," *UPI*, 19 Feb.1988; "Israeli Soldier Kills Mom of Ten Who Stabbed His Partner," *Toronto Star*, 15 Sept. 1986, p. A10; B. Hepburn,

"Israeli Settler Kills Axe Attacker – West Bank Incident Leaves Palestinian Dead," *The Toronto Star*, 15 Nov. 1993, p. A3.
15 D. Fisher, "Disputed Tomb of the Patriarchs: Arabs, Jews, Pray under Same Roof, Under Guard," *Los Angeles Times*, 29 Mar.1986, p. A1.
16 Associated Press, "Gunman Slays 20 at Site of Mosque," *New York Times*, 25 Feb. 1994, p. A1; "Mosque Massacre Incites Arab Rioting," *Miami Herald*, 26 Feb. 1994, p. A1; B. Hutman and A. Pinkas, "Wave of Riots after Hebron Massacre: Kiryat Arba Doctor Slays 39; Over 29 Palestinians Die in Aftermath," *Jerusalem Post*, 27 Feb. 1994, p. 1.
17 R. Friedland and R. Hecht, "The Bodies of Nations: A Comparative Study of Religious Violence in Jerusalem and Ayodhya," *History of Religions*, Nov.1998, vol. 38, no. 2, pp. 101–49; D. Pipes, "The Temple Mount's Indian Counterpart," *Jerusalem Post*, 17 Jan. 2001; Zilberman, *Jerusalem and Ayodhya*.
18 Eaton, "Temple Desecration in Pre-Modern India"; K.N. Panikkar, "A Historical Overview," in *Anatomy of a Confrontation: The Rise of Communal Politics in India*, Sarvepalli Gopal (ed.) London: Zed Books, 1991; Sita Ram Goel, *Hindu Temples: What Happened to Them,* New Delhi: Voice of India, 1998.
19 P. Bacchetta, "Sacred Space and Conflict in India: The Babri Masjid Affair," *Growth and Change*, vol. 31, no. 2, 2000, pp. 255–84; A. Ali Engineer (ed.), *The Bari-Masjid Ramjanambhoomi Controversy*, Delhi: Ajanta Pub., 1990; P. Van der Veer, "'The Gods Must be Liberated!': A Hindu Liberation Movement in Ayodhya," *Modern Asian Studies*, 1987, vol. 21, no. 2, pp. 283–301.
20 N. Harsh, *The Ayodhya Temple Mosque Dispute: Focus on Muslim Sources*, Delhi, India: Penman Publishers, 1993.
21 Bacchetta, "Sacred Space and Conflict in India: The Babri Masjid Affair," p. 265; J. Bajaj (ed.) *Ayodhya and the Future of India,* Madras, India: Center for Policy Studies, 1993.
22 A. Nandy, S. Trivedy, S. Mayaram, and A. Yagnik, *Creating a Nationality: The Ramjanmabhumi Movement and the Fear of the Self*, Delhi, India: Oxford University Press, 1995.
23 Bacchetta, "Sacred Space and Conflict in India: The Babri Masjid Affair," p. 257.
24 D. Mukherji and A. Upreti, "Making of the Mandir," *The Week* (India), 7 June 1998.
25 See G. Sher, *Just Beyond Reach: The Israeli-Palestinian Peace Negotiations, 1999–2001*, Tel Aviv: Miskal-Yediot Acharonot Books and Chemed Books, 2001, pp. 197 and 406; M. Klein, *Breaking a Taboo: The Negotiations for a Final Agreement in Jerusalem, 1994–2001*, Jerusalem: Jerusalem Inst. for Israel Studies, 2001, pp. 61 and 108; Hassner, *War on Sacred Grounds*; M. Curtius, "Holy Site Paramount Among Obstacles to Mideast Peace; Religion: Much of the Israeli-Palestinian Dispute Comes Down to a 36-Acre Compound in Jerusalem," *Los Angeles Times*, 5 Sept. 2000.
26 Eusebius of Caesarea, *Life of Constantine*, F. Winkelman (trans.), secs 3.25–3.33, cited in F.E. Peters, *Jerusalem*, Princeton, NJ: Princeton University Press, 1985, pp. 135–36, and in J. Wilkinson, *Egeria's Travels*, Wartminster: Aris and Phillips, 1999, pp. 16–20.
27 K. Armstrong, *Jerusalem: One City, Three Faiths*, New York: Ballantine Books, 1997, p. 229, citing Eutychius, *Annals*, pp. 16–17; Fowden, "Sharing Holy Places," at p. 140.
28 For Gordon's justification of this site as the location of the crucifixion and resurrection, *see* C. George Gordon, "The Journals of Major-Gen. C.G. Gordon, C.B., at Kartoum," ed. A. Egmont Hake, New York: Negro Universities Press, 1969; John Pollock, *Gordon: The Man Behind the Legend,* London: Constable, 1993; W.H. Gordon, *Events in the Life of Charles George Gordon from Its Beginning to Its End*, London: Kegan Paul, Trench, 1886.

9 Contest or cohabitation in shared holy places?
The Cave of the Patriarchs and Samuel's Tomb

Yitzhak Reiter

Introduction

A visitor to Samuel's Tomb (Hebrew: *Kever Shmuel HaNavi*; Arabic: *Nabi Samwil*) today would be impressed by the peaceful cohabitation in a holy site where Jews and Muslims conduct their prayers simultaneously. The situation in this particular site is extraordinary: this is the only place in the world where a functioning synagogue operates underneath an active mosque, and an open ventilation shaft connects the mosque floor with the Jewish prayer room ceiling in such a way that from the middle of the mosque one can observe the Jews praying below. The mosque is administered by a local imam who is subject to the *waqf* authorities and the Palestinian Authority. The Jewish prayer room is controlled by Israel's IDF Civil Administration of the West Bank as a national park, containing also an archaeological site and nature reserve. Given its location—the highest place overlooking Jerusalem from its outskirts (908 meters above sea level), and the political situation—amidst the Palestinian–Israeli strife over territory and sovereignty, and in view of the record of friction and violence in two other major sacred places where Jews and Muslims conjunct—the Temple Mount/Al-Haram al-Sharif and the Cave of the Patriarchs/Al-Haram al-Ibrahimi—Samuel's Tomb looks like an oasis amid the desert.

At the Cave of the Patriarchs in Hebron, where Muslims and Jews have also shared the sacred site since June 1967, the record of violent clashes peaked with a massacre carried out by a Jewish extremist settler from nearby Kiryat Arba during Muslim prayers in 1994. How can we explain the different reality of these two holy sites, venerated simultaneously by adherents of the two religions who also belong to two peoples embroiled in an intense and ongoing conflict? Why is it that only a strong military regime can guarantee peace and order at the Hebron site, while at the Samuel's Tomb a situation of relative coexistence prevails between Jewish and Muslim worshipers?

In order to address these questions, let me first present the broader context of shared sacred places in Palestine. For adherents of the three great monotheistic religions, Palestine is a holy land. Many sites in this land are associated with important figures in the faith and Holy Scriptures of Jews, Christians, and Muslims.[1] The Cave of the Patriarchs in Hebron is a good example of a place that all three religions see as a holy site of "their" patriarchs, but today only Muslims and Jews worship there and claim sovereignty over the site. The Bible mentions it as the burial plot that Abraham purchased from Ephron the Hittite for his wife Sarah (Genesis 23) for 400 shekels. Jews believe, as mentioned in the Bible, that the three great Patriarchs and their wives are buried there (Genesis 49:27; one tradition also includes Adam and Eve). The Patriarchs are also mentioned many times in the New Testament, and the Byzantines and Crusaders built a church above the cave. Later on Muslims, who view the Patriarchs as "primordial" Muslims, destroyed the church and erected a mosque over the cave. The Cave of the Patriarchs is only one remnant of a syncretic medieval culture of numerous cults which inhabited Palestine to venerate the tombs of saints and turn them into popular prayer rooms and buildings.[2] As the history of the Holy Land shows, an interesting state of coexistence was maintained during the Middle Ages at the tombs of saints in the Galilee; Muslims, and Jews visited the sites and performed similar rituals at them, without interference from the other group. Most of the sacred sites in the Galilee (more than sixty tombs of saints) were maintained by Muslims, though Jews took an active part in the rituals. Likewise, Muslims worshiped and performed rituals at sites maintained by Jews. In some cases, adherents of the two religions held joint ceremonies. A local subculture developed in the Galilee founded on the same traditions and textual sources and shared by all the settlements and religious communities.

There are living examples of a phenomenon from the past in which Jewish and Muslim worship prevailed in dozens of saints' tombs in the Galilee and elsewhere.[3] Today there are at least seven active holy sites in which both Muslims and Jews (and in some cases Christians as well) share a common belief or ritual. In some of these sites they worship simultaneously, while at others, only one group worships while the other is excluded due to the current security and political circumstances. In such cases the barred party claims that if the situation were different its followers would hurry to venerate and worship at the place.

The Temple Mount/Al-Haram al-Sharif is paramount among these holy sites. Muslims worship on the Mount/Haram, while Jews worship at its outer Western Wall. Its centrality in the religious belief of the two communities turned this site into a bone of contention and a place of violent struggle as well as the source for holy war.[4] Rachel's Tomb at the outskirts of Bethlehem and Joseph's Tomb in Nablus are examples of sites that are holy to both Jews and Muslims (although are more central places in the Jewish tradition), but due to political circumstances Muslims are barred from Rachel's Tomb and Jews today have no free access to Joseph's Tomb. A different case is that of David's Tomb on Jerusalem's Mount Zion. This place is holy for Jews and Muslims as well as for Christians, who identify it as the Coenaculum (Cenacle), the room of the Last Supper. In 1948 the place was under exclusively Jewish control but was accessible to all, and each group had its own room and prayer space. Another interesting site is a tomb cave on the Mount of Olives in Jerusalem which Jews identify as the burial place of Chulda the Prophetess, Muslims identify as the grave of Rabi'a al-'Adawiyya and Christians as Saint Pelagia. Inside the cave is a Muslim prayer niche (*mihrab*) close to a carved place in the floor which Jews believe signifies Chulda'a grave. The site is controlled by Muslims, who since 1967 have allowed Jews (and others) to visit and pray there. Perhaps the most interesting place is Elijah's Cave, located at the western slope of the Carmel Mountains in today's Bat Galim neighborhood of Haifa. This place has been venerated since medieval times by Jews, Christians, Muslims, and Druze. Until 1948 it was administered by the Muslim *waqf*, and since the founding of the State of Israel it has been under Jewish control. Nevertheless, today people of the other three religions venerate it on a sporadic and personal level.[5] While it is true that Muslims lost their status in this place, they are not prevented from venerating it.

Returning to the theme of this study, what are the conditions which make peaceful cohabitation between Jewish and Muslim worshipers in one place possible? What makes the situation in Samuel's Tomb and Elijah's Cave different from the Temple Mount in Jerusalem? Can two communities of different religious denominations coexist in a holy site sanctified by both? Anti-religious rivalry and competition have generated hatred, hostility, and rejection of the Other. At the same time, we have seen that in certain historical periods complex political situations have engendered mechanisms of equilibrium resulting in a *modus vivendi* among believers from different religions.[6]

In the context of the struggle over the Holy Land of Palestine/Eretz Israel, holy places are symbols of religious, cultural, and national identity that are harnessed towards the political strife. Therefore, genuine coexistence between the two communities is almost impossible as long as there is no solution to the national problem. Samuel's Tomb and the Cave of the Patriarchs are two outstanding important remains of an historical legacy of places where Jews and Muslims practice their worship side by side. In this study I compare the political reality in the two tombs. Samuel's Tomb symbolizes coexistence and the Cave of the Patriarchs symbolizes mutual hostility between Jews and Muslims.

Are holy sites indivisible?

Based on the record of inter-religious clashes in holy places, Ron Hassner argues that "sacred places are coherent monolithic spaces that cannot be subdivided, they have clearly defined and inflexible boundaries, and they are unique sites for which no material or spiritual substitute is available."[7] His concept of the indivisibility of holy places maintains that because disputes about sacred space involve religious ideals, divine presence, absolute and transcendent values, there is no possibility for compromise. In this regard, a holy site is like a "good," whose value is destroyed if it is divided. At times, division has been imposed by a third party but, as Hassner put it, if this

Contest or cohabitation in shared holy places? 161

happens each party reserves the right to renew the struggle whenever it perceives shifts in the underlying balance of power that sustain the fragile division of space.[8]

In his article in this volume, Hassner adds that "sacred sites provide access, legitimacy, meaning and a sense of community. Inevitably, those same reasons lead religious groups into conflict with competitors who wish to implement conflicting rules regarding access, compete for rightful title, provoke their rival and target its population." He concludes that conflicts between two religious groups over a particular holy place cannot be managed or solved, and that in the long run only separation between the parties in two separate places can avoid violent clashes between them. He also argues that the peaceful situation in shared holy places, such as in Elijah's Cave and Samuel's Tomb, exist only because they are marginal "folk" places rather than official synagogue or mosque sites. Unlike Hassner, I believe that although complete separation might be an ideal situation, its price is too high for at least one of the two religious groups involved, which would have to conduct its rituals in a substitute location and not at the site believed to be sacred. In view of this, one should more carefully examine the details and records of such cases. Through an analysis of the details of two such sites, I attempt here to discover the basic generators of peaceful coexistence versus testified and violent clashes.

My comparison is based on the following research assumption: there is a direct relationship between the political significance of a holy site for each of the two conflicting religious-political communities and the reality between coexistence and hostile and violent manifestations. The political significance of a holy place is influenced by four main parameters which I use in my comparison between the two holy sites under review in this essay: the site's centrality in the religious belief; the site's surrounding human environment and the significance of the holy site for the local residents; the record of sovereignty, control, and administration of the place.

The holy sites' structure and location

The two holy sites considered in this study have a record of being venerated by adherents of the three monotheistic religions: Jews, Christians, and Muslims. Since the post-Crusader period, these sites saw simultaneous worship by Jews and Muslims, with the exception of the period of Jordanian rule in the West Bank, between 1948–67, when Jews had no access to these sites. Samuel's Tomb is situated four kilometers northwest of the Old City of Jerusalem (today, a few hundred meters from the municipal boundaries), overlooking Jerusalem at an altitude of 908 meters above sea level. At the center of the site, in the highest place, a very large church was built during the Crusader period that eventually was turned into a mosque and a Jewish place of worship in the cave underneath. In the center of the mosque is a wooden monument that marks the burial place of the prophet Samuel, which is in the tomb cave below. Near this monument is a round opening of 50 cm. linking the hall with the cave below, from which it is possible to watch the Jews praying in what was the "cave" and now is a synagogue.[9] The 60 square meter cave has an arched ceiling, and in the middle there is a huge gravestone separating the hall into a men's section and a women's section for Jews who come to pray at the tomb.

Jews and Muslims enter the building from the same entrance, and although there is a separate door to serve the Jews, they do not need it. When the Jews enter the main entrance they see in front of them the mosque door. If they arrive prior to the Muslim public prayer, they will hear the *adhan*—the broadcast of the Muslim call to prayer from a loudspeaker that the imam places near the main entrance (and removes directly after the broadcast).

Unlike the situation with the Cave of the Patriarchs in Hebron, Samuel's Tomb is not located in a high density populated area. Only some 200 Palestinians live in the village of Nabi Samwil. Most of the Muslim worshipers are bussed from Jerusalem, particularly on Fridays. Jews do not live near the place itself. Until recently there was no public bus route leading to it, and most Jewish visitors had to use either a private car or taxi, or to walk about one kilometer from Jerusalem's Ramot neighborhood. Today, they can use a public bus.

The Cave of the Patriarchs, however, is located in the city of Hebron, which is populated mostly by Palestinian Muslims and by a minority of Jews. A few hundred of them live in the Old City, but most Jews reside in nearby Kiryat Arba. Since 1967 Hebron has witnessed a series of clashes between extremist Jewish settlers and local Palestinians. The struggle between the two parties involves the city in general and not only the sacred site. Today, Hebron's central holy site is overcrowded with both Jewish and Muslim worshipers.

The current structure over the Cave of the Patriarchs is a Muslim mosque that was built on the remains of a Crusader church. The rectangular stone enclosure is divided into two sections by a wall running between the northwestern section, which includes four cenotaphs (Abraham, Sarah, Jacob, and Leah) each housed in a separate octagonal room, and the southeastern smaller section which functions as a mosque and contains the two cenotaphs of Isaac and Rebecca, and a *mihrab*. The caves under the enclosure are not accessible. Entering from the western entrance, one faces a small door where the *muezzin* makes his call to prayer. On the right hand side is a large corridor; on its western side is what Muslims consider to be the tomb of Joseph (Yusefiyya) and what some Jews regard as the tomb of Esau, which is now closed but which contains a few Korans. On the left side one exits to the open courtyard, which combines the current Jewish prayer halls of Abraham and Jacob. The Abraham hall mostly serves Jewish women worshipers. The Jewish and Muslim sections are separated by a double iron door guarded by Israeli soldiers. On the eastern side of the structure there is an adjacent mosque called the Jawliya Mosque.

Whereas Samuel's tomb is located outside the city of Jerusalem near the ancient route that led from the coastal plain to Jerusalem via Beit Horon (today: Route 443), and only about twenty Muslim families live near the site, the Cave of the Patriarchs is situated in the urban center of Hebron. The most documented event took place during the 1929 Palestinian riots against the background of the Western Wall affair, when 67 Jews were massacred by Palestinians in this city. After 1967 Hebron became a target of Jewish settlers who followed their theological vision of returning to the biblical places as part of a messianic concept. The Jewish settlement movement caused a highly charged situation in Hebron, which became a flashpoint in the Israeli–Palestinian conflict over the land. Thus, the conflict between the city's Arab inhabitants and the Israeli settlers is being reflected in the Jewish–Muslim relationship over the site. Hebron's central holy site is overcrowded by both Jewish and Muslim worshipers, whereas the Samuel's Tomb sees Jews in large numbers (hundreds a day and thousands during special events) and only about a hundred Muslim worshipers (twenty of them village residents), most of them bused by the *waqf* from Jerusalem to attend Friday Muslim services. Overall then, the signs and human presence in and around the site attest to Jewish dominance. The Muslim presence is felt mainly on the Friday day of public prayer, though also via the name of the adjacent Arab village and houses, and in the form of the modest signs in Arabic placed at the entrance to the structure and to the mosque.

The holy site's centrality for religious adherents

Unlike the case of the Temple Mount/Al-Haram al-Sharif in Jerusalem, where Muslims and Jews have different religious and historical narratives of the place, in the cases of Samuel's Tomb and the Cave of the Patriarchs, Jews and Muslims share the same biblical figures and almost the same narrative. The Hebron site became over the course of time one of the central sites of worship for Jews, and is also an important place for Muslims. Samuel's Tomb, however, is of lesser importance—yet is still more important for Jews than other popular saints' tombs (perhaps equivalent in its importance to Rachel's Tomb).

Samuel (*Shmuel* in Hebrew) is an important figure in Judaism, second to Moses although not as central as the Patriarchs. He was the last head of the Israelite tribes in the generation of "the Judges." He was also the only judge who became the leader of all the tribes, leading them to a crushing victory over the Philistines who had previously defeated and enslaved the Israelites.[10]

Samuel was raised in the temple at Shiloh after the death of the priest Eli, who was considered the spiritual leader of the Israelite tribes. Samuel was a prophet who also wrought miracles, such as causing rain to fall in the harvest period. Later generations likened him to Moses and Aaron ("Moses and Aaron among His priests, Samuel among those who call on His name." Psalms 99:6). He was active mainly in Shiloh and Mitzpah, and was buried at Rama.

Samuel's image is more related to popular benediction. His biblical image renders him a suitable figure for popular veneration. Like Moses, John the

Baptist, and other prophets, his birth was bound up with a miracle. From his conception he was dedicated to perform the Lord's work, in the wake of a vow made by his mother, Hannah, who had been barren. Beginning in the thirteenth century, Jewish worship at *Nabi Samwil* even overrode Jewish worship in Jerusalem, which became of secondary importance for a short period, and the main Jewish ceremony in the Land of Israel was the pilgrimage to Rama, namely *Nabi Samwil*.[11] (A possible explanation for this is Crusader persecution of the Jews in Jerusalem.)

Excavations carried out at the site in recent years reveal the existence of a settlement dating from the eleventh century BCE. It is not known whether the site was inhabited in earlier periods. The first sources that associate the site with Samuel's Tomb date from the thirteenth century. Twelfth-century Jewish travelers, for their part, drew no connection between Samuel and *Nabi Samwil*. Indeed Benjamin of Tudela (who visited Jerusalem in 1173) took issue with the Christian tradition, writing that Samuel's Tomb was in Ramla (which the Crusaders confused with Rama), and that the Crusaders moved it to *Nabi Samwil*. "There the Crusaders built a large platform [church] named for Samuel of Shiloh."[12] Beginning from the Crusader period, the site became identified with the tomb of the prophet Samuel. In other words, it was no longer only a place of worship in his honor but also his burial place, which the Crusaders called St. Samuel.

The archaeologists Magen and Dadon believe that the site's sanctity for the Jews in the Second Temple period was adopted by the Byzantine Christians, who also venerated Samuel.[13] Pottery fragments from the Umayyad and Abbasid periods, discovered in the *Nabi Samwil* excavations in the 1990s, mention the name "*Dayr Samwil*."[14] The word "*dayr*" means a Christian monastery; hence we learn that the site bore the name of a monastery that apparently dated from the Byzantine period.

The Crusaders, who considered themselves the successors of the biblical Israelites, identified a large number of Scriptural sites and created their own sacred geography. It was only natural that a biblical connection would be found for a key stop on their way to Jerusalem, and so during the Crusader period *Nabi Samwil* acquired the centrality that was passed down to succeeding generations. It was from *Nabi Samwil*, on the morning of 7 June 1099, in the First Crusade, that the legions of Crusaders first saw Jerusalem and its fortifications after an arduous three-year trek. Richard the Lionheart, who led the Third Crusade, looked down on Jerusalem from this site, but was unable to conquer it from Saladin. The Crusaders "rediscovered" the site and re-sanctified it as a place of worship. It may well have been then that they named the site Mountjoy, afterwards founding a Crusader order there with the same name.

Islam, for its part, accepts and recognizes all prophets and messengers of God who preceded Muhammad—called "the Seal of the Prophets." As a result, all figures that are central to Judaism are also holy in Islam. Samuel's image as recorded in "the narratives of the prophets" (*qisas al-anbiya'*) and enshrined in popular Islamic consciousness, is positive and is very similar to the biblical account.[15] However, his standing in Judaism is much higher than in Islam.

The situation is different regarding the Patriarchs. Jews as well as Muslims view Abraham as the founding figure of their monotheistic faith. According to the Bible, the Lord first appeared to Abraham in Hebron, where he revealed to him his promise that he and his descendants would inherit the land from the Nile to the Euphrates.[16] The Lord ordered Abraham regarding circumcision, and he and his family were circumcised there (Genesis 17). The Cave of the Patriarchs is identified as the plot Abraham purchased from Ephron the Hittite in order to bury his wife Sarah. Hebron was a central city in Palestine and known as the place where King David was anointed and ruled before he chose Jerusalem as his capital. According to Jewish tradition, Jews have sanctified and worshiped in this site from biblical times, with clear historical evidence that this has been the case from the first century CE. The structural basis of the Patriarchs' compound is built with the same type of stones as the Western Wall in Jerusalem, and is thus considered to be Herodian. The Jewish traveler Benjamin of Tudela reported in 1170 that Jews used to bring the bones of their relatives to be buried in the cave next to the graves of the Patriarchs. In his visit to the place he saw barrels full of such bones.

The importance of the site for Christians is also linked to Abraham, who is mentioned 72 times in the New Testament and to Isaac, whose suffering is symbolically related to that of Christ.[17] The Byzantines sanctified the Abrahamic site. They built a church called St. Abrahamius with two entrances, one of which was to give access to Jews. In 570 an Italian priest reported that the Jews used light frankincense and candles.[18] From the thirteenth century, Jews were barred from the place by an order of the Mamluk Sultan Baybars. During the Mamluk period some 20 Jewish families resided in Hebron.

In Islam, Abraham is also regarded as the fundamental ancestor of the monotheistic belief (*hanif*), and as such—the first primordial Muslim. He is known as the Friend of God—al-Khalil—the Arabic name of Hebron. Abraham is also believed to have found the *Ka'ba* in Mecca—the most holy site for Muslims. The Cave of the Patriarchs is named in Arabic after Abraham— al-Haram al-Ibrahimi. A large Muslim endowment (*waqf*) was dedicated to the charity of feeding the poor and the pilgrims,[19] and the trust foundation is attributed to the prophet who endowed it (a few years before Palestine was conquered by Umar) to one of his companions—Tamim al-Dari, in return for his tribe's support of the prophet's camp.[20] For centuries, following Abraham's tradition of hosting, the Tamimi endowment would provide pilgrims with banquet meals.

The Arab geographer Al-Muqaddasi (d. 985) narrated the Muslim tradition according which the structure over the cave was built by the demon, a traditional way of explaining that huge stones such as this perhaps could not be brought by human creatures. The Persian traveler Naser-i-Khosro reported in

1047 CE that he visited the mosque and the surrounding pilgrim dormitories and benefited from the daily meal of lentils and olive oil which the local (Tamimi) *waqf* used to serve, according to him, even for 5,000 pilgrims a day at particular times. The Arab chronicler Mujir al-Din reported in 1496 that the Jawliya Mosque was built by a Mamluk high-ranking officer in 1318. The Jewish Ovadia of Bartinura reported in 1495 that the site was built up with a mosque and that the Muslims respect the site as a sacred place. The cave itself was inaccessible for both Muslims and Jews, and the Muslims used to lower candles into the cave, while the Jews were permitted to pray outside against a small window which they believe is located opposite Abraham's grave, where he himself was praying. During the Mamluk and Ottoman periods, the religious character of the city of Hebron encouraged the forming of Islamic endowments (*awqaf*) around the holy site. Many Hebron Muslim women were named after Sarah, Rebecca, Leah, and Rachel. Unlike Samuel's Tomb, which belongs to a long tradition of popular saint tombs despite the mosque that operated there, the Hebron sacred site was a regular mosque and not a ritual center such as other popular saints' tombs.[21]

In sum, it is very clear that in terms of its religious significance, the Cave of the Patriarchs is a more pivotal site for both Jews and Muslims than Samuel's Tomb. Moreover, the city of Hebron, both throughout history as well as today has strong religious and political import, which explains why Jews in post-Crusader times conducted pilgrimages to the site as a key holy place after the Temple Mount. For Jews, Samuel's Tomb has more importance than it does for Muslims because of Samuel's religious and even political standing, whereas for Muslims he is one more ancient "prophet."

Continuity and change: historical accounts of control and veneration

Nabi Samwil

With the end of the Crusader period, rituals of Jewish and Muslim worship emerged at *Nabi Samwil*.[22] Jewish worship was not possible there until the end of the Crusader period because of the Crusader church that stood at the site. However, in the thirteenth century, Jewish worship at *Nabi Samwil* began to take precedence over prayer in Jerusalem, which took on secondary importance. The major Jewish ceremony at the time in the Land of Israel became the pilgrimage to Rama, namely *Nabi Samwil*.[23] The Jews' popular name for the site was *Sidi Shmuel*, or *Sayyiduna Shmuel*—"our master Shmuel."[24] Ritual ceremonies performed at *Nabi Samwil* symbolically expressed the biblical narrative and literary and mythical images of Samuel that were extrapolated from his life story and filtered by popular interpretation. They included an oath in the name of "our master Shmuel," the vow of the oil and candle-lighting, and giving alms to a charitable trust named for the prophet Samuel. Compilations of the prayers that were customarily recited next to the tomb were made in medieval times.[25] These special prayers were recited by local Jewish venerators, and the atmosphere assumed an ecstatic character enhanced by the consumption of wine.[26] Another custom involved tying pieces of cloth on a tree next to the tomb in what was considered a type of magical act of invoking healing properties.[27] According to medieval sources, Jewish rituals were held side by side with Muslim practices during this period. Two thirteenth-century sources relate that a Muslim structure existed in front of Samuel's tomb.[28] A student of Nachmanides or the Ramban (fifteenth century) relates that he found at the site "a very handsome structure and in front of the structure an Islamic house of worship."[29] However, the head of the Franciscan monastery on Mount Zion writes in 1429 about a chapel of St. Samuel near Jerusalem which was devoted to Jewish worship.[30] Another fifteenth-century source also mentions the Jewish rituals. One tradition has it that the holy Ari—Rabbi Isaac Luria, the greatest of the Safed kabbalists—confirmed the site of Samuel's Tomb and the graves of his parents. Rabbi Meshulam from Valtira, who visited the Holy Land in 1481, says that on the 28th day of the Hebrew month of Iyar, according to tradition believed to be the day Samuel died, more than a thousand Jews from Egypt, Syria, and Babylon would gather at the tomb to pray. The pilgrimage, which took place in the months of Nisan and Iyar, between Passover and Shavuot, was called *ziara* (in Arabic: pilgrimage, seasonal visit to a saint's tomb) by the Jews.[31] Rabbi Ovadia from Bartinura, who passed through the Holy Land in 1489, notes that many Jews visited the tomb and miracles were thought to have occurred at the site. Another traveler, Rabbi Moshe Basula from Pissaro, Italy, who was in the Holy Land between 1521–23, says that the Jews had a special prayer site at which they lit candles, and also mentions a spring.[32] In the sixteenth century, a Jewish Charitable Trust (*hekdesh*) of Our Master Samuel already existed at *Nabi Samwil*. Jewish pilgrims brought candles and oil to light in the cave and donated alms to the institution's trustee. According to the kabbalists, because Samuel led an austere life he ascended to higher realms when he left this world, and so pilgrims fulfilled the commandment to give donations in his honor.[33] The trust financed the site's maintenance and also gave charity to the poor in Jerusalem and to *kollel* students. A caretaker (*shamash*) at the site lit candles every Monday and Thursday.

Beginning in the fifteenth century we already see testimony concerning quarrels between Jews and Muslims over the site's maintenance and the right to worship there.[34] Testimonies of this nature multiplied during the Ottoman period.[35] Occasionally, friction between the two groups led local Muslim officials to bar the Jews from the site for a time or to make them pay an entry fee. Leaders of the Jewish community in Jerusalem would then complain to the Sultan, who would order the governor and the Qadi of Jerusalem to restore the *status quo ante*. For example, a document dating from 1550 describes a complaint lodged by a Muslim from the nearby village of Beit Iksa, according to which the Jews who came to "*maqam al-sayyid Shmu'il*" did not take proper care of their pack-animals and their belongings.[36] Another document cites an order sent to Jerusalem by the Sultan forbidding the authorities to prevent Jews from carrying out a *ziara* (pilgrimage) to the Tomb of the Prophet Samuel whenever they wished.[37] And yet another interesting document, dated 1554, makes reference to a petition that the Jewish community of Jerusalem sent to Istanbul complaining that the Jews had customarily made pilgrimages to an ancient synagogue called "*Sid Nabi Allah Samwil*" but were forbidden to visit the site after it became a mosque. The Sultan ordered the Qadi and the governor of Jerusalem to investigate the complaint and, if it was valid, to stop bothering the Jews on this matter.[38]

The Portuguese traveler de Aveiro wrote in 1560 that the site was maintained by Jews and that all the nations usually referred to it as "Santo Samuel."[39] Some time later, the site was taken away from the Jews and non-Muslim visitors had to pay an entry fee. The Jews then boycotted the site in order to deprive the Muslims of such revenues.[40] A report dated 1590 relates that after appeals by the Jews, they were again given access to the tomb in return for payment.[41]

Testimonies from the seventeenth and eighteenth centuries also describe Jewish and Muslim worship at *Nabi Samwil*, together with continuing friction between the two communities. Vilnay relates that the Muslims showed respect for the Jews by also lighting candles and by serving as guards at the tombs and receiving payment from the Jews by authorization of the governor.[42] According to another account, however, the Mufti of Jerusalem, Sheikh Muhammad al-Khalili, turned the site into a mosque and barred the Jews from entering Samuel's Tomb.[43] The Ottomans endowed (as *waqf*) cultivated lands for the upkeep and renovation of the site.[44] An eighteenth-century report states that the Qadi ordered money to be collected from every Jew wishing to enter the cave and that the president of the Sephardi community in Jerusalem was arrested at his order for leading a group of Jews to the Samuel's Tomb without his authorization.[45]

The Cave of the Patriarchs

There is a record of the Cave of the Patriarchs in Hebron changing hands, i.e., sovereign powers, between Jews, Christians, and Muslims since antiquity. The structure over the cave was turned into a mosque during the long period of Muslim control, and after the thirteenth century Jews were allowed to pray only outside the building against an open window looking into the cave. The claims of both Jews and Muslims for rights in the place encapsulate the entire debate over Palestine territory. Muslims claim that they have controlled the site since the seventh century (with an interval of Crusader rule), while Jews claim to be the originators of the site as a burial cave as is textualized in the Bible (Genesis 23; 49:27). Since the Cave of the Patriarchs functioned as a mosque during the period of Islamic rule in Palestine, it remained so under the British Mandate and Jordanian rule. Until the end of the British Mandate in Palestine, Jews were only allowed to pray at the outer wall against the cave—known as the seventh step of the main entrance stairs.

The political drive: challenging sovereignty since 1967

The history of the two holy sites under review are illustrative of the whole conflict and debate over Palestine and its holy sites—between Jewish Israelis who claim to be the heirs of the ancient biblical Hebrews or Arab (Muslim and Christian) Palestinians who claim a continuous presence at least from the Islamic conquest of Palestine in 636 CE. The following is an account of the political events related to these sites since 1967.

Nabi Samwil

During the thirty years of British rule in Palestine, Jews and Muslims had access to the site, which was under *waqf* ownership and sovereignty. Nuwayhid, however, narrates that Jews were prevented from worship at the site at that time.[46] Since the British Mandate was committed to preserve the Status Quo, i.e., the existing rights at holy places, the Jews did not challenge the sovereign powers of the Muslims as they attempted to do at the Western Wall. During the nineteen years of Jordanian rule of the West Bank, Jews had no access to *Nabi Samwil*.

Jewish worship at *Nabi Samwil* was gradually renewed after 1967 by a group of Bratslav Hassidim. Under the auspices of the Israeli IDF Civil Administration, which is in charge of the area as part of the occupied West Bank, the Jewish group now enjoys freedom of access and worship at the site. At the same time, the Muslim *waqf* still controls the mosque, constituting the entire building excluding the cave, which was gradually turned into a Jewish prayer room, or synagogue. There is a special pilgrimage to the site on Lag Ba'Omer and a *hilula* on the 28th day of Iyar, the traditional date of Samuel's death according to Jewish tradition. In 1971 Israel demolished Arab evacuated houses built on the archaeological remains adjacent to the Tomb structure. The increase in the number of Jewish visitors to the site was particularly striking in the 1990s, following improvements to the access road and the posting of directional signs in Hebrew reading "Tomb of the Prophet Samuel" in place of the previous signs, which used the Arabic name *Nabi Samwil* only. The site's location and the spectacular view it affords also draw many visitors. One Jewish group of Sephardi Jews affiliated with the Shas political party even established a *kollel* in a mobile trailer nearby, and recently they also opened a souvenir shop and kiosk. By so doing they are competing with the original kiosk which is owned by the local Muslims—the family of the imam.

The growing number of Jewish worshipers at the site was also driven by two other developments: the increase of the popular ritual of visiting tombs of saints among Jews in Israel generally, and the political situation which endorsed Jewish religious and nationalist groups to show their presence and to claim possession over popular holy sites, in the belief that their actual veneration would safeguard the place from Israel's concessions to the

Palestinians. The case of Rachel's Tomb near Bethlehem is a good example how these groups succeeded in persuading the Israeli authorities to keep this site outside the territory handed over to the Palestinians following the Oslo Accords. Recently, Israel constructed a special fortified building protected by military forces and a long winding security wall to ensure Jewish control, access and worship.[47] As for the Tomb of Samuel, Palestinians, too, made an effort to increase their presence there and to ensure the continuation of *waqf* authority funds and the bussing of Muslims from Jerusalem to take part in the Friday public prayers.

Since 1967, the political situation between Jews and Muslims who revere the site has been calm and peaceful. Tensions between Jews and Muslims over the control of Samuel's Tomb emerged only after the Baruch Goldstein massacre of 29 Muslims in the Abrahamic site of Hebron in February 1994. One incident only was recorded in that same year, when a Jewish group tried to take control of the structure and remove the Arabic signs (including a sign at the entrance stating that the site was restored by the Supreme Muslim Council during the Mandate period and another stating that the place belongs to the Muslim *waqf*). They also tried to sabotage the loudspeaker system through which Muslims are called to prayer and they affixed a *mezuzah* to the portal of the structure. A fight broke out in which a Muslim youngster (the great-grandson of the *waqf* guard) and a *kollel* student were hurt. After this clash, the IDF Civil Administration took over the entire *Nabi Samwil* site and restored order and the *status quo ante*. The site was entirely fenced to prevent unnecessary friction between Jews and Muslims and to ensure that the sanctity of the place was not violated, particularly on sensitive dates of mass worship. A permanent detail of soldiers was posted by the entrance and metal detectors were used to check all visitors. On Fridays, during the Muslim prayer service, the soldiers closed the entrance of the structure to Jews, who could, however, enter the burial chamber via an external entrance opened especially for this purpose. In 2004 the military guard and fence was removed following a record of coexistence and tranquil relations between the local Muslims and Jewish worshipers.

Nevertheless, peaceful coexistence does not mean that the two parties accept the right or acknowledge the affiliation of the other. Many Jewish visitors that I questioned at the site over the years failed to know or to acknowledge the Muslim attachment to the place. Local Muslims I spoke with were more knowledgeable about the Jewish importance of the place but some of them also related the renewed Jewish veneration after 1967 to political motivations. For example, a seminar paper written by a high-school student from *Nabi Samwil* village emphasizes that there is no evidence that a synagogue existed at the site. "Jews used to pray there, but as part of a general phenomenon, as at other saints' tombs," he wrote. The paper claims that the recent excavations conducted by the Jews destroyed findings from Islamic periods and that nothing was found to indicate a Jewish presence.[48]

The Cave of the Patriarchs

After 1967, the new order in the Cave of the Patriarchs as determined by the then Israeli Defense Minister Moshe Dayan was a spatial and time division between Jews and Muslims. Dayan narrated in his autobiography that after Israel's occupation of the West Bank he visited the site and searched for an arrangement that would give the Jews access to the Patriarchs' caves (as opposed to organized public prayer) without disturbing Muslim worship. First he investigated whether the underground burial cave could encompass Jewish prayers (as in the case of *Nabi Samwil*), and by so doing leave the mosque building untouched by Jews. When this was found to be impossible he opted for a time-and-space-sharing arrangement.[49] Dayan discovered that the Muslims conduct their daily prayer in the Isaac Hall, so he assigned the rest of the building for Jewish worship. He proposed a time and space separation which was agreed upon on 1 August 1967 between the Israeli officials and the Muslim senior *waqf* clerics and the Palestinian Mayor of Hebron—Muhammad 'Ali al-Ja'bari. The signed agreement also stipulated the rules of behavior (modest clothing, no smoking, no alcohol, no sale of candles or drinks). The reality, however, proved to be stronger than the agreement. The growing Jewish veneration of and renewed settlement in Hebron resulted in elevating the Jewish ritual there to synagogue level, thus creating a de facto situation of more space and time for the Jewish prayers—beyond the control of Dayan as Minister of Defense and the military commanders.[50] The Jewish settlers took over the Jacob and Abraham Halls and the open courtyard joining them, which was covered by a cloth for convenience. The Muslim prayer takes place in the Isaac Hall, which since 1979 was shared by Jewish (one-third) and Muslim (two-thirds) worshipers, who were separated by iron dividers. Dayan admitted that he did not want the cave structure to turn into a synagogue, but once it was established without his knowledge, he could do nothing to abolish it.[51] Ironically, Dayan opined that sovereignty on the West Bank holy sites should be Muslim. However, he himself and the Israeli authorities behaved as sovereigns in imposing the new practices that gave the Jews near parity in the site.[52]

The post-1967 situation imposed by Israel is that the Muslim *waqf* holds formal sovereignty over the place, but actual power is vested in the Israeli army. The *waqf* employs three dozen guards working in three shifts and is responsible for cleaning, renovation of the outer structure, keys, and equipment. The Israeli army is responsible for security and public order. Despite attempts to create a peaceful shared space in Hebron, it has been the site of tension and occasional violent outbreaks.

The Muslim public in Hebron viewed the post-June 1967 situation with tremendous hostility. Early in October 1968, a hand grenade exploded at the entrance for Jews, injuring 43 Jewish worshipers.[53] Other incidents took place from time to time. In 1976 Jews and Muslim worshipers defiled the others' Korans, Torahs, and other ritual items.[54] Muslims continuously complained of the Jews' desecration of the site and the expansion of their actual use of the compound. Moreover, in their eyes the Jewish occupation authorities effectively turned a mosque into a synagogue and a military base.[55] They also complained that "once the Jews have got a finger [i.e. the August 1967 agreement]—they demand the whole hand."[56]

The most severe violence at the site was the act of a Jewish extremist, who represented a radical Jewish group in Hebron and nearby Qiryat Arba that believes that the site and the city of Hebron should be Jewish only. On 25 February 1994, during the Muslim Ramadan Friday public prayer (and the Jewish Purim holiday) Baruch Goldstein, a local physician and member of the extremist Kahane (Kach) movement, donned his IDF uniform and weapon, massacring 29 Muslim worshipers and injuring 125 before he was killed by the Muslims on the spot. The Israeli Commission of Inquiry Regarding the Hebron Massacre[57] stated that the mix and friction between Jewish and Muslim prayers in the same place and time, the lack of separation and the privilege enjoyed by Jews to enter the site with their weapons facilitated Goldstein's attack. The commission's recommendations form the basis of the existing post-1994 arrangements: complete separation of the site between Jews and Muslims; no access with weapons; strict security control.

Today the site and surrounding area is guarded by the Israeli army, which employs a double security check of metal detectors and guards: one checkpoint is located on the routes leading to the site, and the other is situated at the two entrances to the building. The space inside the building is physically separated between Muslims and Jews, who also use separate entrances. Weapons are prohibited, with the exception of the military guards during their shift. Muslims use the large Isaac Hall and the adjacent Jawliya Mosque, while Jews pray at two smaller halls: the Abraham Hall, the Jacob Hall and the open (newly cloth-roofed) court between the two small halls. The two sections are separated by a double iron gate, preventing one group from viewing the other with one exception—the small domed room of Abraham's cenotaph, which has open windows to both the Muslim and the Jewish sections (the military authorities informed me, however, that they intend to seal the windows with bulletproof glass). The separation arrangement is not perfect. The muezzin makes his call to prayer from a room located in the Jewish section, and he is given a special escort five times a day to enter this room. Also, a *waqf* office is located in the Adam hall, and the military must make special arrangements to secure the access of *waqf* officials to this office from time to time. A Jewish *mezuzah* was affixed only at the outer entrance door, but was not permitted in the mosque building itself.

The fact that the site is shared under the post-1994 arrangement also raises questions of maintenance, which are coordinated by the Israeli military liaison and the *waqf* administrator. In order to prevent friction and to keep the post-1994 *status quo*, even the most minor work can only done after the approval of high-ranking officials on both sides. On the Israeli side, I have been told, maintenance issues must receive the personal permission of the Minister of

Defense. For this reason, even important maintenance works are often delayed, such as a recent problem of water drainage.

The need of both Jews and Muslims for a larger prayer space during holidays led to a cooperative arrangement between the Israeli military commander and the *waqf* officials, according to which the entire compound is used by each side for ten days of the year, during which the other side cannot use the compound at all. If a Jewish and a Muslim holiday fall at the same time, the two parties negotiate to find a solution: one party delays his use for a day or few hours. As an example, in 2005 the first day of the twelfth Jewish month of Elul coincided with the Muslim celebration of the Prophet Muhammad's nocturnal journey and ascension to heaven (*Al-Isra' wal-Mi'raj*). The parties agreed to divide the use of the compound during the day, a few hours for the complete use of each side. In 2006 the Muslims agreed to delay the *Isra'* celebration to the following day. In preparing the compound for the use of one community, local Jewish and Muslim officers work together to restore utilizations—such as menorah and scrolls of the other group. Prior to the use by Jews of the entire compound, the Muslim prayer rugs are rolled out and put in storage, while before the use of the entire space by the Muslims, the plastic chairs, prayer stands and Torah ark are likewise moved.

The post-1994 arrangements are not the ideal situation for either party. The Muslim administrator says that the new arrangement worsened the rights of the Muslims, since they can use the entire compound only ten days a year, whereas before February 1994 they could use it every day during special hours.[58] The Israeli military liaison reports that in some cases the Jews complain of the high volume of the Muslim call to prayer. This particular issue is constantly being negotiated between the parties.[59]

Conclusion

The Abrahamic site of Hebron is a place of tension where Jews and Muslims are in constant confrontation. This was particularly the case between 1967 and 1994. Since the post-1994 massacre of Muslim prayer-goers, the strict arrangements have successfully prevented the eruption of severe incidents between the two religious groups. It may be concluded that the sharing of a site by means of separation works only under stringent monitoring by a strong security power, such as the Israeli military in the case of the Cave of the Patriarchs, or perhaps by a third party (as was suggested by a team of the Jerusalem Institute for Israel Studies with respect to the Old City of Jerusalem).[60] True, each of the two parties reserves the right to renew the struggle whenever it perceives a shift in the balance of power, as Hassner points out. Yet, the two official sides have managed to keep order, and even to agree on a time-sharing arrangement during holidays and maintenance issues. The key to achieving this stability can be summed-up in three points: 1) strong and strict monitoring and security forces; 2) constant dialogue and coordination between the monitoring power and the administrators of the two parties; 3) careful preservation of the *status quo*. Based on the above I argue that in certain circumstances holy places can be shared/divided provided that a powerful supervisory body monitors the site (as does the IDF in Hebron at present, or possibly an international body in the future) with a strong security force in place to preempt any violation of longstanding rules.

In the context of the struggle over the Holy Land of Palestine/Eretz Israel, sacred places are symbols of religious, cultural and national identity. Therefore, compromise or official recognition of even a de facto division appears almost impossible as long as there is no solution to the national conflict. In the Cave of the Patriarchs the two parties to the conflict accommodated themselves to the post-1967 arrangement of divide-and-share by viewing the current situation as a temporary one that does not demand formal recognition. This psychological delay mechanism, as in the case of *hudna* in Islam, makes possible this divide-and-share situation of a holy place. The fact that such a division was created by a new balance of power does not mean that the parties to the dispute legitimate the other's role in the debated site. Indeed, each of the two religious faiths, which in this case also belong to two rival national communities, still maintains its belief in future exclusive control. However, the two communities over the course of time have come to recognize the strong relationship of the other party to its holy place and have learned to live with only half of its ultimate desire.

Once a situation of two religious communities sharing a sacred place has developed, even if they are engaged in a national and religious-based confrontation, they can learn to accept this shared space and defer their preferred ultimate solution of indivisible control. Notwithstanding the above, I do not argue that the same model of divide-and share should be applied to al-Haram al-Sharif/Temple Mount because these are places of supreme contestation.

In this analysis of the two case studies we have seen four parameters that affect the political situation in these shared holy places. The first is the site's religious importance to each of the two communities involved. The more important a place is perceived to be by its adherents—the more the likelihood that it will engender a situation of conflict. Samuel's Tomb is less important than the Cave of the Patriarchs. Moreover, its religious importance for Muslims is relatively marginal, not different from any other mosque. This is one explanation for why Muslims do not challenge the Jewish presence in this site.

The second parameter is political importance. Hebron as a city and the Abrahamic site are national symbols for both Jews and Muslims, and the 1929 massacre of 67 Jews exemplifies this fact. On the other hand, *Nabi Samwil* has no national importance. It is known as a sacred place and a tourist site without any political importance.

The third parameter relates to the location and human environment. Here again, Hebron, as a heavily populated city settled by Jewish nationalist groups after 1967, is more likely to see escalation than is *Nabi Samwil*, with the small Muslim community that was left after 1967 and whose building and expansion is restricted by Israeli authorities—and this is what actually occurred.

The fourth parameter has to do with continuity or change in sovereign powers and veneration. If the historical record shows continuity of control and veneration of a party, it is less likely that the other party would challenge its existing rights. However, if one party attempts to newly impose itself—the other party is most likely to struggle against the change and to use violence. Samuel's Tomb was venerated by Jews for centuries under Muslim rule during the Mamluk and Ottoman periods. Present-day Muslims acknowledged this fact after 1967 when they did not disturb the Jews from worshiping in the particular space that they used prior to 1948, and this remains so as long as the Jewish side acknowledges the right of the Muslims to control their mosque and conduct prayers without disturbances. The situation is totally different in the case of the Abrahamic site of Hebron. Before 1948, for hundreds of years Jews could only pray outside the structure. But in 1967, Israel imposed a new order of divide-and-share inside the mosque building. Local Muslims challenged the agreement signed between Dayan and Ja'bari, not to mention when this agreement was violated by the Israeli side which took over control of the site. No wonder, then, that the change of a long-existing *status quo* arrangement led to severe clashes between the two conflicting groups.

Analysis of the historical accounts in shared holy places in Palestine leads to another important conclusion: As long as religious group A accepts the sovereignty of religious group B in a particular shared sacred site, group A is more likely to be tolerated by group B and to conduct its rituals with no interference. This was the case in many places in the Galilee under Muslim rule, and as we learn from the case of *Nabi Samwil*. However, a challenge to the sovereignty of the other causes that party to opt for excluding the party that is challenging its rights. Put differently, once a party to the conflict recognizes the sovereign powers of the other party, it could experience greater recognition of its needs and practices in a shared holy site.

Notes

1 T. Canaan, *Mohammedan Saints and Sanctuaries in Palestine*, Jerusalem: Ariel, 1980; E. Reiner, "Pilgrims and Pilgrimage 1099–1517," PhD dissertation, Hebrew University of Jerusalem, 1988 [in Hebrew]; J.W. Meri, *The Cult of Saints among Muslims and Jews in Medieval Syria*, Oxford: Oxford University Press, 2002.
2 *Ibid.*
3 *See* Reiner, "Pilgrims and Pilgrimage 1099–1517."
4 On this see Y. Reiter, *From Jerusalem to Mecca and Back: The Islamic Consolidation of Jerusalem*, Jerusalem: Jerusalem Institute for Israel Studies, 2005 [in Hebrew].
5 The Christian Carmelite order arrives every 14 June to conduct their special celebration of St. Elisha ceremony. See U. Bialer, *Cross on the Star of David: The Christian World in Israel's Foreign Policy, 1948–1967*, Bloomington, Ind.: Indiana University Press, 2005, p. 178.
6 *See e.g.*, the Jaffa 1229 Peace Treaty between Al-Malik al-Afdal and Friedrich II.
7 R.E. Hassner, "To Halve and to Hold: Conflicts over Sacred Space and the Problem of Indivisibility," *Security Studies*, Summer 2003, vol.12, no. 4, p. 13.

8 *Ibid.*, p. 26.
9 Y. Magen and M. Daddon, "Nabi Samwil (Montjoie)", in G. Claudio Bottini, Leah Di Segni and L. Daniel Chrupcala (eds), *One Land – Many Cultures: Archaeological Studies in Honour of Stanislao Loffreda Ofm*, Studium Biblicum Franciscanum, Collectio Maior, vol. 41, Jerusalem: Franciscan Printing Press, 2003, pp. 123–38.
10 J. Ben-Dov, *Nabi Samuel*, Tel-Aviv: Hakibutz Hameuchad, 2006, p. 10 [in Hebrew].
11 Reiner, "Pilgrims and Pilgrimage 1099–1517," p. 250.
12 *Masa'ot Binyamin Metudela*, London: Adler 1907, p. 28 [in Hebrew]. Shmuel Hanavi Synagogue is mentioned in the year 1013 as being administered by the Karaites, but its location is unknown. See S.H. Kook "Notes on 'The History of the Synagogue on the Tomb of Shmuel HaNavi'," *Bulletin of the Israel Exploration Society*, Reader B, Jerusalem: The Israel Exploration Society, 1965, pp. 248–49. (originally vol. 6, pp. 143–44) [in Hebrew].
13 Magen and Daddon, "Nabi Samwil (Montjoie)."
14 *Ibid.*
15 Al-Tha'alibi (died 1062 CE), *Qisas al-Anbiya' al-Musamma 'Arais al-Majalis* (al-Maktaba al-Thaqafiya), p. 232 ff. [in Arabic].
16 Genesis 17:1–21.
17 Elie Shiler, *Mearat Hamachpela*, Jerusalem: Ariel, 1979, p. 93 [in Hebrew].
18 *Ibid.*, p. 97.
19 *See* al-Muqaddasi's account in M.J. Goeije, *Bibliotheca Geographorum Arabicorum*, Leiden, 1906, p. 188; G. Le Strange, *Palestine Pilgrims' Text Society*, 1896, vol. II, p. 89.
20 *Al-Iqta' wa-Awwal Iqta' fi al-Islam* [in Arabic].
21 Shiler, *Mearat Hamachpela*, p. 98.
22 Meri, *The Cult of Saints among Muslims and Jews in Medieval Syria*, pp. 240–42.
23 Reiner, "Pilgrims and Pilgrimage 1099–1517," p. 250.
24 Y. Elitzur, "The Origin of the Tradition on Nabi Samuel, *Kathedra*, Apr. 1984, vol. 31, pp. 75–89 [in Hebrew].
25 S. Asaf, *Old Prayers at Kever Shmuel Ha-Navi* (Jerusalem, n.p. 1948), pp. 71–72 [in Hebrew], quoted by Reiner, "Pilgrims and Pilgrimage 1099–1517," p. 316.
26 Reiner, "Pilgrims and Pilgrimage 1099–1517," p. 319.
27 *Ibid.*, p. 274.
28 *Ibid.*, p. 310.
29 S. Asaf, "Jerusalem," *Compilation of the Hebraic Society of the Exploration of Eretz Israel and its Antiquities in Memory of Luntz*, p. 58 [in Hebrew]; A. Shohat, "The History of the Synagogue on the Tomb of Shmuel haNavi," *Bulletin of the Israel Exploration Society*, Reader B, Jerusalem: The Israel Exploration Society, 1965, pp. 141–45, (originally vol. 6, pp. 81–86) [in Hebrew].
30 Reiner, "Pilgrims and Pilgrimage 1099–1517," at p. 310.
31 For example, in 1538, according to the registers of the Nablus Tax Checkpoint, 128 Jewish pilgrims arrived. *See* Amnon Cohen, "Damascus and Jerusalem," *Sfunot*, 1973, vol. 17, p. 98 as quoted by Reiner, "Pilgrims and Pilgrimage 1099–1517," at p. 288.
32 Magen and Daddon, "Nabi Samwil (Montjoie)."
33 Y. Gliss, *Minhagei Eretz Israel*, Jerusalem: Mossad Harav Kook 1968, p. 275, based on Rabbi Hayim ben Menashe Sithon (the Ralbah) and his book *Eretz Hayim*.
34 A. Shohat, "The History of the Synagogue on the Tomb of Shmuel haNavi."
35 *Ibid.*
36 A. Cohen, *A World Within, Jewish Life as Reflected in Muslim Court Documents from the Sijill of Jerusalem (XVIth Century)* Philadelphia, Penn.: University of Pennsylvania, Center for Judaic Studies, part I, p. 78 (Sijill 23\460).

Contest or cohabitation in shared holy places? 177

37 *Ibid.*, p. 93 (Sijill 28\220).
38 *Ibid.*, p. 98 (Sijill 29\167). A similar document from 1599, see p. 202 (Sijill 80\344a).
39 Shohat, "The History of the Synagogue on the Tomb of Shmuel haNavi."
40 *Ibid.*
41 Y. Ben Zvi, "A Jewish Settlement near the Tomb of Shmuel ha-Navi," *Yediot be-Haqirat Eretz Israel ve-'Atiqoteyha*, 1953, vol. 2, p. 254 [in Hebrew].
42 Z. Vilnay, *Holy Gravestones in Eretz Israel*, Jerusalem: Mosad ha-Rav Kook, 1963, p. 58 [in Hebrew]. In the eighteenth century Jews used to burn dresses and other precious items as sacrifices to God. See Ben Zvi, "A Jewish Settlement near the Tomb of Shmuel ha-Navi," p. 250.
43 Ben Zvi, "A Jewish Settlement near the Tomb of Shmuel ha-Navi," p. 250.
44 Shukri 'Arraf, *Tabaqat al-Anbiya' wal-Awliya' al-Salihin fi al-Ard al-Muqaddasa*, Tarshiha: Author's Edition, 1993, p. 111 [in Arabic].
45 Shohat, "The History of the Synagogue on the Tomb of Shmuel haNavi." For pictures of Nabi Samuel, *see* M. Michelson, M. Milner and Y. Salomon, *The Jewish Holy Places in the Land of Israel*, Tel Aviv, Misrad Ha-Bitachon, [Israel Ministry of Defense Press], 1996, pp. 62–65 [in Hebrew].
46 'Arraf, *Tabaqat al-Anbiya' wal-Awliya' al-Salihin fi al-Ard al-Muqaddasa*, p. 111.
47 N. Shragai, *Al Em HaDerech – The Story of Kever Rachel*, Jerusalem, Sha'arim LeHeker Yerushalayim, 2005, pp. 24–25, 31 [in Hebrew].
48 F.F. Barakat, "*Al-Nabi Samwil bayna al-ams wal-yawm wal-tahdid al-Isra'ili lil-mawaqi' al-athariyya wal-diniyya*," Jerusalem, high school seminar paper, 1997, p.19 [in Arabic].
49 S. Gazit, *The Carrot and the Stick*, Tel-Aviv: Zmora, Bitan, 1985, p. 242 [in Hebrew].
50 Moshe Dayan, *Avnei Derech*, Autobiography, Jerusalem: Idanim, 1976, pp. 498–502 [in Hebrew].
51 *Ibid.*
52 For the post-1967 development, *see* M.Roman, "Jewish Kiryat Arba versus Arab Hebron," Jerusalem: The West Bank Data Project, 1985, pp. 55–68.
53 *Ibid.*
54 Report of the Commission of Inquiry of the Massacre in the Cave of the Patriarchs, Jerusalem, Government Press 1994.
55 Idarat al-Awqaf wal-Shu'un al-Islamiyya – Qism Ihya' al-Turath al-Islami fi Bayt al-Maqdis, *Al-Masjid al-Ibrahimi, Dirasa Watha'iqiyya Musawwara* [The Awqaf Department, The Ibrahimi Mosque, A Documented and Photographed Study], Jerusalem, Waqf Department, 1985, pp. 230–59 [in Arabic].
56 As Sheikh Jamil Hammami once put it in a session at PASSIA (author's notes).
57 Justice Meir Shamgar, Report of the National Commission of Inquiry Regarding the Massacre at the Hebron Cave of Patriarchs, 1994.
58 Conversation with Ya'qub Hijazi, the *waqf* administrator of the site.
59 Conversation with 'Atef Shanan, the IDF commander in charge of the site.
60 The Herzliya Convention 2006: *The Holy Basin of Jerusalem*, Jerusalem: Jerusalem Inst. for Israel Studies, 2006.

10 Treatment of antiquities on the Temple Mount/*Al-Haram al-Sharif* [1]

Jon Seligman

Introduction

Over the last few years the archaeological involvement in the holy places of Jerusalem has become a focus of professional and public concern. Archaeology has held a central place in the political and public debate between Israelis and Palestinians over the management and ownership of the of the complex known to the Jews as *Har HaBayit*—the Temple Mount and to Muslims as *Al-Haram al-Sharif*—the Noble Sanctuary[2] while the question of the site's archaeological protection became aggravated following the destruction of archaeological layers by the Islamic *waqf* (Supreme Muslim Council) between 1996 and 2001 during construction work.[3]

Indeed, the study of nationalism and archaeology has been one of the most hotly debated topics of the last decade. In some political circles, the role of archaeology is perceived as providing "evidence" for a real or presumed connection between modern religious and/or national movements and their ethnic or religious roots, a role embraced by some but rejected by the majority of archaeologists, including this author.[4]

The interrelationship between archaeologists, architects, conservators, and other professionals with Jerusalem's religious and political reality has accompanied modern research of the city since the mid-nineteenth century. Extraordinary relationships have been created between the people and institutions involved—scholars, professionals from the archaeological establishment, academic institutions and archaeologists who work for the religious institutions and representatives of the holy sites' administrators—the *Waqf* on the Temple Mount / *Al-Haram al-Sharif*.

The reason for scholarly interest is clear. This site is the most important center of worship in Judaism and Islam, and has been a focus of pilgrimage for the last three millennia.[5] Yet the desire of various scholars to collect every item or shred of data stood in opposition to the religious reality, which severely limited the possibilities of conducting proper academic research. As the Temple Mount is an active place of worship, maintained by a religious body, regular archaeological excavation was impossible. Nevertheless, detailed archaeological and architectural studies of the sites have been conducted to document the standing structures on site. From time to time it has been possible for archaeologists to carry out limited excavations when renovations or repairs following earth tremors and development took place.

The references made to the Temple Mount in scientific and popular studies of Jerusalem notwithstanding, the complex relationship that developed between scholars and the religious authorities has yet to be fully studied. This essay draws mainly on the available sources, on material in the archives of the Israel Antiquities Authority [hereinafter IAA], and on my own personal experience over the past decade together with my colleague, Dr. Gideon Avni, who worked with me on much of this study.

Archaeological research on the Temple Mount/Al-Haram al-Sharif

Modern archaeological research of the Temple Mount began in the mid-nineteenth century, with the easing of access restrictions for Western travelers and scholars. Prior to that time non-Muslims were banned from entering the sacred site, and information was based on observations from the surrounding buildings. Only a few intrepid explorers and travelers actually visited the Mount and documented some of its elements, though their descriptions were general in nature and did not include the underground spaces.

The situation changed after the Crimean War. Beginning in the late 1850s, Western scholars were allowed to visit the Temple Mount in return for a fee, the Muslim authorities turning a blind eye to activities carried out in exploring the enclosure and its underground spaces. The first scholars who documented the Mount and the subterranean areas in detail were James Thomas Barclay (1858),[6] Ermete Pierotti (1864)[7] and Marquis Charles Melchoir de Vogüé (1864).[8]

However, the most comprehensive documentation of the Temple Mount was prepared between 1864–75 by British scholars working for the Palestine Exploration Fund (PEF): Sir Charles William Wilson from 1864–65, Sir Charles Warren from 1867–70, and Conrad Schick from 1872–75.[9] While all these activities took place with the knowledge and permission of the Ottoman authorities, guards and Muslim religious functionaries on the Temple Mount occasionally interfered with the scholars' work. This nineteenth-century documentation still comprises the main basis for scholarly information concerning the Temple Mount and its underground structures.

At the beginning of the twentieth century a number of attempts were made to conduct studies and excavations, especially in the Temple Mount's underground areas. The most prominent of these was the expedition led by the British noble Montague Brownlow Parker in 1909–10, who sought to find the Ark of the Covenant and treasures from the Temple of Solomon. After some ineffectual excavations in the City of David, the expedition carried out illicit excavations in the Temple Mount, only to be discovered by the Muslim authorities which led to a scrambled escape from Jerusalem.[10]

During the period of British mandatory rule in Palestine, two comprehensive studies were executed, focusing on the Dome of the Rock and the al-Aqsa

Mosque. In 1924 E.T. Richmond published the results of an extensive survey of the Dome of the Rock, carried out in 1918.[11] Between 1938–42, R.W. Hamilton, then the Director of the Department of Antiquities, surveyed the al-Aqsa Mosque and conducted limited excavations in the building while major repairs were under way as a consequence of the 1927 earthquake.[12] These engineering–architectural studies were the result of the need to report on the structural stability of the monuments due to the fear of collapse from weakened foundations, an outcome of years of neglect and as a result of the tremor.

In the 1920s, K.A.C. Creswell compiled a detailed study of the structures of the Temple Mount, including many drawings and photographs, some of which were published in his monumental book *Early Muslim Architecture*.[13] At the same time M. Van Berchem documented and published dozens of ancient inscriptions discovered on the Temple Mount and in the surrounding buildings.[14]

During Jordanian rule in East Jerusalem, only limited archaeological work was carried out at the site and its surroundings. K. Kenyon,[15] who conducted large-scale excavations in Jerusalem, did not devote any attention to the Temple/*Haram* compound.

After 1967 Israeli scholars made a valuable contribution to documenting the Early Islamic monuments on the Temple Mount, most notably Miriam Rosen-Ayalon[16] and Meir Ben Dov.[17] At the same time extensive excavations, under the leadership of Benjamin Mazar and later Ronny Reich, were conducted for the first time to the south and west of the Temple Mount compound, revealing impressive remains from both the Roman and Early Islamic periods.[18]

During the past thirty years, extensive surveys of the Mamluk and Ottoman construction on the Mount have been conducted as a joint effort of the British School of Archaeology in Jerusalem and the Archaeological Department of the *waqf*. The results of these studies were published as two volumes, one by Burgoyne on Mamluke Jerusalem and the other by Natsheh on the Ottoman city.[19] These studies have made a considerable contribution to our knowledge of the structure, history, and development of the Temple Mount enclosure. Nevertheless, it must be emphasized that due to the religious importance and sensitivities of the site, no proper scientific, archaeological excavation has ever been conducted there, save for limited work during the al-Aqsa repairs during the Mandatory period.[20]

How were these scientific studies of the sacred enclosure received by the Muslim religious authorities, the *Waqf*, in charge of the day-to-day running of the site? The sources available for analysis are mainly the descriptions of the scholars themselves, who often were subject to the suspicions and even interference of the believers. From the start, the explorers of the PEF were received with distrust and even animosity during their work in the underground chambers of the Temple Mount. It seems that this suspicion of Western scholarship grew in the face of the secretive as well as farcical actions of the Parker expedition on the Temple Mount.[21]

The attitude of the Muslim *Waqf* toward researchers, and particularly archaeologists, is evident in both their formal and informal relations with the official archaeological authorities and with private individual researchers. As a rule, a consistent reticence by the *Waqf* regarding the research of external archaeologists and architects was observed. This attitude grew during the twentieth century through the British Mandate, Jordanian rule, and into Israeli control. Some elements of the Muslim establishment saw the study of the sacred enclosure by Western scholars not as academic inquiry into the historical development of the site and its archaeological remains, but rather as an attempt to undermine the central status of the Islamic monuments of the site—the Dome of the Rock and the al-Aqsa Mosque. On the other hand, their suspicions of foreign scholars notwithstanding, the *Waqf* was always prepared to cooperate with professional archaeological and conservation organizations that focused on the site's Islamic monuments.

The British Mandate—1917 to 1948

Early on the British authorities reconfirmed the custody of the *waqf* over the *Al-Haram al-Sharif*, a position reaffirmed in July 1922 in Articles 9 and 13 of the League of Nations' provision for a Mandate in Palestine: " … nothing in this mandate shall be construed as conferring upon the Mandatory authority to interfere with the fabric or the management of purely Moslem sacred shrines, the immunities of which are guaranteed."[22] Shortly after the British occupation of Jerusalem in December 1917, it became clear that the historic monuments on the Temple Mount were in very poor physical repair, owing to continual neglect during the last phase of Ottoman rule. Immediately after the British set up their military government in Jerusalem, the first formal contacts were made between the authorities and the *Waqf*. Professional relations were maintained between employees of the Mandatory Department of Antiquities and the professional administration of the *Waqf*. Inspectors working for the Department of Antiquities had free access to almost every place on the Temple Mount, and they were allowed to record, measure, and photograph its major monuments. Throughout the years of the British Mandate, documentation, and surveys continued for preservation purposes, mainly in the Dome of the Rock and the Al-Aqsa Mosque. The *Waqf* recognized such professional activities and good working relations prevailed between the functionaries of both sides. These special relationships were maintained by the directors of the Department of Antiquities, who took a personal and active role in the documentation work.

Department of Antiquities' inspectors routinely visited the Temple Mount together with *Waqf* officials to comprehensively document both the monuments and the everyday activities. Visiting inspectors were often accompanied by professional teams from the Department of Antiquities and professionals from other government agencies.[23]

In parallel to the activities of the Department of Antiquities, the *Waqf* established a Technical Department with the aim of maintaining the monuments.

One of the first actions undertaken by this department was the preparation of a plan to treat the ceramic tiles adorning the Dome of the Rock. Over time the Technical Department, which still exists, became an organ that documented and studied monuments in the field of conservation, often in cooperation with recognized international institutions.

Good professional contacts between the Muslim religious authorities and the official archaeological and architectural organs of the Mandatory government continued until the end of British rule in the country. Surveys and studies of the Temple Mount were conducted through the 1940s as a joint effort of the Department of Antiquities and the *Waqf*.[24]

An excellent example of the processes described here is the treatment of the al-Aqsa Mosque following the earthquakes of 1927 and 1937. The poor state of the Mosque was known well before the quakes, and led to Richmond's recommendation of January 1924 to pull down the dome of the Mosque.[25] Major renovations were conducted on al-Aqsa prior to 1927, during which massive concrete supports were added in the undercroft, disfiguring the space inside of the Double Gate. On 11 July 1927 an earthquake whose epicenter was in the Jordan Valley rocked Jerusalem. A second tremor was felt in the city on 12 October 1937. While the Dome of the Rock remained relatively unscathed, the al-Aqsa Mosque, built above ancient vaults on the Herodian extension of the Temple Mount, was severely damaged, resulting in the collapse of the roof together with many ancient timbers. In view of this the *Waqf* commissioned a report on the monument's physical state from Mahmud Ahmad Pasha, Director of the Department for the Preservation of Arab Monuments of Egypt, which was submitted in May 1938.[26] Major repair works, involving the heavy dismantling and rebuilding of extensive sections of the Mosque were conducted from 1938 to 1942 under Egyptian supervision and sponsorship. In a break from earlier practice, the repairs were professionally, if partially, documented by R.W. Hamilton.[27] For the first time they included limited archaeological excavations within the Mosque and documentation of the large vaulted structures east of the building prior to their removal. Hamilton sums it up thus: "It (the documentation) ... preserved some record, however imperfect, of an ancient building that has now suffered radical and irreversible transformation."[28] In another ground-breaking activity the decorated timbers which had previously adorned Al-Aqsa were taken for preservation to the newly founded Palestine or Rockefeller Museum.

Jordanian Rule

The period of Jordanian rule (1948–67) is hardly represented in the Jordan archives of the Department of Antiquities. A tendency pointing to a deterioration of the cooperation between the Jordanian Department of Antiquities and the *Waqf* can be detected. Evidence of this is provided by a seemingly small incident in 1953, where documentation was required following the collapse of part of the mosaic covering the walls of the Dome of the

Rock. In a letter sent by the Director of the Antiquities Authority, G. Lancaster-Harding, to the renowned expert on Muslim architecture, Professor K.A.C. Creswell, he notes the poor state of the mosaics which were peeling off the walls. Responding to Creswell's request to erect scaffolding so that the mosaics could be examined, Harding observed, "By the law I have no control over any religious buildings which are actually in use, but I might be able to pull a few strings." The issue was passed to the antiquities inspector, Yusef Sa'ad, to handle the case and make contact with the *Waqf*. In a series of letters Sa'ad asks the *Waqf* to close the western door of the Dome of the Rock for three hours to enable photography and documentation. In a blunt reply the *Waqf* refused the request, explaining that it was unwilling for worshippers to be disturbed by photography.[29]

A further example was the renovation of the Dome of the Rock. In 1952 the Jordanians launched an appeal, based on Megaw's report produced during the Mandate period,[30] to resume restoration of the Dome of the Rock. Money donated by various Arab states led to the commencement of the work in 1956 by a Saudi contractor, during which the foundations were reinforced, the mosaic ceiling decoration repaired, the twelfth-century grille around the *Sakhrah* (sacred rock) dismantled, and the heavy lead dome, which had crushed its own supporting structure, was replaced with the now familiar gilded aluminum sheeting. Professional architectural and technical supervision was made possible by the Egyptian government, and the edifice was later carpeted thanks to the Moroccan monarchy. Notably the local Jordanian Antiquities Department seems to have been kept out of the picture, its involvement in preserving the most important monument under its care being minimal, if at all existent. We can only speculate the reasons for keeping the Department of Antiquities out of the decision-making process of the maintenance of the Temple Mount/Haram al-Sharif. Possibly the site was viewed as a holy place to be operated exclusively by the religious authorities or the omission may be due to an inherent weakness in the administrative structure of the department at that time.

Israeli rule

Following the decision of Defense Minister Moshe Dayan on 17 June 1967 permitting the *Waqf* to retain internal administration, the site which had been taken by the Israel Defense Forces only ten days before was returned; the Israeli Police was charged with responsibility for security affairs.[31] With this single decision Dayan created the basis for the *status quo* that has existed until the present day.

Immediately after the Six-Day War Jerusalem was unilaterally reunited on 27 June 1967, At that time, the Knesset passed a number of enabling laws that expanded the municipal area of the city, to include East Jerusalem within Israel. It then enacted legislation to put Arab East Jerusalem under Israeli civil law—as distinct from the military administration which governed the West Bank and the Gaza Strip. In 1980 the Knesset introduced the Basic

Law–Jerusalem Capital of Israel, which included legislation for the protection of the holy places and freedom of access to them.[32]

The Temple Mount, obviously an active religious site, became from August 31, 1967, part of a registered antiquities site consisting of the Old City and its surroundings in accordance with the provisions of the Antiquities Ordinance 1929, later replaced by the Law of Antiquities 1978. Within the Israeli public disputes arose over the interpretation of the level of civil control that could be exercised by the Israeli government and administrative authorities over East Jerusalem. The *Waqf*, for its part, rejected the imposition of Israeli civil rule, claiming that as military occupied territory the *Al-Haram al-Sharif* should come under the rule of international law and UN conventions.[33]

For the first twenty years of Israeli rule in East Jerusalem, the Department of Antiquities and Museums of the Ministry of Education and Culture maintained regular professional contacts with the *Waqf* in all matters concerning the Temple Mount. From time to time departmental inspectors would visit the site, sometimes accompanied by police officers or government representatives. On occasion, mainly when the *Waqf* was engaged in construction or earth moving operations on the Mount, questions arose concerning archaeological supervision and prevention of damage to antiquities; such questions frequently had to be settled at the political level.

During this period, and in particular from the mid-1980s onward, informal relationships were established between archaeologists from the Department of Antiquities and professional staff of the *Waqf*, mainly engineers and architects responsible for development and maintenance work on the site. These relationships consisted primarily of occasional personal meetings in which views and positions were presented in various areas relating to activity in and around the Temple Mount. At the same time, the *waqf* consistently declined to inform Israeli authorities, in an official capacity, of their plans for construction and development on the *Haram* enclosure.

From 1988 the legal situation on the Mount changed following an appeal brought before the Israeli Supreme Court[34] by the Temple Mount Faithful Movement,[35] and in light of consequential directives issued by the State Attorney General, which reviewed the authority and *modus operandi* of government agencies in relation to works on the Mount.[36] In accordance with these directives the Israel Department of Antiquities and Museums, and later the Israel Antiquities Authority, were to conduct regular tours of inspection on the Temple Mount, monitoring work of various types—construction, development and conservation—and submit regular reports accordingly to the Attorney General.[37] During the years 1990 to 1996, good informal relations were maintained between the IAA staff and the professional personnel of the *waqf* active on the Mount. Regular meetings were held, during which information was received and updated, and opinions exchanged as to activities on the Mount. In the course of these conversations, the *Waqf* staff gave the IAA representatives advance notice of planned activities, such as extensive repairs to the Dome of the Rock and preparation of the underground vaults in "Solomon's Stables"[38] for visitors and worshipers. The IAA representatives, for their part, showed the *Waqf* staff their plans for excavation south of the Temple Mount and for developing the area as an archaeological park.

It should be noted that works conducted at this time on the Mount, under the direction of the *Waqf*'s professional departments, generally adhered to universally accepted principles regarding the treatment of historical monuments, with the cooperation and supervision of international professional agencies. Thus, differences of opinion between the IAA staff and the *Waqf* on professional matters were almost non-existent.

Notable in this context is the extensive renovation, by an Irish contractor, of the Dome of the Rock between 1992 and 1994, during which large portions of the dome were replaced. The work, including an extensive conservational survey of the existing dome, was ordered by the *Waqf* and involved many foreign experts who spent many months inside the Temple Mount. During the work, access to the site by Israeli professionals was possible and they were able to communicate their advice.

The situation changed drastically in Autumn 1996 with the active entry of the Israeli Islamic Movement into development projects and management of the Temple Mount. The Israeli Islamic Movement is a militant ultra-religious movement supported by large circles of Israel's Arab community in northern Israel, led by Sheikh Raed Salah of Umm el-Fahm, who rejects any historical Jewish association with the Temple Mount *al-Haram al-Sharif*. In 1996 the *Waqf* began works within the structures known since Crusader times as Solomon's Stables, in order to open them as a mosque now named *Musallah al-Marwani* for Marwan, the first Caliph of the Umayyad dynasty. Later *al-Aqsa al-Qadima*, the passageway under the *al-Aqsa* Mosque leading to the blocked Huldah Gate, was cleared and converted into a prayer area.

The participation of the Islamic Movement in the work to prepare Solomon's Stables for worship involved operations that violated conservation principles for the treatment of historical monuments; in some places antiquities were actually damaged. During these years the IAA's ability to inspect the site and to conduct informal discussion with the *Waqf* was severely curtailed.

Between 1998 and 2000, additional work was carried out in the ancient subterranean passages and vaults beneath the southern part of the Temple Mount. This activity reached a peak toward the end of 1999, when a monumental staircase and entrance was excavated down into Solomon's Stables.[39] In the process a tremendous pit was dug with heavy mechanical machinery without any archaeological supervision, causing major irrevocable changes, in complete contravention of internationally recognized standards of management of sites of universal cultural value[40] and sparking worldwide controversy over the management of the archaeological patrimony of the Temple Mount. The Director of the IAA, Amir Drori, described the event as an "archaeological crime."[41] The resulting political uproar in the Israeli political echelon has not subsided, with intense scrutiny placed upon the actions of the *Waqf*, Israeli police, IAA, and government within the site from the ostensibly apolitical Committee for the Prevention of Destruction to Antiquities on the Temple Mount, a public affairs group that includes a number of well-known intellectuals, cultural figures, and archaeologists. Periodic petitions to the Supreme Court have been made challenging the decisions of these official bodies, although the motions are inevitably rejected as being beyond the court's jurisdiction due to the highly sensitive nature of the site and the fact that the management of the site is considered a policy rather than a legal matter.

Two bulges, one on the southern wall and the other on the eastern, became an issue in 2000. While the structural causes of these bulges was a matter for some debate, with the usual mutual recriminations, the inherent danger of collapse on one hand and the clear understanding that such a collapse would spark unwanted responses from extremists on both sides, on the other, made it imperative to treat the problem urgently. A debate ensued over the thorny subject of who had the competence to repair the wall—and especially, who had the right to do so. With the decline of the influence of the Palestinian Authority on the Temple Mount that resulted from the fallout of the Second Intifada, the Prime Minister's Office decided that the repair would be used as a pretext to enhance the influence of the Jordanians, and avoid conflict over sovereignty of the complex. A team of specialists from the Hashemite Kingdom was invited to investigate the structural needs, and was entrusted with the supervision of the works which were completed in 2004. The *Waqf* officials, who after all receive their salary from the *Awqaf* Ministry in Amman, quickly adjusted themselves to this new reality.

During the years that followed the damage beside Solomon's Stable a series of other maintenance activities were carried out by the *Waqf*. These did not cause further injury to the site but the heightened sensitivities that resulted from their earlier actions aroused suspicion. Thus in July 2007, when the *Waqf* began digging a trench on the eastern side of the Temple Mount for the laying of an electricity cable, tensions reemerged. Though the work had been approved by the police and the IAA, it generated protest from the Committee for the Prevention of Destruction of Antiquities on the Temple Mount who criticized the use of a tractor for excavation supposedly without archaeological supervision on the Temple Mount. This claim is rejected by this author as an inspector of the IAA, was posted on a watching brief throughout the work, ensuring that no damage to antiquities occurred during the operation. Indeed, the very fact that an antiquities inspector could be present during the work, albeit under the auspices of the Israel Police, marks a policy change, the consequences of which are still to be assessed.

Discussion

The Temple Mount has been the focus of continuous reluctance on the part of the Islamic *Waqf* to accept the involvement of outside academic bodies in scientific research at the site. However, this has not prevented the formulation of a series of comprehensive studies of standing monuments at the site based on systematic surveying and documentation.[42] Yet scholars have never been able to conduct archaeological excavations or to properly document the subterranean areas. At times, research activity on the Temple Mount has been conducted in spite of official disapproval or with the averted eye of the official *Waqf* religious administration. Unofficial collaboration on the basis of personal contacts between archaeologists, architects, and engineers of the technical departments of the *Waqf* has enabled occasional archaeological and architectural research at the site without archaeological excavation.

Analysis of the reasons for the unwillingness of the Muslim establishment to cooperate with external academic and research bodies can be explained by the disregard afforded to the importance of research into early periods of the complex. This type of research never offered a component that could strengthen the religious identity of Muslim believers and thus the religious establishment did not see it as a means of furthering its needs. Consequently, official bodies of the *Waqf* have at times expressed their alarm and opposition to research which would, in their view, weaken the hold of Islam on the Mount by uncovering early "non-Muslim" remains. However, claims that have been made concerning attempts by Muslim elements to actively erase all early remains on the Temple Mount have not been conclusively proven. Indeed, some Muslim religious elements have not even displayed interest in these claims as, in their view, Muslim ownership of the *Al-Haram al-Sharif* cannot be challenged. It seems that the opposition to research on the Temple Mount has its primary source in the desire to protect the site's holiness for Islam and to prevent external interference or any attempt to undermine the exclusivity of Muslim control of the Noble Sanctuary that would follow from the possible discovery of earlier remains. The only research approved were projects that contributed directly to the preservation and physical maintenance of the buildings. This was the case, for example, in the 1930s and 1940s, with the extensive repairs of the al-Aqsa Mosque and the massive renovations of the Dome of the Rock in the 1990s. These attitudes have influenced the relationship between the *Waqf* and the Department of Antiquities since the early days of the British Mandate. It is important to note that no official relations between the organizations have ever existed, but nonetheless, unofficial connections and cooperation have been cultivated, especially with the *Waqf* Technical Department.[43]

Except for short periods, the Temple Mount has been under exclusive Muslim religious control since the Arab conquest of Jerusalem in the seventh century CE. Strange as it may seem, in periods when Jerusalem was in non-Muslim hands the importance of the Temple Mount as a Muslim religious focus increased.[44] Despite the rivalry that exists over control for administrative hegemony of the *Al-Haram al-Sharif* between the Hashemite Kingdom of Jordan, the Palestinian Authority and the Islamic Movement,[45] this has not had any impact on the singular belief of the various Muslim elements involved concerning the site's identity and sanctity to the Islamic world. In such a situation there is no need for archaeological and historical research to provide additional proof of that Muslim hegemony. Quite the opposite, research of this type is perceived as a threat, as the exposure of early remains on the Temple Mount could undercut exclusive Muslim control.

Clearly, the Temple Mount/*Al-Haram al-Sharif* is holy both to Judaism and Islam. This basic fact creates an inherent tension between the two faiths. From 1967, this has expressed itself in repeated attempts by extreme national religious Jewish groups to actively express their aspiration to renew Jewish rule of the Mount and even act by force to fulfill it.[46] The result has been the increasingly heightened fears of the Muslim religious establishment to any challenge that might undermine the historical connection of Islam to the site. Accordingly, archaeological research of Israeli scholars close to the Temple Mount, and especially the excavations conducted south of the Mount between 1968 and 1982, are presented as a tool in the political and national conflict and as an Israeli attempt to challenge Muslim control of the site. This attitude has brought about increasing reluctance by official Muslim bodies to allow any research activity inside the complex. It should be recalled that this official reticence existed well before the implementation of Israeli sovereignty over East Jerusalem. As noted above, from the start of modern research in Jerusalem in the nineteenth century, similar claims have been made pertaining to the activities of foreign scholars in the site, and this reserve has continued throughout the years and is not specifically related to the work of Israeli researchers.

Together with the official disinclination to research, there has nonetheless been informal cooperation since 1967 with Israeli scholars studying archaeological and artistic aspects of the Muslim period buildings of the Temple Mount, including inquiries conducted while the *Waqf* turned a blind eye. The work of these scholars and others even won the unofficial appreciation of professional echelons of the *Waqf*.[47]

A comparative analysis of the operations conducted on the Temple Mount during the periods of British, Jordanian, and Israeli rule indicates that at no time have the governmental authorities enjoyed full control of construction and development at the site. The degree to which the Department of Antiquities has been involved in activity on the site has varied. Under British rule, the Department of Antiquities was closely involved in technical matters; the main monuments on the Mount were surveyed and documented and plans were drawn by British architects for the renovation of certain buildings. Employees of the Department of Antiquities during the Mandate period could freely access every corner of the Temple Mount, and they indeed did so, photographing and preparing drawings.

The following Jordanian period seems to have been characterized by limited professional contact between the Department and the *Waqf*. Although Israeli law was imposed on East Jerusalem in August 1967, involvement of the Department of Antiquities and Museums in activities on the Mount was kept informal, at a low level of intensity. During the 1980s, personal professional ties were forged between the technical staff of the *Waqf*—archaeologists, architects, the staff of the Islamic Museum—and archaeologists from the Israeli Department of Antiquities. However, these contacts did not lead to greater involvement on an official level. The informal contacts were strengthened in the early 1990s. At times the *Waqf* informed the IAA of future plans for development and construction at the site. Since 1996, as a result of political changes in the wake of the Second Intifada and the rise of the radical Israeli Islamic Movement, the level of dialogue between the two sides concerning works on the Temple Mount declined, and between 2000 and 2004, IAA inspectors were denied access to the Temple Mount area. Today, with the absence of any informal contact, visual inspection of the site continues while official contacts are maintained under the auspices of the Israeli Police. Certainly the Islamic monuments of the Temple Mount are well-maintained and are afforded the best treatment the world can provide. We can only hope—no insist—that the other aspects of this most important site are provided the same care.

Notes

1. This essay forms part of a research study conducted together with my colleague, Gideon Avni, concerning the history of scholarship, inspection, and perception of the holy sites in Jerusalem during the modern period. I thank Gideon for his help with this essay and his permission to use sections of our mutual work in this article.
2. M. Klein, *The Jerusalem Problem – The Struggle for Permanent Status*, Gainesville, Fla.: University Press of Florida, 2003
3. *See* S. Berkovitz, *The Battle for the Holy Places*, Jerusalem: Hed Arzi, 2000 [in Hebrew]; G. Avni and J. Seligman, *The Temple Mount, 1917–2001 – Documentation, Research and Inspection of Antiquities*, Jerusalem: Israel Antiquities Authority, 2001; Y. Reiter (ed.) *Sovereignty of God and Man: Sanctity and Political Centrality on the Temple Mount*, Jerusalem: Jerusalem Institute for Israel Studies, 2001 [in Hebrew]; J. Seligman and G. Avni, "Between the Temple Mount / *Haram el-Sharif* and the Holy Sepulchre: Archaeological Involvement in Jerusalem's Holy Places," *Journal of Mediterranean Archaeology*, 2006, vol.19, no. 2, pp. 259–88.
4. *See* Seligman and Avni, "Between the Temple Mount," pp. 259–60.
5. The Temple Mount is a 35-acre esplanade containing places holy to Jews and Muslims alike. According to Jewish tradition the Temple Mount, known also as Mount Moriah, is the place where Abraham fulfilled God's test of faith with his son Isaac was Mount Moriah. Later the Divine presence of God came to rest at the site with the building of the First and Second Temples, the destruction of which by the Babylonians and by the Romans came to symbolize the exile of the Jewish people. The compound is Judaism's holiest site. For Muslims the place is also seen as the site of Abraham's test though also as the place to which Muhammad made his nocturnal journey from Mecca upon el-Buraq to pray at the furthest mosque (Al Aqsa) and ascend to the heavens with Archangel Gabriel. Owing to its importance as Islam's third most important shrine, the Aqsa Mosque and the Dome of the Rock were built at the site.
6. J.T. Barclay, *The City of the Great Kings, or Jerusalem as it was, as it is, and as it is to be*, Philadelphia, Penn.: J. Challen, 1858.
7. E. Pierotti, *Jerusalem Explored – Being a Description of Ancient and Modern City*, I-II, London: Bell and Daldy, 1864.
8. E.M.M. de Vogüé, *Le Temple de Jerusalem – Monograph du Haram ech-Cherif*, Paris: Noblet et Baudrie, 1864.

9. C.W. Wilson, *Ordnance Survey of Jerusalem, Made in the Years 1864–1865*, Southampton: Palestine Exploration Fund, 1865; C. Warren, *Plans, Elevations, Sections. Showing the Results of the Excavations in Jerusalem, 1867–70*, London: Palestine Exploration Fund, 1884; W. Morrison (ed.) *The Recovery of Jerusalem – A Narrative of Exploration and Discovery in the City and the Holy Land*, London: Palestine Exploration Fund, 1871; C. Schick, *Die Stiftshutte der Temple in Jerusalem und Tempelplatz der Jetztzeit*, Berlin: Weidmann, 1896. See Gibson and Jacobson for an updated compilation of the nineteenth century archaeological research at the site. S. Gibson and D.M. Jacobson, *Below the Temple Mount in Jerusale: A Sourcebook on the Cisterns, Subterranean Chambers and Conduits of the Haram al-Sharif*, BAR Int'l. Series 637, Oxford: Tempus Reparatum, 1996.
10. N. Shalev-Khalifa, "In Search of the Temple Treasure – The Story of the Parker Expedition in the City of David, 1909–11," 1998, vol. 116, *Qadmoniot*, pp.126–35 [in Hebrew].
11. E.T. Richmond, *The Dome of the Rock in Jerusalem – A Description of its Structure and Decoration*, Oxford: Clarendon Press, 1924.
12. R.W. Hamilton, *The Structural History of the Aqsa Mosque – A Record of Archaeological Gleanings from the Repairs of 1938–1942*, Jerusalem: Department of Antiquities of Palestine,1949.
13. K.A.C. Creswell, *Early Muslim Architecture, I: Umayyads, A.D. 622–750*, Oxford: Clarendon Press, 1969.
14. M. Van Berchem, *Matériaux pour un Corpus Inscripionum Arabicarum*, II: *Syria du Sud, Jerusalem "Haram,"* Cairo: Institut français d'archéologie orientale, 1927.
15. K.M. Kenyon. *Digging Up Jerusalem*. London: Benn, 1974.
16. M. Rosen-Ayalon, *The Early Islamic Monuments of al-Haram al-Sharif – An Iconographic Study*, 1989, vol. 28, Qedem, Jerusalem: The Hebrew University Institute of Archaeology.
17. M. Ben Dov, *In the Shadow of the Temple*, New York: Harper and Row, 1982.
18. B. Mazar *The Mountain of the Lord*, New York: Doubleday,1975; Ben Dov, *In the Shadow of the Temple*.
19. H.M. Burgoyne, *Mamluk Jerusalem: An Architectural Study*, London: World of Islam Festival Trust: 1987; Y. Natsheh, "Architectural Survey," in S. Auld and R. Hillenbrand (eds.) *Ottoman Jerusalem: The Living City 1517–1917*, Part II, London: Altajir World of Islam Trust, 2000.
20. *See e.g.*, Hamilton, *The Structural History of the Aqsa Mosque*.
21. Shlaev–Khlifa, "In Search of the Temple Treasure."
22. Art. 13 of the Mandate.
23. Avni and Seligman, *The Temple Mount*, at pp. 14–20.
24. *Ibid.*, pp. 20–21.
25. *Ibid.*, p. 14.
26. *Ibid.*, pp. 16–18.
27. Hamilton, *The Structural History of the Aqsa Mosque*.
28. *Ibid.*, at iv.
29. Avni and Seligman, *The Temple Mount*, at p. 23.
30. Megaw's report was not published.
31. N. Shragai, *The Temple Mount Conflict*, Jerusalem: Keter, 1995, pp. 18–27. [in Hebrew]; M. Benvenisti 1976. *Jerusalem, The Torn City*. Minneapolis: University of Minneapolis Press, p. 101; A. Ramon, "Beyond the Kotel: The Relation of the State of Israel and the Jewish Public to the Temple Mount, 1967–99," in Y. Reiter, *Sovereignty of God and Man*, at pp.113–42; G. Gorenberg, *The End of the Days: Fundamentalism and the Struggle for the Temple Mount*, New York: Free Press, 2000.
32. Online. Available: http://www.mfa.gov.il/MFA/Foreign%20Relations/Israels%20Foreign%20Relations%20since%201947/1979–80/113%20Basic%20Law-%20Jerusalem-%20Knesset%20Resolution-%2030%20J (accessed 30 Aug. 2008).

33 *See e.g.*, UNESCO Res. 31COM 7A.18 of 2007. Online. Available: http://whc.unesco.org/en/decisions/1281 (accessed 30 Aug. 2008). " ... recalling the relevant provisions on the protection of cultural heritage including, as appropriate, the four Geneva Conventions (1949), the Hague Convention for the Protection of Cultural Property in the Event of Armed Conflict of 1954, the Convention for the Protection of the World Cultural and Natural Heritage of 1972, the inscription of the Old City of Jerusalem and its Walls at the request of Jordan on the World Heritage List (1981) and on the List of World Heritage in Danger (1982), and the recommendations, resolutions and decisions of UNESCO.
34 HCJ 193/1986.
35 The Temple Mount and Eretz Yisrael (Land of Israel) Faithful Movement is a militant fringe Orthodox Jewish movement that wishes to establish a Third Jewish Temple in place of the mosques and reinstitute the practice of ritual sacrifice.
36 Shragai, *The Temple Mount Conflict*, at pp. 94–95; Berkovitz, *sup The Battle for the Holy Places*, at pp. 299–306; Avni and Seligman, *The Temple Mount*, at pp. 27–29.
37 Avni and Seligman, *The Temple Mount*, pp. 27–38.
38 Solomon's Stables is the popular name of an area located beneath the surface of the south eastern corner of the Temple Mount. It is a vaulted structure that supports the platform created by Herod's construction of the walls that surround Mount Moriah. At their western edge they connect directly into the southern end of the eastern Huldah (Triple) Gate passageway. The present name follows the Crusader identification of the vaults with the stables of Solomon.
39 Avni and Seligman, *The Temple Mount*, at pp. 34–37; Reiter, *Sovereignty of God and Man*, at pp. 308–16; S. Berkovitz, *The Temple Mount and the Western Wall in Israeli Law*, Jerusalem: Jerusalem Inst. for Israel Studies, Study Series 90, 2001, p. 62.
40 J. Seligman, "Solomon's Stables, The Temple Mount, Jerusalem: The Events Concerning the Destruction of Antiquities 1999 to 2001," 2007. vol. 56, *'Atiqot*, p. 51 ff.
41 *Ibid.*
42 *See e.g.*, Creswell, *Early Muslim Architecture*, I, pp. 65–131, 323–80; H.M. Burgoyne, *Mamluk Jerusalem: An Architectural Study*, London: World of Islam Festival Trust, 1987; Natsheh, "Architectural Survey."
43 Avni and Seligman, *The Temple Mount*, at pp. 41–42.
44 Reiter, *The Temple Mount*, at p. 156.
45 *Ibid.*, pp. 158–60.
46 Shragai, *The Temple Mount Conflict*, at pp. 83–134; Reiter, *The Temple Mount*, at pp. 297–317.
47 Seligman and Avni, "Between the Temple Mount / *Haram el-Sharif* and the Holy Sepulchre," at pp. 265–69, 274–77.

11 The Shihab Al-Din Mosque affair in Nazareth[1]

A case study of Muslim–Christian–Jewish relations in the state of Israel

Daphne Tsimhoni

The Shihab al-Din affair that agitated Nazareth during 1997–2003 erupted from the intrusion of a group of Islamists into a government-owned square in front of the Basilica of the Annunciation with the insistent demand to build a huge mosque that would overshadow the Basilica. It extended far beyond a local conflict over a piece of land and signified the triangle of Muslim–Christian, Jewish–Christian, and Jewish–Muslim relations in Israel and above all the treatment of the Arab citizens by the Israeli-Jewish government. The affair further demonstrated the significance of Nazareth, the Basilica of the Annunciation and the Christian Holy Places in general to worldwide Christianity and the ability of the international community to put pressure on the Israeli government's decision making regarding the Holy Places. Was the Shihab Al-Din affair a passing episode? Was it a demonstration of Huntington's "clash of civilizations" theory? To answer these questions, this essay will discuss and analyze the affair in historical perspective as based on written documentation, the media and attitudes of Muslim and Christian personalities toward it.

Historical background

The significance of Nazareth and its holy places goes back to the fourth century, when Christianity became the official religion of the Byzantine Empire under Emperor Constantine. Nazareth became the third Christian holy town in significance due to the annunciation of the birth of the Messiah in it. It declined following the Muslim occupation of the Holy Land in 638, suffering most of the years from nature disasters, wars and Bedouin raids. Its population dwindled and there were hardly any Christians left.[2] In 1102 the Crusaders under the leadership of Tancred conquered Nazareth and made it their capital of Galilee. Under their rule the Church of the Annunciation and other churches were rebuilt. By the mid-twelfth century Nazareth became the seat of an archbishop and was described by travelers as expanding and relatively flourishing town. In 1187 Saladin defeated the Crusaders in the battle of Hittin. Nazareth went back to Muslim rule, many inhabitants fled from it; however, pilgrims were still allowed to visit the holy sites of the town. In 1263 the

Mamluks from Egypt headed by Baibars occupied Nazareth, destroyed the churches, and killed many Christians who refused to convert to Islam. Prince Edward reconquered the town in 1271. Finally, the Mamluks reconquered and destroyed Nazareth in 1291. Altogether the Crusaders' rule over Nazareth hardly left a long-lasting mark on the town in the coming generations of Muslim rule. Nazareth remained a small marginal town with hardly any Christian population. The Ottoman occupation of Nazareth and Palestine in 1517 did not make a drastic change of the town's position during its first decades.[3]

The emergence of Nazareth in modern times and the rebuilding of its Christian holy sites took place from the seventeenth century onward. The expanding commercial relations between the Ottoman Sultan Ahmad I and Henry IV, the king of France, and the agreements signed between them improved the position of the Catholics in the Ottoman Empire and facilitated their activities in the Levant. The major actors in Galilee were local semi-independent rulers, first and foremost the Druze Emir Fakhr al-Din II of Mount Lebanon (1585–1632) and Dahir al-Omar (1750–1710) who were interested in improving the economy and position of their province. They made Nazareth the major town of Galilee and encouraged Christians to settle in it. Fakhr al-Din encouraged Franciscan monks to settle down in Nazareth. In 1620, he permitted them to build a church and monastery on the Cave of the Annunciation.[4]

The Franciscans suffered enormous difficulties in building the church particularly from Bedouin raids. Due to the long Maronite tradition of carrying arms and self-protection, uncommon among other Christian communities in the Levant, the Franciscans applied to the Maronite patriarch in Lebanon to send some of his community members for help. These Maronite builders and guards laid down the basis for the renewed Christian population in Nazareth. Other Christian communities first and foremost Greek Orthodox Arabs from Transjordan were also encouraged to settle down in Nazareth and build their churches. Following the collapse of Fakhr al-Din and throughout the seventeenth and eighteenth centuries Nazareth declined. It suffered from Bedouin attacks, during which the Franciscan church and monastery were set on fire and the Franciscans were forced to leave Nazareth.[5]

The position of Nazareth improved during the reign of Dahir al-Omar (1750–1710). A local strong man of Bedouin descent, he improved the economy and security of Nazareth, encouraged the Christians to resettle in the town and allowed the Franciscans to rebuild the new Church of the Annunciation over the ruins of the old church.[6] Indicative of the preferred position of the Christians in Nazareth by its Muslim rulers was the fact that the first mosque in Nazareth, the White Mosque was constructed later on in 1804, near the Church of the Annunciation. It became a *waqf* (endowment) of the powerful Fahum family and the center of the established Muslim families.[7]

Nazareth leaped into modernity during the nineteenth century with the expanding activities of the Western churches intertwined with the Western powers' increasing interests in the Holy Land. The fate of the town, and in

194 *Daphne Tsimhoni*

particular its Christians, had their ups and downs often depending on the goodwill of its regional rulers. It flourished under those Muslim rulers who welcomed western activities that strengthened the economy and security in the area such as Ibrahim Pasha (1831–40), the son of Egyptian ruler Muhammad Ali. He ameliorated the position of the Christians and Jews and welcomed the churches to building their institutions in Nazareth.[8] Western churches expanded their activities following the retreat of the Egyptian army. They built schools, orphanages, hospitals, and pharmacies, thereby laying the basis for the modernized educational-medical services of Nazareth and contributing to the relative prosperity and security of the town. Nazareth, particularly its Christian population, still suffered occasionally from local revolts and Bedouin raids. By the turn of the century due to the development of inland transportation and an improvement of its security, Nazareth became a transit town for commodities from Transjordan to the port of Acre, thereby expanding its economic opportunities[9] These developments further attracted Christians from the rural hinterland to settle down in Nazareth. They played a major role in the town's economy serving as a link between the Muslim local rulers and rural population, on the one hand, and the Western powers and churches, on the other. The Christians became the majority of Nazareth in 1856 and their proportion expanded toward the end of the century (see Figure 11.1). The expansion of the churches' activities found expression in the building of new churches. Travelers of the period noted the Franciscan Church of the Annunciation and the Franciscan Monastery as the most outstanding buildings in Nazareth.[10]

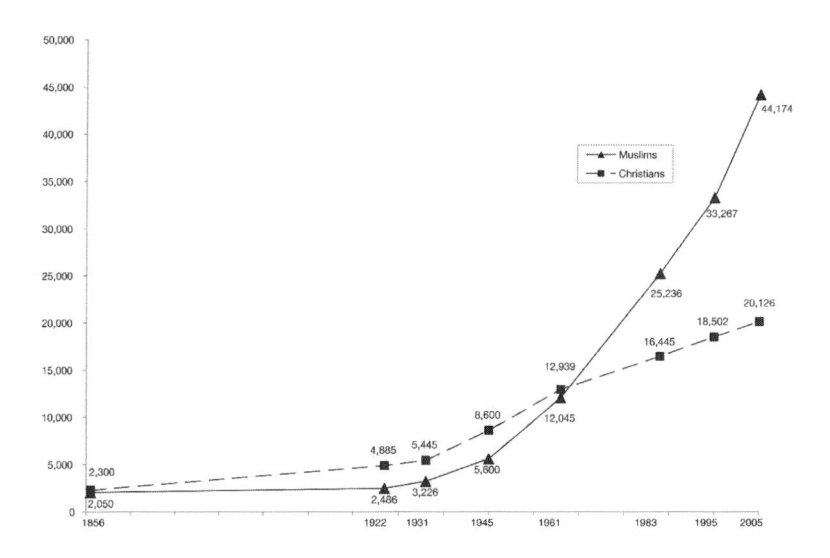

Figure 11.1 Population of Nazareth 1856–2005

Despite their economical and cultural affluence and their demographic majority in Nazareth, the Christians remained a vulnerable ethno-religious group. They continued to depend on the elite local Muslim families and on the Muslim Ottoman central government for their security, and occasionally appealed to the Western powers for their protection. The elite Muslim families on their part welcomed the activities of the churches and the prominence of their holy places, recognizing their contribution to the town's modernization, economy and education. This Muslim–Christian equilibrium found expression in the nomination of the mayors of Nazareth by the Ottoman government. The first mayor, Tannus Qa'war, a Christian dignitary, was nominated in 1875. However, out of nine mayors of Nazareth 1875–1917, just four were Christian.[11]

Muslim–Christian relations in Nazareth have been mistakenly conceived by some Israeli Jewish researchers as constantly inimical, reflecting the oppression of the Christians in Palestine by the Muslim government and majority of the population.[12] In fact, as this historical survey shows, the Christians were invited by the local Muslim rulers of Galilee to live in and develop Nazareth. They lived and even flourished at some periods in symbiosis with their Muslim townsmen depending on the protection of the elite Muslim families. Most of the Muslim attacks on Christians in Nazareth were waged by Muslim Bedouins from outside rather than by Muslim residents of Nazareth.

The British Mandate in Palestine (1917–48) opened a new era of security and prosperity in Nazareth. It became the district town of Galilee with a multi-cultural population of Muslims, Christians of various denominations, and a handful of Jews, as well as British officers and officials. It had a thriving economy, rich religious life, a good education system and strong medical services. However, like many mountain inland towns it was overtaken by the booming coastal towns and the capital city Jerusalem. Although its population doubled from 7,424 in 1922 to 14,200 in 1945, Nazareth remained a relatively small, traditional inland town. Despite the increase in the general population, emigration, particularly of Christians expanded to the developing economic centers in Palestine as well as abroad. Hence, despite their growth in absolute figures, the Christian proportion of Nazareth's total population gradually declined from 73 percent in 1922 to 61 percent in 1944. Hence, Christians still maintained the majority and continued to form the backbone of the middle class in Nazareth. Nazareth's elite comprised affluent Muslim families living in symbiosis with successful Christian merchants and professionals, joined by British officials and their families. The presence of the British government improved the sense of security of the Christians, which found expression in the nomination of the mayors of the town by the British district governors during the mandate: two out of the three mayors were Christian.

The 1948 War and the establishment of the State of Israel considerably changed the position of Nazareth and its socio-ethnic balance. In summer 1948, the Muslim Mayor Yusef Muhammad Ali al-Fahum, together with the

Muslim and Christian dignitaries, surrendered Nazareth to the Israeli army without a struggle. Nazareth became a refugee center for both Christians and Muslims and the churches played an important role in providing food and shelter for the refugees.[13] From then on Nazareth was transformed from a small peripheral town into the major Arab political-national as well as cultural-urban center; it became the unofficial capital of the Arab minority in Israel. As the veteran Christian Arab journalist Atallah Mansour put it, "Nazareth was poised for its golden age under Israeli rule."[14]

The proportion of the Christians of the population of Nazareth has been in a continuous decline since 1948. Having lost their majority during the 1960s, they have declined to approximately 30 percent of the population of Nazareth today, as the above graph demonstrates. This was due first to the settlement in the town of largely Muslim refugees and the expansion of its municipal boundaries to include several Muslim villages in the outskirts. Second, compared with the Muslims, Christians had a much lower birthrate and higher emigration rate. Third, the lack of land for housing in Nazareth induced a continuous, largely Christian migration to the neighboring Jewish development town Natzrat Illit.[15]

Christians were not only the mainstay of the Arab middle class; they also filled the vacuum created by the exodus of the Muslim political leadership during the 1948 War.[16] The political game and the struggle for the local municipal council and position of mayor of Nazareth during the 1950s and 1960s were political-national in nature, rather than ethno-religious. It was not waged between Muslims and Christians per se but rather between small Arab parties based on family/communal loyalties that were affiliated with the Labor Party, the dominant party in Israeli politics until the mid-1970s, on the one hand, and the Communist Party, on the other. Christians of various communities took a prominent role in these small family/communal parties. The Arab parties often created coalitions in the municipality and managed to elect their candidates as mayors. The Communist Party (known as Rakah and later Hadash) was the only party in Nazareth that had an ideological agenda and was the only legal party that expressed Arab nationalism. Christian Arabs, first and foremost Greek Orthodox, were prominent in this party due to historical traditions.[17]

The significant change in the local politics of Nazareth took place following the 1975 municipal elections. Having expanded their supporters to include students and merchants, the Communist Party ran to these elections as the Democratic Front of Nazareth or in short the Front [Jabha]. It won for the first time 66.7 percent of the votes and 11 out of the 17 seats on the municipal council of Nazareth. Its leader, Tawfiq Zayyad was elected as the first Communist mayor of Nazareth. A well-known poet born to a Muslim family, Zayyad was a secular Communist married to a Christian. Zayyad replaced Mayor Sayf al-Din Zu'bi, member of a dignified Muslim family who became a Knesset member of an Arab party affiliated with the Labor Party. Zayyad soon became a Knesset member of the Communist Party on top of his role as mayor. The Communist domination of the local politics in Nazareth as well as Zayyad's excessive political activity soon caused the animosity of the Israeli government. The government viewed the nationalistic expressions of the Communists as a menace to the State of Israel and refused to cooperate with the Communist dominated municipality of Nazareth. A year later in 1976, violent demonstrations took place in Nazareth against the confiscation of Arab lands by the Israeli Government. These events further expanded the breach between the Israeli administration and the Communist-dominated municipality of Nazareth. This explains in part the reservations of the Israeli establishment regarding the Nazareth municipality during the rise of the Islamic movement in Nazareth.[18]

It was under the leadership of Zayyad and the Communist secular Arab nationalist party that Christians reached the peak of their political influence in Nazareth, at the time when they had already lost their majority in the town. This was due to their prominence in all the political parties and in particular in the Communist Party.

Zayyad served as mayor for nearly 20 years until he died suddenly in a car accident in 1994. A charismatic personality and secular Muslim he was accepted not only among secular but also among religious fundamentalist Muslims who did not dare criticize him. Following his sudden death, his young deputy, Ramiz Jeraysi, then 42 years of age, was elected by the municipal council as mayor, a position that he has maintained to this day. Trained as an engineer, he has done his best to run the municipality efficiently. However, he has not been able to cope with the expanding fundamentalist Islamists.

Parallel to the growing political identification of Nazareth as a Communist hub and Christian-dominated town, the influence of the Christian churches in the town increased as well. Since the early 1950s, the Christian churches expanded their institutions to care for the growing needs of the Nazareth population. Owing to insufficient government funding and investments, they continued to provide for Nazareth's educational and medical services.[19]

By contrast, the Muslims of Nazareth did not organize themselves as a religious autonomous community with an institutional infrastructure with their own schools and hospitals. This was due to the traditional position of the Muslims in the Ottoman Empire as part of the ruling elite and the loss of their control over the majority of their endowments (*waqfs*) within the State of Israel. Since the early 1950s, Nazareth suffered economic decline, high unemployment and a high rate of emigration. This reflected the Israeli government's neglect owing to its apprehension that Nazareth was becoming a center of Arab nationalism as well as its general policy toward the Arab minority in Israel. As a preventive step, in 1957 Prime Minister David Ben-Gurion declared the establishment of a new Jewish development town Nazeret Illit on the hills surrounding Nazareth. The new Jewish town soon became the location of regional government offices, industrial investments as well as housing developments at the expense of the development of Nazareth.[20] With limited prospects to develop its industry, economy and housing, Nazareth was doomed to contend with poverty and the exacerbation of both socio-economic and ethno-religious tensions.

While Nazareth lost its Christian majority, its international significance as a Christian pilgrimage center expanded after the 1948 War. During the 1950s, the Franciscans renewed their initiative of the 1920s to construct a new magnificent basilica on that site of the old Church of the Annunciation in order to mark the centenary of their activity in Nazareth. The Israeli government granted a permit to build the new monumental Basilica of the Annunciation in 1954, an exceptional decision in light of the Israeli government's policy in those days of limiting the activities of the churches. This was apparently due to the government's desire to render help to the Catholic Church in its anti-Communist campaign by reducing the high unemployment rate in Nazareth through the inflow of foreign currency and jobs that this enormous project would create. Internationally, this would demonstrate Israeli's respect for freedom of religion and possibly ameliorate its relations with the Vatican that had not yet established diplomatic relations with it. The Israeli authorities were also alert to the Vatican's earlier plans for granting extraterritorial status to the holy sites of Nazareth that were liable to be renewed.[21] Furthermore, after the 1948 War, the major Christian holy places in Jerusalem and Bethlehem came under Jordanian rule and were practically inaccessible to Israeli Christians. Both Israel and the Catholic Church were interested in creating a local focus for the Christians in Israel as well as a pilgrimage center to the worldwide Catholic Church equivalent in stature to the inaccessible holy places in East Jerusalem and Bethlehem.

Following an internal struggle between different sectors within the Vatican as well as Israeli reservations, the Holy See rejected an oriental style design of a huge basilica that would include four towers symbolizing the annunciation to the four corners of the world. It was designed by the famous architect Antonio Barluzzi who had previously designed many buildings for the Catholic Church in the Holy Land. In 1959, Giovanni Muzio was invited to redesign the Basilica. He designed it on the model of a church that he had planned for the Franciscans in Varese, Italy. This design was finally approved by Pope John XXIII in 1960.[22] Having a clearly European design, the new Basilica was intended first for international pilgrims and second for the local worshipers. Among the Christian communities in the town, the local Roman Catholic (Latin) community was just third in size. Contributions by Christians from all over the world made it possible to construct the Basilica and the cloister and to adorn them with specially donated works of art. Consecrated in 1969, it is considered the largest Franciscan basilica in Asia. The local inhabitants of Nazareth refer to it as *al-kanisa al-kabira*, the "Great Church." In order to facilitate construction, the Franciscans bought some neighboring houses from their local owners and evacuated part of a near-by cemetery. Catholic websites and organizations stress the Basilica's size that "towers lower Nazareth" and "overshadows all the other churches and mosques in Nazareth" and note that its construction was "the result of a compromise found by the Catholic Church and the State of Israel."[23] Even though Nazareth had lost its local Christian majority, the new basilica as well as the expansion of other churches emphasized the international Christian connection to Nazareth. Indeed, this Christian expansion contrasted with the limited number of mosques serving the majority Muslim population of the town.

The sources of tension

Chad Emmett, who conducted an anthropological research in Nazareth during the 1980s, described the bonds that united the Christians and Muslims in this town as being those of language, culture, Arab nationalism, and the experience of being a discriminated minority under Israeli rule. However, he noted that they seldom intermarry or live in the same quarters of the city.[24] Emmett further described cases of mutual veneration by both communities of Christian symbols and Muslim symbols as well as mutual participation in the other's religious traditions and festivals, most obviously during the 1950s and 1960s.[25] The noted Christian Arab journalist, ex-member of the Communist Party Salim Jubran, confirms Emmett's analysis. He remembers with nostalgia the past friendly relations between Muslims and Christians in Nazareth. This was possible when secular Arab nationalism was led by the Communist Party that dominated the town's municipality and politics. Christians played a dominant role in that party and set the tone in the Nazareth municipality. According to Jubran, "We both adored Nasser more than we adored Jesus and Muhammad."[26]

Christian–Muslim relations in Nazareth deteriorated in the late 1980s as the outcome of several processes, first and foremost the breakdown of the socio-religious balance. Despite the decline of the Christian majority in the town during the 1960s, Christians maintained their predominance in white-collar professions and in management positions. They continued to dominate public life and civic society as well as socio-cultural associations, such as the Rotary, even though these organizations opened their gates to all regardless of religion and communal affiliation. The majority of the schools and hospitals in Nazareth still belong to the churches. They too are open to all the population regardless of religion and community. In many of these institutions Muslims constitute the majority of students, patients, and sometimes also employees, yet they still feel alienated.

The expansion of education among the Muslims in Nazareth and their entrance into academic professions enhanced competition between Muslims and Christians over the limited white-collar and management positions open to Arabs in Israel. Hence, Christians complain about being pushed out of these positions while Muslims complain about Christian over-representation in them. Furthermore, the dissolution of the Soviet Union and the decline of worldwide Communism drastically diminished the power of the Communist Party and secular Arab nationalism in Israel most obviously in Nazareth.[27]

Furthermore, a large proportion of the Muslim refugees and villagers settled down in the eastern, poorer neighborhoods of the town where environmental development lagged behind and sewage infrastructure was often incomplete. They complained about the lack of proper municipal services as compared with the western quarters where most of the Christians lived.[28] This continuously widening gap combined with an ideological-national vacuum was bound to challenge the old socio-economic order based on the symbiosis between Muslim dignitary families with the middle-class, successful Christians in the town.

Muslim fundamentalism, as Emmanuel Sivan showed, expands among the poor urban classes as well as professionals and intellectuals who have been disappointed by the lure of westernization and modernization.[29] Researchers of the Islamic Movement in Israel have pointed out that its success was mainly due to its social activity, namely, voluntary work, and free or low-cost kindergartens and social work among the Muslim Arab villagers in the center of Israel. The Islamic Movement in Israel has been giving preference to Islamic social justice over the ritualistic precepts of the Islamic creed.[30]

In contrast, the Communist Party in Israel, dominated by Christians and Jews until the 1970s, did not address the socio-cultural needs of the Muslim lower classes and villagers. This was most obvious in Nazareth where the party's branch has been the strongest in the Arab sector in Israel. During the long years of Communist Party domination over the municipal council of Nazareth, they did not develop a public educational-welfare network to take care of the poor, largely Muslim neighborhoods. Furthermore, the Muslim masses never adapted themselves to the position of a discriminated minority lagging behind the Christians. This situation of a marginalized Muslim majority versus an outstanding Christian minority created a feeling of alienation among Muslims of the poor eastern neighborhoods. At the same time, it created among the Christians a sense of cultural superiority combined with the growing insecurity of a minority within an antagonized, frustrated majority Muslim environment.

The Islamic Movement established its party headquarters in Nazareth in 1988, later than in the Muslim "triangle" in the center of Israel. It declared as its agenda the amelioration of living conditions in the poor Muslim neighborhoods and the realization of social justice according to Qur'anic tradition. It stated that the Movement had nothing against Christians; it just intended to provide an Islamic alternative to the many Christian institutions and schools in the town in the absence of sufficient government or municipal ones. Gaining influence in the poor neighborhoods, the Islamists blamed the Communists for attacking Islam, and claimed that the Communist-dominated municipality offended Islam by holding receptions during Ramadan at which spirits were served. Verbal attacks and insults on Christians and Jews became part of sermons in Nazareth mosques. The expansion of the Islamist verbal aggression inevitably developed into the incursion of mosques into Church properties, such as occurred in the Nabi Sa'in *waqf* affair. The entrance of the Islamic Movement into the municipal council following the 1989 elections, its growing power within the council, combined with the continuous decline of the Christian population in Nazareth, were bound to cause further deterioration in Christian–Muslim relations.[31]

The disintegration of Arab secular nationalism under the Communist Party leadership, the rise of the Islamic Movement and the changing demographic balance in Nazareth undermined the existing social order and the Muslim–Christian relations. The Islamic Movement desired to assert the new reality of the Muslim majority in Nazareth. It further wished to "localize" Nazareth and challenge its international Christian affiliation as symbolized by the dominance of the Basilica of the Annunciation over the landscape of Nazareth. All these factors culminated in the Shihab al-Din affair.

The Nazareth 2000 Project and its demise

The rise of the Yitzhak Rabin government in 1992 and the new spirit of the Oslo Peace Accord that it initiated brought about a new agenda for the improvement of the position of the Arab citizens of Israel. This new approach met favorably with the Arab demand for the large-scale development of Nazareth. Both secular Communists and ardent Arab nationalists, the Nazareth Mayor Tawfiq Zayyad (Muslim) and his deputy, Ramiz Jeraysi (Christian Orthodox Arab), welcomed the project as a non-sectarian means to develop its economy and tourism. The Nazareth municipal council approved the Nazareth 2000 Project as such. The project envisioned the Christian 2000 Jubilee and the Pope's planned visit to the Holy Land as a way of putting Nazareth on the tourist world map. It was expected that millions of pilgrims and tourists would throng the city during the millennium year. The project intended to develop the Old City of Nazareth, build museums and create new city gardens as well as tourist trails between the famous churches. A major part of the project was a tourist plaza in front of the Basilica of the Annunciation. The project was supposed to expand the number of hotel rooms, commercial areas, and jobs as well as improve the roads and the general appearance of the town. Beyond that, the project intended to expand tourism to Israel for the 2000-millennium celebrations and form a counterpart to the Bethlehem 2000 celebrations. The government's budget for the project was 40 million dollars, and by 1994, approximately 20 million dollars had been invested mainly in solving traffic problems.[32]

Following the murder of Yitzhak Rabin and the 1996 elections, the right-wing Likud Party headed by Benjamin Netanyahu came to power. The new coalition together with the religious and ultra-Orthodox parties changed the government's agenda regarding the peace accord and the Arab minority in Israel. This change of government orientation brought about the freezing of nearly all government projects and finance connected with the Nazareth 2000 Project.

Professor Raphael Israeli, an ardent right-wing supporter who served as a member of the first Commission of Inquiry into the Shihab al-Din affair (discussed later in this essay), explained the Netanyahu government's change of policy as its reluctance "to face head-on the Nazareth Muslim majority which had by then begun to show signs of discontent concerning the project, fearing lest it would boost the diminished stature of the Christian minority and dwarf their own." To avoid criticizing the role of the Likud government, he pointed out the ultra-Orthodox Sephardic Shas Party and its loathing of Christians and Christianity as a major factor for discontinuing the government's financial support of the Nazareth 2000 Project.[33]

The only part of the project that still went forward was the tourist plaza in front of the Basilica of the Annunciation—a 1955 square meter plot of land that had been a state domain since the Ottoman period and was allotted by the Israel Lands Administration to the municipality of Nazareth for the construction of the plaza. It contained an empty dilapidated Ottoman school building. At the corner of the square, there was a neglected ancient tomb reportedly belonging to Shihab al-Din, a nephew of the glorious Saladin, the Muslim commander who defeated the Crusaders in the twelfth century. Shihab al-Din's tomb had existed since then on that spot, but it had never attracted much attention nor had it been a center of worship. Now the Islamists claimed that the entire area, including the tomb and the plaza, were part of the same *waqf* (endowment property). There were also several stores owned by the Muslim *waqf* altogether comprising 254 square meter of the total 1955 square meter plot. The planned plaza included the renovation of the Shihab al-Din Tomb but not as an integral part of the plaza.

In summer 1997, a contractor hired by the municipality knocked down the old school. However, he soon went bankrupt and the development of the plaza was suspended. The rubble left near the Shihab al-Din Tomb excited the Islamists to take action.[34] Their campaign was led by Abu Nawwaf (Ahmad Salih Hamudah Zu'bi) who had taken his position as chair of the local *waqf* in Nazareth. Salman Abu Ahmad, a civil engineer and leader of the Islamic Movement in Nazareth and member of the municipal council of Nazareth, was the brain and coordinator behind the Islamist campaign. Abu Nawwaf presented the mayor with a plan to build a huge mosque on top of the Shihab al-Din Tomb with a towering 86-meter minaret. However, the municipality, apparently assuming that in the meantime the plaza would be completed, asked him to present plans for further discussion. Considering this as rejection, on December 21, 1997, Abu Nawwaf stormed the square with hundreds of Muslims in tow and erected a huge protest tent, maintaining that the whole square including the demolished school was a Muslim *waqf*. The Israeli authorities reacted slowly and hesitantly. The police did not evacuate the invaders immediately. Had it done so, the whole affair might have been prevented. It took several weeks until the Israel Lands Administration, the official owner of the square, referred the matter to the Nazareth law court where the issue was adjudicated for nearly two years. In the meantime, the police refused to dismantle the tent despite the demands of the municipality.[35]

The struggle of the Islamic Movement for the building of the mosque in front of the Basilica of the Annunciation left no illusion regarding its aims. It was intended to become a symbol of the "Islamization of Nazareth," echoing slogans such as "Islam is the solution" and "Falastin—a Muslim Arab state." It was clear that their immediate target was to obstruct the "Nazareth 2000" Project which symbolized for them the Christian dominance of the town. A more moderate explanation designed to appeal to the Israeli-Jewish audience was provided by Israeli-Jewish lawyer Dan Shafrir, who represented the Muslim *waqf* in Nazareth. In a letter sent to the Israeli government and Knesset members, he explained that by building the Shihab al-Din Mosque, the *waqf* meant to become integrated in the Nazareth 2000 Project. He emphasized that "Nazareth is a mixed town where Muslims live together with Christians" and noted that "the Muslims constitute 70 percent of the town's population."[36] At the height of the struggle in 1999, members of the Communist Party at the municipality of Nazareth recognized the mistake they had made in neglecting the poor Muslim neighborhoods of Nazareth and in overemphasizing the religious aspect of the millennium celebrations over their cultural, social, and economic aspects. They further acknowledged that insufficient consideration had been given to Muslim sites as part of the 2000 Project.[37]

It later became apparent that the treatment of the issue by the Netanyahu government was motivated by the desire to win votes for the Likud party. According to his own testimony, it was Danny Greenberg, then a consultant of Prime Minister Netanyahu and the Likud Party (but not the Likud government), who promoted the idea of erecting a big mosque in front of the Basilica of the Annunciation. He hoped in this way to win Likud votes from the Muslims of Nazareth. According to rumors, the erection of the protest tent by the Islamic Movement on the eve of Christmas 1997 was coordinated with Greenberg and, following instructions from the political level, the police left it untouched. Later on, Greenberg played down his role maintaining that he had just been following the line taken from more central figures in the Netanyahu government and the Likud Party as well as from the religious ultra-Orthodox parties.[38]

The conflict further deteriorated following the municipal elections in November 1998, in which the Shihab al-Din issue was played off between the weakening Communist Party that promoted Palestinian Arab secular nationalism, and the rising force of the Islamic Movement, that placed Islam above nationalism. The Communist Party, the Democratic Front, headed by the mayor-elect Ramiz Jeraysi, of a Christian Orthodox Arab family, won nine seats (held by four Christian and five Muslim members); the United Nazareth Party, in which the Islamic Movement was the major group, won ten seats. This new balance of power prevented the establishment of a municipal council. Together with the deepening inter-communal political conflict, it caused the paralysis of municipal activity for many months. All this time a prolonged discussion of the matter took place in the law courts of Nazareth and Tiberias without arriving at any clear decision while the police abstained from taking firm action. It was clear that matters would come to head.

In the meantime the Muslims reinforced the walls of the tent with bricks and concrete to withstand the vagaries of winter. With daily prayers, the newly functioning mosque became a regular feature of the city center, and work on the plaza in preparation for the millennium was suspended. The affair now became known as the "Shihab a-Din controversy." The Islamists claimed that the entire area, including the tomb and the plaza, was part of the same *waqf* property, and they applied the powerful mobilizing symbol of Saladin (via his nephew) to raise passions and enlist the support of the Muslims in Nazareth and elsewhere.

The outbreak of violence

The following Easter, April 3–4, 1999, riots broke out in Nazareth. On Easter eve a fistfight occurred between members of the Islamic Movement in the protest tent and several Christian drunkards. Early the next morning, members of the Islamic Movement joined by Muslim villagers from the vicinity of Nazareth, rioted in the town center. Even though a large police force was mobilized at the outskirts of Nazareth, it stood by watching the scene erupt, abstaining for hours from stopping the attacks. The Islamists started attacking Christian passers-by. Christian women driving their cars were dragged off and badly beaten. Muslims who were considered by the Islamists to be collaborators with the Christians were also attacked. Among them was Atif Fahum, chair of the White Mosque, near the Basilica of the Annunciation who was on his way to greet his Christian friends on their holiday. He was particularly shocked by the fact that the police force that was present did nothing to stop the rioters. Shops and businesses on the main street, as well as government offices, were vandalized.[39] Northern District Police Commander Alik Ron explained later on Israeli television and radio news broadcasts that he had received orders from "higher political levels" to let his forces stand by and abstain from interfering. Only following his insistent demands was he allowed to put an end to the riots.[40]

The riots received nationwide circulation and deeply shocked many people of Nazareth, particularly the attacks on women and the delayed interference by the police to stop the violence. As the veteran Christian Arab journalist and author Atallah Mansour put it, "the pogrom went on for two days until the international press raised a hue and cry against Israel law enforcement policies," but none of the leaders of the mob was arrested.[41] The Islamists on the other hand tended to play down these riots by putting the blame on "several young urchins" that did not cause any serious damage.[42] Siham Fahoum Ghanim, an ex-council member of Nazareth in the pro-Islamist party, disclosed in her book some Muslim perspectives of the riots that partially confirm journalistic and media reports on the attacks on Nazareth Christians. According to Ghanim, the Easter riots were a reaction to the attack of several Christians on Muslims at the Shihab al-Din Square on Easter Sunday eve. On Easter Sunday and Monday, Christians and Muslims attacked each other. At least 30 people were wounded, while the police apprehended at least 12 people. On Monday, the minarets called upon Muslims to assemble and defend the Shihab al-Din Holy Place. Police Commander Alik Ron refused the Muslims demand to hold a legal demonstration and prevented the entry of car caravans from the neighboring villages.[43]

It is noteworthy that Muslims as well as some Israeli Jewish academicians who empathize with Palestinian-Arab nationalism either belittled or completely ignored the riots and attacks on the Christians of Nazareth and the delayed police intervention in the violent riots on Easter 1999.[44] This is demonstrative of the growing influence and identification of Palestinian Arab nationalism with Islam. Even more indicative is a conflicting narrative suggested by Raphael Israeli. His account reflects the approach of the Commission of Inquiry, i.e., that, the Easter riots emanated from the Muslim–Christian confrontation within the municipal council of Nazareth. Israeli tried to justify the police abstention from enforcing law and order on the rioters. "Skirmishes gradually became a general problem, with police refraining from interference lest they be accused by both parties of exacerbating or encouraging the rift."[45] He found another excuse in the police reaction to the violent demonstrations that had taken place a year earlier in September 1998 in the Muslim town of Umm al-Fahm in protest against the closure of 500 dunams of the Roha agricultural lands near that town by the military authorities. The police was then denounced for its violent suppression of the demonstrations, using tear gas and rubber bullets for the first time against Israeli demonstrators, thereby causing scores of wounded. Again, the police was accused of using excessive force to suppress the October 2000 riots in which 13 Arab demonstrators were shot by police. This led to the establishment of an official judicial commission of inquiry headed by Supreme Court Justice Theodore Orr. The Orr Commission Report, considered the police treatment of the Umm al-Fahm demonstrations as one of the major Arab grievances leading up to the October 2000 riots, later known as the Second (al-Aqsa) Intifada. Israeli takes these denouncements as an excuse for the laxity of the police in interfering in the Nazareth riots. "Why should they [the police] take physical risks in their zeal to fulfill their duty, only to end up reprimanded by the politicians and scorned by public opinion?"[46] Israeli's account focuses on the basic failure of the Israeli Government's duty to enforce law and order upon all its citizens, including the Arab ones. It unintentionally confirms the Arab Christian grievance that the government tended to ignore its duty in the Nazareth riots since Arab Christians, and not Jews, were targeted.

While the police failed in their duty to keep law and order, local Christian dignitaries, community activists, and clergy did their best to stop the riots and the attacks on Christians. As soon as he heard of the riots in the town center, Fuad Farah, then chair of the Orthodox Arab Council in Israel, immediately rushed to the Shihab al-Din Square and appealed to Abu Nawwaf to stop the riots. However, he refused to sign any document agreeing to the construction of the Shihab al-Din Mosque. He also approached several Muslim dignitaries of the town and urged them to make an open call to stop the riots immediately, but none dared to face the Islamist mob publicly. According to Farah, Mayor Jeraysi did not dare appear in the streets of Nazareth either.[47] In his book, Farah denounced Arab national organizations that refrained from denouncing the attacks on Christians, ignoring what the Christians had done for the sake of all of the Arab population, Muslims and Christians alike, in the 1948 War and after.[48]

At this point attempts were made to present the campaign to build the Shihab al-Din Mosque as part of the Palestinian national struggle against the "Israeli occupation" by raising the banner of "Shihab al-Din and al-Aqsa are the heart of Palestine." Palestinian Arab nationalists in Israel including some Christian politicians supported the Islamic Movement renovation campaign for al-Haram al-Sharif (the Temple Mount) under the slogan "Al-Aqsa is in Danger," considering it as a national no less than a religious campaign.[49] However, the organ of the Balad Arab national secularist party *Fasl al-Maqal* on April 16–22, 1999, denounced that trend. Afif Ibrahim wrote, "We were not logical when we lifted this banner. The shrine of Shihab al-Din is just an issue between the municipality [of Nazareth] and the Islamic Movement over a piece of land."

During this difficult situation, Abd al-Salam Manasra, a native of Nazareth, General Secretary of the High Islamic Sufi Council in Jerusalem and the Holy Land, made a bold gesture by walking through the rioting mob together with Christian Orthodox dignitaries. Recalling these events Manasra said, "We have never had any problem with the Christians of Nazareth, the rioters came from the villages. Warned about the danger involved, I said: Let them attack me before they attack them [the Christians]. So we walked together from one roadblock to another until they were all dismantled."[50]

The absence of responsible government action and the urgent need to restore law and order had their impact on the growing identification of the Arab public organizations with Islam. The chair of the General Committee of Arab Mayors and Local Councils in Israel, Muhammad Zaydan, urgently convened an ad hoc committee of seven members in attempt to calm the riots. The committee was composed of Knesset members from the Communist and the Ra'am Parties, Islamic Movement members as well as Arab mayors from the Galilee. It is significant that no Christian member was included. On April 4, 1999, the committee published its call for the cessation of the violence. It urged a return to "the relaxed friendly relations that had existed in Nazareth before." According to this, the *waqf* committee would continue its negotiations with the Israeli government for the building of the mosque. The Chairman Zaydan would follow them up while the Nazareth municipality would refrain from interference. The Islamists naturally considered this decision as a clear support of the semi-representative Arab councils committee in the building of the mosque. Some even maintain that the Christians consented to the building of the mosque while they ignore the circumstances in which the declaration was issued.[51]

Viewing these circumstances, an urgent meeting of an ad hoc reconciliation committee convened in which Muslim and Christian dignitaries and religious leaders from Nazareth and the Arab sector elsewhere in Israel participated, including lawyer Tawfiq Abu Ahmad, a relative and supporter of Salman Abu Ahmad, the leader of the Islamic Movement in Nazareth. A day later on April 5, 1999, the committee came out with a declaration signed by six Muslim and six Christian religious leaders, including the Greek Catholic Archimandrite Emile Shoufani, headmaster of the St. Joseph College in Nazareth and one of the outstanding Greek Catholic clerics in Nazareth. The declaration denounced violence against any holy places [art.1]. The Christian brethren and religious leaders declared that "they have no claim of ownership of the Shihab al-Din plot of land" [art. 2]. "The Christian brethren and dignitaries" further expressed their support in the struggle of their Muslim brethren regarding the liberation of their blessed *waqf* lands [art. 3]. All the participants of the meeting urged the government to find an early solution for the Shihab al-Din issue, "the authorities being responsible for the crisis and the tension in the town of Nazareth." The declaration ended with a call to restore the peaceful situation that had existed before and "adhere to morality and fraternity."[52]

It was clear that the grave situation, the realization of the lack of public security and the Christian apprehensions that they were liable to face future violence without protection enabled Abu Ahmad to manipulate the Christian dignitaries into signing this public declaration that conformed to the aims of the Islamic Movement. Raphael Israeli refers to the Christian leaders' signature on this document as a clue to their being "torn between their loyalty to other fellow Arabs ... and their horror at the threat of being crushed by the Muslim majority and the mounting aggressiveness of the Islamists."[53] He overlooks the main issue, namely the absence of the Israeli security and law enforcement authorities as if there were only Muslim and Christian players in the Nazareth arena. Members of the Islamic Movement in Nazareth later interpreted this declaration as a proof of the support of the majority of the people of Nazareth, including Christian leaders, in the building of the disputed mosque.[54] Siham Fahoum-Ghanim confirms this pressure telling in her book of several Islamist sheikhs who demanded that the Christian leaders declare their consent to the erection of the Shihab al-Din Mosque as a pre-condition to the restoration of order.[55]

The riots agitated the heads of the Catholic Church in Israel and abroad. The Franciscan Custodian of the Holy Land wrote a letter to Prime Minister Netanyahu on April 8 in which he urged the government to "safeguard the religious interests and sensibility of all the communities in this country. ... The authorities could have easily intervened and hindered the bloody confrontation." He ended warning that "favoring extremists today only creates terrorist problems tomorrow."[56] Latin Patriarch Michel Sabbah expressed in his Easter message his concern of the "critical situation between Muslims and Christians in Nazareth." He put the blame on the general election campaign that was "feeding this tension for electoral interests."[57] In the coming weeks, Israeli embassies in the west were flooded by protests and questions by the Vatican and various Christian organizations regarding the violence and the dispute in Nazareth.[58] The churches in Nazareth closed their gates in protest; their representatives met government officials and expressed their concern, as well as that of the Vatican, regarding the Israeli government's treatment of the riots and their strong opposition to the construction of the mosque in front of the Basilica.[59]

Israeli officials apparently did not take these protests seriously. A government source told the *Jerusalem Post* daily newspaper that "the General Security Service is convinced that if the dispute is not resolved, Moslem violence will intensify. There's almost no doubt that justice is on the side of the Christians, but at the same time, even the city's Christians along with the mayor, want to see a compromise reached that will calm the city."[60] With an eye to the coming general elections on May 17, the compromise as conceived by the government was to side with the Islamist demands in Nazareth. In doing so, the government ignored long-term effects of the conflict in both the local and the international arenas.

Rather than punishing the rioters, representatives of the Likud and several religious parties who were members in the government coalition visited the Islamic Movement protest tent in the disputed square and publicly expressed their support for the building of the mosque in front of the Basilica. Moshe Katsav, then Minister of Tourism and in charge of Arab affairs in the Netanyahu government, told Israel television Channel One in an interview on Friday, April 9, 1999, that he personally supported the Muslim demand to erect the Shihab al-Din Mosque. Salman Abu Ahmad, the local leader of the Islamic Movement in Nazareth, welcomed the Katsav declaration as "a ray of light," noting that his party had not yet decided whether to vote for Netanyahu-right wing Likud or Barak-Labor party in the coming general elections. Several spokesmen of the Islamic Movement admitted in television interviews that their demand for the mosque on the disputed land stemmed from their desire to change the Christian atmosphere of Nazareth, since "the Muslims constitute the majority of the population in the town." Abu Nawwaf warned on television that he "will burn all Nazareth" if the demand to build the mosque was rejected.[61]

Government commissions of inquiry

On April 11, 1999, the Netanyahu government decided to establish a ministerial committee of four headed by Tourism Minister Katsav in order to report to the Prime Minister about "proposals for the resolution of the dispute between Muslims and Christians regarding the contended square in Nazareth." About a week later, on April 18, 1999, the Israeli government discussed the Nazareth issue and upon accepting the recommendation of the ministerial committee, decided to allocate the Islamic Movement 504 square meters of the disputed square for the construction of the mosque. Government officials were well aware that just 254 square meters of it (the Shihab al-Din tomb—135 square meters, and the shop complex—119 square meters) might be proved to be Muslim endowment (*waqf*) property in the forthcoming court decision. The government further decided to allocate a patch of land elsewhere in Nazareth in order to build another big mosque. However, the Islamic Movement rejected the government's offer.[62]

A few days earlier, on April 14, Interior Minister Eli Suissa of the ultra-Orthodox Shas Party, appointed yet another four-member commission of inquiry including Amram Kal'aji, official of the Interior Ministry as chair, two ex-officials (Efrayim Lapid and Gad Aviner), and Professor Raphael Israeli of the Hebrew University of Jerusalem. All were renowned hardliners regarding the Arabs in Israel. The commission was nominated in order to provide an independent forum for fact-finding and recommendations for a solution for the crisis. According to Israeli, the commission in fact served no more than a "cover up" for the government's pre-made decision to allow the building of the Shihab al-Din Mosque.[63] It is significant that the terms of reference of both commissions did not include an in-depth discussion of the Easter 1999 riots nor the possible detention of riot instigators and their punishment.

The commission, appointed by Interior Minister Suissa, heard testimonies from Muslim and Christian inhabitants of Nazareth as well as from members of the municipality and the Islamic Movement. Its main concern was with possible reactions of the Islamic Movement to its decisions. Local Christians presented their views discreetly, apprehensive of possible Muslim violent responses against them. Only evangelical Christians with American passports dared to testify openly. Neither officials of the Religious Affairs, Foreign Affairs, and Justice Ministries, nor academicians, who were acquainted with the Christian communities and the Christian world, were consulted on the issue. Officials who did caution against the government decisions in this matter were shunted aside.[64] Matters calmed down for several weeks in anticipation of the May 17, 1999 general elections. The mood among the people in Nazareth was that if the right-wing Likud Party were to win, the Islamic Movement would get the upper hand, and if the Labor bloc would win, the Christians and the moderate Muslims in Nazareth would strengthen their position. Labor, led by Ehud Barak, was swept into power. The new Labor-led coalition government hesitated for several months to deal with the issue. Barak explained to the Arabic newspaper *Kul al-Arab* on September 9, 1999 that "reconciliation and dialogue are needed in order to solve this sensitive issue" and that he had decided to appoint a special ministerial committee to study the issue and present its recommendations so to enable the preparations for the 2000 celebrations to proceed.[65]

This second ministerial committee, headed by Internal Security Minister Professor Shlomo Ben-Ami, Jerusalem Affairs Minister Haim Ramon, Interior Minister Nathan Sharansky, and Culture and Sports Minister Matan Vilnay, did not probe matters too deeply. This committee too was mainly concerned with the Islamic Movement's reactions and met just twice with the municipal council of Nazareth. Furthermore, it did not invite experts and officials acquainted with the issue to testify on the possible implications of the affair on the local inter-communal relations in Nazareth as well as on the reaction of the international Christian community. The committee declared its intentions to reach a "painful compromise." It tended to base itself on the conclusions of the commission nominated by the previous Interior Minister Suissa, which had presented its recommendations in September 1999 to the new Labor government. Its recommendations were to allow the building of the Shihab al-Din Mosque on a 700 square meters plot that would be extracted from the planned tourist plaza, thus expanding the 504 square meters allowed by the Netanyahu ministerial committee. One member, Professor Raphael Israeli, presented his minority recommendation not to exceed the 504 square meters allowed for the building of the mosque by the previous Netanyahu government.[66] However, even Israeli did not challenge the idea of allowing the Islamists to build their mosque on the disputed square. He warned against worldwide Christian protests against the building of the enlarged mosque, ignoring the fact that these would come anyway if the mosque were to be built there, regardless of its size.

In early October 1999, some details of the Ben-Ami committee's proposed compromise were handed to the various parties of the conflict and aroused great concern among the municipality and the Christians of Nazareth. At the same time, Ben-Ami admitted that he was aware that the disputed square was state land and not a Muslim *waqf*, as claimed by the Islamic Movement.[67] On October 5, less than three weeks after it had commenced its work, the Ben-Ami committee published its decision to allow the Islamic Movement to build a mosque in front of the Basilica on 700 square meters out of the 1955 square meters disputed square (compared with the 504 square meters that the Netanyahu government had offered) and to allot another 10 dunams of state land (compared with the four dunams that the Netanyahu government had offered) elsewhere in Nazareth for religious and social purposes. The cornerstone would be laid several weeks later, on November 8, 1999, and the mosque itself was to be built after the termination of the 2000 celebrations, according to a plan that would be approved by the government. A police station would be constructed on the edge of the square to keep order. As part of the compromise, the protest tent was to be taken down prior to the laying of the cornerstone. The decision was adopted by the Barak government and became a binding regulation.[68]

Just a day after the publication of the committee's decision, the district court of Nazareth published its decision regarding the ownership of the disputed land. The court's decision of October 3 maintained that the entire disputed square of 1955 square meters was state domain. It refuted the claims of the Muslim *waqf* that the whole square was a holy place and a Muslim *waqf* and found those claims to be baseless. The court declared its decision final.[69] A further decree by the Tiberias court on October 25, 1999 ordered the demolishing of the Islamic Movement's protest tent and the awnings around it, for there was no disagreement that they had been built illegally.[70] Raphael Israeli expressed his disappointment with the Labor government that although "had committed itself to the rule of law, did not await the verdict of the district court."[71] In fact, Ben-Ami and Barak were aware of the court's decisions before making their own, as shown above, which makes the disappointment even greater.

As expected, the Islamic Movement welcomed the government decision, while the Nazareth Mayor Jeraysi, in attempt to avoid direct confrontation with the Islamic Movement, declared that any settlement between the government and the Islamic Movement would be acceptable to the municipality. On October 7, 1999 the Islamic Movement held a press conference at which it praised the government's support of its cause. It warned the Vatican to "abstain from interfering with the local affairs of Nazareth." Otherwise, it warned, the local Christians would be hurt and the Movement would appeal to the Muslim world for support and cause the cancellation of the 2000 celebrations in Nazareth.[72]

The conflict in Nazareth and the Barak government decisions were intensely covered by the Israeli Hebrew media, presented as a local internal conflict between Christians and Muslims in Nazareth in which the Israeli government was obliged to intervene as a moderator. Government spokespersons did not refer to the government responsibility for keeping law and order and the security of all its citizens. An exception was the leading Israeli daily *Ha'aretz* that reported daily on the events in Nazareth and warned that any concession to the Islamic Movement would be taken as a prize for their aggression and the breaking of the law and would further stimulate violence. It called on the government to reconsider its decision in the light of the court's decision.[73] *Ha'aretz* correspondent on Arab affairs, Yossi Alghazi, warned against the implications of the government decision on Nazareth. He quoted Arab complaints of the government's indifference towards the Muslim fundamentalists' violence as long as it was directed against Arabs rather than Jews: "If Nazareth is set on fire, Tel Aviv will suffer burns as well."[74]

News of the Barak government's decision aroused protests by the churches locally as well as worldwide. The Vatican declared its absolute objection to the construction of the mosque in front of the Basilica. It maintained that former Foreign Minister Ariel Sharon had promised the Pope John Paul II on his visit to the Vatican on April 26, 1999 that the Israeli government would not permit the construction of a mosque in front of the Basilica. As the Israeli government did not withdraw its decision in favor of building the mosque, the churches warned that they would close their gates on the coming Christmas and that the Pope might cancel his planned visit to the Holy Land. They criticized the government for being shortsighted and motivated by the narrow interest of raising votes in the elections and ignoring all other considerations. The decision also caused accusations by the Arab public of a divide-and-rule policy.[75] Having appealed to Prime Minister Barak against the permit to build the Shihab al-Din Mosque, the three patriarchs of Jerusalem (the Greek Orthodox Patriarch Diodoros I, the Latin Patriarch Michel Sabbah, and the Armenian Patriarch Torkemen Manoogian) together with the Custos of the Holy Land, Giovanni Battistelli, published a strong protest against the decision to build the mosque. They declared that all the sanctuaries in the land would be closed in protest on November 22–23, 1999.[76]

Nevertheless, Ben-Ami declared that the government would proceed with his committee's recommendation to build the mosque despite the court's decision and the protest of the churches. He explained that the issue was a political one and therefore required a compromise rather than a legal solution. He claimed that the land was state domain and the government had therefore a free hand to allot it to the Islamic Movement, regardless of the court's decision.[77] By that time, unfinished digging and construction blocked the main road of Nazareth. The nearby tourist marketplace was paralyzed because of the uneasy access to it caused by the unfinished restorations as well as by the agitation surrounding the Islamist protest tent. Contractors for the millennium celebrations cancelled their contracts.

In line with the decision of the Ben-Ami committee, the protest tent was pulled down by the Islamic Movement on November 8, in preparation for the mosque's cornerstone-laying ceremony. In a last-minute attempt to cancel the government decision, a delegation of American Catholic cardinals visited Jerusalem in early November and appealed to members of the Ben-Ami ministerial committee to have the decision revoked. Although they found understanding among professional officials, Jerusalem Affairs Minister Haim Ramon, who was in charge of the issue, put them off. They left Israel disappointed and warned that they would lobby in the United States Congress as well as with President Bill Clinton in order to prevent the building of the mosque.[78]

Palestinian leader Yasser Arafat and the Mufti of Jerusalem made a last-minute effort to dissuade the Islamic Movement from building the mosque, or at least delay it. Several Arab countries made similar appeals. Prince Abdallah Ibn Saud promised a generous donation for removing the mosque to another site in Nazareth. The Lebanese paper *al-Safir* maintained that the Mufti of Cairo declared the future prayers at the planned Shihab al-Din Mosque as null and void.[79] These attempts by the Arab world were motivated by their awareness of the deep dissension within the Arab community in Nazareth and in Israel at large; the deepening dispute over the mosque was liable to endanger their Arab national identity and unity. They also bore in mind the forthcoming negotiations regarding the status of Jerusalem and apprehended that Israel might use the conflict in Nazareth as a pretext to question the capability of the Palestinian Authority to govern the holy places.

The construction of the Shihab al-Din Mosque

The cornerstone ceremony of the new Shihab al-Din Mosque took place on November 23, 1999. Thousands of members of the Islamic Movement attended, including three Knesset members of Ra'am (Arab Democratic Party), in which the moderate wing of the Islamic Movement participated. Despite its promise, the Israeli government did not send a representative to the ceremony. In protest the churches closed their doors for two days, on November 22 and 23; the Vatican publicly accused the Government of Israel of discriminating against the Christians and ignoring its commitment to the protection of the Holy Places. The issue became a hot topic in both the local and international media. Ben-Ami tried pathetically in a television interview to explain that the ministerial committee that he headed was bound to follow decisions of the previous government even though he personally had reservations about the issue.[80] The Barak government's public support of the Islamic Movement in the Nazareth conflict aroused deep disappointment and desperation among church leaders and the Christian public in Israel, particularly in Nazareth.[81] A host of assumptions and theories spread in Nazareth suggesting that the Barak government decision in favor of the Islamists was part of a pre-arranged collusion with them before the elections in attempt to win their votes. Israeli supports these theories and brings as a clue Barak's promise to create a separate Arab district centered in Nazareth, including an Arab university.[82] There is no doubt that the Barak government gave in to the Islamists demands, but there is no clue that this was a pre-arranged collusion. After all, the Likud government initiated the affair. The Labor government is to blame for following its predecessors' steps rather than imposing law according to the court's decisions.

In early 2000, things looked ostensibly calm in Nazareth. The Islamists pulled down their protest tent but erected a hydraulic pillar, enabling the tent to be put up and pulled down quickly, and spread carpets all over the square to prove their possession. The 1999 Christmas and New Year celebrations that coincided with the Ramadan passed seemingly in an atmosphere of reconciliation. The two parties in the municipal council were more prepared to reach a compromise that would enable the municipality to function. The Islamist council members joined the mayor's coalition; some were appointed as deputies to the mayor as well as to other well-paid influential positions.

Saturday, March 25, 2000, the Catholic holiday commemorating the annunciation to the Virgin Mary of the impending birth of her baby Jesus, was scheduled as the date of the long-expected visit of Pope John Paul II as part of his pilgrimage to the Holy Land. Owing to the ongoing conflict in Nazareth, the town was marginalized in this visit. The Pope arrived in a helicopter that landed in nearby Natzrat Illit where its Jewish mayor welcomed him. The entourage proceeded to the Basilica of the Annunciation where the mayor of Nazareth together with numerous cardinals greeted the Pope and entered the Basilica. No ceremony took place in front of it. Many people gathered in the disputed square to greet the Pope, including members of the Islamic Movement and the *waqf* council of Nazareth. They waved a salute, as Dan Rabinowitz so empathically describes, "on their own terms" with a clear message, that "the Muslims who are the majority of Nazareth … [are] playing hosts to the ultimate visitor from Rome."[83] The Islamist campaign leader later put it, "I was prepared to travel to Rome and discuss the affair with the Pope as an equal but canceled my trip because I resisted the demand to give up the building of the mosque in advance."[84] There were banners greeting the Pope as well as quotations in Arabic from the Holy Qur'an that might sound offensive to Christians. Despite their pledge, the Islamists did not dismantle the hydraulic tent and the mosque's loudspeaker interrupted the mass inside the Basilica. The worldwide BBC and CNN coverage of the event showed Christians singing and protesting against this interruption.

The years 2000–2001 drastically changed the political arena as well as Jewish–Arab relations in Israel. The Second (al-Aqsa) Intifada began in October 2000, this time with the involvement of Israeli Arab citizens. Twelve Israeli Arabs, all of them Muslim, were shot dead by the police in these riots. In Nazareth police snipers shot dead three demonstrators and wounded others. Following new elections, Ariel Sharon the leader of the Likud Party became Prime Minister in March 2001, thereby replacing the Labor coalition government. It was against this background that the Islamic Movement made its preparations to build the Shihab al-Din Mosque.

In line with the Barak government's decision, the Nazareth Islamic Movement, and *waqf* called for a competition which was won by a Jordanian architect. They then submitted the required plan for the Shihab al-Din Mosque to the Nazareth District Planning Committee that approved it. On November 21, 2001 the Israel Land Administration, confirmed the plan to build the mosque on the disputed square, thereby seeming to remove the last bureaucratic obstacle to the commencement of construction. The Islamic Movement still needed to wait for the official confirmation to be signed by the legal consultant of the Israel Land Administration.[85]

Viewing these events, Christian leaders of all churches overcame their differences, convened in Jerusalem and established an unprecedented ad hoc Christian coalition, "the International Coalition for Nazareth," that included nearly all the churches in Israel. With American evangelicals as spokesmen, the coalition demanded that the Israeli government revoke its decision to allow the building of the Shihab al-Din Mosque. Despite their continuous protests, the Barak government stuck to its permission to the Islamists. The Islamic Movement, on its part, appealed to the Supreme Court to allow the works to commence. Following an internal debate, the Islamic Movement decided to start digging the basement of the Shihab al-Din Mosque prior to obtaining the official written permit. They started the work on New Year's Eve 2002 as a symbolic act "despite the Christians fury."[86]

The Custos of the Holy Land together with the International Coalition for Nazareth appealed to Prime Minister Sharon to undo the mistake done by the previous governments "for the sake of Nazareth, for the sake of the Holy Land's three monotheistic faiths and for the sake of the future security of the State of Israel." It warned against allowing the "fringe group of extreme Islamists" to complete "a provocative Mosque adjacent to the Basilica" and stressed the tremendous strain on Christian–Muslim, Jewish–Christian, and, in the end, Muslim–Jewish relations that it would create.[87] In a further letter, the International Coalition for Nazareth warned against "a government's appeasement of a small, violent and racist group ... If the government does not act decisively to stop this now, the tide of growing extremist activity will never be turned back." The letter stated that "The Israel Government should uphold the integrity and sanctity of all Christian Holy Places in Israel and guarantee free access to the holy sites according to its international obligations. Therefore, the Israeli government should nullify the permit to build the mosque and go back to the original plan of building a public open space there."[88]

In the meantime, the *waqf* in Nazareth, assuming that the government would continue to close its eyes, proceeded to pour the foundations of the Shihab al-Din Mosque in defiance of the court decision. Despite complaints from the International Christian Coalition, the Israeli police, bearing in mind the riots of the 2000 Intifada, refused to intervene out of fear of a Muslim backlash.

Reversing the government's decision

The Christian coalition found an open ear and empathy with the new American President George W. Bush who had entered office in January 2001 with the support of evangelist churches. Being a devout Christian, Bush was attentive to pleas from the Vatican as well as from American Catholic and Protestant leaders to prevent the building of the Shihab al-Din Mosque. Israeli Hebrew and Arabic newspapers reported on discussions of the issue in meetings and phone calls between Prime Minister Sharon and President Bush. Apparently as a response to the American intervention, the Israeli cabinet decided on January 8, 2002 to stop construction works on the disputed square due to the dissention that it aroused between Israel and the Christian world. The cabinet further nominated Public Works Minister Nathan Sharansky to head a ministerial commission to study the issue and submit recommendations for a solution to the dispute within two weeks. The cabinet decision met with opposition from Muslim Knesset members as well the chair of the Committee of the Heads of the Arab Municipal Councils who protested against the new government commission. They viewed it "as motivated by the desire to approach the Christian world" and held that it "was opposed by the desire of the Arab people."[89] This stand demonstrates the growing Islamization of the Arab national cause in Israel and the strengthening ties between the Islamists and the Committee of the Arab Local Councils that was supposed to be a national representative body of all the Arab local councils in Israel, Muslims, and Christians alike.

The new ministerial commission included some members of the previous Ben-Ami ministerial commission, including the chair Sharansky himself. It convened its first meeting on January 15, 2002, bearing in mind that Prime Minister Sharon was determined to discontinue the construction of the Shihab al-Din Mosque. Urging the commission to present its decision as soon

216 *Daphne Tsimhoni*

as possible, Sharon emphasized the illegality of the work on the Shihab al-Din site and stressed that it created an anomalous situation which should end immediately. The commission visited the Shihab al-Din site, met with the sides involved and heard the grievances of the Islamists. Sharansky, who had signed the previous Ben-Ami commission's decision to allow the building of the Shihab al-Din Mosque, now said that the issue should be re-examined "viewing the experience of the recent years. It is not pleasant to become an arbitrator between the Christian and Muslim worlds; we'd rather that they arrive at an understanding on their own."[90] Sharansky's words left no doubt about Prime Minister Sharon's change of mind and the Israeli government's growing awareness of the international significance of Nazareth and increasing American pressure to obey international commitments as well as the local court decisions.

The establishment of the Sharansky Commission outraged the Islamic Movement and local Arab national leadership that had demonstrated a growing sympathy with the Islamic cause. Throughout January 2002, the Islamic Movement conducted demonstrations in Nazareth against the Sharansky Commission in which thousands took part. Muslim Knesset members of the Ra'am party, in which the moderate branch of the Islamic Movement participated, urged the government to issue the permit for building the mosque "that had already been agreed upon." Tawfiq al-Khatib, head of the Committee of Heads of the Arab Local Councils asked, "Why doesn't the Sharon Government respect compromises that have been agreed upon by previous governments?"[91] Salman Abu Ahmad, the Islamist deputy mayor of Nazareth warned against renewed disturbances if the construction of the mosque was to be suspended. "The Muslims," he said, "were determined to build the mosque."[92]

Catholic reactions to the Sharansky commission were cautious. Father David Yaeger, spokesperson of the Franciscan Custody of the Holy Land, warned against any delay in the commission's work. The work at the Shihab al-Din site was continuing despite assurances by the government that it had stopped according to the court's decision. He further criticized the three Israeli governments that had treated the issue as a local tribal one and ignored scores of appeals by local and international church leaders on the affair.[93]

Referring to the Sharansky Commission, the veteran Likud leader and former Defense Minister Moshe Arens criticized the two previous governments that had taken the role of conciliator between Muslims and Christians with an eye on Muslim votes. "The government," he asserted, "is in charge of law enforcement and should take measures against those who break it. Furthermore, building the mosque in front of the Basilica is a provocation against millions of Christians who consider it as one of the holiest places. The Sharon government should not hesitate to enforce law despite the vocal demonstrations of the Islamic Movement."[94]

The process of reversing the previous governments' decisions regarding the Shihab al-Din Mosque took longer than Sharon expected. Finally, in March 2002, the Sharansky Commission published its recommendation to ban the construction of the Shihab al-Din Mosque in the disputed square. Sharansky explained the decision as influenced by the worldwide Christian opposition to the planned mosque as well as the Israeli obligation to safeguard the holy places and protect the rights of its minorities and their freedom of religion. The government, he said, offered the *waqf* seven alternative locations available for the immediate building of the mosque elsewhere in Nazareth. He promised to restore Shihab a-Din's Tomb, without altering it status. In addition, the government called for the implementation of the Nazareth Municipality's original plan that had been prepared in advance of the Pope's visit in 2000, to turn the disputed square into an open plaza for tourists.[95] The Vatican and local church leaders expressed their satisfaction at the decision of the Sharansky ministerial commission.

It took another year until the magistrates' court of Nazareth issued a demolition order for the Shihab al-Din Mosque on March 6, 2003.[96] The Islamic Movement appealed to higher authorities and the case went all the way to the district court in Nazareth and the Israeli Supreme Court that rejected the appeal and confirmed the demolition order in June 2003.[97] During that year, the Islamic Movement weakened due to internal dissension between the more moderate faction that was prepared to compromise with the government and the more extreme faction that rejected any cooperation or recognition of the authority of the State of Israel. In the 2003 general elections the Ra'am Party won just two seats instead of five gained in the previous elections. The general atmosphere in the West became less favorable toward the Muslims following the September 11, 2001 attack on the United States and the defeat of Saddam Hussein. All these brought about the more decisive attitude of the Israeli government toward the Islamic Movement. In May 2003, the police arrested several leaders of the Islamic Movement charged with activities against Israel's security. Above all, the direct pressure put by President Bush on Prime Minister Sharon made the Israeli government take firm action against the building of the Shihab al-Din Mosque.

Early in the morning of July 1, 2003, without any advance warning, government bulldozers demolished the constructions of the Shihab al-Din Mosque's basement. This was a secretly planned operation apparently taking orders directly from Prime Minister Ariel Sharon. Guarded by massive presence of the police, the demolishing of the mosque's basement took several hours and passed without violence. Members of the Islamic Movement in Nazareth were taken by surprise. They did their best to rally huge protest demonstrations but just a few scores attended. Their efforts to organize a general strike in Nazareth failed.[98] "This is a black day," conceded Abu Nawwaf at the Shihab al-Din Mosque while promising to continue the procedures to get a permit and build the mosque.[99] On the same day of the demolition, the security authorities took further steps to limit the activities of the Islamic Movement. A police announcement allowed tourists to renew visits to the Temple Mount in Jerusalem. There was no doubt about the close connection between these two operations.

Nathan Sharansky praised the demolition as the victory of law enforcement and admitted that the previous governments were wrong in fearing the reactions of the Islamists. Joseph Dan, professor of Jewish philosophy of the Hebrew University and the Shalem conservative research center, analyzed the demolishing of the Shihab al-Din Mosque in the context of Samuel Huntington's theory of the world's clash of civilizations. According to Dan, the demolition of the mosque was an exceptional victory in view of the ongoing decline and marginalization of the Christians by the growing Islamic dominance in the Middle East. "It was only the unbridled support of three bodies—the Vatican, the European Union and the United States—that enabled the Israeli government to take the decision to destroy the mosque in Nazareth."[100] In my opinion, the word "pressure," rather than "support," would have been a more appropriate description. The Israeli government's policy would have been more sensible had it abstained altogether from interfering in the local delicate communal balance in between Muslims and Christians in Nazareth. It should have heeded the call of Aviezer Ravitzky, professor of Judaic Studies, that Israel should abstain from becoming the spearhead of the West in the "clash of civilizations" between the West and the Muslim world.[101]

The construction of the tourist plaza according to the original Nazareth 2000 plan started soon after. It was completed in 2005 but remained enclosed behind bars. Its inauguration was deferred due to apprehensions of the government and the churches that the Islamists were liable to convert the plaza into an open mosque. In early March 2006, a bizarre Jewish–Christian homeless family launched an explosives attack inside the Basilica of the Annunciation explaining that they wanted to attract worldwide attention to their desperate situation. Luckily, they did not cause any serious damage. The following days, big demonstrations took place in Nazareth organized by the Committee of Heads of the Arab Local Councils. Both Muslim and Christian leaders participated in protesting the lack of proper government protection "against attacks on Arabs." Some Islamists took advantage of the situation. They broke into the barred tourist plaza and attempted to pray there, but the police forced them out.[102] This event formed the de facto inauguration of the plaza that has remained open since then. Though empty most of the daytime, on Fridays the Islamists occasionally perform open prayers at the square lifting banners and flags of the Islamic movement. However, this phenomenon has not yet been institutionalized.

Currently, in December 2008, life in Nazareth seems to have returned to normal. The main road has been repaired and new shops have opened on it, decoration and preparations for the Christmas celebration and traditional processions are at their peak. The number of visitors and pilgrims has expanded. Local hotels are full; there are new plans for increased tourism and start of renovation of the Old Town of Nazareth. The first steps of recovery might be also noticed in the returns of the municipal elections of Nazareth. In all three elections to the mayor seat since 1998 Jeraysi won over the Islamist candidate though with a slight percentage of votes. The municipal council elected in 2003 included eight Communist Democratic Front (Jabha) members, one independent member (pro-nationalist secular Balad Party) and eight members of the United List [muwahhada] the core of which is Islamist. Mayor Jeraisi had to come into terms with the Islamists in order to enable the municipality function. In the November 2008 municipal elections the Communist Democratic Front representation expanded to nine members; that of the Islamist United List diminished to seven and another two seats were won by nationalist pro-Balad members. This means that moderate Muslims might gain back their power and that for the first time since 1998 the municipal council of Nazareth could function without coming into terms with the Islamists.[103]

At the same time, one can feel the growing influence of Islam on the town in the *muezzin* loudspeakers' calls for prayers and the growing numbers of Muslim women who wear the Muslim dress and head covers. An underlying tension between the Islamists and the Christians bursts out from time to time and obstructs the recovery of Nazareth. It finds expression in loud Muslim prayers outside of the Church of the Annunciation and occasional violence toward Christians, particularly on Christian and Muslim holidays. This tension is symbolized by a banner strung up between two trees by an Islamic group on the approach to the Basilica of the Annunciation proclaiming Allah to be the "Unbegotten, Supreme, One and Only God," to be construed as a provocation to Christians. Mayor Jeraysi tries to explain his abstention from taking any action to stop this provocation by ridiculing it as the work of "some marginalized fanatics": Instructing its removal would aggravate tensions with the fundamentalists and embarrass the moderate Muslim majority with whom we wish to cooperate."[104]

Muslim and Christian perspectives of the Shihab al-Din affair

Was the Shihab al-Din Mosque affair a forgettable passing episode? Islamist leaders openly profess that they have not given up the idea to rebuild the Shihab al-Din Mosque at the tourist plaza. Salman Abu Ahmad, the figure behind the campaign, expresses the view of many Islamists that the disputed square as well as all of Nazareth and the Holy Land is a Muslim *waqf* despite the rejection of the Islamist claims by two Israeli courts. He believes that the Islamic Movement lost the battle only temporarily and looks for a future opportunity to renew the campaign. Hence, the Islamic Movement refused to accept the government's offer to build their mosque and Islamic center on a state land elsewhere in Nazareth. He insists that the Shihab al-Din Mosque should be built in front of the Basilica of the Annunciation as a cultural-political assertion no less than religious one. Salman Abu Ahmad believes that this goal can be achieved by peaceful democratic means, by winning the municipal elections. Abu Ahmad and other Islamists count on the demographic process that has turned Nazareth into a Muslim majority town and on the growing Islamization of the Muslim citizens of Nazareth. According to him, an Islamist-dominated municipal council will be able to convert the tourist plaza into a mosque. Commenting on Christian apprehensions regarding the imposition of Islamic codes on the public life in Nazareth, he mentions that "alcoholic beverages should not be served to the municipality parties as a matter of common sense."[105]

Abd al-Salam Manasra, general secretary of the High Islamic Sufi Council in Israel, represents a more moderate Islamism. He carefully expresses his basic support of building the Shihab al-Din Mosque in front of the Basilica, "maybe in ten years time ... We are in favor of building the mosque but won't kill ourselves for this end." He resents the Islamic Movement's activity because, according to him, their extremeness caused the loss of the whole project. They should have realized, he says, that no one, including Prime Minister Sharon, could withstand President Bush's pressure to prevent the building of the mosque.[106] In contrast to the Islamists, members of the White Mosque, the first mosque in Nazareth situated on a higher spot next to the Basilica of the Annunciation, clearly dissociate themselves from "those people of the mosque downtown and their aspirations. This [White Mosque] is an honorable mosque."[107] Their attitude represents the established Muslim families in Nazareth. They have lived together with the Christians for generations and appreciate the churches' contribution to the town's economy, education, and tourism. They don't feel threatened by it.

Siham Fahum-Ghanim, an ex-council member and supporter of the Islamist cause in the Nazareth crisis, maintains that the Islamic Movement in Nazareth emerged out of the frustration of the Muslim masses from the growing socio-economic gap between them and the Christians. The essence of the crisis is a conflict of identities. Religion is a very important component in the self-identity of the Muslims, by far more than in the identity of the Christians. The Muslims, particularly the younger generation, have become obsessed with the building of the mosque. She warns against the Crusader war that president Bush declared and its risks to Muslim–Christian relations in Nazareth. She also offers a compromise in Nazareth whereby only the first story of the mosque would be completed without the minaret.[108]

The idea of building the Shihab al-Din Mosque in front of the Basilica of the Annunciation gained support by Muslim Arab nationalists such as the Committee of the Heads of the Arab Local Councils. Some Muslim Arab academicians consider the issue within the local context only, ignoring the international significance of Nazareth and its holy places to worldwide Christianity. They tend to idealize the Muslim–Christian relations and put the blame for the Shihab al-Din controversy solely on the Israeli government. They do not reject the idea of building a moderate mosque in front of the Basilica.

Rassem Khamaisi, a town planner and professor of geography at the University of Haifa, acknowledges the expansion of the Muslim–Christian rift in Nazareth as in the Arab population in Israel at large, echoing the global trend of the expression of self-identity by ethnic and religious minorities; economic, political, and social factors often exacerbate these tensions. Khamaisi does not openly support the building of the Shihab al-Din Mosque. However, he considers the planning of Nazareth from a local perspective only; he believes that tourism cannot form the basis of the town's economy and ignores the international significance of Nazareth and its holiness to worldwide millions of Christians. He observes that the solution for the Shihab al-Din conflict can only take place by improving the socio-economic conditions of the Muslims in Nazareth and by maintaining a greater discourse between the various groups and communities within the Arab minority in Israel.[109]

Yusuf Jabarin, lecturer on town planning at the Technion, puts the blame for the crisis on the conceptual planning of the plaza that did not involve the people of Nazareth in its planning process. Still, he has no doubts about the good intentions of the planners. Findings of a survey that he conducted in Nazareth in summer 2004 showed that the vast majority put the major blame for the Nazareth crisis on the Israeli government and secondary blame on the Islamic Movement.[110] To my mind, the application of a modern concept of town planning is not a sufficient reason for the Nazareth crisis. The planned plaza was not enforced on Nazareth; the mayor of Nazareth and his deputy initiated it and the town's council approved it.[111] He ignores the socio-religious process that brought about the rise of the Islamic Movement in Nazareth. It was the Movement's aggressiveness toward the Christians and the deterioration of Muslim–Christian relations that culminated in the Shihab al-Din crisis.

Ahmad Ashkar, a Muslim native of the village Iksal near Nazareth, believes that the root of the Shihab al-Din crisis lies both in the jealousy and marginalization that many Muslim feel toward the Christians. In a booklet published in 2000, Ashkar discusses at length what he considers as the over-representation of the Christians in public positions and in the Christian schools in Nazareth which he considers as the outcome of nepotism while a large proportion of the destitute in Nazareth are Muslims. Ashkar denounces the Islamic Movement for their "confessionalism" and collaboration with the Zionist state that aims to break down the Arab Palestinian society. He further blames the Christian churches that, by declaring their strike against the building of the Shihab al-Din Mosque, deteriorated the conflict in Nazareth into a communal religious issue between Muslims and Christians, thereby playing into the hands of the Islamic Movement and the State of Israel. The key for the solution as offered by Ashkar is to convert the Christian schools into "mixed schools" and to stop what he considers the discrimination against the Muslims. He preaches for the separation between religion and state and the promotion of Arab national feelings above the religious ones.[112]

The Shihab al-Din Mosque crisis and particularly the April 1999 riots caused great agitation among the Christians of Nazareth and in Israel at large. It demonstrated once more their vulnerability and dependence on outside forces for their security. It made them realize that the foundation of the Shihab al-Din Mosque was demolished only because of pressure by the international church and above all by President George Bush. The growing influence of the Islamic Movement and its aggressive attitudes towards the

Christians, the gradual loss of the Christian atmosphere of Nazareth, and the damages caused to its economy and civic society have caused many of them to despair. While some tend to migrate to larger cities with a Jewish majority within Israel, others have emigrated to the West. Among those who remain there is a growing tendency to acquiesce in Muslim dominance; some even empathized with the Islamists' grief over the destruction of the base of the Shihab al-Din Mosque.

The major trend among the Christians, including members of the secularist Communist Party, is to preserve the Christian "face" of Nazareth regardless of its Muslim majority. As Ramzi Hakim, the municipality spokesman put it, "Nazareth is holy for the indigenous Christians as well as for worldwide Christianity. It should therefore retain its Christian characteristics regardless of the declining proportion of Christians in the town, in the same way that Mecca is holy for worldwide Islam and should therefore retain its Muslim characteristics regardless of the religion of its population."[113]

Despite the relative success of the Democratic Front in the 2008 municipal elections, many Christians express their fear that a municipal council with an Islamist majority is just a matter of time due to demographic developments, i.e., higher birthrate of Muslim lower classes than that of the Christians and a continuous migration of Christians from Nazareth. Christians apprehend that an Islamist-dominated council would be liable to issue regulations in order to give Nazareth a Muslim "face," such as restrictions on its public lifestyle, limitations on women's appearance in public, and their dress or limitations on the public drinking of alcoholic beverages. It would also be liable to renew the reconstruction of the Shihab al-Din Mosque. Utterances by Islamist activists such as Salman Abu Ahmad as mentioned above enhance their apprehensions. Christian leaders express their belief that the Israeli central government would have to intervene in order to stop such attempts at their very outset owing to its commitments to safeguard freedom of religion and the holy places in the State of Israel. Otherwise, they believe, the international community would have to intervene once more on their behalf.

Christian journalists and intellectuals observe the Shihab al-Din affair as a symptom of the treatment of Arabs, basically Muslims, by the Israeli government. Interviewed several times on Israeli radio, Lutfi Mash'ur, the noted editor of the *Sinara* Arabic paper in Nazareth, denounced the involvement of Israeli politicians as the major cause of the Shihab al-Din conflict. The veteran Christian journalist and author Atallah Mansour pointed out in his book the prolonged discriminatory policy of the State of Israel toward its Arab citizens, particularly with regard to the Muslims, as the major cause of the Shihab al-Din crisis. Being largely a rural population in 1948, they suffered more than the Christians from land confiscations. Lacking their own community schools and proper government public educational system, many Muslims attend Christian church schools where they feel marginalized and alienated. They are jealous of the Christians who, having become a minority in Nazareth still dominate its public economy and civic life. Feeling powerless and unable to confront the government and win back their rights, the Muslims turn their frustration against their Christian neighbors.[114]

As can be expected, the drive for restoring unity between Christians and Muslims in Nazareth emphasizes the "common enemy"—the Israeli government—and the need for Arab national unity in order to struggle against it.[115] Fuad Farah, chairman of the Orthodox National Arab Council in Israel, observes that in the Shihab al-Din affair, the Israeli government took advantage of the differences among the Arabs and used them to its own advantage, shifting the attention of the Arab people away from their real problems. It wished to demonstrate the chaos and dangers that the Christians and the holy places in Jerusalem would face if they were to be transmitted to the Palestinian Authority rule. It aimed to prove that only Israel could protect the Christians in the Holy Land. It also tried to shift the traditional support of the Christian church centers in East Jerusalem away from the Palestinian Arab cause, especially in the issues of the Palestinian refugees and the future government in Jerusalem. Farah calls the Arab leadership to suppress with an iron fist any attempt to sew dissension and conflict within the Arab people, particularly against the Christians who form the weakest section of it, and calls for a Muslim–Christian–Druze dialogue on a national as well as on a religious basis.[116]

With the passage of time international evangelical Christian activists have become more cautious about their victory in the Shihab al-Din Mosque affair. They express concern that this supposed Christian victory might prove to be a two-edged dagger as it is liable to cause local Christians to be identified with the United States and the international church or with the Christian West in its confrontation with the Muslim East. They fear that such identification would expose them to alienation and violence on the part of the local Muslims. They observe that the desirable solution for the indigenous Christians should therefore be their greater integration within Israeli society. The Israeli government should demonstrate a greater amount of goodwill toward that end; the international Christian world should support but cannot replace that goodwill.[117]

The role of Israeli governments in the Shihab al-Din affair

As shown earlier in this essay, the Israeli governments of both Netanyahu's Likud and Barak's Labor played their role in exacerbating the Shihab al-Din controversy. This was the culmination of the Israeli governments' treatment of the Arab minority as a fifth column that was liable to cooperate with Israel's Arab enemies to annihilate Israel or to eliminate its raison d'être as a nation-state of the Jewish people. Until the 1980s, the Israeli governments preferred to accommodate with the return to Islam rather than cope with the emergence of secular Palestinian Arab nationalism. Hence, Israeli authorities closed their eyes to the emergence of Muslim fundamentalist organizations in the hope that struggles between the two movements would weaken them both.

Furthermore, beyond ignorance and shortsightedness, the Israeli treatment of the Shihab al-Din affair reflects the complex collective identity of the Jewish majority in Israel. The Israeli veteran philosopher Joseph Agassi observes that despite the establishment of the State of Israel as the nation-state of the Jewish people, "[the Israeli Jews] have retained the features of a national minority rather than a liberated people." This fact "has prevented them from acting the way the ruling majority should act when dealing with minorities (both as individuals and groups) in its vicinity."[118] Hence, rather than enforcing law and order as governments should do, both the Netanyahu and Barak governments preferred to make deals with those who broke the law; they acted like an ethnic group that seeks alignments with other groups rather than a democratic national government that enforces law on all of it citizens equally.

Moreover, the Israeli governments' agenda was instinctively influenced by the memories and experiences of the Jews as minorities in both Christian Europe and the Muslim world. The Jewish experience of hundreds of years of persecution in Christian Europe has had a continuous impact on the Jewish attitude toward the Christians in Israel despite the very different historic role of the Christians in the Middle East. Indeed, modern anti-Semitism partially rooted in the mediaeval Christian church attitudes toward the Jews, and the Christian extensive missionary activities during the nineteenth and early twentieth centuries to proselytize Jews added to the feelings among Jews that the Christians will always try to eliminate them. Interfaith dialogue and the official rapprochement policy of the Vatican toward the Jews and Israel have not considerably changed the ill feelings that many Jews in Israel still have toward worldwide Christianity.

These latent feelings found a clear expression in an interview that Shlomo Ben-Ami gave to the veteran Israeli journalist Uri Avnery shortly before the 1999 general elections. Professor of Spanish History Ben-Ami had been born in Muslim Morocco and, would soon become the Internal Security Minister in the Barak Labor government. He commented on the relations of Jews with Islam and Christianity saying: "No doubt, Christianity is the eternal enemy. With Islam, it has been easier. It [Islam] did not emerge from us. Its relations with us have not been ideal and without hate. I do remember pogroms ... on the other hand, Muslims and Jews visited together graves of Jewish saints."[119]

Jewish experience under Islam was much more favorable than their treatment in Christian Europe until the nineteenth century. Despite their disabilities as *dhimmis*, they were allowed freedom of worship, vast measures of autonomy as well as security of life and property. Hardly any pogroms or attempts to convert the Jews to Islam occurred until the nineteenth century.[120] Jews and Christians had a similar position as *dhimmis* under Islam, and vied with each other on the same professions and services of the Muslim rulers, a competition which nurtured antagonism between the two minorities.

The role of indigenous Christians as advocates and spokespersons of Palestinian Arab nationalism since its inception and specifically, within the Communist Party during the first decades of the State of Israel, aroused the

Israeli political establishment's suspicion towards them as the spearheads of the Arab nationalist struggle against the State of Israel. The non-violent support of the Arab church superiors in Jerusalem for the Palestinian Arab struggle against the Israeli occupation of the West Bank during the first Palestinian Intifada (uprising) further strengthened the animosity of the Israeli governments toward their Christian Arab citizens.[121]

Summary and conclusions

The Shihab al-Din affair in Nazareth emerged from the background of the breakdown of the traditional Muslim–Christian equilibrium in the town. The loss of the Christian majority, the expansion of the Muslim poor and the growing social gaps between Christians and Muslims together contributed to the rise of the Islamic Movement in Nazareth and led it to challenge the Christian dominance in the economy and civic society of Nazareth. The Islamists' initiative to build the huge Shihab al-Din Mosque in front of the Basilica of the Annunciation was an expression of their desire to obliterate the Christian "face" of Nazareth and its affiliation with worldwide Christianity and replace it with a Muslim "face" instead. The deterioration of the affair from a local case of law-breaking into an international problem was due to a great extent to the mismanagement of the conflict by the Israeli authorities, their long-time negligence of the Arab minority and their compromising attitude toward the Islamists' demands. The Israeli governments treated the Shihab al-Din affair as a local religious-sectarian-tribal issue between the Muslims and Christians of Nazareth, ignoring the significance of Nazareth and the holy places to millions of believers all over the world and the international implications of the issue.

Hence, the international community, primarily President George Bush and the Vatican, put pressure on Prime Minister Sharon to demolish the foundation of the mosque that had been built in breach of the Israeli court decisions but with the consent of several Israeli authorities. The affair demonstrated the interaction of the local arena with the international one and the significance of the Christian holy places to worldwide Christianity. It further demonstrated the growing influence of Islam on the national identity of the Arabs in Israel as well as the vulnerability of the Christian Arabs and their growing dependence on an outside protecting force in the absence of the government law enforcement. The acceptance of the Islamists' demands nearly made the local Nazareth conflict part of the global struggle between the Christian West and Arab Islam as envisioned by President Bush. The major conclusions of this study conform to the warning of the noted Professor of Jewish Studies Avi Ravitsky that, due to its unique position in the Middle East and among the international community as well as the fragile inter-communal relations within the state, Israel should abstain from becoming a spearhead of the West in any future "clash of civilizations."

On the face of it, matters seem to have returned to normal in Nazareth. However, a latent desire to rebuild the Shihab al-Din Mosque still exists among many Muslims in Nazareth and waits for an opportunity to come to the fore. It is part of their desire to "localize" Nazareth, to dilute its international Christian significance and assert its Arab Muslim majority.

A further conclusion of this study is that an overall change of the government's policy toward the Arab minority in Israel is required in order to repair the situation: first, treating the Arabs of all denominations as equal citizens rather than meddling in their communal religious affairs and maneuvering between religious groups; second, improving the economic conditions in Nazareth, encouraging new investments, placing high priority on the construction of new housing and providing work opportunities particularly for the educated young people. Above all, Israel should keep its international commitments of ensuring the religious freedom and security of the holy places. Taking this road should ease the tension in Nazareth and make it a thriving tourist town based on inter-communal co-operation rather than a hub of fundamentalist holy wars.

Notes

1 This essay was written at the Truman Research Institute, the Hebrew University of Jerusalem. Thanks are due for the assistance given.
2 A. Mansur, *The History of Nazareth from Ancient Times to Present Days*, Egypt: Author's pub., 1924, pp. 35–43 [in Arabic]; C.F. Emmett, *Beyond the Basilica: Christians and Muslims in Nazareth*, Chicago, Ill.: University of Chicago Press, 1995, pp. 15–21; G. Salameh, *Nazareth, The Town and its Development Toward the End of the Ottman Rule*, unpub. M.A. thesis, University of Haifa, 1982, pp. 1–10 [in Hebrew].
3 Emmet, *Beyond the Basilica*, pp.19–20; Mansur, *The History of Nazareth from Ancient Times to Present Days*, p. 43
4 Mansur, *The History of Nazareth*, p.45; Salameh, *Nazareth*, p. 11; Emmett, *Beyond the Basilica*, p. 21.
5 Mansur, *The History of Nazareth*, pp. 45–46; Salameh, *Nazareth*, pp. 12–13.
6 Emmett, *Beyond the Basilica*, pp. 22–23; Mansur, *The History of Nazareth*, p. 61, Salameh, *Nazareth*, p. 16.
7 Emmett, *Beyond the Basilica*, pp.136–37. The mosque was constructed in 1805–6 according to Mansur, *The History of Nazareth*, p. 61.
8 M. Ma'oz, *Ottoman Reforms in Syria and Palestine 1840–1861*, Oxford: Clarendon Press, 1968, pp. 138–39; Salameh, *Nazareth*, pp. 19–29, 31–34.
9 Salameh, *Nazareth*, pp. 50–62.
10 *Ibid.*, p. 37 and sources therein.
11 List and description of the Nazareth mayors in N. Zu'rub-Qa'war, *The History of Nazareth*, Nazareth: Venus Press, 2000, pp. 336–54 [in Arabic].
12 Prominent among these is Raphael Israeli, a renowned professor of Islam at the Hebrew University of Jerusalem, who bases his assumption on nineteenth-century consular reports regarding the oppression of Christians in the Jerusalem and Nablus areas. Although he admits that he found no specific reference to such oppression of the Christians in Nazareth, he asserts that "There is no reason to assume that the fate of Nazareth Christians was any better." R. Israeli, *Green Crescent Over Nazareth: The Displacement of Christians by Muslims in the Holy Land*, London: Frank Cass, 2002, pp. 11–12.
13 B. Morris, *The Birth of the Palestinian Refugee Problem, 1947–1949*, Tel-Aviv: Am Oved, pp. 268–72 [Hebrew edn]; A. Mansour, *Narrow Gate Churches, The*

Christian Presence in the Holy Land Under Muslim and Jewish Rule, Pasadena, Calif.: Hope Pub. House, 2004, pp. 276–77.
14 Mansour, *Narrow Gate Churches*, p. 278.
15 D. Rabinowitz, *Overlooking Nazareth: the Ethnography of Exclusion in Galilee*, Cambridge: Cambridge Univesity Press, 2000, pp. 34–8.
16 D. Tsimhoni, "The Political Configuration of the Christians in the State of Israel,", *Ha-Mizrah He-Hadash*, 1989, vol. 32, pp. 139–64 [in Hebrew].
17 The affiliation of the Orthodox Arabs with the Communist Party go back to the activity of Russian Orthodox educational institutions in Nazareth during the late nineteenth century that appealed first and foremost to the indigenous Orthodox Arabs. Following the 1917 Bolshevik revolution and the disappearance of the Russian institutions, many Orthodox Arabs preserved their loyalty to Russia by shifting it to the Communist Party. Others joined the Communist Party as the outcome of their search for secular national identity following the breach within the Orthodox Patriarchate of Jerusalem between the Greek upper hierarchy and the Arab community priests and laity. For further details *see* D. Tsimhoni, "The Arab Christians and the Palestinian Arab National Movement During the Formative Stage", in G. Ben-Dor (ed.), *The Palestinians and the Middle East Conflict*, Ramat Gan, Turtledove Publishing, 1978, pp. 73–98; D. Tsimhoni, "The Greek Orthodox Patriarchate of Jerusalem During the Formative Years of the British Mandate in Palestine", in *Asian and African Studies* (Journal of the Israel Oriental Society, University of Haifa), vol. 12, no. 1 (March 1978), pp. 77–121.
18 Emmett, *Beyond the Basilica*, pp. 260–65.
19 For their history and description *see* Mansur, *The History of Nazareth*, at p. 278; Zu'rub-Qa'war, *The History of Nazareth*, at p. 382 ff.; Fuad Farah, *The Living Stones: the Christian Arabs in the Holy Land*, Nazareth: Venus Press, 2003, pp. 164–77 [in Arabic].
20 Rabinowitz, *Overlooking Nazareth*, pp. 6, 26–51.
21 U. Bialer, *Cross on the Star of David, the Christian World in Israel's Foreign Policy 1948–1967*, Jerusalem: Yad Ben Zvi Institute, 2006, pp. 27, 35, 173–74 [in Hebrew]; *Nazareth Today, Souvenir of the new Basilica of the Annunciation recently open for worship*, [Author not indicated], Jerusalem: Franciscan Printing Press, n.d., p. 17 ff.
22 For the internal struggle within the Catholic Church regarding the plan of the New Church of the Annunciation see: M. Halevi, "Religion, Symbolism and Politics: The Planning and Building of the Modern Church of the Annunciation in Nazareth," *Kathedra*, no. 126 (December 2007), Jerusalem: Yad Ben-Zvi Press, 2007, pp. 83–102 [in Hebrew].
23 See for instance, V. Vekselman, "Christmas Tour of the Holy Land," 18 Dec. 2001, Olga's Gallery. Online. Available: http://www.abcgallery.com/list/archive.html. Accessed: Feb. 1, 2009; Emmett, *Beyond the Basilica*, pp. 73, 105.
24 Emmett, *Beyond the Basilica*, pp. 227–40.
25 *Ibid.*
26 My interview with Salim Jubran, 23 Dec. 2003.
27 D. Tsimhoni, "The Christians in Israel: Between Religion and Politics," in E. Rekhes (ed.) *The Arabs in Israel: Dilemmas of Identites*, Tel-Aviv: Dayan Center for Strategic Studies, Tel Aviv University, 1998, pp. 63–69, [in Hebrew]; Emmett, *Beyond the Basilica*, pp. 227–54.
28 Emmett, *Beyond the Basilica*, p. 265 ff.
29 Emmanuel Sivan, *Radical Islam: Medieval Theology and Modern Politics*, New Haven, CT: Yale University Press, 1985.
30 R. Paz, *The Islamic Movement in Israel Following the Elections to the Local Authorities* Tel Aviv: Dayan Center, Tel Aviv University, 1989, p. 20 [in Hebrew]; E. Rekhess, *The Arab Minority in Israel: Between Communism and Arab*

Nationalism, 1965–1991 Tel-Aviv: Dayan Center, Tel Aviv University, 1993, pp. 152–54 [in Hebrew]; T. Mayer, *The Awakening of the Muslims in Israel*, Giv'at Haviva: Institute for Arab Studies, 1988, pp. 65–72 [in Hebrew]; R. Israeli, *Muslim Fundamentalism in Israel*, London: Brassey, 1993.

31 Tsimhoni, "The Christians in Israel," at pp. 66–67; Emmett, *Beyond the Basilica*, at pp. 265 ff.
32 For details of the project and its reasoning see Raphael Israeli, *Green Crescent Over Nazareth*, pp. 70–77; C.M. Sennott, *The Body and the Blood: The Holy Land's Christians at the Turn of a New Millenium, a Reporter's Journey*, New York: Public Affairs, 2001, pp. 203–7; Emmett, *Beyond the Basilica*, pp. 69–70; Y. Jabarin,"The Right for the Town: The Case of the Shihab al-Din Crisis in Nazareth," *Mikan* no. 1 (Dec. 2005–Jan. 2006) p. 14 [in Hebrew].
33 Israeli, *Green Crescent Over Nazareth*, pp. 78–82.
34 Israeli, *Green Crescent Over Nazareth*, p. 78 ff.
35 *Ha'aretz*, 19 Apr. 1999.
36 Advocate Dan Shafrir to the members of the Knesset, the Israeli government and chiefs of staff of the ministries, 23 Apr. 1998, Copy of letter in Hebrew on file with author.
37 My interview with Ramzi Hakim, then secretary of the municipality of Nazareth, 21 Nov. 1999.
38 *Ha'aretz*, 11 Oct. 1999; N. Barne'a, "Who Rang the Bells", *Ha-Ayin ha-Shvi'it*, 2 May 2002 [in Hebrew]; Sennott, *The Body and the Blood*, at pp. 208–11.
39 Sennott, *The Body and the Blood*, pp. 221–24; *Ha'aretz*, 27 Apr. 1999, interview with Atif Fahum, the son of Yusuf Muhammad Fahum, mayor of Nazareth, 1947–49.
40 Israel Television Channel One, Fri., 9 Apr. 1999 and Israeli Radio Channel Two, Sat., 10 Apr., 1999; Alik Ron repeated his assertion in his testimony (3 Sept. 2001) before the official Orr Judicial Commission of Inquiry Investigating the Riots of the 2000 al-Aqsa Intifada. News1. Online. Available www.nfc.co.il (accessed 5 Feb. 2006). The full report of the commission: Online. Available http://elyon1.court.gov.il/heb/veadot/or/inside5.htm [in Hebrew] (accessed 1 Feb. 2009).
41 Mansur, *Narrow Gate Churches*, pp.281–82.
42 My interview with Salman Abu Ahmad, 22 Dec. 2005.
43 Siham Fahoum-Ghanim, *Challenges and Changes in the History of Nazareth: the Muslim–Christian Relationships*, Nazareth: author's pub., 2003, pp. 302–18 (in Arabic); cf. Mansur, *Narrow Gate Churches*, pp. 281–82; Sennott, *The Body and the Blood*, p. 5.
44 See e.g., D. Rabinowitz, "Strife in Nazareth," *Ethnography*, Mar. 2001, vol. 2, no. 1, pp. 105–6.
45 Israeli, *Green Crescent Over Nazareth*, p. 103
46 Israeli, *Green Crescent Over Nazareth*, pp. 103, 111–12.
47 My interview with Fuad Farah, 29 Dec. 2005.
48 Farah, *The Living Stones*, at pp. 115–16; my interview with him 22.5.2007
49 On the Muslim–Christian solidarity regarding al-Haram al-Sharif, see Y. Reiter, *From Jerusalem to Mecca and Back*, Jerusalem: Jerus. Institute for Israel Research, 2005, pp. 84–95 [in Hebrew]; N. Luz, *Al-Haram Al-Sharif in the Arab Palestinian Public Discourse in Israel: Ideintity, Collective Memory and Social Construction*, Jerusalem: Florsheim Institute for Policy Studies, 2004, pp. 33–39 [in Hebrew].
50 My interview with Abd al-Salam Manasra, 30 July 2003.
51 Copy of the comuniqué. For the Islamist perspective, see Fahoum-Ghanim, *Challenges and Changes in the History of Nazareth*, at pp. 312–18.
52 Photocopy of the declaration in *ibid.*, p. 319. See also Israeli, *Green Crescent Over Nazareth*, at pp. 94–95.
53 Israeli, *Crescent Over Nazareth*, p. 95.

54 My interview with Salman Abu Ahmad, 22 Dec. 2005, and with Sheikh Ahmad Natur, 4 Jan. 2006.
55 Fahoum-Ghanim, *Challenges and Changes in the History of Nazareth*, at pp. 312–18.
56 Copy of letter by the Franciscan Custos of the Holy Land, 8 Apr. 1999.
57 Latin Patriarchate Easter Message, 4 Apr. 1999. Online. Available http://www.al-bushra.org/latpatra/easter1999.htm (accessed 1 Feb. 2009).
58 Israeli, *Green Crescent Over Nazareth*, at pp. 95–96.
59 *Time Magazine*, 10 May 1999.
60 *Jerusalem Post*, 6 Apr. 1999.
61 *Arabesque*, Israeli Television, 17 Apr. 1999; *Ha'aretz*, 12 Oct. 1999.
62 *Ha'aretz*, 19 Apr. 1999; Israeli, *Green Crescent Over Nazareth*, at pp. 93–94, 97.
63 Israeli, *Green Crescent Over Nazareth*, pp. 96–97.
64 *Ha'aretz*, 11 Oct. 1999. My interviews with officials and witnesses who requested to remain anonymous.
65 *Kul al-Arab*, 10 Sept. 1999.
66 For a detailed discussion of the commission's work, *see* Israeli, *Green Crescent Over Nazareth*, at pp.115–33.
67 *Ha'aretz*, 3 Oct. 1999.
68 *Ha'aretz*, 6 Oct. 1999.
69 The District Court of Nazareth decision in file 1173/98, 3 Oct. 1999. The full text of the court's decision was published in *al-Sinara*, 15 Oct. 1999 [in Arabic].
70 For the courts' decisions and a description of the legal battle, see Israeli, *Green Crescent Over Nazareth*, at pp. 135–45.
71 Israeli, *Green Crescent Over Nazareth*, p.145.
72 *Ha'aretz*, 7, 8 Oct. 1999.
73 *See e.g.*, *Ha'aretz,* 19 Oct. 1999.
74 *Ha'aretz*, 13 Sept. 1999.
75 *Ha'aretz*, 6 Oct. 1999; *Ha'aretz,* 27 Apr. 1999 reported on Sharon's meeting with the Pope (details were not published) and on Sharon's personal objection to the construction of the Mosque in front of the Basilica.
76 A copy of the protest, 4 Nov. 1999, addressed to all ambassadors, local Christians, Christian pilgrims, and travel agents.
77 *Ha'aretz*, 11 Oct. 1999.
78 *Ha'aretz*, 20 June, 22 and 23 Nov., 1 Dec. 1999.
79 *Ha'aretz*, 20 June, 22 and 23 Nov., 1 Dec. 1999; *Kul al-Arab*, 3 Dec. 1999.
80 Ben-Ami's interview on Israeli Television, Channel 1, 23 Nov. 1999.
81 My interview with Father (now Bishop) Elias Chacour, 18 Dec. 1999.
82 Israeli, *Green Crescent Over Nazareth*, at pp. 98–99.
83 Rabinowitz, "Strife in Nazareth," at, pp. 94–96, 107–8.
84 My interview with Salman Abu Ahmad, 22 Dec. 2005.
85 *Ynet news*, 22 Nov. 2001; *Jerusalem Post*, 14 Dec. 2001.
86 *Ynet news* 1 Jan.2002; *Ha'aretz*, 30 Dec. 2001; *Jewish Telegraphic Agency*, 30 Dec. 2001.
87 Letter delivered by the Christian coalition to Sharon on 6 Jan., 2002, Online. Available: http://helpnazareth.org (accessed 15 Jan, 2003).
88 Copy of the International Coalition for Nazareth letter to the Government Committee, 17 Jan. 2002.
89 *Al-Sinara*, 11 Jan. 2002.
90 *Ha'aretz*, 16 Jan. 2002; *Ynet news*, 24 Jan. 2002.
91 *Kul al-Arab*, 25 Jan. 2002; Protocols of meetings of the Knesset, 1, 8, 21, 22, 24 Jan. 2002.
92 *Ynet news* 9 Jan. 2002; *Ha'aretz* and *Jordan Times*, 11 Jan. 2002.
93 *Ha'aretz*, 22 Jan. 2002.
94 M. Arens, "Repairing the Mistake in Nazareth," *Ha'aretz*, 22 Jan. 2002.
95 *Israelinsider*, 4 Mar. 2002.

96 *Ha'aretz*, 6 Mar. 2003.
 97 *Ha'aretz*, 26 June 2003.
 98 *Ha'aretz*, 1, 2 July 2003; *Al-Sinara, Kul al-Arab*, 4 July 2003.
 99 *San Francisco Chronicle*, 6 July 2003.
100 Joseph Dan's interview with the Israel Broadcasting Service Channel Two, 1 July 2003; *Ha'aretz*, 2 July 2003.
101 "Will the Jews Be the Arrowhead in the 'Clash of Civilizations?'" S. Della Pergola and A.Yovel (eds.) The President's Study Forum on World Jewish Affairs, Jerusalem: Institute of Contemporary Jewry, Hebrew University, series A (2004), pp. 25–33 [in Hebrew].
102 *Ha'aretz*, 4 Mar. 2006; *al-Sinara*, 12 Mar. 2006.
103 Returns of the 2008 local councils elections. Online. Available: http://www.haaretz.co.il/hasite/images/printed/P121108/2008.htm (accessed 5 Feb. 2009).
104 My interview with Fuad Farah, 1 Dec. 2008; numerous reports on the web, for instance interviews with Jeraysi and Christian leaders: "Not a single Christian in birthplace of Christ: Muslim intimidation could make 'land of Jesus' barren in 15 years" Posted: 24 Sept. 2007. Online. Available: http://www.worldnetdaily.com/news/article.asp?ARTICLE_ID=57797 (accessed 5 Feb. 2009); Y. Tommer, "Come to Nazareth!" Posted 24 Dec. 2008 Online. Available: http://english.ohmynews.com/articleview/article_view.asp?no=384480&rel_no = 1 (accessed 5 Feb. 2009).
105 My interview Salman Abu Ahmad, 22 Dec. 2005.
106 My interview with Abd al-Salam Manasra, 26 June 2006.
107 My interview with the White Mosque members, 26 June 2006.
108 Fahoum-Ghanim, *Challenges and Changes in the History of Nazareth*, pp. 256–64, 433–36.
109 R. Khamaisi, *The Nazareth Area: A Metropolitan Outline for Governance Planning and Development*, Jerusalem: Floersheimer Institute for Policy Studies, 2003, pp. 21–27, 43, 56 [in Hebrew]. See also Khamaisi, Chapter 7 in this volume.
110 Jabarin, "The Right for the Town" at pp. 12–19.
111 *Ibid.*, p.19.
112 A. Ashkar, *The Self Destruction – the Nazareth Example: Boundaries of the Conflict and its Secrets in the Shihab al-Din Square*, Ramallah: al-Mashriq, 2000, pp. 31–86, 113–15 [in Arabic].
113 My interview with Ramzi Hakim, 21 Nov. 1999.
114 Mansour, *Narrow Gate Churches*, pp. 279–80, 288.
115 *Arabesque*, Israel Television, August 29, 1999; numerous articles in the local Arabic newspapers, e.g., *Kul al-Arab*, 27 Feb. 1998; *Kul al-Arab*, 18 Apr. 1999.
116 Farah, *The Living Stones*, at pp. 113–18.
117 My interview with Danny Kopp, 1 Aug. 2003, and with David Parsons, media and public relations of the International Christian Embassy in Jerusalem, 22 June 2006.
118 J. Agassi, *Between Faith and Nationality: towards an Israeli National Identity*, Tel Aviv: Papyrus, 1993, p.223 [in Hebrew].
119 *Kolbo* (Haifa), 3 May 1999 [in Hebrew].
120 Bernard Lewis, *The Jews of Islam*, Princeton, NJ: Princeton University Press, 1984; Norman Stillman, *The Jews of Arab Lands in Modern Times*, Philadelphia, Penn.: Jewish Pub. Society, 1991.
121 For details *see*: D. Tsimhoni, *Christian Communities in Jerusalem and the West Bank Since 1948: An Historical, social and Political Study*, London: Praeger, 1993, pp. 167–202.

12 Holy shrines (*maqamat*) in modern Palestine/Israel and the politics of memory[1]

Mahmoud Yazbak

As the cradle of Judaism and Christianity and with Jerusalem as the third canonical Holy City in Islam, Palestine through the centuries has resonated in the minds of millions of believers as the "Holy Land." Taking their inspiration from the Scriptures in which their faith is grounded and responding to the customs shaped by subsequent expressions of tradition, followers of all three religions naturally came to attribute holiness to the numerous shrines and other sacred places that dotted the country, whether they called it Terra Sancta, *eretz ha-qodesh* or *al-ard al-muqaddasa*. In his recent comprehensive study, Josef Meri describes how this "sacred topography" was constructed:

> Devotees created and sustained "sanctity" by building shrines, tombs, and other commemorative structures, writing about sacred [sites] and performing rituals. Sacred topography encompasses those distinguishing characteristics of a place that its inhabitants, writers and travelers *identified* as holy—monuments, such as tombs, sepulchers, mausoleums, houses, shrines, mosques, synagogues, and churches, as well as natural sites, such as mountains, wells, rivers, and caves.[2]

Meri outlines a long tradition of pilgrims and travelers to the Holy Land, physically "mapping" its sacredness through the pilgrimages (Arabic: *ziyara*, Hebrew: *aliya le-regel*) they undertook there while recollecting the country's sights and smells in the travelogues and itineraries they wrote for their co-religionists "back home." There was also an "inner-spiritual" figurative mapping, as the sacred places they mention are *mubarak*, embued with *baraka* (blessing). Besides *baraka* Muslim writers use such descriptions as "friendly atmosphere (*uns*), awe (*mahaba*), reverence (*ijlal*) [and] dignity (*waqar*)," while among Jews we find such terms as "awesome" (*nora'*) and "holy" (*qadosh*) to describe the intangible nature of the sacredness these pilgrimage sites embodied for them.[3]

The origin of most ancient shrines is, of course, shrouded in legend. As happened throughout the Middle East, Jews, Christians, and Muslims in Palestine absorbed traditions of sanctuaries that had existed long before the rise of the monotheistic religions. Even as local populations left behind their pagan beliefs and adopted monotheism, ancient shrines retained their sanctity the sites themselves in many cases now transformed to serve the changed sociopolitical constellations arising from the new creed. As the last monotheistic religion to appear, Islam not only embraced most of the figures venerated by Jews and Christians but also adopted many of their symbols, shrines, and saints. Shrines dedicated to prophets in Judaism or saints in Christianity became holy for Muslims too. In fact, few such shrines have a written history that antedates the advent of Islam and most were then, as Meri puts it, "rediscovered" during the Middle Ages.[4] The impetus for this may well have come from political events, for example when the Mamluk Sultan al-Malik al-Zahir Baybars (r. 1260–77) decided to put an end to the disruptive presence of the Franks and subsequently restored many of Palestine's shrines:

> Baybars was clearly sending a message that he was the patron of the Holy Land, the Hijaz [containing the Muslim holy cities of Mecca and Medina] and elsewhere. He was also reviving the veneration of the prophets, companions [of the Prophet Muhammad], and other holy persons to whose shrines *ziyara* was to become an established custom among the ruling elite and the common people alike.[5]

Around the same time, in the 1270s, we find the traveling scholar 'Ali ibn Abi Bakr al-Harawi putting together his *Kitab asl-Isharat ila Ma'rifat al-Ziyarat*, the oldest pilgrim guide to survive, in which he records a long list of shrines all venerated simultaneously by Muslims, Christians, and Jews.[6] Muslims and Jews routinely served together as keepers at the same shrines and Jewish travelers to the Holy Land would often rely on Muslim guides to show them the holy places in the Galilee and elsewhere. Similarly, there are many reports of Muslims, Jews, and Christians visiting the same *maqamat* and praying at the same tombs of holy men.[7] Jewish travelers who visited the Galilee and Lebanon during the Mamluk and Ottoman periods have left us vivid descriptions of the common practice of Jews and Muslims visiting the same shrines. Meri quotes a source from the early thirteenth century mentioning such sites in Safad, Kefar 'Amuqa, 'Alma and Bar'am:

> In Safad there [was the Tomb of] Rabbi Hanina b. Hyrkanus, in which there are sixteen recesses. We encircled them, weeping. (...) Two [Muslims] remain their continually to attend to the light and supply oil in honour of the righteous man (*zaddiq*). In Kfer 'Amuqa, we found the sepulcher of Jonathan, son of Uziel,[8] over which there is a great tree. The [Muslims] bring oil to it and have a light burning there in his honour (...). They make here their vows, too, to his glory.[9]

Then again Meri refers to the report made by Rabbi Moshe Basula from Pissaro, Italy (1480–1560) of Muslims, Jews, and others coming together in several places to worship, make vows, and seek cures.[10]

What cannot fail to strike the modern reader in these accounts is the level of sharing and the degree of mutual respect among the worshipers of all three religions: "Indeed, all sacred places contributed a sense of harmony and continuity to a given locality in the eyes of Jews, Christians and Muslims, who, though emphasizing their own holy sites, recognized the holiness of sites to devotees of other faiths."[11] Two late fourteenth-century Muslim sources—one by the chief *qadi*, Muhammad al-'Uthmani, and the other by the geographer al-Dimashqi—describe a Muslim *ziyara* to the cave on Mt. Meron near Safad, known in Jewish tradition until today as the tomb of the second century Talmudic sage Shimon Bar Yochai, author of the *Zohar* ("The Shining Light"). Al-'Uthmani writes that "the site of Meron contains waterwheels and pools in a cave from which water trickles. On an appointed day of the year, on the 15th of the Jewish month of Iyyar (Passover), a great gathering of Jews would congregate there from near and faraway. They dig there a canal around that place. Water flows into that canal more than is customary. Jews take that water [back with them] to distant lands."[12]

Jewish sources and travelers frequently mention how Jews and Muslims from the Meron area would come together at the shrine on holy days in order to pray for rain[13] and organize the annual festival for Rabbi Shimon, known in Arabic as Sheikh al-Shu'la ("Sheikh of the burning light"). A big bonfire would be lit to commemorate the anniversary of the Rabbi's death, giving rise to its Arabic name, 'Id al-Shu'la, "the feast of the burning light."[14] This is, of course, the Jewish festival of Lag be-Omer. "Mingling together in a popular festival, Arabs and Oriental Jews [*Sephardim*] used to sing special songs, in Arabic, in the Rabbi's honor."[15]

Today the annual pilgrimage to Mt. Meron is as popular as ever. The thousands of "Oriental Jews" who flock there each year originated in the nearly one million Oriental Jews the young state of Israel brought to Palestine in the early 1950s to help fill the empty space the Zionists had created there in 1948.[16] No longer are there Muslim neighbors to join them in the celebrations, and the songs they sing are no longer in Arabic.[17] And there is one other difference: all Islamic symbols that before the establishment of Israel used to mark the shrine as a Muslim holy site have been removed and all signs of the cave's sacredness for other religions have been erased.

Yet, today, while Muslim and Christian *ziyarat* and *mawasim* (s. *mawsim*, annual mass pilgrimage) to shrines in Palestine have almost totally disappeared, a strong Jewish cult of saints is flourishing in Israel and the names of Baba Sali and Abuhatzera, for example, are familiar to large numbers of Israelis.[18] How do we explain this phenomenon, especially as we remember that erasing the Arabness of immigrant Jews from Middle Eastern and North African countries was crucial to Zionism's Ashkenazi hegemony? As it had eradicated Palestine's shared Judeo-Islamic heritage, Israel vigorously set about de-Arabizing ("westernizing") the newly arrived "Oriental" Jews or *mizrahim*.[19] In her studies on Mizrahi identity Ella Shochat poignantly analyzes this as follows:

The Middle Easternness of Jews questioned the very definitions and boundaries of the Euro-Israeli national project. The cultural affinity that Arab-Jews shared with Arab-Muslims was in many respects stronger than that which they shared with European Jews—a fact that threatened the Zionist conception of a homogeneous nation, modeled on the European-nationalist definition of the nation-state.[20]

As they gradually emerged from under the sub-Ashkenazi identity their *'aliya* to Zion[21] had entailed, there came the awareness that for Arab Jews, as Shochat writes, "existence under Zionism has meant a profound and visceral schizophrenia, mingling stubborn self-pride with an *imposed self-rejection* (...). The assimilative project has partially 'succeeded,' at least in terms of dismantling a vast civilization of the Jews of the Muslim world."[22] But she gives this the following twist:

The myth of the melting pot promoted by Euro-Israeli ideologues was in fact taking place in the 1950s and 1960s, but not in the ways the dominant Euro-Israeli institutions foresaw and imagined. (...) We Arab Jews (...) crossed a border and ended up in Israel, *but our millennial 'Arabness' did not thereby suddenly cease.* Nor did it remain static in a previous historical incarnation. How could we change our language, our cuisine, our music, our ways of thinking overnight?[23]

"How could we change," she might have added, "our religious customs overnight?" From here it is a small step to lay bare, as she does, "the deep roots of Mizrahi antagonism to the Ashkenazi establishment, the variegated forms of their resistance—sometimes even unconscious, sometimes even politically misconceived, but a resistance that can be found in the crevices of a social system Mizrahim are slowly learning to master, oppose, and change."[24]

And it is as a form of *resistance*, I suggest, that we should view the Mizrahi revival of the cult of saints in Palestine/Israel, as it seeks to drive another wedge in the social system Israel's Mizrahim want to "oppose".

In comparison, Palestinian *mawasim* were an essential component of folklore and popular practices of religion for many generations. The *mawasim* of Nabi Musa, near Jerusalem, and Nabi Salih, near Ramla, took place each year in April, that of Nabi Rubin, south of Jaffa, from approximately mid-August until mid-September. As festivals of mass pilgrimage, these *mawasim* provided people with welcome opportunities to meet relatives from other parts of the country, to engage in business transactions, to seek prospective marriage partners, etc.[25]

Records of the Supreme Muslim Council kept in the Abu Dis Archives contain detailed data on the administration and budgets involved in the organization of Palestinian *mawasim* during the Mandate period. The festival of al-Nabi Rubin annually attracted thousands of Palestinians to the shrine, 15 km south of Jaffa, from the surroundings of Jaffa itself, Ramla, Lydda, Gaza, and many other southern localities that celebrated the *mawsim* with scout parades and commercial activities. The *mawsim* and *ziyara* would start in mid-August, after the orange picking season had come to an end, and continue for one whole month. A large camp would be set up in the dunes, accommodating during the Mandate period more than 50,000 visitors. The *waqf* of Nabi Rubin owned 32,000 dunams,[26] most of which were rented out to *fellahin* from nearby villages, and its income was used to sponsor, among other things, a large soup kitchen (*simat*) and a pumping system to provide water and other facilities for the huge gatherings in al-Nabi Rubin's *mawsim*.[27] Besides its religious aspects, the *mawsim* ranked as probably the most important social gathering in the Jaffa region, as is evident from a popular saying among Jaffa's women who allegedly tried to encourage their husbands to take part: "*Ya bitrubinni ya bitalliqni*" ("Take me to the Rubin festival or you must divorce me").[28]

No al-Nabi Rubin *mawasim* or *ziyarat* were held after 1948. More than 97 percent of the indigenous population of Jaffa, Lydda, Ramle, and their rural regions had been expelled and turned into refugees, languishing in hastily thrown up camps on the other side of the armistice lines that marked the new reality the establishment of Israel had generated. All of the Nabi Rubin *waqf*'s lands were confiscated by the state. The mosque was destroyed and the mosque's minaret, initially left standing, collapsed later. The shrine itself was converted into a Jewish holy site.[29]

The history of the *maqam* of al-Nabi Rubin is emblematic for nearly all of the shrines in post-1948 Palestine that through the centuries were shared by and sacred for Muslims, Christians and Jews. Most of these sites are now exclusively Jewish—followers of the other two religions have been robbed of their historical rights to them and the shrines are now controlled by official or unofficial Jewish religious administrations that have erased all Muslim religious symbols and generally prevent Muslim devotees from visiting these sites and making their vows there. One should also recall that the indigenous Palestinian population that survived the onslaught in 1948 and became part of the State of Israel—about 150,000 people—were immediately placed under an official military regime that lasted for 18 years (1948–66) and that vastly restricted their freedom of movement and expression. Although now, according to international law, citizens of the State of Israel, Palestinians during that period could not travel outside their home village or town without having obtained special permission from the military governor. This meant that they were cut off from the churches, mosques and holy shrines that had survived and were forbidden to maintain and repair them. It also meant that when the military regime was removed, many of the shrines that once belonged to the shared sacred topography of Palestine had been confiscated, destroyed or Judaized. Numerous shrines were left to disintegrate, the ownership of others moved from the Custodian for Absentees Property to Israeli citizens who turned them into restaurants, museums, pubs and discos or even cow sheds.[30]

In 1950 the Israeli Government Committee for the Preservation of Muslim Religious Buildings, Jerusalem, published a report by L.A. Mayer and J. Pinkerfeld,

Some Principal Muslim Religious Buildings in Israel, in Hebrew, Arabic, and English, documenting some of the Muslim shrines then still existing and purporting to demonstrate they were well taken care of following the establishment of the State of Israel. In many cases, there is no trace left of the shrines mentioned today, the buildings having been destroyed by decision of the various official governmental or municipal offices. Jaffa's shrines and mosques are a good example. The Mayer-Pinkerfeld report lists only seven of the more than 25 Muslim religious buildings existing in Jaffa in 1949.[31] Two of these, the Raslan and Dabbagh mosques, were totally demolished. The Siksik Mosque (in Jaffa) was first turned into a Bulgarian restaurant and a nightclub and today serves as a warehouse for a plastics factory and a social club for Bulgarian Jews.[32] The Tabiyya Mosque (in Jaffa) was first put under the control of the Custodian of Absentees Property and then handed over to a Christian family who converted it into a church, called "The House of Simon the Tanner,"[33] which means the site is no longer accessible to the town's Muslims.[34] The al-Wihda Mosque (in Jaffa) was converted into the Zikhron Ya'akov Synagogue,[35] the al-Jami'ah Mosque (in Jaffa) became a nightclub, and the al-Nuzha Mosque (in Jaffa) was left abandoned for years, its interior desecrated by the prostitution that was practiced there. The Mosque of Wadi Hunayn (today's Nes Ziona) and that of Yazur (today's Azur) have also been converted into synagogues, Ge'ulat Israel Synagogue and Sha'are Tzion, respectively.[36] The majority of the other sites the report mentions met a similar fate, such as the famous al-Jami' al-Ahmar Mosque in Safad, whose marvelous architectural structure Mayer and Pinkerfeld describe in detail.[37] This hallmark Muslim religious site is today a banquet hall for weddings and similar functions, and during the general elections of 2006 functioned as the headquarters for the Kadima party.[38]

Israeli governments have routinely desecrated Muslim cemeteries. In the Jaffa area part of the 'Abd al-Nabi cemetery and *maqam* are now hidden under a public park and the Tel Aviv Hilton Hotel. Similarly, part of an urban expressway runs over a section of the Taso cemetery on the outskirts of Jaffa, after it was expropriated for the purpose,[39] while the main road north out of Haifa to Acre has obliterated part of the cemetery that lay east of the Ottoman town, an office building of the Israel Electric Company occupying the rest.[40]

Of the shared shrines that survived but which Israel has turned into exclusively Jewish sites, the shrine of al-Khadir is a good example. For Muslims, al-Khadir is a Muslim saint who was widely worshiped already throughout the medieval Middle East. Like their Muslim neighbors, Palestinian Jews also worshiped at al-Khadir shrines, which for them are associated with Eliyahu ha-Navi, the biblical Prophet Elijah. Al-Khadir shrines could be found all the way from Egypt to Yemen, but the cult of Eliyahu ha-Navi was unique to Palestine, Egypt, and Syria.[41] In many cases, Christian visitors worshiped at the same shrines, as they connected them with Mar Eliyas, St. George. But whether as al-Khadir, Eliyahu ha-Navi or Mar Eliyas, the shrine was a shared sacred space, with all three religions converging on the same spot.[42]

Historically, the great majority of shrines of al-Khadir/Elyahu ha-Navi/Mar Eliyas in Palestine appear to have been established or rediscovered subsequent to the Crusader occupation of the Holy Land (1099–1187), thereby turning Palestine into possibly the most important geographical center for Muslim, Christian, and Jewish shrines of al-Khadir until 1948.[43]

An ancient shrine of al-Khadir exists on Mt. Carmel, overlooking the village (later city) of Haifa. Through the ages Muslims, Jews, Christians, and Druze made pilgrimages to this site.[44] Worshipers of each of these communities developed their own specific beliefs about the shrine's powers and sanctity, as they prayed and prostrated themselves in the presence of the prophet, asking him to intercept for them with Allah or God. All ascribed healing power to the shrine, especially for mental illnesses. Outside the cave visitors would arrange big parties after they had made their vow in the name of the Prophet for which they would prepare copious meals to be shared with friends and relatives, with part of the food always distributed to the poor in gratitude to the prophet.

During the Mamluk and Ottoman periods, the sacred cave al-Khadir on the Carmel and its *waqf* were administered by Muslim families, the last of whom were the al-Hasan family.[45] In 1948 they were expelled and fled to Lebanon as refugees, while Israel's Ministry of Religions took over the al-Khadir shrine and its *waqf*, posting new signs at the entrance of the cave that avoid all mention of the place's non-Jewish history and its shared sanctity.[46] The cave's interior and the shrine itself were completely redone so as to serve only Jewish worshipers.[47] With all inscriptions now only in Hebrew and all religious symbols exclusively Jewish, al-Khadir on Mt. Carmel has been turned into out-of-bounds territory for Israel's Muslims and Christians, with the exception of the Carmelites from the nearby monastery, who pray there every June 14 and individual Druze and Muslims who sometimes visit the place for personal oaths.[48]

A similar fate befell the shrine of al-Nabi Samu'il (in Arabic), the biblical Prophet Samuel, in the village of Ramah, near Jerusalem. We have Jewish records going back to the twelfth century of pilgrimages to the shrine of Samuel.[49] In Islam, too, Nabi Samu'il is venerated as a saint and Muslims from the surrounding villages would make their pilgrimage to the shrine.[50] Records show that for many generations Muslims as well as Jews would offer their prayers and bring votive offerings here, making the tomb an important center where Jews and Muslims interacted.[51]

A mosque bearing the name of Nabi Samu'il situated near the shrine also dates back to the twelfth century.[52] While this was a main shrine for Muslims, Jewish pilgrims as well regularly found they had free access to it throughout the year.[53] Records (*sijill*) of the *shari'a* court of Jerusalem dating back to the sixteenth century show that the main Jewish pilgrimage to Nabi Samu'il's shrine was held during the spring, especially in April and May.[54] Both Jewish and Muslim travelers from the eighteenth century have left us vivid descriptions of Jewish *ziyarat* to this shrine, which took place eight days before the

Jewish festival of Shavuot. Arab Jews would visit the site on that day and spend the entire night praying in the surrounding yard.[55] Though some local leaders and notables reportedly tried on occasion to halt Jewish pilgrimage to Nabi Samu'il's shrine, the Ottoman Central Authorities reiterated the right and "long tradition" of Jewish pilgrims to visit the shrine and practice their belief there. In decrees from 1722 and 1735, the Ottoman Sultan ordered the Qadi of Jerusalem to punish anyone who tried to prevent Jewish believers from visiting the shrine, "as they had always done in the past."[56] The shrine's Muslim caretakers made sure votive candles would burn there continually. Muslim peasants from nearby villages believed that the shrine had special powers to ensure adequate quantities of rain during the winter months.[57] A popular belief held that God withheld rain in punishment. When that happened, the whole peasant community would approach the saint to intercede for them with God: in procession the *fellahin* would raise their hands towards the sky, and pray: "O Prophet Samuel, give us to drink! O Lord of Heaven, give us to drink ... O ye Lord, wet the calycotome villosa, for we have come to Samuel to ask his mediation for water."[58]

Israel's occupation of the West Bank in 1967 put an end to these *ziyarat* and here, too, the shrine quickly became dominantly Jewish. The Muslim *Waqf* Administration and Islamic Affairs Department began launching complaints with the Israeli military governor of the West Bank as early as 1972 when Jewish settlers were already trying to take over the site.[59] In the late 1980s a Jewish religious institution joined the settlers in their efforts.[60] The *Waqf* administration then focused all its efforts on trying to keep at least the mosque above the shrine in Islamic hands.[61] Today, Muslims venerate in the mosque while Jews pray underneath in the cave (see also Reiter's essay in this volume, Chapter 6).

Symbolic of the despair among Palestinians at the way Israel continues to dispossess them of their land and confiscate their sacred spaces is the fate that befell the Tomb of Joseph/Yusef near Nablus.[62] Until 1948 this was a shared Jewish–Muslim shrine.[63] In 1948 (officially annexing it in 1950) Nablus became part of the Kingdom of Jordan, which meant that the shrine became inaccessible to devotees from Israel, both Jewish and Muslim.

The occupation of the West Bank by Israel in June 1967 brought a total reversal of this state of affairs. Although located in an entirely Muslim area, this shrine, too, quickly became exclusively Jewish, set off and heavily protected by the Israeli army. In 1980 it was taken over by Jewish settlers who turned it into a Jewish seminary (*yeshiva*). All Muslims, even those living next door, were forcefully prohibited from entering the shrine. Following the outbreak of the al-Aqsa Intifada in September 2000, ignited by the visit to Haram al-Sharif by Israel's then opposition leader Ariel Sharon and the subsequent killing in the clashes that it provoked of a large number of Palestinians by Israeli troops, Nablusi residents in utter desperation decided it was better for the shrine not to belong to anyone at all than to be usurped by one particular religion and partially destroyed the site by setting fire to it.[64]

This, of course, was not just a matter of groups of Jewish religious extremists taking over shared sacred places, but of official policy. When, in 1967, Israel occupied the 22 percent of Palestine it had failed to conquer in 1948, for Israeli politicians this opened vistas of "Greater Israel," *Eretz Israel ha-Shlema*, and Jewish religion—or the Zionist-nationalist interpretation of it—became a prominent tool in "reclaiming" the West Bank as part of Israel: the official call for settlements by Jewish colonizers there was heard within days of the June war.

It is the messianic fervor that the Zionist discourse seems to have absorbed after 1967 that has turned this nationalistic drive for more territory into the lethal disruptive force it has been for close to 40 years now on the West Bank and in the Gaza Strip. Early on, it meant mass confiscation of Palestinian land, first for military purposes, but then most of it was handed over to Israeli settlers.[65] Gush Emunim (Bloc of the Faithful), for example, achieved one of its first successes as early as April 1968 when it settled in the heart of the Old City of Hebron/Al-Khalil. Enjoying the full protection of the Israeli army, it has terrorized the indigenous Muslim population ever since.[66]

What we find at work here, of course, is that "element of artifact, innovation and social engineering that enters into the making of nations."[67] Hobsbawm explains this with the insight that "nationalism comes before nations" and that "nations do not make states and nationalism but the other way round."[68] For the light he can help throw on Israel's confiscation of Palestine's sacred topography, I quote Hobsbawm at some length:

> Again, while the Jews, scattered throughout the world for some millennia, never ceased to identify themselves, wherever they were, as members of a special people quite distinct from the various brands of non-believers among whom they lived, at no stage, at least since the return from the Babylonian captivity, does this seem to have implied a serious desire for a Jewish political state, let alone a territorial state, until a Jewish nationalism was invented at the very end of the nineteenth century by analogy with the newfangled western nationalism.[69]

Hobsbawm immediately follows this by explaining:

> It is entirely illegitimate to identify the Jewish links with the ancestral land of Israel, the merit deriving from pilgrimages there, or the hope of return there when the Messiah came—as he so obviously had *not* come in the view of the Jews—with the desire to gather all Jews into a modern territorial state situated on the ancient Holy Land. One might as well argue that good Muslims, whose highest ambition is to make the pilgrimage to Mecca, in doing so really intend to declare themselves citizens of what has now become Saudi Arabia.[70]

In 1948, for those Palestinians who had somehow remained within the territory of the new State of Israel, the abuse of their Islamic holy shrines proved especially painful as it robbed them of the solace and comfort the large majority of them would seek in the embrace of religion and tradition.[71] After being pushed into marginality, Palestinians under Israeli occupation have sought recourse to their old traditions to help them develop new forms of community and identity and so confront the outside enemy. Holy shrines in contemporary Palestinian society are being revived or re-invented to help build or re-imagine a new identity that can help people cope with the daily aggression that threatens their existence.[72]

Each year, Christian and Muslim Palestinians from Bethlehem and its environs get together in the gardens of the Greek Orthodox Monastery of Mar Eliyas (Elijahu ha-Navi/al-Khadir), located on the outskirts of the district of Bethlehem, to celebrate the Saint's name day on May 6. On the preceding day, groups of Muslim and Christian men, women and children gather under the olive trees and hold picnics. Christians may go into the church to deliver loaves of bread specifically baked in celebration of the event. Together, Muslims and Christians light candles and leave jars of olive oil in the church.[73]

On the day itself, visitors (Christians and Muslims) form a long queue outside the church awaiting their turn to place around their neck a heavy chain that is attached to the structure's wall, which they will kiss three times and then step over. According to local tradition, the chain was found in a cave beneath the monastery. The cave and the monastery are dedicated to Mar Eliyas because it is believed this was the spot where the prophet sought refuge from the persecution of Queen Jezebel and had bound himself with this chain. Greek Orthodox priests explain the fervent attachment of the locals to the chain as an expression of the people's deep devotion to the prophet:

> Those who enchain themselves with it bind themselves to the saint and make themselves one with him. All the votive offerings they bring, like the oil for the lamps, the bread and the candles, express this self-dedication. Eliyas is a mediator between God and the people. And they can talk to him when they cannot talk to God.[74]

Believers explain that, by worshiping the chain, they call on Mar Eliyas to deliver them from the afflictions they are made to suffer, just as God delivered Eliyas from his. For local Muslims "the chain is linked to the al-Khadir shrine in the nearby village of the same name." Muslims and Christians approaching the Mar Eliyas chain believe that it alleviates all kinds of illnesses, especially psychological, that it brings good luck and protects against bad luck and the evil eye.[75]

In 1983, Christian as well as Muslim Palestinians from Bayt-Sahur (near Bethlehem) reported repeated sightings of the Virgin Mary in the shadowy depths of an underground cistern beneath the market square of the town. Prompted by public pressure, the Bayt-Sahur municipality built a shrine over the cistern for the use of Muslims and Christians of all denominations, and called it Be'er al-Sayyida, the "Well of our Lady." The exterior architecture is distinctly modern, and apart from a cross that tops it, bears less resemblance to a church than to a traditional Muslim *maqam*. Inside, the walls are covered with icons and paintings of Christian subjects but one also finds a significant number of Qur'anic verses, inscriptions, paintings and pictures with clear Islamic subjects left there by the faithful.[76]

Religious practices at the shrine similarly reflect the town's heterogeneous character.[77] As the shrine belongs to the municipality, representatives of all communities can make reservations for events they want to hold there. Both Muslims and Christians collect water from the cistern in the back of the shrine as a healing substance that brings good luck and blessings. When the municipality built the new shrine of Be'er al-Sayyida, it meant it to be for all those living in the town and its surroundings: "The municipality builds for all the people, and the people all own and can use the well."[78] Moreover, the initiative meant to create a "space" between the communal "inner" domain of faith and the "outside" they see as aiming to destroy them—a boundary that marks their separation from the ubiquitous Israeli army troops and Jewish settlers, the two most salient symbols of occupation. Strongly aware of their Palestinian identity, Bayt-Sahurians in this way are able to imagine themselves as a "nation in waiting," and as Muslims and Christians, engage in a collective struggle for mutual survival against the external enemy.

Significantly, there is considerable variety in the way Christians and Muslims gathering in al-Khadir seek comfort from the shrine. Some use the site just for picnicking, others to take a blessing from the chain, others again to redeem a promise and ask for the Prophet's blessing. Similarly, the shrine of Be'er al-Sayyida and the way it consolidates this mixed Palestinian community has created a public space in which residents of Bayt-Sahur can embrace and celebrate an image that joins them in a trans-communal identity.[79]

Finally, there is one incident in which we find the Israeli authorities not just encouraging (as with the illegal Jewish settlers in the occupied West Bank) but actively promoting the "cult of saints" and sponsoring the re-invention of a particular shared *maqam*. This occurred as early as 1948, at the crucial period in the nearly complete destruction and expulsion of Palestinian society. This is the cult of Nabi Shu'ayb, traditionally venerated throughout Palestine by all of the country's Muslims, including the Druze. Until 1948, the *ziyara* of Nabi Shu'ayb had much the same features we find in many other traditional visits to shrines throughout in Palestine. It was neither an official holy day nor did it attract mass pilgrimage from outside the Galilee. The shrine served as a place of vow taking (*nidhr*) for Druze and Sunni Muslims.[80] Soon after 1948, following the expulsion of Palestine's Sunni Muslims, the *maqam* became exclusively Druze.[81]

This is not the place to discuss why the Zionists allowed the Druze to remain—no Druze village was destroyed in 1948. Suffice it to note that already in the early 1930s the Zionist movement began cultivating "friendly ties" with Palestine's Druze population, especially after they learned that the community was eager to preserve a position of neutrality so as to safeguard its "particularist" nature.[82] Before 1948, Firro explains, "the usefulness for the Zionists of a tiny minority of not more than 13,000 ... stemmed from their alleged ability to convince the leaders of the Druze communities in Syria and Lebanon to stay out of the conflict, pleading that only their non-interference could safeguard the 'weak' and 'small' community in Palestine."[83] After 1948, Israel quickly and aggressively worked to alienate the Druze minority from the other Palestinians in the new state, part of the divide-and-rule tactics of the military regime I mentioned above.[84] Simultaneously, the Druze were turned into a "showcase for the world at large of the 'benevolent attitude' [Israel] was willing to adopt towards 'non-hostile' minorities within its territory."[85] And it was the *maqam* of Nabi Shu'ayb where this "inseparability of religion and nationalism" was now played out.[86] In December 1948 the shrine served as the location where the first Druze took their oath in the Israeli army, a custom that was consolidated in April 1949 as the *ziyara*, held under the official auspices of the Israeli authorities, came to symbolize the coalescing interests of both sides. The next step came in 1954 when the Israeli authorities recognized the *ziyara* of Nabi Shu'ayb as an official Druze holiday, extending it over three, later even four days. Significantly, we find that at the same time the Druze religious and political leaders together with the Israeli Ministry of Religious Affairs agreed to "abolish" the feast of al-Fitr—which the Druze community had always celebrated together with the country's Sunni Muslims—making it clear that Israel succeeded in "fostering among the Druzes an awareness that they are a separate community." Firro speaks of a hyphenated "Israeli–Druze" consciousness that underpinned the politics of how the community chose to memorialize its own recent history.[87]

This essay was written under the shadow of the Separation Wall the Israeli government is rapidly completing in the occupied West Bank. But the politics of memory embodied by the monstrous Separation Wall also represents Israel's ultimate denial of the shared Judeo-Islamic heritage of a large part of the country's population; Mizrahim and Palestinians alike. What, then, of the Holy Land and the future of our shared past? As a Palestinian historian in search of hope for change, I return to Ella Shochat:

> For Arab Jewish communities, the traumatic move to Israel came in the wake of the partition of Palestine, a process of which they had no control and in which they like the Palestinians, were the objects and not the subjects of history, even if this objectification for Palestinians took on a different, infinitely more violent form.[88]

And I join her as she looks ahead and tries to envision a road back to that shared Arab-Muslim culture—the shared Judeo-Islamic heritage I have been concerned with here—in which lie her own roots as an Iraqi Jew, telling us to avoid the blind spots of the conventional modes of analyzing Israeli politics and society. What is desperately needed for critical scholars is a de-Zionized decoding of the peculiar history of Mizrahim, one closely articulated with Palestinian history.[89]

It puts me in mind of Sheikh al-Shu'la, Rabbi Shimon Bar Yohai, and the big bonfires with which Muslims and Jews used to commemorate the anniversary of his death. Mt. Meron, after all, is not far from Nazareth, where I live.

Notes

1 I wish to thank my good friend Dick Bruggeman for his invaluable assistance and encouragement. Many thanks to Mr. Khadir Salameh of the Aqsa Museum and the staff of the Abu Dis Archives.
2 J.W. Meri, *The Cult of Saints among Muslims and Jews in Medieval Syria*, Oxford: Oxford University Press, 2002, p. 12 (emphasis added).
3 *Ibid.*, pp. 20–29.
4 *Ibid.*, p. 27.
5 *Ibid.*, pp. 259–60.
6 A.B. Abi Bakr Al-Harawi, *Kitab al-Isharat ila Ma'rifat al-Ziyarat*, annotated by J. Sourdel-Thomine, Damascus: Institut Français de Damas, 1953 [in Arabic]; Meri, *The Cult of Saints*, p. 7.
7 A. Cohen and A.S. Pikali, *Yehudim be-Beit ha-Mishpat ha-Muslemi, Hevra, Kalkala ve-Irgun Qehilati bi-Yerushalayim ha-'Uthmanit ba-Me'ah ha-Shesh 'Esre* (Jews in the Muslim Religious Court. Society, Economy and Communal Organization in the Sixteenth Century, Documents from Ottoman Jerusalem), Jerusalem: Yad Izhak Ben-Zvi, 1993, pp. 109, 112, 114–15, 117, 122 [in Hebrew].
8 Local Muslims called it the *maqam* of Abu As'ad al-Darir ("the blind"). See M. 'Abbasi, *Qura Qada Safad fi 'Ahd al-Intidab*, Nazareth: al-Hakim Liltiba'h, 1996, p. 154 [in Arabic].
9 Meri, *The Cult of Saints*, at pp. 243–44.
10 *Ibid.*, p. 244.
11 *Ibid.*, p. 14.
12 The original manuscript was published by B. Lewis, "An Arabic Account of the Province of Safed – I," *Bulletin of the School of Oriental and African Studies*, 15 (1953), p. 480 ff. The translation here is Meri's, *The Cult of Saints*, at p. 247. See also M. bin Ibrahim al-Dimashqi, *Kitab Nukhbat al-Dahr fi 'Aja'ib al-Barr wa al-Bahr*, Baghdad: Maktabat al-Muthanna, n.d., p. 118 [in Arabic]; Sh. 'Arraf, *Tabaqat al-Anbiyya' wa-al-Awliyya' al-Salihin fi-l-Ard al-Muqadassa*, 2 vols., Tarshiha: Akhwan Makhkhul, 1993, vol. 2, p. 203 [in Arabic].
13 A. Ya'ari (ed.), *Igrot Eretz Yisra'el she-Katvu ha-Yehudim ha-Yoshvim ba-Aretz el-Ahihem she-ba-Gula mi-Yame Galut Bavel ve-'ad Shiyvat Ziyon she-be-Yameinu* (Letters from Eretz Israel, written by Jews settled there to their Brethren in the Diaspora, from the Days if the Babylonian Exile to the Return of Zion in our own Days), Ramat Gan: Masada, 1971, p. 113 [in Hebrew].
14 Z. Vilna'i, *Ariel, Ensiklopedia le-Yediy'at Eretz Yisra'el* (Encyclopaedia of the Knowledge of Eretz Yisrael), Tel Aviv: Yediot Acharonot, 1977, pp. 7911–18 [in Hebrew].
15 Ibid., p. 7917.
16 Cf. Ilan Pappe, *The Ethnic Cleansing of Palestine*, Oxford: One World, 2006, pp. xi–xii, and passim.
17 For a concise and vivid description of today's Jewish holy festival in Mt. Meron, see Y. Bilu, *Lelo Metzarim, Hayav ve-Moto shel Rabi Ya'aqov Wazana* (Without Bounds. The Life and Death of Rabbi Ya'acov Wazana), Jerusalem: Magnes Press, 1993, pp. 22–24 [in Hebrew].
18 U. Kupferschmidt, "A Morrocan *Tzadiq* in Israel: The Emergence of the Baba Sali," in E. Rabbie, M. S. Nihon, and J. G. Frankfort (eds), *Bijdragen en Mededelingen van*

het Genootschap voor de Joodsche Wetenschap in Nederland gevestigd te Amsterdam, Amsterdam: Genootschap voor de Joodsche Wetenschap in Nederland gevestigd te Amsterdam, 2002, vol. 11, pp. 252–53.

19 The term *Mizrahim* to denote Arab Jews, i.e., Jews who had come (or had been brought) to Israel from Middle Eastern or North African countries, "began to be used in the early 1990s by leftist non-Ashkenazi activists who saw previous terms such as *bnei edoth hamizrah* [lit.: descendants of the eastern ethnicities] as condescending; non-European Jews were posited as 'ethnicities,' in contradistinction to the unmarked norm of 'Ashkenaziness' or Euro-Israeli 'Sabraness,' defined simply as Israeli. 'Mizrahim' also gradually replaced the term 'Sephardim' (literally referring to [Jews] of Spanish origin"; Ella Shochat, "The Invention of the Mizrahim," *Journal of Palestine Studies*, 1999, vol. 29, no.1, p. 13.

20 Ella Shochat, "Rupture and Return: A Mizrahi Perspective on the Zionist Discourse," *The MIT Electronic Journal of Mid. East Stud.* 2001, vol. 1, Online. Available: http://web.mit.edu/cis/www/mitejmes/issues/200105/shohat.htm (accessed 8 May 2006). Earlier she writes: "Of course, there was a kind of regional geo-cultural Jewish space from the Mediterranean to the Indian Ocean, where Jews traveled, exchanged ideas, under the aegis of the larger Islamic world, into which they were culturally and politically interwoven, even if they retained their Jewishness within that realm. They were shaped by Arab-Muslim culture and helped shape that culture in a dialogical process that resulted in their specific Judeo-Arabic identity."

21 That is, immigration to Israel; this is the same term Hebrew uses for pilgrimage but shorn by Zionism of its religious connotation, similar to, e.g., *'avoda*, "work," which for religious Jews expresses "the worship of God through work."

22 Shochat, "The Invention of the Mizrahim," at p. 15 (emphasis added).

23 *Ibid.*, pp. 16–17 (emphasis added).

24 *Ibid.*, p. 18.

25 For more information on these *mawasim* before the establishment of the State of Israel, see T. Canaan, *Mohammedan Saints and Sanctuaries in Palestine*, London: Journal of the Palestine Oriental Society, 1927, pp. 193–216; Kamil J. Asali, *Mawsim al-Nabi Musa fi Filastin, Tarikh al-Mawsim wa-al-Maqam*, Amman: Jordan University Press, 1990; 'Arraf, *Tabaqat al-Anbiyya, Tabaqat al-Anbiyya' wa-al-Awliyya' al-Salihin fi-l-Ard al-Muqadassa*, at pp. 575–86 [in Arabic].

26 Archives of the Higher Muslim Council, Abu-Dis, *Markaz Ihya' al-Turath al-Islami*, Reports of annual income of Nabi Rubin's irrigated and un-irrigated crops, file no. 3/4,4/328/16; see also survey map of the Nabi Rubin's compound area prepared in 1922, file no. 10/1,6/22/16 [in Arabic].

27 Archives of the Higher Muslim Council, Abu-Dis, *Markaz Ihya' al-Turath al-Islami*, file no. 10/1,5/22/16, from the *waqf* administrator of Jaffa to the head of the Higher Muslim Council in Jerusalem, 20 Dec. 1922 [in Arabic].

28 For a detailed description of the Nabi Rubin's *mawsim*, see A.H. al-Bawwab, *Mawsu'at Yafa al-Jamila*, 2 vols., Beirut: al-Mu'asasa al-'Arabiyya lildirast wa-al-Nashr, 2003, pp. 1353–70 [in Arabic].

29 Author's visit to the site, 10 Oct. 2006.

30 Holy sites in Palestine before 1948 belonged to and were administered by the Islamic endowment authority (the *waqf*), which was recognized by both the Ottoman Empire and the British Mandatory Government. See Y. Reiter, *Ha-Waqf be-yirushalayim 1948–1990* (Islamic Awqaf in Jerusalem 1948–90), Jerusalem: Makhon Yirushalayim Leheker Yisra'el, 1991, p. 44 [in Hebrew]; H. Gerber, *Ottoman Rule in Jerusalem 1890–1914*, Berlin: Klaus Schwarz Verlag, 1985, pp. 183–94. Together with their real estate when not destroyed, Israel confiscated all these endowments, which it first transferred to the so-called "Custodian of Absentee Property," then to the state, which then sold them on to Israeli public

bodies and private Jewish citizens. For a full discussion of official Israeli policies toward Islamic *waqf* properties, *see* M. Dumper, *Islam and Israel, Muslim Religious Endowments and the Jewish State*, Washington, D.C.: Institute for Palestine Studies, 1997; Reiter, *Ha-Waqf be-yirushalayim 1948–1990*, pp. 13–14.
31 L.A. Mayer and J. Pinkerfeld, *Some Principal Muslim Religious Buildings in Israel*, Jerusalem: Ministry of Religious Affairs, 1950, pp. 33–39.
32 Author's visit to the site, 15 Aug. 2006. *See also* Archives of Tel Aviv Municipality, Group 4, file no. 2241, document no. 877/62J.
33 Author's visit to the site, 15 Aug. 2006; Mayer and Pinkerfeld, *Some Principal Muslim Religious Buildings in Israel*, at p. 34.
34 *See e.g.*, a report of *Ha'aretz*, 1 July 2001, 16 Sept. 2005, *Ma'ariv* 3 Apr. 1983 [in Hebrew]. Cf. also D. Yahav, *Yafo, Kalat ha-Yam* (Jaffa, Bride of the Sea), Tel Aviv: Tammuz, 2004, pp. 31–48 [in Hebrew].
35 Yahav, *Yafo, Kalat ha-Yam*, p. 47.
36 *Ha'aretz*, 16 Sept. 2005; 23 Sept. 2005: A report of the Chief Engineer of the Municipality of Tel Aiv, 9 Jan. 1962.
37 Mayer and Pinkerfeld, *Some Principal Muslim Religious Buildings in Israel*, at pp. 44–53.
38 *See Ha'aretz*,1 Mar. 2006, *al-Ittihad*, 1 Mar. 2006. For other examples, *see* Pappe, *The Ethnic Cleansing of Palestine*, at pp. 217–19. For a full report concerning the fate and conversion of 70 Islamic holy sights in Israel administered under its Absentees Property Law, *see* www.Palestine-info/arabic.htm. *See also* M. Rapaport, "Pa'am Haya Kan Misgad" (Once A Mosque Stood Here), *Ha'aretz*, 16 Sept. 2005 [in Hebrew].
39 *Ha'aretz*, "ha-'Aravim be-Yafo (The Arabs in Jaffa)", 28 May 1981; S. Jiryis, *The Arabs in Israel*, Beirut: The Institute for Palestine Studies, 1969, p. 120.
40 Reiter, *Ha-Waqf be-yirushalayim 1948–1990*, at p. 110.
41 *See* A. J. Wensinck, "al-Khadir," Encyclopedia of Islam, new edn, Leiden: E.J. Brill, 1986–2002, vol. 4, pp. 902–5.
42 J.W. Meri, "Re-appropriating Sacred Space: Medieval Jews and Muslims Seeking Elijah and al-Khadir," *Medieval Encounters: Jewish, Christian and Muslim Culture in Confluence and Dialogue*, 1999, vol. 5, pp. 1–28. Canaan lists twenty shrines of al-Khadir in different towns and villages, many of them honored by Muslims and Christians. For further information, *see* Canaan, *Mohammedan Saints and Sanctuaries in Palestine*, at pp. 120–25.
43 A detailed survey of Christian and Muslim shrines of al-Khadir and Elijah in Palestine can be found in A. Augostinovic, *El-Khadir and the Prophet Elijah*, trans. by E. Hoade Jerusalem: Franciscan Printing Press, 1972.
44 M. Yazbak, *Haifa in the Late Ottoman Period, 1864–1914: A Muslim Town in Transition*, Leiden: E. J. Brill, 1998, pp. 207, 214, A. Ovadiah, "Elijah's Cave, Mount Carmel," *Israel Exploration Journal*, 1966, vol. 16, p. 285.
45 Yazbak, *Haifa in the Late Ottoman Period, 1864–1914*, p. 137.
46 The following is a quotation of part of the sign:

> ELIJAH'S CAVE, one of the most sacred caves in Eretz Israel. Tradition holds that Elijah the Prophet stayed here on his way to his momentous confrontation with the prophets of the Ba'al on the Carmel: "and Elijah said ... now herefore send and gather to me all Israel unto Mount Carmel"
>
> (Kings, 1:18)

> In the following paragraph the sign mentions that "the renovation [sic!] of Elijah's Cave was undertaken at the initiative of the Haifa Tourism Development Association in cooperation with the Municipality of Haifa, the Ministry for Religious Affairs and the Ministry of Tourism" (author's visit to the cave, Aug. 2006).

47 G. Barka'i and E. Sheller (eds) "Hamkomot Ha-kdoshim laDruzim baCarmel," *Ariel, Ktav 'Et le-Yedi'at Eretz Yisra'el*, 142 (2000), p. 45, [in Hebrew]; A. Brans, "Sodoteiha shel Me'arat Eliyahu," *Moreshet Derekh*, 1996, vol. 66, pp. 4–9 [in Hebrew].
48 About the central place of al-Khadir in the consciousness of Muslim and Christian residents of Haifa, see R. Da'eem, "*Agadot Qdoshim Loqaliyot me-Pi Mesaprim Notzrim ve-Muslemim ba-Heqsher shel Me'arat Eliyahu ha-Navi ve-Minzar Eliyahu ha-Navi be-Hayfa*" (Local Sacred Legends as told by Christians and Muslims about the Cave and Shrine of the Prophet Elija), unpublished M.A. thesis, University of Haifa, 2005 [in Hebrew].
49 Meri, *The Cult of Saints*, at pp. 240–42.
50 Canaan, *Mohammedan Saints and Sanctuaries in Palestine*, at pp. 45, 76, 229.
51 Cohen and Pikali, *Yehudim be-Beit ha-Mishpat ha-Muslemi*, at p. 110.
52 'Arraf, *Tabaqat al-Anbiyya*, at pp. 106–9.
53 R. Ben Ya'akov, "Ha-Ziyara' 'al Qivre Tzadiqim" (The Ziyara [Pilgrimage] to the Graves of Holy Men), *Masa'ot*, 1996, vol.1, p. 26 [in Hebrew].
54 Cohen and Pikali, *Yehudim be-Beit ha-Mishpat ha-Muslemi*, document nos. 105 and 108, pp. 115, 117.
55 Ben Ya'akov, "Ha-Ziyara' 'al Qivre Tzadiqim," at p. 26.
56 A. Cohen, A.S. Pikali, and O. Salama, *Yehudim be-Beit ha-Mishpat ha-Muslemi, Hevra, Kalkala ve-Irgun Qehilati bi-Yerushalayim ha-'Uthmanit ba-Me'ah ha-Shmona 'Esreh* (Jews in The Muslim Religious Court, Society, Economy and Communal Organization in the Eighteenth Century, Documents from Ottoman Jerusalem), Jerusalem 1996, pp. 121–22.
57 Such beliefs were common everywhere in Palestine, and Muslims, Christians, and Jews each practiced their own type of rain procession; see Canaan, *Mohammedan Saints and Sanctuaries in Palestine*, at p. 229.
58 *Ibid.*, pp.229–30.
59 I would like to thank the Department of the Waqf Affairs in Ramallah for allowing me access to its archives; see file Nabi Samu'il, No. MAR/145/57, Correspondence between the *Waqf* Council and the Israeli Military Authorities, during May 1972.
60 *Ibid.*, Report written by the head of the Islamic Waqf Department of Jerusalem to the head of the Waqf Department of the West Bank, 21 May 1991.
61 *Ibid.*, File no. 3/17/112/808, 26 Aug. 1992; a report attached to this file contains a complaint about the Muslim keeper of the site, alleging he is collaborating with the Jewish settlers; *see also*, a letter of Sheikh Sa'd al-Din al-'Alami, the Head of the Higher Islamic Administration of Jerusalem, to the Israeli Defense Minister, complaining that the Israeli Civil Administration in the occupied West Bank had put fences around the mosque in order to turn it into a tourist site, and insisting that "this aggression must be stopped, because it causes unrest and anger, but will not give the aggressor any legitimacy." There are dozens of similar complaints.
62 About the history of the shrine, *see* al-Harawi, *Kitab al-Isharat ila Ma'rifat al-Ziyarat*, at p. 24; 'Arraf, vol. 2, pp. 43–47. Traditionally, Islamic sources associate the tomb with the biblical Joseph, the son of Jacob. However, confronted with the violent behavior of the Jewish settlers, local Muslims today follow Ihsan al-Nimr (*Tarikh Jabal Nablus wa-al-Balqaa'*, vol. 4, Nablus: Jam'iyyat 'Ummal al-Matabi', 1975, p. 175) who claims the tomb belongs to a certain Sheikh Yusuf whom he does not further identify; others claim this is the seventeenth century Sheikh Yusuf Duwaykat [Online. Available: http:/www.islamonline.net; http://ar.wikipedia.org (accessed 8 May 2006). *But cf. also* M.M. al-Dabbagh, *Biladuna Filastin*, Beirut, 1988, vol. 6, p. 277.
63 Vilna'i, *Ariel, Ensiklopedia le-Yediy'at Eretz Yisra'el*, at pp. 2795–99.
64 "Israel withdraws from the Tomb of Joseph, 7 Oct. 2000" Online. Available http://www.ynet.co.il/articles (last accessed 8 May 2006).

65 By 1972 Israel had confiscated over 1.5 million dunams, almost 28 percent of the West Bank, by 2000 this had risen to almost 42 percent. On the way Israeli politics and messianic settler movements found each other after the June war of 1967. See Ilan Pappe, *A History of Modern Palestine. One Land, Two Peoples*, Cambridge: Cambridge University Press, 2004, pp. 200–204.
66 Seared into the memory of most Palestinians, for example, is the murder, on 25 Feb. 1994, of 29 Palestinian worshipers during Friday prayers in Al-Khalil's al-Haram al-Ibrahimi Mosque, committed by Dr. Baruch Goldstein, a Jewish settler and a physician in the Israeli Defense Forces (IDF).
67 Eric Hobsbawm, *Nations and Nationalism since 1780: Programme, Myth, Reality*, Cambridge: Cambridge University Press, 1990, p. 10.
68 *Ibid.* I hardly need to add that he is joined in this by many others, among them Ernest Gellner, who has so often been quoted for the following: "Nations as a natural, God-given way of classifying men, as an inherent though long-delayed political destiny, are a myth; nationalism, which sometimes takes pre-existing cultures and turns them into nations, sometimes invents them, and often obliterates pre-existing cultures, *that* is a reality" [emphasis in the original] E. Gellner, *Nations and Nationalism*, New York: Cornell University Press, 1991, pp. 48–49. See also Benedict Anderson, *Imagined Communities*, 2nd ed., London: Verso, 1991.
69 Hobsbawm, *Nations and Nationalism since 1780*, pp. 47–48.
70 *Ibid.*
71 *Cf.* Pappe, *The Ethnic Cleansing of Palestine*, at p. 217.
72 G. Bowman, "Nationalizing the Sacred: Shrines and Shifting Identities in the Israeli-Occupied Territories," *Man*, 1993, vol. 28, no.3, p. 433.
73 Women who made vows for the saint usually walk for long distances to reach the monastery. This description is based on a report from 26 May 2005. For full details of the ceremony, *see* Online. Available www.Elaph.com/Reports/2005/5/61462.htm. (accessed 8 May 2006).
74 Bowman, "Nationalizing the Sacred," at p. 434.
75 Canaan, *Mohammedan Saints and Sanctuaries in Palestine*, pp. 79–80.
76 Bowman, "Nationalizing the Sacred," at p. 439.
77 The population of Bayt Sahur is estimated to be 15,000, two-thirds being Christians; see http://Palestine-info.info.
78 Bowman, "Nationalizing the Sacred," at p. 450.
79 *Ibid.*, p. 453.
80 For the history of the *ziyara* to the *maqam* of Nabi Shu'ayb, *see* K.M. Firro, "Druze *maqamat* (Shrines) in Israel: From Ancient to Newly-Invented Traditions," *British Journal Middle Eastern Studies*, 2005, vol. 32, no. 2, pp. 227–32.
81 *Ibid.*, p. 223. As a "gesture" to the Druze community, the Israeli Government allocated to the shrine about one hundred dunams (of territory the state had first confiscated) and sponsored the construction of new buildings around it.
82 *Cf.* K.M. Firro, *The Druzes in the Jewish State: A Brief History*, Leiden: E.J. Brill, 1999, p. 23.
83 *Ibid.*, p. 4. The following quote may shed some light on the mindset of the Zionist leadership at the time: "In fact, this nation – the Druze – has special features and a special destiny that set it apart from other nations. In certain ways, it is similar to the Jewish nation because of a fundamental characteristic. Here, too, *religion and nationalism are so united* that it is difficult to separate between them" [emphasis added].
84 *Ibid.*, pp. 71–127. On page 94, in a chapter tellingly called "Towards Symbiosis," Firro quotes David Ben-Gurion: "We must foster among the Druze an awareness that they are a separate community vis-à-vis the Muslim community."
85 *Ibid.*, p. 4.

86 A month before, on 14 November, religious Druze leaders had prepared the move by claiming that "the historical relationship between the Druzes and the Jews went all the way back to the time of Moses, the name of the Druze saint, Shu'ayb, being Arabic for Jethro, the father-in-law of Moses."; *see* Firro, *The Druzes in the Jewish State*, p. 74. It seemed to disturb no one that as a religious sect, *al-Durziyya*, the Druze trace their origin back no further than to the early eleventh century CE; *ibid.*, p. 12.
87 Firro, "Druze *maqamat* (Shrines) in Israel," p. 239; *see also* Firro, *The Druzes in the Jewish State*, at pp. 243–50.
88 Referring back to the "profound and visceral schizophrenia" Zionism has meant for Israel's Arab Jews, she realistically adds in brackets: "(This is not to suggest that once in Israel Mizrahim have not been part of this violence against Palestinians.)"
89 Shochat, "The Invention of the Mizrahim," at p. 18.

13 Self-empowerment through the sacred culture and representation in the urban landscape
The Mosque of Hassan Bey and the Arab community of Jaffa

Nimrod Luz

Introduction

In this essay I explore the relations between the construction of social and political power and the politics of sacred places in urban communities through the analysis of changes in the architectural environment in Tel Aviv-Jaffa. My main goal is to reconstruct and analyze the struggle over the control and the use of the Hassan Bey Mosque as part of the community need for self-empowerment. I argue that the public and legal struggle conducted in Tel Aviv-Jaffa through the 1970s by its Muslim community reflects the strategies of a subordinate group to achieve better representation in the urban landscape, as part of its broader need to gain more control and live according to its cultural-religious codes.

In the aftermath of the 1948 War, Jaffa's Arab community declined from 70,000 people to a devastated community of less than 4,000. Jaffa, considered the "bride of Palestine" (*Arus Filastin*) and its intellectual center, thus became an obsolete and decaying suburb of the relatively new Jewish city of Tel Aviv.[1] The growing needs of the State of Israel led to the expropriation of Arab real estate and lands, some of which were religious institutions, such as mosques and cemeteries. One of these is the Hassan Bey Mosque, built in 1916 by the Ottomans on the outskirts of Manshiyyah, the biggest Muslim suburb of Jaffa. During the 1948 War it was used as a sniper post to inflict casualties on the Tel Aviv population. The history of the Mosque is not unlike that of the historic Arab town—once the center of a growing and lively neighborhood, and since 1948 a neglected, dilapidated building, inaccessible to its former community. During the 1970s and 1980s the Mosque became the focus of a lengthy public and legal debate, as it was slated to be leased and turned into a tourist shopping center. The struggle resulted in the Mosque's repossession by the Jaffa Muslim community and its renewal as a center for religious practice.

The Hassan Bey Mosque is yet another case study illustrating the inseparability of religious and sociopolitical forces in society. In this particular instance it is almost impossible to differentiate between the two, for the two forces are used interchangeably to promote and sustain the political needs of the Muslim community. The conflict over the Mosque is intrinsically connected to the political struggle of a minority group to express itself within the city's landscape and to challenge the hegemonic position of the majority group. The Hassan Bey affair demonstrates the ways in which the Jaffa community operates in order to reclaim its cultural assets, to enhance its cohesion as a group against the dominant majority (hegemonic prevailing discourse and agencies), and to better represent itself in the city. I maintain that these are all part and parcel of the long and fraught process of self-empowerment of the Arab community of Jaffa.

My objectives are threefold: 1) to explore the Hassan Bey affair as an example of a minority group's politico-cultural struggle to challenge the dominant group and to work cohesively to augment its role in the daily management of its life; 2) to outline the historical narrative of the struggle (what actually took place on the ground and within the community) using in-depth interviews and municipal archival documents; 3) to analyze the political use of the religious sacred place within the context of a cultural conflict between hegemonic and subordinate groups.

Theoretical context

Kong has focused our attention on the importance of religious places and landscapes in cultural geography.[2] It is readily apparent that religious places are always highly sensitive and often evoke dramatic and contentious social and political encounters. In fact, as already claimed by Needham, sacred places are by nature contested places, as the sacred is a contested category.[3] I further argue that sacredness is not an inherent feature of a place, but is socially constructed. Consequently, sacred places offer pertinent case studies for considering the ways different forces construct and produce them as such. Sacred places can be appropriate lenses to explore how the cultural labor of rituals in specific historical situations, and the hard work of memory, design, construction, and control, produce the importance of these places.[4] Analysis of sacred places should consider not the numinous and transcendental nature of such places, but rather the power relations of domination and subordination, inclusion and exclusion, and other forms of social encounters, which may be considered under the theme of the politics of a place.[5] To understand why the Arab population of Jaffa channeled its struggle to become more prominent mostly through sacred landmarks, it is important to understand the connection between politics, hegemony, and resistance.

The notion of hegemony is generally connected with the work of Antonio Gramsci, the Italian Marxist theorist.[6] Gramsci explored the ways dominant groups inflict social order and the common understanding of "the right order of things" (commonsensical views) upon society at large and subordinate groups in particular. Hegemony, according to Gramsci, is the prevailing commonsense view formed in culture that sets the tone and dictates the accepted notions of what is good/true/right/legal. Civic institutions that inform values, customs, and spiritual ideals, and induce what he called spontaneous consent to the status quo diffuse it. Gramsci's understanding of hegemony is highly relevant to any social theory as it recognizes and postulates the coexistence and constant conflict among dominant and subordinate groups in society. Further, it acknowledges the existence of groups (at times opposing and usually not coordinated) within the dominant and subordinate classes. For this reason Williams referred to hegemony not just as the conscious system of ideas and beliefs, but as "the whole lived social process" as practically organized by specific and dominate meanings and values.[7]

There are a few advantages to this concept of hegemony. By looking at hegemony as a whole way of life, all parts of society are included within it, i.e., dominant and subordinate groups. This approach avoids reification of society as it does not regard hegemony as a static or fixed state of affairs but rather as a process, defined by Gramsci as a moving equilibrium. Thus, boundaries and consensual norms are always shifting and being negotiated among the dominant and subordinate groups. Indeed, cultural hegemony has a dynamic nature and non-impermeable boundaries. By viewing hegemony as such, we can explore this concept as a site of constant coercion (by force or consent) and resistance. Again following Williams, this sense of ideology is applied in abstract ways to the actual consciousness of both dominant and subordinate classes.[8] When imposed on subordinate groups (different consciousness), it always entails different forms of conflict and struggle. Consequently, ways and means of counter-hegemony are being formed and sites of resistance are sought after and utilized as part of the process. In a sense, the Hassan Bey affair is best seen as forming ways of counter-hegemony by creating a site of resistance and an alternative reading of the power geometries inflicted by the powers that be. Alternative readings and interpretations of the cultural landscape are none other than challenges to the commonsensical world view, i.e., forms of resistance.

Resistance may be defined as the behavior and cultural practices of subordinate groups that contest hegemonic social formation and threaten to unravel the strategies of domination. Consciousness is not necessarily essential to its constitutions.[9] Resistance may be regarded as the ability of people to alter things and realities through myriad tactics and behaviors. It constitutes the capacity of subordinate groups to create means of counter-hegemony or form alternative worldviews and norms. Resistance can be mapped as it has visible expressions and therefore takes place.[10]

Pile argues forcefully that the very existence of geographies of resistance indicates that people are positioned differently in unequal and multiple power relations. The existence of this inequality (i.e., the existence of hegemonic and subordinate groups) is projected on the ground in the formation of uneven and differentiated power-geometries and landscapes (i.e., physical manifestations) of inequalities. Resistance seeks to challenge, subvert, and alter power relations in a way that will lead to the creation of alternative spatialities to those created hitherto by hegemonic groups and state discourse. Through alternative spatialities, or sites of resistance, people can challenge, mitigate, or completely avoid the effects of hegemonic power on their daily lives. As Pile notes, resistance is less about particular acts than about the desire to find a place in a certain power geography where space is denied.[11] In order to accomplish this, the group's mobilization is required, which is why Pile is persuasive in saying that resistance is about mass mobilization in deference to common interests. The pertinent question is what triggered the mobilization? Castells' analysis of urban movements offers a solid understanding:

> Urban movements, and indeed all social mobilizations, happen when in their collective action and at the initiative of a conscious and organized operator, they address one or more structural issues that differentiate contradictory social interests, These issues, or their combination, define the movement, and the people they may mobilize, the interests likely to oppose the movement, and the attitude of institutions according to their political orientation. ... The social issues providing the 'goals' of an urban movement represent the connection in action between the movement and the whole society.[12]

Put simply, mobilization will take place when the goal as formulated by the group leaders will appeal to a meaningful number of people. The goals and the reactions to the group's recruitment cannot be separated from the reality in which people live. In the Israeli context as experienced in the Tel-Aviv–Jaffa municipality, the issue of repossessing the Mosque, of reclaiming part of the Arab community's history and cultural assets was enough to mobilize a substantial part of the group. By looking at the Mosque of Hassan Bey as a site of resistance, I will portray the events and the process of reconstituting the place within the context of the fragile and changing hegemony and counter-hegemony equilibrium. Further, I will describe the operators and key agents in both types of groups and penetrate the complex mosaic of different groups and interests that were (and still are) influential actors in the re-inscribing this mosque into the urban landscape.

The making of a landmark

At the beginning of World War I (August 1914) a new governor was appointed over Jaffa, an Ottoman officer by the name of Hassan Bey al-Jabi.[13] During his short sojourns in Jaffa, Hassan Bey launched a few development ventures.[14] These were apparently intended to render futile his subordinates' aspirations in view of the waning of the Ottoman Empire's power. Hassan Bey became notorious for being a cruel, merciless, and obtuse commander with a particular thirst for bribes.[15]

Self-empowerment through the sacred culture 253

These traits are readily apparent in his initiative to build a mosque that would carry his name in the suburb of Manshiyyah. He handpicked a desirable plot by the seaside confiscating it from its Christian Arab owner. On the very same day he registered the land under his name and ordered that construction materials should be gathered from the surrounding area. He went as far as to plunder building sites in Tel Aviv, Ramle, and Rishon leZion some ten miles away, obtaining by force the necessary materials. It would seem that forced labor was the main source of workers for construction of the mosque. People, mostly Muslims, were grabbed at random on the streets to contribute workdays under duress.[16] By the time of his departure to a new post in May 1916, the mosque was already completed.[17] The following description of the building from a letter to the Supreme Muslim Council in 1941 is still appropriate:

> The Mosque is fashioned in the Ottoman style and it is built of stones. Its measures are 21 m. by 28 m. Its main entrance is reached with a staircase from the north and it opens into a courtyard paved in its entirety save a part of it, which was designated as a garden.[18]

The building was well-planned and proportioned, and when set amongst the small and simple houses of Manshiyyah, it cut a fine and impressive figure in the local landscape. In 1923 the Supreme Muslim Council—the leading Muslim authority of the time—embarked on a series of renovations and religious building constructions, one of which was the Mosque of Hassan Bey.[19] However, this was not about affixing a new door to the building or building a new washing facility. This was also part of the full-scale ethno-national struggle between Muslims and Jews which was taking shape under the British Mandate.[20] Hassan Bey Mosque was a religious building, but it was more—it was a Muslim landmark of the city of Jaffa which faced off against the flourishing and fast-growing Jewish city of Tel Aviv. Its strategic location on the northern borders of Jaffa was responsible for the role it played during the turbulent times of 1947–48 when armed conflict erupted between the two sides. From December 1947 to May 1948 Arab snipers were regularly stationed at Hassan Bey and used its minaret as a shooting platform while firing on the streets of Tel Aviv.[21] During that period the municipal borders of the two towns became not just highly charged ethnic-national borders, but an active war zone. The role played by the Mosque is still vivid and evocative in the collective memory of both communities. One may argue, of course, if and how much this was relevant during the 1970s and 1980s when the site was being fought over by the Arab community. But as the following anecdote from an interview with an Arab activist from Jaffa reveals, these memories are still part of the "past of the place" on both sides. 'Abd Satil is the current head of Rabita, an Arab organization for the social welfare of Jaffa citizens. He was born in the State of Israel and for him the Mosque is part of the history and cultural heritage of his community. When asked about the Mosque these were his recollections:

Manshiyyah was a very rich neighborhood. ... it was mainly Muslim as the Christians lived nearer to the center. Apparently it was also a place where people gathered and made plans [i.e. military plans—N.L.] and during the war they shot from the minaret. I remember having this meeting with someone in Tel Aviv, from the Likud Party, and he told me he was shot at from the building and asked me: Why do you renovate Hassan Bey?[22]

On April 28, 1948 forces of the Irgun Zevai Leumi captured the neighborhood of Manshiyyah.[23] This was also the crucial gambit for the final surrender of Jaffa to Jewish forces on May 13, 1948.[24] By the time of Jaffa's official surrender, most of the population had already left the city. Manshiyyah was totally evacuated from its former residents and the Mosque of Hassan Bey ceased to act as a religious center and venue for congregational gathering and worship. In the years to follow it stood as a decaying symbol of the urban Arab past and, as the development plans of the Tel Aviv municipality progressed, as the last relic of the neighborhood of Manshiyyah. The prominent minaret standing on its own became a sign of the triumphant Jewish-Zionist project and a living landmark of the past existence of the Arab community and its catastrophe.

Changing the equilibrium—hegemony at work

On May 13, 1948 Arab Jaffa surrendered. Less than 4,000 inhabitants, roughly 5 percent of the city's former population, remained.[25] From then on Jaffa's small Arab community was confined to a few neighborhoods situated close to the historic center while Manshiyyah, the northern suburb, was resettled with new Jewish immigrants. In Jaffa, as in many other places, the new state was confronted with the issue of absentee properties. This legal term refers to Arabs who did not report to the Israeli authorities by a certain date and therefore were considered to be absent. In the post-war atmosphere and in view of the constant demand for land, Israel issued laws that enabled state agencies to confiscate and use former Arab lands, houses, and property. A new government office was eventually established, the Custodian of Absentee Property, in order to control and facilitate the transfer of these assets to several state agencies. On March 14, 1950 the Israeli Knesset issued the Law of Absentees' Property.[26] Section 19a of this law declares that the Custodian of Absentee Property can only release land and property to the state Development Authority. This section was the most efficient mechanism to ensure that any land belonging to former Arab owners would mostly be sold to Jewish agencies or the Jewish private sector.[27]

The Mosque of Hassan Bey came under this category of absentee property. Accordingly, in the years to follow the shattered Muslim community of Jaffa was prevented from any access to or use of this building. For most of this time the Mosque was deserted and devoid of any social activity. During the

1950s a few ideas were proposed, such as giving a social worker access to the Mosque in order to use it as a youth center.[28] Generally speaking, the building remained closed and unattended from 1948 onward. This state of affairs inevitably resulted in the building's continuous deterioration and use as a venue for illegal activities such as narcotics and prostitution.[29] Throughout the 1960s and 1970s most of Manshiyyah's houses were razed to the ground in accordance with the city's development plans.[30] Against the background of the rapidly disappearing neighborhood and the urban void taking shape, the Mosque became even more conspicuous. It became, using Lynch's theoretical concepts, a landmark in the city's landscape.[31] Its imageability—that is, the intensity of feelings and emotional associations it aroused and provoked—increased, indeed soared dramatically.

A shift in state policy towards its Arab citizens took place in 1965. An amendment (Section 29b) to the Law of Absentees' Property led to the formation of a new legal entity called the Muslim Charitable Trust. This Trust was composed of committees appointed in six municipalities all over Israel where Muslim communities and Muslim confiscated land and properties were located. The Trusts were ostensibly created to enable Muslim communities to take direct control of assets that were until then in the hands of the state. In fact, however, these trusts could only manage those properties in their municipal areas that were released to them by the Custodian. Thus, instead of gaining access to a significant part of the community's former property, the Trust' duties were reduced to dealing with only the part that the Custodian was willing to release. It should be stressed that the Custodian only approved development plans for abandoned property on those occasions when the Trust could produce a future lease or sale contract with a Jewish third party.[32] The money derived from those would-be transactions was then, and only then, to be used for the benefit of the community. But these were not the only obstacles facing those committees. A special committee of the Israeli Government was in charge of appointing members of the Trust. The committee members were drawn from various state authorities, such as the Ministries of Defense, Finance, Agriculture, and Interior, the Israel Lands Administration, etc. Under such circumstances, one need not be surprised that these committees were nothing more than another mechanism (in effect, a state agency) that was devised to facilitate the easy appropriation of Muslim property into Jewish hands. The Jaffa Trust was first appointed on November 23, 1967.[33] Its members, to say the least, were not considered to be pillars of the community. People in Jaffa still refer to them today as collaborators; some would even go as far as calling them traitors.[34] The governmental committee made sure that the people appointed to the Trust were cooperative and accommodating to the general needs of the municipality development plans. In this way, the state ensured that a very sensitive and delicate task that might have contributed significantly to the generally poor Arab communities would be entrusted to people who were, at best inept, at worst self-serving, criminal personalities. Ahmad Asfur, a former member of the Jaffa Trust, described the manner in which these trusts actually operated:

During the sixties Charitable Trusts were founded. They took simple people from the streets and gave them jobs. The Trust was a sovereign body like the Vatican, but those who were appointed for the jobs did not know their rights and always yielded and surrendered to the master.[35]

The Jaffa Trust was to play a crucial part in the orchestrated effort to transform the neglected Mosque of Hassan Bey into a tourist center. As suggested by Gramsci, hegemonic and subordinate classes are multifaceted and often fractured. It is with the help of strategic allegiances that a group opposing the Trust within the Jaffa community managed to manipulate hegemonic powers in order to win back the sacred place, a part of the community's cultural and religious heritage. This achievement could only be accomplished by understanding how hegemony works and by learning how to manipulate it. My argument here is that this was possible only because the project concerned a sacred object and important cultural icon in the ideological landscape of the Jaffa Arab community.

"Like a thorn in the side of development"—urban planning as a hegemonic force

According to the Tel-Aviv Jaffa Master Plan of 1954 and the 1968 Urban Building Plan, the Manshiyyah area was designated as part of the city's Central Business District (CBD). The area of the Mosque was slated for lucrative up-market housing, commercial buildings and business trade centers.[36] In all proposed plans it was taken for granted that the CBD would include all of Manshiyyah, and the route along the sea (to the west of the Mosque) would function as a major urban route connecting Jaffa with the central and northern parts of Tel Aviv. It appeared clear that the issue of the Mosque was not taken into account. In due course special measures had to be suggested to do away with the Mosque in order to prevent any obstruction to the development plan. Gershon Peres, the entrepreneur and contractor of the Hassan Bey transaction, discloses how this "urban need" was addressed. Peres unveils the hidden transcript of the way various forces, hegemonic agents, and agencies coordinated the Mosque affair.[37] According to Peres, he was approached by three individuals who were all public figures—Joshua Rabinowitz, the mayor of the city at the time; Shmuel Toledano, the Prime Minister's Adviser on Arab Affairs; and Aharon Danin, the first-born child of Tel Aviv and a veteran of the Israel Lands Administration. Together they formed a plan that would ultimately rid the city of what was, according to development plans (and their own personal opinions), an obstacle. In order to accomplish the plan they needed to secure the consent of the Jaffa Trust. By acting as a go-between for various state and city agencies and the Jaffa Trust, Peres successfully negotiated the transaction. The official transcript as recorded by the law firm acting on behalf of the Trust tells a different story altogether. In a letter to a member of the city council,[38] they name the active party in the transaction as the Jaffa Trust and its members, who decided to act on behalf of their decaying and neglected Mosque. They were the ones who approached the contractor and they implore the city council to approve the plan and allow the renovations to begin. It was important for the Trust members to be depicted as the initiators of the leasing of the Mosque, and not as a rubber stamp to a Jewish initiative. In view of later developments, such as the assassination of a future head of the Trust in 1986, it would seem that these measures were not frivolous. Be that as it may, in 1974 a secret contract was signed between the Edgar Construction Company (Peres and associates) and the Jaffa Muslim Charitable Trust, according to which the building would be leased for 49 years and be renovated as a tourist shopping center. Nearly four years of secret negotiations ended with the legal act of the Trust approving the contract. Throughout the early 1970s when the negotiations were taking place, a growing number of people in Jaffa learned of the situation with growing discontent. However, unlike former cases in which religious Muslim endowments were taken from the community, this time it met with community opposition. This opposition was about to set a precedent and change the course of events.

I demonstrated earlier how hegemony, as the prevailing state of affairs, worked in the case of the Mosque by dictating and shaping public norms. In addition, the hegemony of the legal system, through its various civic institutions and agents, induced spontaneous consent from both hegemonic and subordinate groups. Now I will focus on counter-hegemony and ways of resistance as formulated within the Jaffa Muslim community.

A site of (and for) resistance

As early as August 1973 a member of the Trust, Zuhdi Siksik, petitioned the Tel Aviv District Court to obtain an injunction to stop the planned leasing of the Mosque.[39] The court granted an injunction and it appeared that for a short period the negotiations over the Mosque had ceased, but it was only a temporary halt. Nevertheless, the Mosque was to become a site of resistance against the indoctrination by hegemonic forces. The key figure responsible in the Hassan Bey affair was Abd Badawi Kabub, a Muslim bus driver from Jaffa who made the Mosque his own private crusade for more then a decade. Kabub was born in Jaffa and as a young man he went to work for the Dan Cooperative Bus Company.[40] While working as an apprentice he was offered something that was a rarity for a Muslim Arab Israeli citizen—membership in the cooperative. After becoming a shareholder, he came into daily contact with Jewish workers and patrons. These contacts would prove important later on. Upon learning from the newspapers about the Hassan Bey transaction and the general misconduct of the Jaffa Trust, Abd Kabub decided to launch a public campaign to save the Mosque. Abd Kabub and a few others from Jaffa's Muslim community established a non-profit association called the al-Maqasid al-Khayriyya al-Islamiyya (the Islamic Philanthropic Association).

Shortly before this association was founded, a new mayor, Shlomo Lahat, was elected to Tel Aviv-Jaffa in 1974. Although the new municipal coalition was ideologically affiliated with a more nationalistic party (Mahal), Lahat and his new officials turned out to be more empathetic to the Jaffa Arab community then their predecessors.

In November 1975 the Tel Aviv-Jaffa deputy mayor, Yigal Grippel, issued a public statement according to which the municipality did not favor the promotion of the tourism center plan on the site of the Mosque.[41] This came in response to an application for a building permit submitted by the Edgar Company to the Tel Aviv-Jaffa Local Planning and Building Commission. Grippel was attuned to the new voices coming from Jaffa and mostly to the work of Abd Kabub's association. Abd Kabub worked both from within the community as well as outside of it. He approached the deputy director general of the Ministry of Religious Affairs and convinced him to act on behalf of the community's interests, i.e., to try and save the Mosque. Later on he coordinated a visit of six leading Qadis from around Israel to the site accompanied by the director general of the Ministry of Religious Affairs. The outcome of this visit was an official report made by the Qadis that was sent to the director general on January 20, 1976. In this document they essentially contradict a former *Shari'a* opinion and state clearly that according to the *Shari'a*, a mosque cannot be sold or leased.[42] The director general acted accordingly and notified the deputy mayor that he opposed any plan that would change the nature of the building. Abd Kabub's greatest achievement thus far was that the formal authorization of the municipal permit approving the plans for renovating the Mosque area itself turned into a prolonged public and legal debate. Throughout that period Abd Kabub regularly organized public prayers at the Mosque site, thus restoring the pre-1948 function of the place. Abd Kabub and members of the Trust were also responsible for fundraising campaigns and active promotion of the Mosque as a sign and symbol of Islam and authentic Palestinian heritage among Muslim communities and leaders on both sides of the Green Line.[43]

A new and decisive turn in favor of the Mosque took place in 1977. For the first time since 1948, the Labor Party lost the reigns of power to the Likud. Abd Kabub and others enjoyed close relations with members of the new government.[44] Ahmad Asfur, who served as treasurer of the Association, was involved in political activity within the Jaffa community to promote the party of the future Minister of Finance, Yigal Hurvitz. The national political changes also had an impact on the local level, and the members of the Jaffa Trust were forced to resign. Hurvitz managed to pull some strings to make sure that the newly appointed Trust included mostly the members of the al-Maqasid Association, with Abd Kabub acting as head.[45] Under his capacity as Minister of Finance, Hurvitz issued a writ on May 25, 1980 that expropriated the Mosque from the hands of the Tel Aviv-Jaffa municipality. In late October 1981, a prayer protest was organized at the Mosque. More then 2,000 people from Jaffa and other Muslim communities around Israel

Self-empowerment through the sacred culture 259

attended a prayer session that was set for Friday noon of the Muslim New Years Eve.[46] Abd Kabub, as head of the new Trust, invited the Mayor of Tel Aviv-Jaffa and other dignitaries such as David Glass, Director General of the Ministry of Religious Affairs, and also the Mufti of Jerusalem and the Al-Aqsa Mosque. Throughout the prayer some of the attendees called for Jihad and circulated a pamphlet that narrated the anti-Muslim attitude of the Israeli government. Speaking after the prayer, the Mayor appealed to the Trust members to finalize a plan for restoring the Mosque and concluded by saying, "I hope we can put this matter behind us and build not just a mosque in this place but also a Muslim archive for the history of the Arabs in Jaffa. I hope that the Mosque will become the foundation stone for peace and solidarity between the two peoples."[47] Careful reading of his speech reveals that he was still under the impression that the former reconstruction plan was in effect. Apparently, the writ was kept secret since on 11 November 1981 the city council held a meeting in order to approve the renovation plan of the Mosque. Only then did the mayor notify the council members that the Mosque was no longer under the municipality's authority.[48] The Mosque was handed over to the official charge of the Muslim Charitable Trust in Jaffa. For the first time since the formation of the State of Israel, the Mosque was returned to a Muslim community—that of Jaffa. However, as the state does not allocate funding for non-Jewish religious buildings, it took the Jaffa community no less than fifteen years to complete the renovations and resume the pre-1948 functions of the place.[49] It would seem that it is easier to counter the hegemonic discourse than to actually alter political and social hegemonic forces.

Resistance, hegemony, and the politics of sacred places

Castells argues that social mobilization happens at the initiative of conscious and organized operators.[50] Abd Kabub was indeed a very conscious operator who enjoyed help and support from members of his respective community. By the very nature of his acts, he functioned as a counter-hegemonic agent, but nevertheless managed to operate within the system and achieve his goals without creating militant confrontations that would have ultimately damaged his main task of reclaiming the Mosque as a place of prayer for the community. Two main factors contributed to the successful end (from the viewpoint of the Jaffa community) of the Hassan Bey campaign. The first is related to the fractured nature of hegemony; the second is directly concerned with the culture-politics of sacred places. The plans for the transformation of the Mosque originated with hegemonic civic institutions and agents. Countering these plans and discourse was an act that required intimate knowledge of how hegemony works and acquaintance with its institutions, language, and most of all its deficiencies. Abd Kabub proved to be the right man at the right time. The nature of hegemony is elusive—it is what Williams tried to sum up as the articulate and formal meanings, values, and beliefs which a dominant class develops and propagates.[51] As astutely observed by Victor Herzberg, the lawyer acting on behalf of the Jaffa Trust under Abd Kabub:

> Abd Kabub was a leader head and shoulders above the community of Jaffa ... he was also a member in Dan and this vested him with special rights ... he had certain characteristics that enabled him to live with Jews and at the same time to be a proud Arab ... he had Western elements in his tactics.[52]

But even Abd Kabub was accused at times of being a collaborator and was undermined by members of his own community.[53] That is, subordinate groups are also fractured and in order to work cohesively they must be constantly mobilized. Abd Kabub was successful (at least most of the time) because the goal as defined by him appealed to a significant part of his group.

Abd Kabub and other members of al-Maqassid—and later when they operated as the Jaffa Trust—were familiar with the hegemonic Jewish society. They knew how to talk and to whom, how to submit a petition and how to use the media. At the same time, they were cautious not to appear as a threat to the majority group's sense of control—indeed hegemony. In addition, they enjoyed the political changes of the 1970s in which new players and new groups from within the majority and hegemonic society became decision-makers. Put plainly by Ahmad Asfur: "Peres went to his friends from the Labor Party, so naturally we went to their opponents."[54] The nature of resistance was such that it enabled the hegemonic side to live with it and accept the claims as legitimate. One may argue that the struggle was won through litigation, that is, through the formal state institutions and not within the realm of hegemony—counter-hegemony relations. In an interview with David Glass, Director General of the Ministry of Religious Affairs at the time, he revealed clearly that it was not the legal technicalities but his informal subjective understanding that we (i.e., the Jewish majority) need not deprive the minority of its religious symbols:

> In this case we had a hunch that above all there were illegal dealings involved. But this was not the main issue; the main thing was my own personal world view of respecting the religious rights of minorities. We would have cried bitterly if anyone would have built onto a synagogue.[55]

Put simply, it was the resistance that mattered more than the actual legal proceedings. And indeed, if that were not true other buildings that were confiscated or expropriated over the years would still be in the possession of their Muslim communities.[56] Glass and others from within the hegemonic majority were more attentive to the subordinate community in this particular case because of the building's sacred nature and in view of the community's organized resistance. The subordinate group's challenge to the hegemonic discourse focused on a symbolic and sacred object. By not stressing the ethnic and national aspects of the conflict, but by focusing instead on the community's religious needs, the subordinate group managed to recruit help from within the hegemonic majority. The debate over the Mosque did not entail any serious effort to offer counterclaims regarding the sanctity of the place. Rather, the conflict revolved around the politics of sacred places and the importance of the place as a cultural landmark. Van der Leeuw identifies four kinds of politics in the construction of sacred space.[57] The most appropriate for the case of Hassan Bey is the politics of property, whereby a sacred place is appropriated, possessed, and owned, its sacredness maintained through claims and counterclaims to its ownership. The Mosque of Hassan Bey was not an active religious building for nearly forty years. There are known cases in which a mosque changed its designation and ceased to be a mosque. The Mosque's repossession by the community was facilitated by the politics of property—a fight over not just the place itself but over its symbolic meaning and history. What I define here as the culture-politics of the place is the context of the struggle not just over a religious place but also of the place of the subordinate group culture and world-view and the way these were used and channeled for the conflict. The use of a cultural icon was used not just to gain sympathy and consent among the Jewish hegemonic elements in society, but also to mobilize the Muslim community to work together towards the goal. When asked about his reasons for fighting over the Mosque, Ahmad Asfur, who identified himself as secular and anti-religious, commented: "I wanted the Mosque to stay because it is part of my history and part of my culture. I want not only my grandson to see the minaret and learn about his heritage but your Jewish grandson too, who will learn there were other people here."[58]

Conclusions

This essay has considered some aspects of a conflict over the control and use of a mosque in the city of Tel Aviv-Jaffa. To a great extent, the public and legal struggle over the Mosque was a manifestation of the ongoing ethnic-national clash between hegemonic and subordinate groups in the city's urban culture. Drawing upon Gramsci's understanding of hegemony as a moving equilibrium, I have portrayed the events within the context of resistance and counter-hegemonic actions on the part of the Muslim community of Jaffa. The essay highlights the symbolic and ideological nature of the urban landscape, indeed the city's built environment, and the need of people to be represented within it in accordance with their worldview or cultural codes. The fight over a symbol and the Muslim community's eventual success in retaining one of its historic and religious icons should be seen as part of a continuous struggle for self-empowerment. Representation in the city landscape is meaningful above and beyond the actual possession of a religious building, as the case of Hassan Bey so clearly demonstrates. The fact that the Mosque was nearly lost and erased from the urban landscape and subsequently was reclaimed by the community turned it into a symbol and sign of the community's ability to unite and fight for other common goals. The formation of the Rabita, a self-organized movement for the Arab population in Jaffa in 1979, cannot be viewed as isolated from the struggle over the Mosque that began in the early 1970s. The conflict transformed the Mosque into a symbol of a glorified and lost past and a threatened cultural heritage. The context of the struggle may be best understood as part of the politics of sacred places within a hegemony–counter-hegemony setting.

Notes

1 For the Jaffa past as depicted by Palestinians, see Online. Available: www.palestine remembered.com (accessed 20 Oct. 2002). For a description of the conquest of Jaffa and the spatial outcomes of Israeli policy shortly after the war, *see* A. Golan, *Wartime Spatial Changes: Former Arab Territories Within the State of Israel, 1948–1950*, Tel Aviv: Ben-Gurion University Press 2001, pp. 75–133 [in Hebrew].
2 L. Kong, "Geography and Religion: Trends and Prospects," *Progress in Human Geography*, 1990, vol. 14, no. 3, pp. 355–71; *ibid.*, "Ideological Hegemony and the Political Symbolism of Religious Buildings in Singapore," *Environment and Planning D: Society and Space*, 1993, vol. 11, pp. 23–45; *ibid.*, "Negotiating Conceptions of 'Sacred Space': A Case Study of Religious Buildings in Singapore," *Transactions of the Institution of British Geographers*, new series, 1993, vol. 18, pp. 342–58; *ibid.*, "Mapping 'New' Geographies of Religion: Politics and Poetics in Modernity," *Progress in Human Geography*, 2001, vol. 25, no. 2, pp. 211–33.
3 R. Needham, cited in D. Chidester and E.T. Linenthal (eds) *American Sacred Space*, Bloomington, Ind.: Indiana University Press, 1995, pp. 1–35, at 5.
4 Kong, 2001, "Geography and Religion: Trends and Prospects," at p. 213.
5 Chidester and Linenthal, *American Sacred Space*, at p. 17.
6 A. Gramsci, *Selections from Prison Notebooks*, New York: International Publishing, 1971.
7 R. Williams, *Marxism and Literature*, Bath: Oxford University Press, 1977, p. 109.
8 *Ibid.*, p. 109.
9 D. Heyness and G. Parkash, "Introduction: the Entanglement of Power and Resistance" in D. Heyness and G. Parkash (eds) *Contesting Power: Resistance and Everyday Social Relations in South Africa*, Delhi: Oxford University Press, 1991, pp.1–22, at p. 3.
10 S. Pile, "Introduction. Oppositional, Political Identities and Spaces of Resistance," in S. Pile and M. Keith (eds) *Geographies of Resistance*, London and New York: Routledge, 1997, pp.1–32, at 2.
11 *Ibid.*, p. 16
12 M. Castells, *The City and the Grassroots*, Berkeley and Los Angeles, Calif.: University of California Press, 1983, p.123.
13 M.M. Dabagh, *Biladuna Filastin*, Jerusalem: Matbuat al-Khukuma, 1972, p. 190 [in Arabic].
14 S. Tolkowsky, *The Gateway of Palestine: A History of Jaffa*, London: Routledge, 1924, pp. 163–64.
15 A. Shlush, *My Life Story 1870–1930*, Tel Aviv: Mizrachi, 1941, p. 196 [in Hebrew].
16 Abd Badawi Kabub, 2003 personal interview.
17 Dabagh, *Biladuna Filastin*, p. 190
18 Cited in S. Hamuda, *Masjid Hassan Bey*, Bait Safafa: Hassan Abu Daw, 1985, p. 15 [in Arabic].
19 *Ibid.*, p.16.
20 Y. Porat, The *Emergence of the Palestine-Arab National Movement 1918–1927*, London: Frank Cass, 1974.

Self-empowerment through the sacred culture 263

21 Hamuda, *Masjid Hassan Bey*, p.19
22 Satil, personal interview, 2001.
23 Tel Aviv-Jaffa Archive 14–84/ 310; H. Lazar, *The Conquest of Jaffa*, Tel Aviv: Shelah, 1961, p. 196 [in Hebrew]
24 A. Golan, *Wartime Spatial Changes: Former Arab Territories Within the State of Israel, 1948–1950*, Beersheva: Ben-Gurion University, Negev Press, 2001, p. 87 [in Hebrew].
25 *Ibid.*, p. 87.
26 37 *Sefer Chukim*, 20 Mar.1950, pp. 86–101 [in Hebrew].
27 Golan, *Spatial Changes*, at p. 18.
28 Tel-Aviv Jaffa Archives, 2239/d-310.
29 Abd Badawi Kabub, 2003, personal interview.
30 R. Fabian, *Jaffa – A Narrative of Politics and Architectural Urbanism*, unpublished MA thesis, Harvard University, 1999, p. 95.
31 K. Lynch, *The Image of the City*, Cambridge, Mass.: M.I.T. Press, 1960, pp. 45–46.
32 Victor Herzberg, 2003, personal interview.
33 Tel Aviv-Jaffa Archive 7(24)-146-1495.
34 Nasim Shakar, 2001, personal interview; Abd Satil, 2001, personal interview; Ahmad Asfur, 2003, personal interview.
35 Asfur 2003, personal interview.
36 Tel Aviv-Jaffa Archive, 22-1-1968-1 (2216).
37 The term "hidden transcript" was formulated in. J.C. Scott, *Domination and the Arts of Resistance*, New Haven, CT and London: Yale University Press, 1990. It refers to the ways subordinate groups find ways to resist hegemony. I assign it here to denote the fact that hegemonic groups also use hidden transcripts when engaged in contacts with subordinate groups.
38 Tel Aviv-Jaffa Archive, 7(24)-146-1495.
39 *Maariv*, 31 Aug. 1973.
40 Abd Kabub, 2003, personal interview.
41 *Ha'aretz*, 26 Oct. 1975.
42 Tel Aviv-Jaffa Archive, 07(26)-52.
43 Abd Kabub, 2003, personal interview; Ahmad Asfur 2003, personal interview.
44 Ahmad Asfur 2003, personal interview.
45 *Ibid.*
46 *Ha'aretz*, 2 Nov. 1981.
47 Lahat, cited in *Ha'aretz,* 2 Nov. 1981.
48 Tel Aviv-Jaffa Archive, 11–05.81-14-2386.
49 I am currently engaged in a project that focuses on the role of the Mosque within the community and vis-à-vis the Jewish urban majority after the 1980s expropriation.
50 Castells, *The City and the Grassroots*, at p. 123.
51 Williams, *Marxism and Literature*, p. 110.
52 Victor Herzberg, 2003, personal interview.
53 *Ha'aretz*, 29 July 1981.
54 Asfur, 2003, personal interview.
55 David Glass, 2002, personal interview.
56 Glass himself offers us the example of the Jamasin graveyard that was taken from the community and used as the plot for the Hilton Hotel in Tel Aviv.
57 G. Van der Leeuw, *Religions in Essence and Manifestations*, Princeton, N.J.: Princeton University Press, 1938. (repr. 1986).
58 Asfur 2003, personal interview.

14 The head of Husayn Ibn Ali

Its various places of burial and the miracles that it performed

Khalid Sindawi

On the tenth day of *Muharram* (Ashura' Day)[1] in the year 61 of the *Hijra* (10.10.680), the Battle of Karbala' broke out between Husayn Ibn Ali (the Prophet Muhammad's grandson) and the armies of Caliph Yazid Ibn Muawiya (who ruled 680–83) on the western bank of the Euphrates River. Husayn and many of his family and supporters were slaughtered, and Husayn's head was brought to Caliph Yazid in Damascus along with Husayn's wives and sisters.[2] Husayn's head was decapitated by Shimr b. Dhi al-Jawshan al-Dababi (d. 686). At the battle's end, Shimr stuck Husayn's head on the point of his javelin and gave the javelin to Khawli b. Yazid al-Asbahi to carry from Karbala' to Kufa, to the governor's palace. When the caravan arrived in Kufa, the head was presented to Ubaydallah b. Ziyad (d. 686), the district governor, on behalf of Caliph Yazid.

Subsequently Ibn Ziyad called for Umar b. Jabir al-Makhzumi and ordered him to parade around the city carrying the heads of Husayn and his followers. Umar obeyed the governor's order. The following day Ibn Ziyad called for Shimr and Khawli and instructed them to take 1,500 warriors to present Husayn's head to Caliph Yazid in Damascus. As they marched through the towns, they were commanded to expose and display the decapitated heads and the prisoners to the local inhabitants.

In the towns of Takrit, Musil, Qarib al-Daawat, Hims, Balbak and Damascus[3] the residents celebrated the news of Husayn's death: they decorated the town gates, waved banners, blew trumpets, and gathered in the streets to rejoice.[4] In the towns of Qinnisrin, Shiyzar, Kafr Tab, Saybur, and Hamah,[5] residents locked the city gates and began mourning Husayn's murder; they threw stones at the bearers of the heads and cursed them.

Eventually the head reached the palace of Caliph Yazid in Damascus and was presented to him set in a golden bowl (in similar fashion to the head of John the Baptist, which was brought to Herod on a golden platter).[6]

The sources differ regarding Yazid's attitude towards the head. Some sources note that Yazid regretted Husayn's murder, while mainly Shi'ite sources note that Yazid rejoiced at Husayn's death and drank wine over his head.[7]

The Head's burial places

While Husayn's body was interred in Karbala'[8] three days after the battle, there are differences of opinion regarding the exact burial place of his head. Sources note eight possible cities or locations where the head might be buried.

Damascus

Some sources state that Yazid kept Husayn's head in his weapons stores, and after his death the head was buried in Damascus near the al-Faradis Gate, today known as *al-Masjid al-Ras* ("the mosque of the head").[9] Other sources note that the head remained in the weapons stores until the period of the Umayyad caliph Sulayman Ibn Abd al-Malik (ruled 715–17) and then buried. Some claim that the head was buried in a wall in the governor's palace in Damascus or in the city cemetery.[10]

al-Raqqa[11]

According to this version, the head was buried in a mosque in the city of al-Raqqa on the Euphrates. This version notes that Yazid sent Husayn's head to the Al Abu Mait tribe, which was related to Caliph Uthman b. Affan (who ruled from 644 until his murder in 656). The explanation was that Yazid sent them Husayn's head so that it might appear as if Yazid was avenging the death of Caliph Uthman. Members of the Al Abu Mait tribe buried Husayn's head in their mosque in al-Raqqa.[12]

Karbala'

Many Shi'ite sources note that Husayn's head was returned to Karbala' and buried together with the rest of his body 40 days after he was killed, i.e., on the 20th of the month of *Safar*.[13] Every year on this date the Shi'ites visit Husayn's grave in a ceremony called "The Visit of the Forty"[14] or the *Marrad al-Ra's* ("visit of the return of head to the body").

Madina

According to this version, Caliph Yazid sent the head to the governor of Madina, Amr b. Sa'id b. al-'Ass (d. 690), who buried it in the Baqi al-Gharqad cemetery[15] next to Husayn's mother Fatima, the daughter of the prophet Muhammad.

In this context Ibn Taymiyya (d. 1328) says it is reasonable to assume that the head was indeed buried in Madina, because during periods of social ferment against the government it was customary to return the bodies of rebels to members of the rebel's tribe. This is what al-Hajaj b. Yusif al-Thaqafi (d. 714) did to the body of Abdallah b. Zubayr (d. 692) after Abdallah was killed and crucified.[16]

Aleppo, Syria

In this version it is claimed that Husayn's head was buried in Aleppo after its return from Damascus, on Mt. Jawshan.[17]

Near the city of Marw[18] in Khurasan

Several sources note that Husayn's head was buried near the city of Marw in Khurasan, at a distance of a *farsakhayn*[19] (about 10 km) and a mosque was built above the head's tomb. The head was brought to Khurasan by Abu Muslim al-Khurasani (d. 755). After he conquered Damascus he moved the head to Marw.[20]

However, the researcher Suad Mahir casts doubt on this version, writing that Abu Muslim did not enter Damascus at the time that it was conquered by his troops, and that it is unthinkable that an Abbasid Caliph would permit Abu Muslim to move the head to Marw for burial. She adds, "If any Abbasid caliph reached Husayn's head, he would have disclosed the fact to the people so that they would hate the Umayyads even more."[21]

Najaf[22] in Southern Iraq

The author of the book *Madi al-Najaf wa-Hadiruha*[23] ("The City of Najaf Past and Present") notes the tradition of the imam Ja'far al-Sadiq (the sixth Shi'ite imam, d. 765), which relates that Husayn's head is buried in Najaf near the grave of his father Ali, and a mosque was built over the tomb of Husayn's head. The place is called *al-Ghariyyan*[24] ("place of two white domes"). In Suad Mahir's opinion this is a weak and unreliable tradition with no basis in the sources.

Asqalan[25] (today: Ashkelon in South Israel)

Some of the traditions note that Yazid commanded his men to march through various towns while carrying Husayn's head until they reached Asqalan, and the city's governor buried it in the city.[26] The sources do not note when the head was moved to Asqalan or when it was buried, nor do they note the name of the city governor who buried the head.

Muhammad Zaki Ibrahim, in his book *Maraqid al-Bayt bil-Qahira*, asks why Asqalan, of all cities, was chosen as the burial place of Husayn's head since at the time the city did not have a large Shi'ite population nor Husayn supporters. He adds that it is possible that the head was buried in Asqalan, close to Jerusalem on one hand, and close to the sea on the other hand. If the city were ever in danger of foreign conquest it would be possible to remove the head easily and transport it to Shi'ite communities in North Africa by sea to prevent it from falling into enemy hands.[27] According to Zaki, the choice of Asqalan as the burial place of the head is understandable. Asqalan is an important strategic location—the head could be moved easily in the face of impending conquest by foreigners.

Cairo

Most of the sources which believe Hussein's head is buried in Cairo stress that it was transferred to Cairo from Asqalan during the period of Fatimid rule (909–1171). Al-Sharani[28] says that Husayn's sister Zaynab (d. 682) moved her brother's head and buried it in Egypt.

Another opinion holds that the head was moved from Asqalan to Cairo via the sea during the period of Fatimid rule by Sayf al-Mamlaka with al-Qadi al-Mu'tamin b. Miskin during the reign of Caliph al-Mustansir billah al-Abdi (ruled 1094–1101), on the tenth day of the month of *Jumada al-Akhira* in the year 548 of the *Hijra*/1153.[29]

At the same time, al-Maqrizi (d. 1441) notes that the head arrived on the 18th of *Jumada al-Akhira* (Sept. 18, 1153) of the same year, and adds that it was moved from Asqalan to Egypt by the governor of Asqalan, who was called Tamim.[30]

The manuscript *Tarikh Amid* by Ibn al-Awraq in the British Museum (No. 5803) notes that Husayn's head was moved from Asqalan to Egypt in the year 549 of the *Hijra*/1154.

In his book *al-Ishara ila Ma'rifat al-Ziyarat*, al-Harawi notes that the head was moved to Cairo after Palestine was conquered by the Crusaders, in the year 549 of the *Hijra* (1154), but some claim that the head was moved to Cairo before the Crusader conquest of Palestine.

The Fatimids, upon witnessing the Crusader conquest of Syria and parts of Palestine, feared for the fate of Husayn's head.

During the period of rule of the Fatimid Caliph al-Faiz (Abu al-Qasim Isa al-Faiz binasrallah (ruled 1149–54), one of his officers, an Armenian convert to Islam called al-Salih b. Ruzzayk (d. 1163),[31] built a mosque which he called *Jami' al-Salih Talai* (near the gate called Bab Zuwayla) in Cairo in 1160. Husayn's head was to have been buried in this mosque after it arrived from Asqalan. Al-Salih b. Ruzzayk sent a delegation to bring the head, which was transported from Asqalan quickly. However, it was not buried in the mosque designated for the purpose, but was interred instead in the large rear cellar (al-Sirdab al-Khalfi al-Aam) in the palace of al-Zumurrud. A year later it was moved to another burial site, which stands today at the entrance to the Khan al-Khalili quarter.[32]

In the opinion of the researcher Lapidas, the Fatimid purpose in moving Husayn's head was to raise Cairo's status as a pilgrimage destination as well as to strengthen Shi'ite faith during the twelfth century.

We should not forget that the Fatimid state was a Shi'ite Ismaili one, and there was competition between the Ismaili and Imamiyya factions. The Imamiyya considered Karbala' to be the major religious center and the pilgrimage to Husayn's grave as more important than the pilgrimage to the Ka'ba.

Perhaps during the period of the Fatimid state the Ismailis hoped to compete with the city of Karbala' and convert Cairo into a site of pilgrimage to the head of Husayn.

Miracles performed by Husayn's Head during its travels

The principal miracles associated with Husayn's head are its ability to speak and to influence events taking place near it. Husayn's head usually spoke during the night—and sometimes all night—until the break of dawn. The first time the head was said to speak, at the entrance to the city of Kufa,[33] it called out verses from the Qur'an from the story of the cave "*Surat al-Kahf*" and the verse was heard, "Or deemest thou that the companions of the cave and the inscription are a wonder among our portents?"[34]

It spoke for the second time in the house of Khawli b. Yazid al-Asbahi, who kept the head overnight. A voice was heard in the night calling verses from the chapter of the poets, but the verse that was heard most clearly was the following: "Those who do wrong will come to know by what a (great) reverse they will be overturned."[35]

On the third occasion, the head spoke in the home of a Jewish rabbi in the city of Qinnisrin, and conducted a conversation with him. The rabbi requested of Husayn's head that his grandfather Muhammad intercede on his behalf on Judgment Day.

The authors who wrote about these miracles sought to prove that, even after his death, Husayn's spirit remained intact and powerful, and although he no longer had a body, his spirit hovered about, maintaining a continuing presence on earth and working miracles after his death.

Traditions about miracles that took place near Husayn's Head

The tradition of the pillar of light

This tradition relates that a pillar of light descended from heaven onto Husayn's head when he was in Kufa and in Damascus.[36] The motif of prophetic light is very common in religious literature in general, including Shi'ite *Qisas al-Anbiya* writings. For example, the light of Muhammad shone on Seth's face, and it is told that a pillar of light shone from the head of Hud when he was in his infancy. Shi'ite sources relate stories about the light of Adam that glowed on Seth's forehead. They also describe a pillar of light that appeared when Abraham was born, causing the angels to marvel.[37]

The miracle of the hand

Another tradition tells of a related miracle that occurred during journey of the caravan bearing the head and the female prisoners. When the caravan stopped to rest on the way from Kufa to Damascus, a hand appeared and carved the following words with a pen of iron on one of the roof beams of the monastery: "How can you ask the nation who killed Husayn, whose grandfather was Muhammad, to plead on behalf of the people on Judgment Day?" The hand usually appeared near Husayn's head.[38]

The miracle of turning the dirhams to clay and black stones

Yet another tradition relates that on the way to Damascus, the same caravan stopped near a monk's cell. The monk saw Husayn's head and paid a sum of 10,000 dirhams to the bearers of the head in exchange for allowing him to keep the head during the night. When the head's bearers woke in the morning, they discovered that the monk's dirhams had turned to clay and black stones with verses from the Qur'an written on them.[39]

The story of Ibn Luhaya

Ibn Luhaya was part of the delegation that carried Husayn's head and the other heads to Damascus. He testified that during the journey they stopped to rest, drinking wine until they became drunk, and then left Husayn's head in a closet. That same night Ibn Luhaya heard thunder and saw lightning, and suddenly was astounded to see the gates of heaven open and the prophets descending. The first to reach earth were Adam, Abraham, Ishmael, Isaac, and Muhammad. After them came the angels Israfil, al-Karubiyyun, al-Ruhaniyyun, and al-Muqarrabun. They all assembled near the Head, comforting the prophet Muhammad and asking that he grant his permission to avenge Husayn's blood. The prophet refused their request, indicating that he himself would judge Husayn's killers on the day of the resurrection.[40]

The story of the servant who carried Husayn's Head over his head from Asqalan to Cairo

The writer Salah al-Din al-Ayyubi, known as al-Malik al-Nasir (ruled 1169–93) learned of a servant who had held an important position under the previous ruler, and knew the whereabouts of his hidden treasures. The servant was brought before the ruler Salah al-Din and was interrogated regarding the treasure's location, but the servant refused to reveal the information. The ruler became angry and ordered him punished. The officer of punishments took the servant away, cut his hair, shaved his head, placed beetles on his head, and tied them down. This was the harshest possible punishment, because a person could not endure the beetles since they would make holes in his head until the victim died. The officer of punishments repeated this procedure a number of times, but the servant did not suffer any pain and the beetles kept dying. The officer of punishments wondered and said to the servant, "I am sure that there is some secret here; you must reveal it to me." The servant answered: "My head is protected because I bore the Head of Husayn from

Asqalan to Cairo on my head; it seems that Husayn is protecting my head." Then the officer of punishments forgave the servant and freed him.[41]

Summary

Why are there believed to be a number of sites where Husayn's Head is buried? Husayn was the grandson of the Prophet Muhammad and as a saint he bestowed importance upon and sanctified a site. There are several possible reasons for the tradition of multiple sites:

1. *The security aspect*: The presence of the Head at strategic locations promoted population growth at these sites. People were drawn to a grave purported to contain the Head of the prophet's grandson Husayn. The burial place then attracted permanent settlement, which in turn promoted population growth in areas considered militarily sensitive and requiring of defense. (Another example of this phenomenon is the city of Mazari al-Sharif in Afghanistan.)
2. *The religious aspect*: The importance of the locations is claimed to be the burial site of Husayn's Head is associated with the possibility of uniting people around a religious ideal in the person of the holy Husayn. People claimed to receive from him emanations of righteousness, honesty and respect between man and man and between man and God. It is understandable that competition grew among various cities for the honor of being the burial place of the Head (for example, between Karbala' and Cairo). The burial site becomes holy by virtue of the presence of the holy relic.
3. *The economic aspect*: A reason perhaps more understandable to modern sensibilities is the desire to promote economic development among residents of the various sites where Husayn's Head was allegedly buried. The tomb of the Head attracts many pilgrims who make the journey in order to enjoy the blessing of the tomb and its relic. These holy sites draw large numbers of people.

Regarding the miracles performed by Husayn's Head

Husayn Ibn Ali was the third imam after his father Ali and his son Hasan. In Shi'a tradition, imams are deemed to have a rapport with the early prophets.[42] In this context, Shi'ites view the imams as links in the eternal dynasty of the chosen who have appeared continuously in the world since the days of Adam, a dynasty which continued down to Muhammad, the last of the prophets, and after him through to the imams. The imams were considered to be worthy of the status of prophets. They were able to perform miracles as a means of proving their status to those who refused to pledge loyalty to the imam and to recognize their obligation of *walaya* (loyality to the Imam).

Shi'ite hagiography does not differ in principle from any other hagiographic literature: as the material presence of the imams receded from the lives of the faithful, the religious experience and their marvelous and sublime abilities became increasingly powerful. The miracles said to be performed by Husayn Ibn Ali's Head stress Husayn's worthiness as an imam. Similar to saints, Husayn maintains his power even in the absence of his body, as his spirit remains hovering among the faithful on earth and he continues to perform miracles after his death.

Notes

1 "The tenth," observed on the tenth of *Muharram*. For more details, *see* K. Sindawi, "Ashura' Day and Yom Kippur," vol. 38, 2001, *Ancient Near Eastern Studies*, pp. 200–214.
2 For details on the Battle of Karbala', *see e.g.*, M. Al-Tabari *Ta'rikh al-Umam wa-al-Muluk*, Beirut: Dar al-Kutub al-Ilmiyya Press, 3rd edn, 1991, pp. 3–5; 346 [in Arabic].
3 For details on these towns, *see e.g.*, Sh. Yaqut, *Mu'jam al-Buldan*, Beirut: Dar Ihya al-Turath Press, 1979, vol. 2, pp. 38–39; vol. 5, pp. 223–25; vol. 2, pp. 302–5; vol. 1, pp. 435–55; vol. 2, pp. 463–70 [in Arabic].
4 For more details, *see e.g.*, K. Sindawi, *The Maqatil in Shi'ite Literature*, unpublished PhD thesis, Ramat Gan: Bar Ilan University, 2000, p. 217 [in Hebrew].
5 Yaqut, *Mu'jam al-Buldan*, vol. 4, pp. 403–4; vol. 3, p. 383; vol. 4, p. 470; vol. 2, pp. 300–301.
6 It should be noted that the Shi'ite authors stress the connection between Husayn Ibn Ali and John the Baptist in order to depict Husayn as a saint. Shi'ite authors see them both as chosen by God and exemplars of perfection. The Shi'ites believe that Husayn is the successor in the line of prophets, and emphasize the continuity of prophecy for the purpose of transmitting the *wasiyya* (heritage), and after the prophets, among the *'imams* in a continuous dynasty. The *wasiyya* was transmitted to the prophets by means of the *Awsiya'* (heirs) of the prophets. According to the Shi'ites, John the Baptist was a prophet.
  In my examination of Shi'ite literature, mainly biographies of John the Baptist, I found several points of similarity between John and Husayn. The authors of the Shi'ia were influenced by John's biography, selecting various details of his life story and inserting them into their compositions. They adapted his story to suit their audience, dressing John in Shi'ite Islamic "costume" in order to endow Husayn with John's holy characteristics, including his descent from a holy family line. The similarities between John and Husayn are expressed in the following details: their conception and birth, their nursing, the choice of their respective names, their glowing faces, the constant crying, and weeping of heaven at their death, the fact that both of their heads spoke after their decapitations, etc.; for more details *see* Khalid Sindawi, "Husayn Ibn Ali and Yahya Ibn Zakariyya in the Shi'ite Sources: A Comparative Study," *Islamic Culture*, 2004, vol. 78, no. 3, pp. 37–54.
7 Most Shi'ite sources note that Caliph Yazid rejoiced over the killing of Husayn and that he even recited a poem that quotes from the song of Abdallah ibn al-Ziba'ra (d. 636) expressing joy over the killing of Husayn. For more details, *see* N. Ibn Nama, *Muthir al-Ahzan wa-Munir Subul al-Ashjan*, Tehran, s.n, 1899 p. 55; L. Abu Mikhnaf, *Maqtal al-Husayn Alayhi al-Salam*, ed. Umar Abu al-Nasr, Beirut: Dar Umar Abu al-Nasr, 1971, p. 132, A. Ibn Tawus, *al-Lahuf Ala Qatla al-Tufuf*, Najaf: al-Haydariyya Press, 1951, pp. 102, 104; A. al-'Isfahani, *Maqatil al-Talibiyyin*, ed. Kazim al-Muzaffar, 2nd edn, Najaf: al-Haydariyya Press, 1965, p. 80; I. al-Qurashi *Uyun al-Akhbar wa-Funun al-Athar*, ed. Mustafa Ghalib, Beirut: Dar al-Andalus Press, n.d., p. 119 [in Arabic].

However, historical sources written by the (orthodox) Sunnis note that Yazid never meant for his men to kill Husayn, behaved honorably towards Husayn's wives, sisters and family members when they arrived at his palace in Damascus, and deeply regretted Husayn's death. For more details *see,* A. Ibn Taymiyya, *Sual fi Yazid,* ed. Salah al-Din al-Munjid, Beirut: Dar al-Kitab al-Jadid, 1976, p. 17; A. Ibn Taymiyya, *Minhaj al-Sunna al-Nabawiyya,* Cairo: al-Amiriyya and Bulaq Press, 1903, vol. 2, p. 49; *compare with* Ibn Kathir I. *al-Bidaya wa-al-Nihaya,* ed. Abu Milhim et al. (Beirut: Dar al-Kutub al-Ilmiyya Press, n.d.), vol. 8, p.198; M. Ibn Tulun, *Qayd al-Sharid fi Akhbar Yazid,* ed. Muhammad Zinhum Azb, Cairo: Dar al-Sahwa Press, 1st edn, 1986 p. 65–67; F. al-Hudayb, *Surat Yazid Ibn Muawiya fi al-Riwayat al-Adabiyya,* Riyad: Dar Aja Press, 1995, pp. 69–76 [in Arabic].
8 Husayn's tomb is called *al-Ha'ir.*
9 S. Ibn al-Jawzi, *al-Muntazam fi Tarikh al-Muluk wa-al-Umam,* Beirut: Dar al-Fikr Press, 1995, vol. 4, p. 159; M. Al-Adawi, *Kitab al-Ziyarat Bi-Dimashq,*ed. Salah al-Din al-Munjid, Damascus: al-Majma' al-'Ilmi al-Arabi, 1956, p. 25; Y. Ibn Abd al-Hadi *Thimar al-Maqasid fi Dhikr al-Masajid,* Beirut: French Institute, 1943, p. 99.
10 M. Ibn Shahrashub, *Manaqib Ali b. Abi Talib,* Beirut: Dar al-Andalus Press, 1991, vol. 4, p. 71 [in Arabic].
11 A well-known town on the banks of the Euphrates, a three day walk from the city of Harran. For details on the city, *see* Yaqut, *Mujam al-Buldan,* vol. 3, pp. 58–60.
12 Y. Ibn Abd al-Hadi, *al-Maqasid fi Dhikr al-Masajid,* Beirut: French Institute, 1943, p. 310 [in Arabic].
13 The second month of the Arabic calendar.
14 On the visit of the *Arbain* at Husayn's grave, *see* M. Ayoub, "Arbain," in *Encyclopaedia Iranica,* vol. 2, p. 275, ed. Ehsan Yarshater, London: Boston and Henely, 1985, p. 275. *See also* J. Shubbar, *Adab al-Taff,* Beirut: Muassasat al-Alami Press, 1969, vol. 41, p.1 [in Arabic].
15 For more details on this cemetery, *see* Yaqut al-Hamawi Shihab al-Din Abu 'AbdAllah, *Mu'jam al-Buldan,* 1997, vol. 3, p. 530.
16 For more details, *see* M. al-Tabari, *Tarikh al-Umam wa-al-Muluk,* Beirut: Dar al-Kutub al-Ilmiyya Press, 3rd edn, 1991, vol. 3, p. 530 [in Arabic].
17 M. Ibn Shihna, *Ta'rikh Halab,* Tokyo: Institute for the Study of Language and Cultures of Asia and Africa, University of Foreign Studies, 1990, p. 78; M. Mahran, *Al-'Imam al-Husayn Ibn Ali,* Beirut: Dar al-Nahda al-Arabiyya Press, 1990, p. 160; A. al-Khui, *Masir Ras al-Husayn wa-Mawdi' Dafnihi,* Karbala, 2001, pp. 6–7.
18 For details on Marw, *see,* Yaqut, *Mujam al-Buldan,* vol. 5, pp. 112–16.
19 A unit of land measure used in Islamic books of law. It is equal to a league of 18,000 feet, or 3½ miles in length, or intervening space between two things. For more details, *see e.g.,* E. Lane, *An Arabic-English Lexicon,* Beirut: Librairie du Liban, 1877, vol. 6, p. 2369 (s.v. frs); T. Hughes, *Dictionary of Islam,* New York: Scribner; Welford; London: W.H. Allen, 1885, p. 124.
20 Mahran, *Al-'Imam al-Husayn Ibn Ali,* p.160.
21 *Ibid.*
22 A city in southern Iraq where Husayn's father Ali Ibn Abu Talib is buried. For more details on this city, *see* Yaqut *Mu'jam al-Buldan,* vol. 5, pp. 271–72.
23 This is based upon Suad Mahir's quote. For more details, *see* S. Mahir, *Mashhad al-Imam Ali fi al-Najaf wa-Ma Bihi min al-Hadaya wa-al-Tuhaf,* Cairo, Dar al-Maarif, 1969, p. 153 [in Arabic].
24 The double form of the word *al-Ghariyy.* It should be noted that there were two ancient structures in Kuffa also known by the name *al-Ghariyyan* to which this article does not refer. These two buildings were long. The first structure was the tomb of a man called Malik while the second was the grave of a man called Aqil; both of these men were friends of Judhayma al-Abrash (or al-Abras) (d. 268). The

two structures were called *al-Ghariyyan* because the king, al-Nu'man ibn al-Mundhir (d. 608), would paint the two structures with the blood of people he killed in his rages. For more details on the subject, *see* J. Ibn Manzur, *Lisan al-Arab*, Beirut: Dar al-Fikr and Dar Sadir Press, 1990, vol. 15, p. 122, entry "Ghrw."

25 For details on the city of Asqalan, *see* Yaqut, *Mujam al-Buldan*, vol. 4, p. 122.
26 S. al-Shablanji, *Nur al-Absar fi Manaqib Al Bayt al-Nabi al-Mukhtar*, Beirut: Dar al-Ilmiyya Press, 1985, p. 234; A. al-Harawi, *al-Isharat Ila Marifat al-Ziyarat*, Damascus: The French Institute for Arabic Studies, 1953, vol. 1, p. 32 [in Arabic].
27 M. 'Ibrahim, *Maraqid Al-Bayt bi-al-Qahira*, Cairo: al-Ashira al-Muhammadiyya Press, 4th edn, 1986, p. 33.
28 Al-Khui, *Masir Ras al-Husayn wa-Mawdi' Dafnihi*, pp. 6–7.
29 Al-Shablanji, *Nur al-Absar fi Manaqib Al Bayt al-Nabi al-Mukhtar*, p. 234.
30 A. al-Maqrizi, Kitab al-Mawaiz wa-al I'tibar bi-Dhikr al-Khutat wa-al Athar al-Ma'ruf bi-al-Khutat al-Maqriziyya, Beirut: Dar al-Kutub al-Ilmiyya Press, 1988, vol. 2, p. 328.
31 On his life, *see* A. Badawi, *Diwan al-Wazir al-Misri Talai Ibn Ruzzayk*, Cairo: Maktabat Nahdat Misr, al-Risala Press, 1960, pp. 1–27.
32 Lapidas, *The History of the Islamic Society*, Cambridge: Cambridge University Press, 1988, pp. 216–17.
33 A. Khawarizim, *Maqtal al-Husayn*, Najaf: al-Zahra Press, 1948, pp. 109–10.
34 Qur'an, 18:9.
35 Qur'an, 23:227.
36 Abu Mikhnaf, *Maqtal al-Husayn Alayhi al-Salam*, pp. 107, 124–25; Khawarizim, *Maqtal al-Husayn*, pp. 123–24; Ibn Nama, *Muthir al-Ahzan wa-Munir Subul al-Ashjan*, p. 40.
37 For more details, *see* U. Rubin, "Pre-existence and Light: Aspects of the Concept of *Nur Muhammad*," *Israel Oriental Studies*, 1975, vol. 5, pp. 62–119.
38 Ibn Nama, *Muthir al-Ahzan wa-Munir Subul al-Ashjan*, p. 52; Ibn Tawus, *al-Lahuf Ala Qatla al-Tufuf*, Najaf: al-Haydariyya Press, 1951, p. 98 [in Arabic].
39 M. Ibn Shahrashub, *Manaqib Ali b. Abi Talib*, Beirut: Dar al-Andalus Press, 1991, vol. 4, p. 67 [in Arabic].
40 Ibn Tawus, *al-Lahuf Ala Qatla al-Tufuf*, p. 98; Khawarizim, *Maqtal al-Husayn*, p. 88.
41 M. Ibn Abd al-Ãahir, *al-Rawêa al-Bahiyya fi Khutat al-Muaziyya al-Qahira*, ed. Dr. Ayman Fuad al-Sayyid, Cairo: Maktabat al-Dar al-Arabiyya lil-kitab, 1996, pp. 30–31 [in Arabic].
42 *See e.g.*, M. Amir-Moezzi, *The Divine Guide in Early Shi'ism, The Esotericism in Islam*, trans. David Streight, New York: State University of New York Press, 1944, pp. 99–115.

Bibliography

General bibliography

Books and articles

Abtahi, H. (2001) "The Protection of Cultural Property in Times of Armed Conflict: The Practice of the International Criminal Tribunal for the Former Yugoslavia," *Harvard Human Rights Journal*, vol. 14, p. 1.

Abu El-Haj, N. (2002) *Facts on the Ground: Archeological Practice and Territorial Self-Fashioning in Israeli Society*, Chicago, Ill.: University of Chicago Press

——(2002) "Producing (Arti) Facts: Archeology and Power during the British Mandate of Palestine," *Israel Studies*, vol. 7, p. 33.

Albright, M. (2006) *TheMighty and the Almighty: Reflections on America, God and World Affairs*, New York: HarperCollins.

Amir-Moezzi, M. (1994) *The Divine Guide in Early Shi'ism, The Esotericism in Islam*, trans. David Streight, New York: State University of New York Press.

Anderson, B. (1991) *Imagined Communities*, 2nd edn, London: Verso.

Anderson, J. N. D. (1951) "The Religious Element in *Waqf* Endowments," *Journal of the Royal Central Asian Society*, vol. 38, pp. 292–99.

Appleby, R. S. (2000) *The Ambivalence of the Sacred*, Lanham, Md.: Rowman and Littlefield.

Arab Studies Society. (Feb. 2003) *East Jerusalem Multi Sector Review Project*, Final Report, Jerusalem.

Armatta, J. (August–September 2003) "Systematic Destruction of Cultural Monuments" in *Bosnia Report*, new series 35. Online. Available: http://www.bosnia.org.uk/bosrep/report_format. cfm?articleid = 1010&reportid = 160 (accessed 2 Aug. 2008).

Armstrong, K. (1997) *Jerusalem: One City, Three Faiths*, New York: Ballantine Books.

Ashgar, A. E. (ed.) (1990) *The Bari-Masjid Ramjanambhoomi Controversy*, Delhi: Ajanta Pub.

Ashis, N., Trivedy, S., Mayaram, S., and Yagnik, A. (1995) *Creating a Nationality: The Ramjanmabhumi Movement and the Fear of the Self*, Delhi: Oxford University Press.

Augustinović, A. (1972) *"El Khader" and the Prophet Elijah*, trans. E. Hoade, Jerusalem: Franciscan Printing Press.

Auld, S. and Hillenbrand, R. (eds) (2000) *Ottoman Jerusalem – the Living City 1517–1917*, London: Altajir World of Islam Trust.

Avni, G. and Seligman, J. (2001) *The Temple Mount 1917–2001 – Documentation, Research and Inspection of Antiquities*, Jerusalem: Israel Antiquities Authority.

Ayalon, E. (1982) "Nebi Yamin (Kever Binyamin, Kfar Saba)," *Archaeological News*, vol. 78–79, pp. 41–42.

Ayoub, M. (1985) "Arbain," in Ehsan Yarshater (ed.) *Encyclopaedia Iranica*, vol. 2, p. 275, London: Boston and Henely.

Azaryahu, M. (1993) "From Remains to Relics: Authentic Monuments in the Israeli Landscape," *History and Memory*, vol. 5, no. 2, pp. 82–103.

Bacchetta, P. (2000) "Sacred Space and Conflict in India: The Babri Masjid Affair," *Growth and Change*, vol. 31, no. 2, pp. 255–84.

Baer, G. (1962) *A History of Land Ownership in Modern Egypt: 1800–1950*, London: Oxford University Press.

Bajaj, J. (ed.) (1993) *Ayodhya and the Future of India*, Madras: Center for Policy Studies.

Bar, D. (2004) "Recreating Jewish Sanctity in Jerusalem: The Case of Mount Zion and King David's Tomb between 1948–67," *Journal of Israeli History*, vol. 23, no. 2, pp. 233–51.

——(2008) "Reconstructing the Past: The Creation of Jewish Sacred Space in the State of Israel, 1948–67," *Israel Studies*, vol. 13, no. 3. pp. 1–21.

Barclay, J. T. (1858) *The City of the Great Kings, or Jerusalem as it was, as it is, and as it is to be*, Philadelphia, Penn.: J. Challen.

Barnes, J. R. (1987) *An Introduction to Religious Foundations in the Ottoman Empire*, Leiden: E. J. Brill.

Barron, J. B. (1922) *Mohammedan Wakfs in Palestine*, Jerusalem: Green Convent Press.

Ben-Ami, I. (1998) *Saint Veneration Among the Jews in Morocco*, Detroit, Mich.: Wayne State University Press.

Ben Dov, M. (1982) *In the Shadow of the Temple*, New York: Harper and Row.

Ben Israel, H. (1998) "Hallowed Land in the Theory and Practice of Modern Nationalism", in B. Z. Kedar and R. J. Zvi Werblowsky (eds), *Sacred Space: Shrine, City and Land,* Macmillan and the Israel Academy of Sciences and Humanities.

Benvenisti, M. (1996) *City of Stone: The Hidden History of Jerusalem*, trans. M. K. Nunn, Berkeley, Calif.: University of California Press.

——(2002) *Sacred Landscape: The Buried History of the Holy Land Since 1948*, trans. Maxine Kaufman-Lacusta, Berkeley, Calif.: University of California. Press.

Berger, P. (1950) "The Internationalization of Jerusalem," *Jurist*, vol. 10, p. 357.

Berkovitz, S. (2001) *The Temple Mount and the Western Wall in Israeli Law*, Jerusalem: Jerusalem Institute for Israel Studies, Study Series 90.

——(2006) *How Dreadful is this Place: Holiness, Politics, and Justice in Jerusalem and the Holy Places in Israel*, Jerusalem: Karta Pub.

Berman, S. (1987) "Antiquities in Israel in a Maze of Controversy," *Case Western Reserve Journal of International Law*, vol. 19, pp. 343, 346–47.

Bialer, U. (2005) *Cross on the Star of David: The Christian World in Israel's Foreign Policy, 1948–1967*, Bloomington, Ind.: Indiana University Press.

Bigelow, A. (2002) "Practicing Pluralism in Malerkotla, Punjab," *Items and Issues*, vol. 3, nos 1–2, p. 10.

——(2004) *Sharing Saints, Shrines, and Stories: Practicing Pluralism in North India*, Doctoral Dissertation, Dept. of Religious Studies, University of California, Santa Barbara.

Binchy, D. A. (1941) *Church and State in Fascist Italy*, London: Oxford University Press.
Bowman, G. (1993) "Nationalizing the Sacred: Shrines and Shifting Identities in the Israeli-Occupied Territories," *Man*, vol. 28, no. 3, p. 431–60.
Breger, M. J. and Ahimeir, O. (eds) (2003) *Jerusalem: A City and Its Future*, New York: Syracuse University Press.
Brenner, N. and Kell, R. (eds) (2005) *The Global Cities Reader*, London: Routledge.
Bronner, Y. and Gordon, N. (21 Apr. 2008) "Beneath the Surface: Are Jerusalem's Digs Designed to Displace Palestinians?" *Chronicle of Higher Education (Chronicle Review)*, p. B5–6.
Brooks, R. (ed.) (2007) *The Wall: Fragmenting the Palestinian Fabric in Jerusalem*, Jerusalem: International Peace and Cooperation Center, IPCC.
Brooks, R., Khamaisi, R., Nasrallah, R., and Abu Ghazaleh, R. (2005) *The Wall of Annexation and Expansion: Its Impact on the Jerusalem Area*, Jerusalem: International Peace and Cooperation Center, IPCC.
Burger, J. (2005) *The Draft United Nations Declaration on the Rights of Indigenous Peoples*, International Council on Human Rights Policy, February Workshop, Online. Available http://www.ichrp.org/paper_files/120_w_05.doc (last accessed 12 Aug. 2008).
Burgoyne, H. M. (1987) *Mamluk Jerusalem: An Architectural Study*, London: World of Islam Festival Trust.
Canaan, T. (1927, repr. 1980) *Mohammedan Saints and Sanctuaries in Palestine*, London: J. Palestine Oriental Society, Jerusalem: Ariel.
Castells, M. (1983) *The City and the Grassroots*, Berkeley and Los Angeles: University of California Press.
Chad, E. F. (1995) *Beyond the Basilica: Christians and Muslims in Nazareth*, Chicago, Ill.: University of Chicago Press.
Chesler, P. and Haut, R. (2002) *Women of the Wall: Claiming Sacred Ground of Judaism's Holy Sites*, Woodstock, Vt.: Jewish Lights Pub.
Chidester, D. and Linenthal, E. T. (1995) "Introduction," in D. Chidester and E. T. Linenthal (eds), *American Sacred Space*, Bloomington, Ind.: Indiana University Press, pp. 1–35.
Cohen, A. (1994) *A World Within, Jewish Life as Reflected in Muslim Court Documents from the Sijill of Jerusalem (XVIth Century)*, Philadelphia, Penn.: University of Pennsylvania, Center for Judaic Studies, part I, p. 78 (Sijill 23\460).
Cohen, R. (2008) *Saving the Holy Sepulchre: How Rival Christians Came Together to Rescue their Holiest Shrine*, Oxford: Oxford University Press.
Cohen, S. B. (1977) *Jerusalem; Bridging the Four Walls*, New York: Herzl Press.
Cohen-Hattab, K. and Shoval, N. (2006) "Tourism Development in a Condition of a Cultural Conflict: 'Nazareth 2000' as a Case Study," unpublished paper.
Cole, J. (2002) *Sacred Space and Holy War: The Politics, Culture, and History of Islam*, London: I. B. Tauris.
Collins-Kreiner, N. (2000) "Pilgrimage Holy Sites: A Classification of Jewish Holy Sites in Israel," *Journal of Cultural Geography*, vol. 18, p. 57.
Corn, G. S. (2005) "Snipers in the Minaret – What is the Rule?" The Law of War and the Protection of Cultural Property: A Complex Equation, *The Army Lawyer*, vol. 28, p. 28.
Cosgrove, D. E. (1984) *Social Formation and Symbolic Landscape*, London: C. Helm.
Creswell, K. A. C. (1969) *Early Muslim Architecture, I: Umayyads, A. D. 622–75*, Oxford: Clarendon Press.

Cunningham, R. B. (2005) *Archeology, Relics, and the Law*, 2nd edn, Durham, N.C.: Carolina Academic Press.

Cust, L. G. A. (1929) *The Status Quo in the Holy Places, with an Annex on the Status Quo in the Church of the Nativity, Bethlehem by Abdullah Effendi Kardus*, Harrow: Printed for the Gov't of Palestine by H.M.S.O., pp. 46–48. repr. as facsimile edn, Jerusalem: Ariel, 1980.

Dana, N. (2003) *The Druze in the Middle East: Their Faith, Leadership, Identity, and Status*, Brighton: Sussex Academic Press.

De Francisis, M. E. (1989) *Italy and the Vatican: The 1984 Concordat Between Church and State*, New York: Peter Lang.

De Jong, A. (1983) "The Sufi Orders in Palestine," *Studia Islamica*, vol. 58, p. 159.

Detling, Karen J. (1993) "Eternal Silence: The Destruction of Cultural Property in Yugoslavia," *Maryland Journal of International Law and Trade*, vol. 17, pp. 41–75.

De Vogüé, E. M. M. (1864) *Le Temple de Jerusalem – Monograph du Haram ech-Cherif*, Paris: Noblet et Baudrie.

Dumper, M. (1994) *Islam and Israel, Muslim Religious Endowments and the Jewish State*, Washington, DC: Institute for Palestine Studies.

——(2002) *The Politics of Sacred Space: The Old City of Jerusalem in the Middle East Conflict*, Boulder, Colo.: Lynne Rienner.

Durkheim, E. (1915) *The Elementary Forms of the Religious Life*, London: Allen and Unwin.

Eagen, S. (2001) "Preserving Cultural Property: Our Public Duty: A Look at How and Why We Must Create International Laws that Support International Action," *Pace International Law Review*, vol. 13, no. 2, pp. 407–48.

Eaton, R. M. (2000) "Temple Desecration in Pre-Modern India," *Frontline*, vol. 17, nos 25 and 26.

Emmett, C. F. (1995) *Beyond the Basilica: Christians and Muslims in Nazareth*, Chicago, Ill.: University of Chicago Press.

Englard, I. (1994) "The Legal Status of the Holy Places in Jerusalem," *Israel Law Review*, vol. 28, p. 589.

Eordegian, M. (2003) "British and Israeli Maintenance of the Status Quo in the Holy Places of Christendom," *International Journal of Middle Eastern Studies*, vol. 35, pp. 307–28.

Ernst, C. W. (1995) "India as a Sacred Islamic Land," in Donald S. Lopez (ed.), *Religions of India in Practice*, Princeton, NJ: Princeton University Press, pp. 556–63.

Esposito, J. L. (2002) *Unholy War: Terror in the Name of Islam*, New York: Oxford University Press.

Eusebius of Caesarea. (1985) *Life of Constantine,* trans. F. Winkelman, secs 3. 25–3. 33, cited in Peters, F. E. *Jerusalem*, Princeton, NJ: Princeton University Press, pp. 135–36.

Fabian, R. (1999) *Jaffa – A Narrative of Politics and Architecture/Urbanism*, unpublished MA thesis, Harvard University.

Fenster, T. (2004) *The Global City and the Holy City: Narratives on Knowledge, Planning and Diversity*, London: Pearson Prentice Hall.

Ferrari, S. (1996) "The Future of Jerusalem: A Symposium: The Religious Significance of Jerusalem in the Middle East Peace Process: Some Legal Implications," *Catholic University Law Review*, vol. 45, p. 733.

Firro, K. M. (1999) *The Druzes in the Jewish State: A Brief History*, Leiden: E. J. Brill.

——(2005) "Druze *maqamat* (Shrines) in Israel: From Ancient to Newly-Invented Traditions," *British Journal of Middle Eastern Studies*, vol. 32, no. 2, pp. 217–39.

278 Bibliography

Forrest, C. (2007) "The Doctrine of Military Necessity and the Protection of Cultural Property During Armed Conflicts," *California Western Law Review*, vol. 37, p. 177.

Francioni, F. and Lenzerini, F. (2003) "The Destruction of the Buddhas of Bamiyan and International Law," *European Journal of International Law*, vol. 14, p. 619.

Friedlander, R. and Hecht, R. (Nov. 1998) "The Bodies of Nations: A Comparative Study of Religious Violence in Jerusalem and Ayodhya," *History of Religions*, vol. 38, no. 2, pp. 101–49.

Gellner, E. (1991) *Nations and Nationalism*, New York: Cornell University Press.

Gerber, H. (1985) *Ottoman Rule in Jerusalem 1890–1914*, Berlin: Klaus Schwarz Verlag.

Gibson, S. and Jacobson, D. M. (1996) *Below the Temple Mount in Jerusalem, A Sourcebook on the Cisterns, Subterranean Chambers and Conduits of the Haram al-Sharif*, BAR International Series 637, Oxford: Tempus Reparatum.

Gordon, C. G. (1969) "The Journals of Major-Gen. C. G. Gordon, C. B., at Kartoum," ed. A. Egmont Hake, New York: Negro Universities Press.

Gordon, W. H. (1886) *Events in the Life of Charles George Gordon from Its Beginning to Its End*, London: Kegan Paul, Trench.

Gorenberg, G. (2000) *The End of the Days: Fundementalism and the Struggle for the Temple Mount*, New York: Free Press.

Gramsci, A. (1971) *Selections from Prison Notebooks*, New York: International Publishing.

Green, L. C. (1993) *The Contemporary Law of Armed Conflict*, Manchester: Manchester University Press.

Guinn, D. E. (2006) *Protecting Jerusalem's Holy Sites: A Strategy for Negotiating Sacred Peace*, Cambridge: Cambridge University Press.

Hadden, J. K. (March 1987) "Toward Desacralizing Secularization Theory," *social Forces*, vol. 65, pp. 587–611.

Hadzimuhamedovic, A. "Transnational Meaning of the Bosnia-Herzegovinian Architectural Heritage and Its Post-War Reconstruction." Online. Available: http://www2.units.it/~vplanet/atti/Hadzimuhamedovic.doc (accessed 29 Oct. 2005).

Halperin-Kaddari, R. (2000–2001) "Women, Religion and Multiculturalism in Israel," *UCLA Journal International Law & Foreign Affairs*, vol. 5, p. 339.

Hamilton, R. W. (1949) *The Structural History of the Aqsa Mosque – A Record of Archaeological Gleanings from the Repairs of 1938–1942*, Jerusalem: Department of Antiquities of Palestine.

Hapgood D. and Richardson, D. (1984) *Monte Cassino*, New York: Congdon and Weed.

Harsh, N. (1993) *The Ayodhya Temple Mosque Dispute: Focus on Muslim Sources*, Delhi: Penman Publishing.

Harvey, D. (1979) "Monument and Myth," *Annals of the Association of the American Geographers*, vol. 69, pp. 362–81.

——(2003) "The Right to the City," *International Journal of Urban and Regional Research*, vol. 27, no. 4, pp. 939–41.

Hasson, S. (1996) *The Cultural Struggle over Jerusalem*, Jerusalem: Floersheimer Institute for Policy Studies.

Hassner, R. E. (2009) *War on Sacred Ground* Ithaca, N.Y.: Cornell University Press.

Hayden, R. M. (2002) "Antagonistic Tolerance: Competitive Sharing of Religious Sites in South Asia and the Balkans in Holy Places," *Current Anthropology*, vol. 43, no. 2, pp. 205–31.

Herscher, A. and Riedlmayer, A. (2000) "Monument and Crime: The Destruction of Historic Architecture in Kosovo," *Grey Room*, vol. 1 (Autumn), pp. 108–22.

Herzliya Convention (2006) *The Holy Basin of Jerusalem*, Jerusalem: Jerusalem Institute for Israel Studies.
Hilmi Efendi, O. (1899) *A Treatise on the Laws of Evqaf*, trans. Tyser and D. G. Demetriades, Nicosia: Government Printing Office.
Hoade E., Fr. (1942) *Guide to the Holy Land*, Jerusalem: Franciscan Press.
Heyness, D. and Parkash, G. (1991) "Introduction: The Entanglement of Power and Resistance" in D. Heyness and G. Parkash (eds.) *Contesting Power: Resistance and Everyday Social Relations in South Africa*, Delhi: Oxford University Press, pp. 1–22.
Hoexter, M. (1984) "Le contrat de quasi-alienation des awq'af a Alger a la fin de la domination turque: etude de deux document d'ana'," *Bulletin of the School of Oriental and African Studies*, vol. 47, pp. 243–59.
——(1997) "Adaptation to Changing Circumstances: Perpetual Leases and Exchange Transactions," in *Waqf* Property in Ottoman Algiers," *Islamic Law and Society*, vol. 4, no. 3, pp. 319–33.
Hughes, T. P. (1895) *Dictionary of Islam*, London: W. H. Allen.
Huntington, S. (1998) *The Clash of Civilizations and the Remaking of World Order*, New York: Touchstone Books.
Israeli, R. (1993) *Muslim Fundamentalism in Israel*, London: Brassey, 1993.
——(2002) *Green Crescent Over Nazareth, The Displacement of Christians by Muslims in the Holy Land*, London: Frank Cass.
——(2002) *Jerusalem Divided: The Armistice Regime. 1947–1967*, Portland, Oreg.: Frank Cass.
Jiryis, S. (1969) *The Arabs in Israel*, Beirut: Institute for Palestine Studies.
Johnston, D. and Sampson, C. (1994) *Religion, the Missing Dimension of Statecraft*, New York: Oxford University Press.
Juergensmeyer, M. (2000) *Terror in the Mind of God: The Global Rise of Religious Violence*, Berkeley, Calif.: University of Calif. Press.
Katz, K. (2005) *Jordanian Jerusalem: Holy Places and National Spaces*. Gainesville, Fla.: University Press of Florida.
Keawar, Z. N. (2000) *History of Nazareth*, Nazareth: Venues Publishing.
Kenyon, K. M. (1974) *Digging Up Jerusalem*. London: Benn.
Key Fowden, E. (2002) "Sharing Holy Places," *Common Knowledge*, vol. 8, no. 1, pp. 124–46.
Khamaisi, R. and Nasrallah, R. (2006) *Jerusalem: The City of Lost Peace*, Jerusalem: Int'l Peace and Cooperation Center, IPCC.
Klein, C. (1971) "The Temple Mount Case," *Israel Law Review*, vol. 6, p. 263.
Klein, M. (2001) *Breaking a Taboo: The Negotiations for a Final Agreement in Jerusalem, 1994–2001*, Jerusalem: Jerusalem Institute for Israel Studies.
——(2003) *The Jerusalem Problem – The Struggle for Permanent Status*, Gainesville, Fla.: University Press of Florida.
Knox, P. and McCarthy, L. (2005) *Urbanization: An Introduction to Urban Geography*, Englewood Cliffs, NJ: Prentice Hall.
Komurcu, M. (2002) "Cultural Heritage Endangered by Large Dams and its Protection under International Law," *Wisconsin International Law Journal*, vol. 20, p. 233.
Kong, L. (1990) "Geography and Religion: Trends and Prospects," *Progress in Human Geography*, vol. 14, no. 3, pp. 355–71.
——(1993) "Ideological Hegemony and the Political Symbolism of Religious Building in Singapore," *Environmental and Planning D: Society and Space*, vol. 11, pp. 23–45.

—— (2001) "Mapping 'New' Geographies of Religion: Politics and Poetics in Modernity," *Progress in Human Geography*, vol. 25, no. 2, pp. 211–33.

—— (1993) "Negotiating Conceptions of 'Sacred Space': A Case Study of Religious Buildings in Singapore," *Transactions of the Institution of British Geographers*, vol. 18, pp. 342–58.

Kupferschmidt, U. M. (1987) *The Supreme Muslim Council, Islam under the British Mandate for Palestine*, The Hague: E. J. Brill.

—— (2002) "A Morrocan *Tzadiq* in Israel: The Emergence of the Baba Sali," in E. Rabbie, M. S. Nihon, and J. G. Frankfort (eds) *Bijdragen en Mededelingen van het Genootschap voor de Joodsche Wetenschap in Nederland gevestigd te Amsterdam*, Amsterdam: Genootschap voor de Joodsche Wetenschap in Nederland Gevestigd te Amsterdam, vol. 11, pp. 273–93.

La Greca, P. (ed.) (2005) *Planning in a More Globalized and Competitive World*, Proceedings of 41 ISoCaRP International Society of City and Regional Planners Congress, The Hague: Gangmi Editore.

Lane, E. (1877) *An Arabic-English Lexicon*, Beirut: Librairie du Liban.Lapidas, I. (1988) *The History of the Islamic Society*, Cambridge: Cambridge University Press.

Lapidoth, R. (2003) "Freedom of Religion and Conscience in Israel," in M. Breger (ed.) *The Vatican–Israel Accords: Political, Legal, and Theological Contexts*, Notre Dame, Ind.: University of Notre Dame Press.

Lauterpacht, E. (1968) *Jerusalem and the Holy Places*, London, The Anglo-Israel Association.

Layish, A. (1966) "The Muslim *Waqf* in Israel," *Asian and African Studies*, vol. 2, p. 59.

Lefebvre, H. (1996) *Writing on Cities*, Cambridge, Mass.: Blackwell.

Lewis, B. (1953) "An Arabic Account of the Province of Safed – I," *Bulletin of the School of Oriental and African Studies*, vol. 15, pp. 477–88.

—— (1984) *The Jews of Islam*, Princeton, N.J.: Princeton University Press.

Liangyung, W. (1999) *Rehabilitating the Old City of Beijing*, Vancouver: UBC Press.

Lincoln, B. (2003) *Holy Terrors: Thinking About Religion After September 11*, Chicago, Ill.: University of Chicago Press.

Louër, L. (2007) *To Be an Arab in Israel*, London: Hurst.

Luz, N. (2005) *The Arab Community of Jaffa and the Hassan Bey Mosque: Collective Identity and Empowerment of the Arabs in Israel*, Jerusalem: The Floershimer Institute for Policy Studies.

Mahmutcahajic, R. (2000) *Bosnia the Good: Tolerance and Tradition*, Budapest: Central European University Press.

Majdalany, F. (1957) *The Battle of Cassino*, Cambridge, Mass.: Riverside Press.

Mansour, A. (2004) *Narrow Gate Churches, The Christian Presence in the Holy Land Under Muslim and Jewish Rule*, Pasadena, Calif.: Hope Publ. House.

Ma'oz, M. (1968) *Ottoman Reforms in Syria and Palestine 1840–1861*, Oxford: Clarendon Press.

Martin, E. M. and Appleby, R. S. T. (eds) (1991–95) *The Fundamentalism Project*, vols. 1–4, Chicago, Ill.: University of Chicago Press.

Mason, P. (1993) "Pilgrimage to Religious Shrines: An Essential Element in the Human Right to Freedom of Thought, Conscience and Religion," *Case Western Reserve Journal of International Law*, vol. 25, p. 619.

Mayer, L. A. Pinkerfeld, J. and Hirschberg, H. Z. (1950) *Some Principal Muslim Religious Buildings in Israel*, Jerusalem: Ministry of Religious Affairs.

Mazar, B. (1975) *The Mountain of the Lord*, New York: Doubleday.
Meri, J. W. (1999) "Re-appropriating Sacred Space: Medieval Jews and Muslims Seeking Elijah and al-Khadir," *Medieval Encounters: Jewish, Christian and Muslim Culture in Confluence and Dialogue*, vol. 5, pp. 1–28.
——(2002) *The Cult of Saints among Muslims and Jews in Medieval Syria*, Oxford: Oxford University Press.
Minerbi, S. I. (1990) *The Vatican and Zionism*, trans Arnold Schwartz, Oxford: Oxford University Press.
Morrison, W. (ed.) (1871) *The Recovery of Jerusalem – A Narrative of Exploration and Discovery in the City and the Holy Land*, London: Palestine Exploration Fund.
Natsheh, Y. (2000) "Architectural Survey," in S. Auld and R. Hillenbrand (eds.) *Ottoman Jerusalem: The Living City 1517–1917*, Part II, London: Altajir World of Islam Trust.
Norwich, J. J. and Sitwell, R. (1966) *Mount Athos*, New York: Harper and Row.
O'Faircheallaigh, C. (2008) "Negotiating Cultural Heritage? Aboriginal-Mining Company Agreements in Australia," *Development and Change*, vol. 39, p. 25.
O'Keefe, R. (1999) "The Meaning of 'Cultural Property' under the 1954 Hague Convention," *Netherlands International Law Review*, vol. 26, p. 1.
——(2004) "World Cultural Heritage: Obligations to the International Community as a Whole?" *International and Comparative Law Quarterly*, vol. 53, p. 189.
Ovadiah, A. (1966) "Elijah's Cave, Mount Carmel," *Israel Exploration Journal*, vol. 16, pp. 285–87.
Panikkar, K. N. (1991) "A Historical Overview," in S. Gopal (ed.) *Anatomy of a Confrontation: The Rise of Communal Politics in India*, London: Zed Books.
Papastathis, C. K. (1993) "The Status of Mount Athos in Helenic Public Law," in Anthony-Emil N. Tachraos (ed.) *Mount Athos and the European Community*, Thessalonika: Institute for Balkan Studies.
——(1996) "The Hellenic Republic and the Prevailing Religion," *Brigham Young University Law Review*, vol. 4, p. 815.
Pappe, I. (2004) *A History of Modern Palestine. One Land, Two Peoples*, Cambridge: Cambridge University Press.
——(2006) *The Ethnic Cleansing of Palestine*, Oxford: One World.
Park, C. C. (1994) *Sacred Worlds: An Introduction to Geography and Religion*, New York, Routledge.
Partsch, K. J. (1995) "Protection of Cultural Property," in D. Fleck (ed.) *The Handbook of Humanitarian Law in Armed Conflicts*, Oxford: Oxford University Press.
Pentzopoulos, D. (2002, first pub. 1962) "Description of the Turkish-Greek dispute and its effects on the region's population," in *The Balkan Exchange of Minorities and its Impact upon Greece*, London: Hurst, pp. 199–219.
Peters, F. E. (1986) *Jerusalem and Mecca: The Typology of the Holy City in the Middle East*, New York: New York University Press.
Pickthall, M. (2000) *The Meaning of the Glorious Qur'an*, New York: Tahrike Tarsile Qur'an.
Pierotti, E. (1864) *Jerusalem Explored – Being a Description of Ancient and Modern City*, I–II, London: Bell and Daldy.
Pile, S. (1997) "Introduction. Oppositional, Political Identities and Spaces of Resistance," in S. Pile and M. Keith (eds) *Geographies of Resistance*, London and New York: Routledge, pp. 1–32.
Pinkerfeld, J. (1960) "David's Tomb," *Louis M. Rabinowitz Fund for the Exploration of Ancient Synagogues*, vol. 3, pp. 41–44.

Bibliography

Pollock, J. (1993) *Gordon: The Man Behind the Legend*, London: Constable.

Poulos, A. (2000) "The 1954 Hague Convention for the Protection of Cultural Property in the Event of Armed Conflict: An Historic Analysis," *International Journal of Legal Information*, vol. 28, p. 1.

Prott, L. (1988) "Cultural Rights as Peoples Rights in International Law," in J. Crawford (ed.) *The Rights of People*, Oxford: Clarendon Press.

—— (1997) "The Development of Legal Concepts Connected with the Protection of the Cultural Heritage," in R. Blanpain (ed.) *Law in Motion*, Hague: Kluwer Law International.

Qooq, S. H. (1965) "Notes on 'The History of Synagogue at Shmuel Hanavi Tomb,'" *Bulletin of the Israel Exploration Society*, Reader B, Jerusalem: The Israel Exploration Society, pp. 248–49. (originally vol. 6, pp. 143–44).

Rabinowitz, D. (2000) *Overlooking Nazareth, the Ethnography of Exclusion in Galilee*, Cambridge: Cambridge University Press.

—— (2001) "Strife in Nazareth: Struggles over the Religious Meaning ofPlace," *Ethnography*, vol. 2, no. 1, pp. 93–113.

Raday, F. (2003) "Culture, Religion and Gender," *International Journal of Constitutional Law*, vol. 1, pp. 663, 668–69.

—— (2007) "Claiming Equal Religious Personhood: Women of the Wall's Constitutional Saga," in W. Brugger and M. Karaynni (eds.), *Religion in the Public Sphere: A Comparative Analysis of German, Israeli, American and International Law*, Berlin and New York: Springer, pp. 243–52.

Rahamimoff, A. (2002) *Outline Plan for Nazareth, 2020: Final Report*, Nazareth: Municipality of Nazareth and Interior Ministry.

Reich, R., Avni G., and Winter, T. (1999). *The Jerusalem Archaeological Park*, Jerusalem: Israel Antiquities Authority.

Reiter, Y. (1996) *Islamic Endowments in Jerusalem*, London: Frank Cass.

—— (2007) "'All of Palestine is Holy Muslim *Waqf* Land' – A Myth and Its Roots," in R. Shaham (ed.) Law, Custom, and Statute in the Muslim World, Studies in Honor of Aharon Layish, Leiden and Boston: E. J. Brill, pp. 172–97.

Reiter, Y. Eordegian, M. and Abu Khahuf, M. (2000) "The Holy Places: Introduction" and "Between Divine and Human: The Complexity of Holy Places in Jerusalem," in Maoz, M. and Nusseibeh, S. (eds) *Jerusalem: Points of Friction – and Beyond*, Leiden and Boston, Mass.: E. J. Brill.

Richmond, E. T. (1924) *The Dome of the Rock in Jerusalem – A Description of its Structure and Decoration*, Oxford: Clarendon Press.

Rivera, D. (2003) "Taino Sacred Sites: An International Comparative Analysis for a Domestic Solution," *Arizona Journal of International and Comparative Law*, vol. 20, p. 443.

Roberts, A. and Guelff, R. (eds.) (1989) *Documents on the Laws of War*, Oxford: Clarendon Press.

Roman, M. (1985) "Jewish Kiryat Arba versus Arab Hebron," *The West Bank Data Project*, Jerusalem: West Bank Data Project, pp. 55–68.

Ronen, Y. (Oct. 2005) "The Demolition of Synagogues in the Gaza Strip," *ASIL Insight* of 17 Online. Available: http://www.asil.org/insights/2005/10/insights051017.html (accessed 10 Oct. 2008).

Rosen-Ayalon, M. (1989) "The Early Islamic Monuments of al-Haram al-Sharif – An Iconographic Study," *Qedem*, vol. 28, Jerusalem: The Institute of Archaeology, The Hebrew University of Jerusalem.

Ross, D. (2004) *The Missing Peace: The Inside Story of the Fight for Middle East Peace*, New York: Farrar, Straus, & Giroux.

Rubin, U. (1975) "Pre-existence and Light: Aspects of the Concept of *Nur Muhammad*," *Israel Oriental Studies*, vol. 5, pp. 62–119.

Rubin Peled, A. (2001) *Debating Islam in the Jewish State: The Development of Policy Toward Islamic Institutions in Israel*, Albany, NY: SU New York Press.

Rumpf, C. (1995) "Holy Places" in R. Bernhardt (ed.), *Encyclopedia of Public International Law*, vol. 2, pp. 863–66.

Sassen, S. (2002) "Cities in a World Economy," in S. S.Fainstein and S. Campbell (eds) *Reading in Urban Theory*, 2nd edn, Oxford: Blackwell, pp. 32–56.

Schick, C. (1896) *Die Stiftshutte, der Temple in Jerusalem und Tempelplatz der Jetztzeit*, Berlin: Weidmann.

Scott, A. J. (2000) *The Cultural Economy of Cities*, London: Sage Publications.

Scott, J. C. (1990) *Domination and the Arts of Resistance*, New Haven, CT and London: Yale University Press.

Scott, J. and Simpson-Housley, P. (1991) *Sacred Places and Profane Spaces: Essays on the Geographics of Judaism, Christianity, and Islam*, New York: Greenwood Press.

Seidemann, R. M. (2004) "Bones of Contention: A Comparative Examination of Law Governing Human Remains from Archaeological Contexts in Formerly Colonial Countries," *Loyola of Los Angeles Law Review*, vol. 64, pp. 545–46.

Seligman, J and Abu Raya, R. (2001) "A Shrine of Three Religions on the Mount of Olives: Tomb of Huldah the Prophetess; Grotto of Saint Pelagia; Tomb of Rabi'a Al-'Adawiyya," *Atiqot Holy Places*, vol. 42, pp. 221–36.

Seligman, J. and Avni, G. (2006) "Between the Temple Mount /*Haram el-Sharif* and the Holy Sepulchre: Archaeological Involvement in Jerusalem's Holy Places," *Journal of Mediterranean Archaeology*, vol. 19, no. 2, pp. 259–88.

Sells, M. (1996) *The Bridge Betrayed: Religion and Genocide in Bosnia*, Berkeley, Calif.: University of Calif. Press.

Sennott, C. M. (2001) *The Body and the Blood, The Holy Land's Christians at the Turn of a New Millenium,a Reporter's Journey*, New York: Public Affairs.

Shapira, A. (2004) *Israeli Identity in Transition*, New York: Greenwood/Praeger.

Sher, G. (2006) *Just Beyond Reach: The Israeli-Palestinian Peace Negotiations, 1999–2001*, New York: Routledge.

Sherrard, P. (1982) *Athos: The Holy Mountain*, Woodstock, N.Y.: Overlook Press.

Shochat, E. (1999) "The Invention of the Mizrahim," *Journal of Palestinian Studies*, vol. 29, no. 1, pp. 5–20.

——(2001) "Rupture and Return: A Mizrahi Perspective on the Zionist Discourse," *The MIT Electronic Journal of Middle East Studies*, vol. 1. Online. Available: http://web.mit.edu/cis/www/mitejmes/issues/200105/shohat.htm.

Sindawi, K. (2001) "Ashura' Day and Yom Kippur," *Ancient Near Eastern Studies*, vol. 38, pp. 200–214.

——(2004) "Husayn Ibn Ali and Yahya Ibn Zachria in the Shi'ite Sources: A Comparative Study," *Islamic Culture*, vol. 78, no. 3, pp. 37–54.

Sivan, E. (1985) *Radical Islam: Medieval Theology and Modern Politics*, New Haven, CT: Yale University Press.

Smith, J. Z. (1978) *To Take Place: Toward a Theory in Ritual*, Chicago, Ill.: University of Chicago Press.

Soloveitchik, Rabbi J. D. (1992) *The Lonely Man of Faith*, New York: Doubleday.

Stark, R. and Bainbridge, W. S. (1985) *The Future of Religion*, Berkeley and Los Angeles, Calif.: University of Califonia Press.
Stillman, N. (1991) *The Jews of Arab Lands in Modern Times*, Philadelphia, Penn.: The Jewish Publication Society.
Strickart, F. (2007) *Rachel Weeping: Jew, Christianity and Muslims at the Fortress Tomb*, Collegeville, Minn.: Liturgical Press.
Telushkin, J. (1991) *Jewish Literacy: The Most Important Things To Know About The Jewish Religion, Its People, and Its History*, New York: HarperCollins.
Thomason, D. (1990) "Rolling Back History: The United Nations General Assembly and the Right to Cultural Property," *Case Western Reserve Journal*, vol. 22, p. 47.
Tobler, T. (1868) *Nazareth in Palestine*, Berlin.
Tolkowsky, S. (1924) *The Gateway of Palestine: A History of Jaffa*, London: Routledge, repr. 1941.
Trevelyan, R. (1981) *Rome '44: The Battle for the Eternal City*, New York, Viking Press.
Tsimhoni, D. (1978) "The Christians in Israel: Between Religion and Politics," in "The Greek Orthodox Patriarchate of Jerusalem during the Formative Years of the British Mandate in Palestine", *Asian and African Studies* (Journal of Israel Oriental Society, University of Haifa), vol. 12, no. 1 (Mar. 1978), pp. 77–121.
——(1993) *Christian Communities in Jerusalem and the West Bank Since 1948, An Historical, Social and Political Study*, London: Praeger, 1993.
Van Berchem, M. (1927) *Matériaux pour un Corpus Inscripionum Arabicarum*, II: *Syria du Sud, Jérusalem "Haram"*, Cairo: Institut français d'archéologie orientale.
Van der Leeuw, G. (1938, repr. 1986) *Religions in Essence and Manifestations*, trans. from the German original of 1933, Princeton, NJ: Princeton University Press.
Van der Veer, P. (1987) "'The Gods Must be Liberated!': A Hindu Liberation Movement in Ayodhya," *Modern Asian Studies*, vol. 21, no. 2, pp. 283–301.
Vekselman, V. (18 Dec. 2001) "Christmas Tour of the Holy Land," Olga's Gallery. Online. Available: http://www.abcgallery.com/list/archive.html (accessed 1 Feb. 2009).
Vilnay, Z. (1986) *Sepulchral Monuments in Palestine*, 3rd edn, Jerusalem: Achiever.
Voinot, L. (1948) *Pèlerinages judéo-musulmans du Maroc*, Paris: Larousse.
Walters, R. and Bruce, S. (1992) *"Secularization: The Orthodox Model,"* in Steve Bruce (ed.), *Religion and Modernization: Sociologists and Historians Debate the Secularization Thesis*, London: Oxford University Press, pp. 8–30.
Wangkeo, K. (2003) "Monumental Challenges: The Lawfulness of Destroying Cultural Heritage During Peacetime," *Yale Journal of International Law*, vol. 28, p. 183.
Warren, C. (1876) *Underground Jerusalem: an Account of the Principal Difficulties Encountered in its Exploration and Results obtained*, London: R. Bentley.
——(1884) *Plans, Elevations, Sections. Showing the Results of the Excavations in Jerusalem 1867–1870*, London: Palestine Exploration Fund.
Watson, G. (1997–98) "Progress for Pilgrims? An Analysis of the Holy See-Israel Fundamental Agreement," *Catholic University Law Review*, vol. 47, p. 497.
Wiegers, G. A. (2004) "Holy Cities in the Perspective of Recent Theoretical Discussions in the Science of Religion," in Alain Le Boulluec (ed.) *A la recherche des villes saintes, Actes du Colloque Franco-Néerlandais, "Les villes saintes," Collège de France, 10 et 11 mai 2001* (Bibliothèque de l'École des hautes études. Sciencesreligieuses, 122) red. A. le Boulluec, 1–13. Turnhout, Brepols.
Wiessner, S. (1999) "Rights and Status of Indigenous peoples: A Global, Comparative and International Legal Analysis" *Harvard Human Rights Journal*, vol. 12, p. 57.

Wilkinson, J. (1995) "Visits to Jewish Tombs by Early Christians," in *Jahrbuch Fur Antike Und Christentum Erganzungsband*, vol. 20, pp. 425–65, Munster: Aschendorffsche, Verlagsbuchhandlung.
——(1999) *Egeria's Travels*, Wartminster: Aris & Phillips.
Williams, R. (1977) *Marxism and Literature*, Bath: Oxford University Press.
Wilson, C. W. (1865). *Ordinance Survey of Jerusalem, Made in the Years 1864–1865*, Southampton: Palestine Exploration Fund.
Yazbak, M. (1998) *Haifa in the Late Ottoman Period, 1864–1914: A Muslim Town in Transition*, Leiden: E. J. Brill.
Yiftachel, O. (2006) *Ethnocracy: Land and Identity: Politics in Israel/Palestine*, Philadelphia, Penn.: University of Pennsylvania Press, pp. 136–42.
Zander, W. (1973) "On the Settlement of Disputes about the Christian Holy Places," *Israel Law Review*, vol. 8, no. 3, pp. 331–66.
——(1982) "Jurisdiction and Holiness: Reflections on the Coptic-Ethiopian Case," *Israel Law Review*, vol. 17, no. 3, pp. 245–73.
Zilberman, I. (1997) *Jerusalem and Ayodhya – A Profile of Religious and Political Radicalism*, Jerusalem: Jerusalem Institute for Israel Studies.
Zubcevic, A. (2007) "Islamic Sites in Bosnia: Ten Years After," in *Islamica Magazine*, Online. Available: http://www.islamicamagazine.com/issue-15/islamic-sites-in-bosnia-10-years-after-the-war.html (accessed 27 July 2008).

Documents

Agreement on the Gaza Strip and the Jericho Area, Signed 4 May 1994, Cairo, UN Doc. A/49/180 S/1994/727 (Annex) of 20 June 1994. Repr. in 33 *ILM* (1994), pp. 626–720, also in 28 *Israel Law Review* (1994), pp. 452–543.
Agreement Providing for the Accession of Greece to the European Community (1979) *Official Journal of European Community*, L 291, vol. 22, 19 Nov. 1979, p. 186.
Antiquities Ordinance 1929, 1 *Laws of Palestine* 28.
Australian Heritage Protection Act 1984, § 4.
Basic Law: Jerusalem, Capital of Israel, in *LSI* 34 (30 July 1980), p. 209, sec. 3.
Bosnia and Herzegovina Commission to Preserve National Monuments, 38th Sess. of the Commission. Online. Available: http://www.aneks8komisija.com.ba/main.php?id_struct = 66&lang = 4 (accessed 8 Aug. 2008).
Buddhas of Bamyan. Online. Available: http://en.wikipedia.org/wiki/Buddhas of_Bamyan.
Bureau of Democracy, Human Rights, and Labor, US Dep't of State, *Israel and the Occupied Territories* (4 Mar. 2002), Online. Available: http://www.state.gov.g/drl/rls/hrrpt/2001/nea/8262.htm (accessed 4 Sept. 2008).
Bureau of Near Eastern Affairs, US Dep't of State, *Sharam El-Sheikh Fact-Finding Committee Report* (Apr. 30, 2001) http://www.state.gov/p/nea/rls/rpt/3060.htm.
Canadian Constitution Act 1982, RSC (1985), App. II, No. 44, Sched. B, Pt. II, s. 35(1).
Central Bureau of Statistics. (2005) *Statistical Abstract of Israel, no. 56*, Jerusalem.
"Central Portion of the Jerusalem Area: Principle of Holy Places," *United Nations Map*, no. 229 (Nov. 1949).
Commission on Human Rights, Principles, and Guidelines for the Protection of the Heritage of Indigenous Peoples, E/CN. 4/Sub. 2/2000/26.
Commission on Human Rights, CHR Resolutions 1998/70, 1999/9 and 2000/18 on the situation of human rights in Afghanistan.

Bibliography

Commission on Human Rights, CHR Resolution 2004/36 (2004) on the Elimination of all Forms of Religious Intolerance *55th meeting 19 April 2004* chap. XI – E/2004/23 – E/CN. 4/2004/127.

Committee on Economic Social and Cultural E/1993/22, at para. 186.

Concordat between the Holy See and Italy, 11 Feb. 1929, Art. 1, repr. in National Catholic Welfare Conference, *Treaty and Concordat Between the Holy See and Italy: Official Documents* 1929.

Convention No. 169 Concerning Indigenous and Tribal Peoples in Independent Countries, adopted 1989, repr. in 1989, vol. 28, *International Law Materials*, p. 1382.

Convention with Respect to the Laws of Custom of War on Land (1899) Online. Available: http://www. icrc. org/ihl. nsf/FULL/140?OpenDocument (last accessed 8 Aug. 2008).Copy of letter by the Franciscan Custos of the Holy Land, 8 April 1999.

Country Reports on Human Rights Practices -2000, Released by the Bureau of Democracy, Human Rights, and Labor, 23 Feb. 2001, US Dept. of State, "The Occupied Territories (Including Areas Subject To The Jurisdiction Of The Palestinian Authority)" Online. Available: http://www.state.gov/g/drl/rls/hrrpt/2000/nea/882. htm (last accessed 5 Aug. 2007).

Cultural Heritage Laws/Legislations nationales sur le patrimoine culturel. Online. Available http://portal.unesco.org/culture/en/ev.php.

Decision on the Commission to Preserve National Monuments, adopted by the Presidency of Bosnia and Herzegovina, 21 Dec. 2001. Online. Available http://www.aneks8komisiga.com.ba/main.php?id_struct=82&lang=4 (accessed 8 Aug. 2008).

Declaration Concerning the Intentional Destruction of Cultural Heritage (2003) UNESCO Doc. 32C/25, 17 July 2003 at Art. s 3 and 4.

Declaration on the Responsibilities of the Present Generations Towards Future Generations (1997)UNESCO Doc. 29C/Res. 44, 12 Nov. 1997, at Art. 4.

Department of Interior, Regulations Implementing NAGPRA, 60 *Federal Register* 62134, 62143.

Egyptian Law on the Protection of Antiquities No. 117 (1983). Online. Available: http://www.unesco.org/culture/natlaws/index (accessed 21 Nov. 2008).

Fourth Geneva Convention on 8 Dec. 1949. Online. Available: http://www.icrc.org/ihl.nsf/WebSign?ReadForm&id=375&ps=P (last accessed 8 Aug. 2008).

Fundamental Agreement between the Holy See and the State of Israel, 30 Dec. 1993, 33 *ILM* 153 (1994).General Assembly Res. 55/254 (2001) on the Protection of Holy Sites A/RES/55/254.

General Assembly Res. 58/128 (2004) on Promotion of Religious and Cultural Understanding, Harmony and Cooperation A/RES/58/128.

General Assembly Res. (1998): 53/165, 1999: 54/185 and 2001: 55/119 concerning the destruction of Bamiyan Buddhas in Afghanistan.

General Assembly Third Committee, 15th Sess., mtgs. 10212–1027 (1960).

General Comment No. 23 of the Committee to Eliminate Racial Discrimination 51st. sess., 18 Aug. 1997.

General Framework Agreement for Peace in Bosnia and Herzegovina of 1995, 14 Dec. 1995. Online. Available: http://www.ohr.int/dpa/default.asp?content_id=380 (last accessed 8 Aug. 2008).

Government of Palestine, Department of Statistics, *Village Statistics, 1945*, Jerusalem, n. d. (1946).

Hague Convention with Respect to the Laws and Customs of War on Land (1907). Online. Available: http://www.icrc.org/ihl.nsf/FULL/195?OpenDocument (last accessed 8 Aug. 2008).

Hague Convention for the Protection of Cultural Property in the Event of Armed Conflict (1954), *UNTS* 215 (24 May 1954).

Hashemite Jordan Kingdom-Israel General Armistice Agreement, 3 Mar. 1949, 42 *UNTS* 304 (1949). *Holy Places – Common Heritage of Mankind*, 27 Sept. 2003, Foundation for the Culture of Peace Madrid, Spain, at Annex III para. 1–3 (on file with the authors).

Human Rights Committee General Comment No. 22CCPR/C/21/Rev. 1/Add. 4, 30 July 1993.

International Covenant on Civil and Political Rights Art. 18, 999 *UNTS* 171, 16 Dec. 1966.International Covenant on Civil and Political Rights of 1966, adopted by General Assembly Resolution 2200 A (XXI) 16 Dec. 1966.

Intergovernmental Committee for the Protection of the World Cultural and Natural Heritage Operational Guidelines for the Implementation of the World Heritage Convention WHC. 05/2, UNESCO, 2 Feb. 2005.

Israel–Jordan Peace Treaty. (26 Oct. 1994), Art. 9. 34 *ILM* 43–66 (1995). Online. Available: http://www.mfa.gov.il/mfa/

Israeli–Palestinian Interim Agreement on the West Bank and the Gaza Strip, 1995. Signed 28 Sept. 1995. Excerpted in 36 *ILM* (1997), pp. 551–647. Also Online. Available: http://www.mfa.gov.il/mfa/home.asp (accessed 10 Aug. 2008).

Krishnaswami, A. (1960) *Study of Discrimination in the Matter of Religious Rights and Practices* E/CN. 4/Sub. 2/ 200/Rev. 1.

Latin Patriarchate Easter Message 4 April 1999. Online. Available: http://www.al-bushra.org/latpatra/easter1999.htm (accessed 1 Feb. 2009).

Military Directive No. 327 On the Matter of Protecting Holy Places, 12 July 1969. NAGPRA, 25 USC §§ 3001–13 (2000).

Nazareth Today, Souvenir of the new Basilica of the Annunciation recently open for worship, [author not indicated] Jerusalem, Franciscan Printing Press, n. d.

New Mexico Attorney General Op. No. 87–31, available at 1987 WL 27033087, 16 USC § 41 0rr-7 (2000).

New Zealand Historic Places Act 1993. Online. Available: http://www.legislation.govt.nz/act/public/1993/0038/latest/DLM300511.html (accessed 20 Jan. 2009).

Niec, H. *Cultural Rights: At the End of the World Decade for Cultural Development in Intergovernmental Conference on Cultural Policies for Development*, UNESCO 1998, CLT-98/Conf. 210/Ref. 2.

Palestine Facts, *What Happened at Joseph's Tomb in October 2000?* Online. Available: http://www.palestinefacts.org/pf_1991to_now_alaqsa_josephstomb. php (accessed 28 Aug. 2008).

Palestine (Holy Places) Order in Council, 25 July 1924, repr. in Enrico Molinaro, *Negotiating Jerusalem*, Jerusalem, PASSIA Pub., 2002, at annex 2.

Peace between the State of Israel and the Hashemite Kingdom of Jordan (26 Oct. 1994). Online. Available: http://www.mfa.gov.il/MFA/Peace+Process/Guide+to+the+Peace+Process/Israel-Jordan+Peace+Treaty.htm (last accessed 8 Aug. 2008).

Philippine Constitution (1987) Art. XIV, sec. 16. Online. Available: http://www.chanrobles.com/philsupremelaw1.htm (accessed 20 Aug. 2008).

Proposed Legal System for the Holy Places – Common Heritage of Mankind (27 Sept. 2003) Foundation for the Culture of Peace Madrid, Sapin (on file with Leonard Hammer).

Protection of Holy Places Law 1967, trans. in Ruth Lapidoth and Moshe Hirsch, *The Jerusalem Question and Its Resolution: Selected Documents*, The Hague: Kluwer, 1994, p. 169.

Protocol Concerning the Redeployment in Hebron and Note for the Record (17 Jan. 1997) *ILM* 1997, vol. 36, p. 650.

Protocol I to the Hague Convention for the Protection of Cultural Property in the Event of Armed Conflict (1954), 249 *U.N.T.S.* 358.

Protocol II to the Hague Convention for the Protection of Cultural Property in the Event of Armed Conflict (1999), 38 *I.L.M.* 769.

Protocols of Meetings of the Knesset (January 2002). Online. Available: www.cbs.gov.il/publications/local_authorities 2005/pdf/207_7300. pdf (accessed 15 Dec. 2008).

Recommendation concerning the Safeguarding and Contemporary Role of Historic Areas (1976) UNESCO Doc. 19C/Annex I, Records of the General Conference, 19th Session Nairobi, 26 Oct. to 30 Nov. 1976, p. 20, 26 Nov. 1976, ISBN 92-3-101496-X. Online. Available: http://unesdoc.unesco.org/images/0011/001140/114038e.pdf#page=136 (accessed 28 Aug. 2008). Also in UNESCO, *Conventions & Recommendations of UNESCO Concerning the Protection of the Cultural Heritage*, Geneva: UNESCO, 1985, p. 191.

Recommendation on Participation of People At Large in Cultural Life and Their Contribution to It (1976) UNESCO Doc. 19C/Annex I Records of the General Conference, 19th Sess., Nairobi, 26 Oct. to 30 Nov. 1976, p. 29, 26 Nov. 1976, ISBN 92-3-101496-X. Online. Available: http://unesdoc.unesco.org/images/0011/001140/114038e. pdf#page = 136 (accessed 28 Aug. 2008).

Regulations for the Execution of the Convention for the Protection of Cultural Property in the Event of Armed Conflict, Art. s 2 and 4 Online. Available http://www.icomos.org/hague/hague.regulations.html (accessed 8 Aug. 2008).

Report of the Commission of Inquiry of the Massacre in the Cave of the Patriarchs (1994) Jerusalem: Gov't Press.

Report by His Britannic Majesty's Government on the Palestine Administration, 31 Dec. 1923, Online. Available: http://domino.un.org/unispal. nsf/d80185e9f0c69a7b852 56cbf005afeac/cc87d3bf6e0759f3052565e800573851!OpenDocument (accessed 4 Sept. 2008).

Report of the International Commission on the Western Wall, The Development of the Dispute (1931) Investigations and Testimonies in Jerusalem. The Jewish Memorandum. The Ruling. The King's Statement. With Pictures, London: H.M.S.O.

Report by Special Rapporteur on Freedom of Religion or Belief, E/CN. 4/2005/61.

Regulation of Ownership and Investment in Real Estate by Non-Saudis, Art. 5, Royal Decree No. M/15, 17/4/1421H, 19 July 2000.

Report of the Special Rapporteur on the Situation of Human Rights and Fundamental Freedoms of Indigenous Peoples, E/CN. 4/2003/90.

Rome Statute of the International Criminal Court (1998). Adopted and opened for signature on 17 July 1998, by the United Nations Diplomatic Conference of Plenipotentiaries on the Establishment of an International Criminal Court, A/CONF. 183/9 of 18 July 1998, 2187 *UNTS* 3, EIF: 1 July 2002.

Saudi Arabian General Investment Authority, Real Estate Law (2004). Online. Available: www.sagia.gov.sa/innerpage.asp?COntentID=89&Lang = en

State of Israel (1964) Jerusalem: Central Bureau of Statistics, Census of Population and Housing, 1961, Publication 17: Muslims, Christians and Druze in Israel.

State of Israel (1983) Jerusalem: Central Bureau of Statistics, Census of Population and Housing, 1983.

State of Israel (1999) Jerusalem: Central Bureau of Statistics, Census of Population and Housing, 995, No. 7, vol. 1.Treaty of Berlin, Art. 62, 83 Parl. Papers 13 July 1878

Treaty of Sèvres, Art. 13, 1920 *UKTS.* No. 11 (Cmd. 961), *American Journal of International Law,* vol. 15, pp. 179–295.

Treaty on the Protection of Artistic and Scientific Institutions and Historic Monuments (Roerich Pact) Washington, 15 April 1935. Available: http://www.icrc.org/ihl. nsf/FULL/325?OpenDocument (accessed 8 Aug. 2008).

Treaty with Turkey and other Instruments Signed at Lausanne, Art. 16, 24 July 1923, 28 *UNTS* 12, in *American Journal of International Law,* vol. 18 Supp., pp. 1–115.

UN Declaration on the Elimination of All Forms of Intolerance and of Discrimination Based on Religion or Belief, see, 35 *Ybk. United Nations,* 25 Nov. 1981, New York: UN, 1985, pp. 879–83.

UNESCO (1968) General Conference 15th sess., Res. 3. 343.

UNESCO (1972) Res. 3. 422 of 17/10–21/11,1972, 17th sess., at 61.

UNESCO (1976) Doc. 19C/Annex I, Records of the General Conference, 19th sess., Nairobi, 26 Oct. to 30 Nov. 1976, p. 20, 26 Nov. 1976, ISBN 92-3-101496-X,Online. Available: http://unesdoc.unesco.org/images/0011/001140/114038e.pdf#page=136 (accessed 8 Aug. 2008).

UNESCO Convention on the Protection of World Cultural and Natural Heritage,Doc. No. 17 C/106, 15 Nov. 1972, cited in 11 *ILM* (1973), p. 1358).

UNESCO World Heritage Convention. Online. Available: http://whc.unesco.org/en/ conventiontext/ (accessed 14 Aug. 2008).

United States Dept. of War (1902) *The War of the Rebellion: A Compilation of the Official Records of the Union and Confederate Armies* (ser. III) 148, 151–53.

United States Institute for Peace, *First Declaration of Alexandria of the Religious Leaders of the Holy Land* (Jan. 2002), Online. Available HTTP:http://www.usip.org/ religionpeace/alexandria_declaration. html (accessed 26 Aug. 2008).

Universal Declaration on Cultural Diversity (2001) UNESCO Doc. 31C/Res. 25, 2 Nov. 2001.

Universal Declaration of Human Rights Art. 18, UNGA Res. 217 (III 1948). Online. Available http://www.un.org/Overview/rights.html (accessed 12 Aug. 2008).

World Bank Operational Policy 4. 10, *Indigenous Peoples,* July 2005. Online. Available http://wbln0018.worldbank.org/Institutional/Manuals/OpManual. nsf/0/0F7D6F3F 04DD70398525672C007D08ED?OpenDocument (accessed 8 Aug. 2008).

World Commission on Culture and Development, *Our Cultural Diversity – Report of the World Commission on Culture and Development 1995.*

World Heritage Convention 1972. Online. Available: http://whc.unesco.org/pg.cfm? cid=246 (accessed 28 Aug. 2008).

Cases

Attorney General of the Government of Israel v. Adolf Eichmann, (1961) Dist. Ct. Jerusalem, 36 *I.L.R.* 5 (reprinted in relevant part in *American Journal of International Law,* 1962, vol. 56), *aff'd,* 36 *I.L.R.* 277 (1962): Court Documents – Indictment (21 Feb. 1961).

Bosnia and Herzegovnia v. Serbia and Montenegro: Application of the Convention on the Prevention and Punishment of the Crime of Genocide (26 Feb. 2007). Online. Available: http://www.icj-cij.org/docket/index. php?p1 = 3&p2 = 3&k = f4&case = 91&code = bhy&p3 = 4.

Cyprus v. Turkey (Merits) (10 May 2001) Appl. 2578/94, *ECtHR Reports* 2001-IV 284.

549/1993 *Hopu and Bessert v. France* (1997) UN Human Rights Committee, CCPR/C/60/D/549/1993/Rev. 1.511/1992
Lansmann v. Finland (1994) UN Human Rights Committee, CCPR/C52/D/511/1992.
Prosecutor v. Blaskic (29 July 2004) ICTY 11, and Appeal, http://www.un.org/icty/blaskic/appeal/judgement/index.htm.
Prosecutor v. Kordic and Cerkez (2001) ICTY Trial Chamber III, Judgement of 26 Feb. 2001, at para. 809. Online. Available: http://www.un.org/icty/kordic/trialc/judgement/index htm.
Prosecutor v Krstic (2001) ICTY 8 (2 Aug. 2001). Online. Available http://www.un.org/icty/krstic/TrialC1/judgement/index.htm (decision upheld in *Prosecutor v. Krstic* [2004] ICTY 7 (19 Apr. 2004). Online. Available: http://www.un.org/icty/krstic/Appeal/judgement/index.htm.
Prosecutor v. Miodrag Jokic, Case No. IT-01-42/1-A (30 Aug 2005) Online. Available: http://www.un.org/icty/jokic/appeal/judgement/index.htm (accessed August 2008).
Prosecutor v. Milosevic [2004] ICTY 8 (16 June 2004). Online. Available: http://www.un.org/icty/milosevic/trialc/judgement/index.htm.
United States v. Goering (1946) *International Military Tribunal*, vol. 1, p. 293.
United States v. Schultz, 178 F. Supp. 2d 445, 446 (2002) aff'd 333 F.3d 393 (2d Cir. 2003).
Wana the Bear v. Com. Constr., Inc., (1982) 180 *Cal. Rptr.* 423, 426, n. 7 (Cal. Ct. App).

Hebrew bibliography

Books and articles

Agassi, J. (1993) *Between Faith and Nationality: towards an Israeli National Identity*, Tel Aviv: Papyrus.
Asaf, S. "Jerusalem," (1928) *Compilation of the Hebraic Society of the Exploration of Eretz Israel and its Antiquities in Memory of Luntz*, Jerusalem:The Hebraic Society of the Exploration of Eretz Israel and its Antiquities.
——(1948) *Old Prayers at Kever Shmuel Ha-Navi*, Jerusalem: n.p.
Bar, D. (2007) *Sanctifying a Land: The Jewish Holy Places in the State of Israel: 1948–1968*, Jerusalem: Yad Ben Zvi and Ben-Gurion Institute in the Negev, pp. 30–35.
Barka'i, G. and Sheller, E. (eds.) (2000) "Druz Holy Places on Mt. Carmel," *Ariel, Ktav 'Et le-Yedi'at Eretz Yisra'el*, vol. 142, p. 45.
Barne'a, N. [2002] "Who Rang the Bells," *Ha-Ayin ha-Shvi'it*, 2 May.
Ben-Dov, J. (2006) *Nebi Samuel*. Tel-Aviv: Hakibutz Hameuchad.
Ben Zvi, Y. (1953) "A Jewish Settlement Near the Tomb of Shmuel ha-Navi," *Yediot be-Haqirat Eretz Israel ve-'Atiqoteyha*, vol. 2, p. 254.
Berkovitz, S. (1997) *The Legal Status of the Holy Places in Jerusalem*, Jerusalem: Institute of Israel Studies.
——(2000) *The Battle for the Holy Places: The Struggle over Jerusalem and the Holy Sites in Israel, Judea, Samaria and the Gaza District*, Or Yehuda, Israel: Hed Arzi.
Bialer, U. (2006) *Cross on the Star of David, the Christian World in Israel's Foreign Policy 1948–1967, Jerusalem: Yad Ben Zvi.
Bilu, Y. (1993) "Without Bounds. The Life and Death of Rabbi Ya'acov Wazana," Jerusalem: Magnes Press.
Canaan, T. (1980) *Mohammedan Saints and Sanctuaries in Palestine*, Jerusalem: Ariel.

Bibliography 291

Cohen, A. (1973) "Damascus and Jerusalem," *Sfunot*, vol. 17, p. 98.

Cohen, A., Simon-Pikali, E., and Salama, O. (1996) *Jews in The Muslim Religious Court, Society, Economy and Communal Organization in the Eighteenth Century, Documents from Ottoman Jerusalem*, Jerusalem: Yad Ben-Zvi.

Halevi, M. (Dec. 2007) "Religion, Symbolism and Politics: The Planning and Building of the Modern Church of the Annunciation in Nazareth," *Cathedra*, no. 126, Jerusalem: Yad Ben-Zvi Press, pp. 83–102.

Jabarin, Y. (Dec. 2005–Jan. 2006) "The Right for the Town: The Case of the Shihab al-Din Crisis in Nazareth," *Mikan*, no. 1 pp. 12–19.

Luz, N. (2004) *Al-Haram Al-Sharif in the Arab Palestinian Public Discourse in Israel: Identity, Collective Memory and Social Construction*, Jerusalem: The Floresheim Institute for Policy Studies.

Da'eem, R. (2005) "Local Sacred Legends as told by Christians and Muslims about the Cave and Shrine of the Prophet Elijah," unpublished M.A. thesis, University of Haifa.

Dayan, M. (1976) *Avnei Derech: Autobiography*, Jerusalem: Idanim.

Gazit, S. (1985) *The Carrot and the Stick*, Tel-Aviv: Zmora, Bitan.

Gliss, Y. (1968) *Customs of the Land of Israel*, Jerusalem: Mossad Harav Kook.

Goitein, S. D. and Ben-Shemesh, A. (1957) *Muslim Law in the State of Israel*, Jerusalem: Gvilim.

Golan. A. (2001) "From Arab Towns to Israeli Cities: Lod and Ramle During and After the War of Independence," *Yahadut Zmanenu*, vol. 14, pp. 263–89.

——(2001) *Wartime Spatial Changes: Former Arab Territories within the State of Israel, 1948–50*, Beer Sheva: Ben-Gurion University of the Negev Press.

Goren, Rabbi S. (5728–1968) "The Holy Places in Light of Halakha," *Machanayim*, vol. 116, p. 7.

Hakohen, A. (5764–2004) "'How Awesome is the Place': Holy Sites: Court, Law and Sanctity," *Sha'arei Mishpat*, vol. 3, pp 73–471.

Hildesheimer, M. (5724–1964) "A Portrait of Rabbi Azriel Hildesheimer," *Sinai*, vol. 54, p. 67.

Kahana, S. Z. (1981) "Stories of Pilgrimage to the Tombs of the Righteous and to the Holy Sites of the Land of Israel," *Yeda-Am*, vol. 54, pp. 44–45.

Kedar, B. Z. (1999) "Wars as Historical Turning Points," in A. Susser (ed.) *Six Days – Thirty Years: A New Look at the Six-Day War,* Tel Aviv: Am Oved, pp. 17–28.

Khamaisi, R. (2003) *The Nazareth Area: A Metropolitan Outline for Governance Planning and Development*, Jerusalem: Floersheimer Institute For Policy Studies.

Kitzis, G. (1980) "28 Iyyar: Pilgrimage to the Tomb of Samuel the Prophet," *Kardom* vol. 10–11, pp. 62–64.

Lazar, H. (1961) *The Conquest of Jaffa*, Tel Aviv: Shelah.

Lichtenstein, Y. (5760–2000) "Visiting and Praying at Gravesites – Supplicating the Dead?" *Techumin*, vol. 20, p. 188.

Limor, O. (2006) "Saint Pelagia's Tomb: Sin, Penitence and Salvation on the Mount of Olives," *Cathedra*, vol. 118, pp. 13–40.

Luncz, A. M. (1891) *Guide to Eretz Israel and Syria*, Jerusalem: published by the author.

Y. Magen and M. Dadon (2003) "Nebi Samwil (Montjoie)," in G. C. Bottini, L. Di Segni, and L. D. Chrupcala (eds), *One Land – Many Cultures: Archaeological Studies In Honour Of Stanislao Loffreda Ofm*, Studium Biblicum Franciscanum, Collectio Maior, 41, Jerusalem: Franciscan Printing Press, pp. 123–138.

Mayer, T. (1988) *The Awakening of the Muslims in Israel*, Giv'at Haviva: Institute for Arab Studies.

Meni, M. (1953) "The Harvest Festival in Hebron," in Y.-T. Lewinsky (ed.), *The Book of Festivals: The Jewish Festivals, their Value, Customs and Influence on Jewish Life and Literature from Ancient Times to the Present*, Tel Aviv: Dvir, pp. 198–200.

——(1965) *To Know the Land*, Ein-Charod, Hakibutz Hameuchad.

Michelson, M., Milner, M., and Salomon,Y. (1996) *The Jewish Holy Places in the Land of Israel*, Tel-Aviv, Misrad Ha-Bitachon (Defense Ministry).

Morris, B. (1997) *The Birth of the Palestinian Refugee Problem, 1947–1949*, Tel-Aviv: Am Oved.

Ramon, A. (2001) "Beyond the Kotel: The Relation of the State of Israel and the Jewish Public to the Temple Mount (1967–99)" in Y. Reiter, *Sovereignty of God and Man: Sanctity and Political Centrality on the Temple Mount*, Jerusalem: The Jerusalem Institute for Israel Studies, pp. 113–42.

——(ed.) (2003) *The Jerusalem Lexicon*, Jerusalem: The Jerusalem Institute for Israel Studies and the Jerusalem Foundation.

Reiner, E. (1988) *Pilgrims and Pilgrimage 1099–1517*, PhD dissertation, Hebrew University of Jerusalem.

——(2001) "Destruction, Temple and Holy Place: on Issues of Time and Place during the Middle Ages," *Kathedra*, vol. 97, pp. 47–64.

Reiter, Y. (ed.) (2001) *Sovereignty of God and Man: Sanctity and Political Centrality on the Temple Mount*, Jerusalem: Jerusalem Institute for Israel Studies

——(2005) *From Jerusalem to Mecca and Back, The Islamic Consolidation of Jerusalem*, Jerusalem: The Jerusalem Institute for Israel Studies.

Rekhess, E. (ed.) (1998) *The Arabs in Israel: Dilemmas of Identites*, Tel-Aviv: Dayan Center for Strategic Studies Tel Aviv University, pp. 63–72.

Rekhess, E. (1986) "Islamic *Waqf* in Acre," unpublished M.A. thesis, The Hebrew University of Jerusalem.

——(1989) "An Assessment of the Reform in the Muslim *Waqf* Institution in Israel – The *Waqf* in Acre," *HaMizrah HeHadash*, vol. 32, pp. 21–45.

——(1991) *Islamic Awqaf in Jerusalem, 1948–90*, Jerusalem: The Jerusalem Institute for Israel Studies.

Rekhess, E. (ed.) (1998) *The Arabs in Israel: Dilemmas of Identites*, Tel-Aviv: Dayan Center for Strategic Studies Tel Aviv University, pp. 63–72.

——(2001). *Sovereignty of God and Man: Sanctity and Political Centrality on the Temple Mount*. Jerusalem: The Jerusalem Institute for Israel Studies.

Rosman, Y. (1984) *Leadership in the al-Khalwatiyya Sufi Organization*, M.A. thesis, Tel-Aviv University.

Rubin, U. (2000) "The Direction of Prayer in Islam: On the History of a Conflict Between Rituals," *Historia*, vol. 6, pp. 5–29.

——(2008) *Between Arabia and the Holy Land: A Mecca-Jerusalem Axis of Sanctity*, Jerusalem: Jerusalem Studies in Arabic and Islam (volume 34, forthcoming).

Seligman, J. (2007) "Solomon's Stables, "The Temple Mount, Jerusalem: The Events Concerning the Destruction of Antiquities, 1999 to 2001," *'Atiqot*, vol. 56, pp. 33–54.

Shalev-Khalifa, N. (1998) "In Search of the Temple Treasure – The Story of the Parker Expedition in the City of David, 1909–11," *Qadmoniot*, vol. 116, pp. 126–35.

Sher, G. (2001) *Just Beyond Reach: The Israeli-Palestinian Peace Negotiations, 1999–2001*, Tel Aviv: Miskal-Yediot Acharonot Books and Chemed Books.

Shiler, E. (1979) *The Cave of the Patriarchs*, Jerusalem: Ariel.

Shlush, A. (1941) *My Life Story 1870–1930*, Tel Aviv: Mizrachi.
Shohat, A. (1965) "History of the Synagogue on the Tomb of Shmuel ha-Navi," *Bulletin of the Israel Exploration Society*, Reader B, Jerusalem: The Israel Exploration Society, pp. 141–45 (originally vol. 6, p. 81–86).
Shragai, N. (1995). *The Temple Mount Conflict*, Jerusalem: Keter.
——(2005) *Al Em HaDerech – The Story of Kever Rachel*, Jerusalem, Sa'arim LeHeker Yerushalayim.
Sindawi, K. (2000). *The Maqatil in Shi'ite Literature*, unpublished Ph.D. thesis, Ramat Gan: Bar Ilan University.
Sivan, E. (1988) *Arab Political Myths*, Tel Aviv: Am Oved.
Travels of Binyamin Metudela (1952) ed. A. Adler, London.
Tsimhoni, D. (1978) "The Arab Christians and the Palestinian Arab National Movement During the Formative Stage," in G. Ben-Dor (ed.) *The Palestinians and the Middle East Conflict*, Ramat Gan: Turtledove Publishing, pp. 73–98.
——(1989) "The Political Configuration of the Christians in the State of Israel," *Ha-Mizrah He-Hadash*, vol. 32, pp. 139–64.
Vashitz, Y. (1947) *The Arabs in Palestine*. Israel: Merhavia.
Vilnay, Z. (1926) "Tombs of Saints in the Arab Tradition," *Eretz Yisrael Yearbook*, pp. 115–32.
——(1963) *Holy Gravestones in Eretz Israel*, Jerusalem: Mosad ha-Rav Kook.
——(1977) *Ariel, Encyclopedia of the Knowledge of Eretz Yisrael*, Tel Aviv: Yediot Acharonot.
Wachtfogel, Rabbi Y. Y. (1968), "The Synagogue that was Destroyed," *Noam*, vol. 11, pp. 15–20.
Ya'ari, A. (ed.) (1971) "Letters from Eretz Israel, written by Jews settled there to their Brethren in the Diaspora, from the Days of the Babylonian Exile to the Return of Zion in our own Days), Ramat Gan: Masada.
Yahav, D. (2004) Jaffa, Bride of the Sea, Tel Aviv: Tammuz.
Yiftachel, O. and Kedar, A. (2000) "On Power and Land: Israel's Land Regime," *Teoria VeBikoret*, vol. 16, pp. 67–100.

Documents

Abandoned Property Law—1950 *Sefer Chukim* 14/3/50 at 86.
Israel Antiquities Law Art. 29(iii), 885 *Sefer Chukim* 76, 1978.
Regulations on the Protection of Sacred Spaces for the Jewish People – 1981 *Kovetz Takanot* 4252, at 1212.
Regulations on the Protection of Sacred Spaces for the Jewish People (Amendment), 1989, *Kovetz Takanot* 5237 at 190.
Regulations-1981 *Kovetz Takanot* 4252 at 1212.

Cases in Hebrew

882/94 *Alter et al. v. Government et al.* (not published).
623/00 *Ishak Halil Jabana et al. v. the National Center for the Development of the Holy Sites et al.* (unpublished).
2085/97 *Sheikh Rahid Salah v. Israel Development Authority* (not published).
Coptic Patriarchate v. Government of Israel, 33(1) *Piskei Din* 225 (1979).
Coptic Patriarchate v. Minister of Police, 25(1) *Piskei Din* 226 (1971).

4128/00 *Director General of the Prime Minister's Office, et al. v. Anat Hoffman, et al, Piskei Din* 57(3) 289.

257/89 *Hoffman et al. v. Government of Israel et al.*, 48(2) *Piskei Din* 265.

3358/95 *Hoffman et al. v. Government of Israel et al.*, 54(2) *Piskei Din* 345 (2000).

4128/00 *Hoffman et al. v. Government of Israel et al.*, decided April 4, 2003, located at: http://elyon1.court.gov.il/files/00/280/041/G13/00041280.g13.pdf (last visited, August, 2008)

Kawasma v. Minister of Defense, 35(1) *Piskei Din* 617 (1981).

4238/00 *Matuali Abu Jabana, et al. v. the Minister of Religious Affairs, et al., Takdin* 2003 (3) at 1350.

7957/05 *Ma'arava v. Prime Minister of Israel*, decided 15 Sept. 2005 (not published).

28/1940 *Mudir el Awkaf v. Keren Kayemet of Israel and Others*, 7 *PLR* 242 (1940).

222/68 (1970) *Nationalist Circles, et al. v. the Minister of Police, Piskei Din* 24(2) 141.

3338/99 (2000) *Pakovich v. State of Israel*, 54 (3) *Piskei Din* 667.

267/88 *Reshet Kollelei haIdra v. the Local Administrative Court, Piskei Din* 43(3) 728.

Shahin et al. v. Commander of IDF Forces in the Area of Judea and Samaria, 41(1) *Piskei Din* 197 (1987).

8666/99 *Temple Mount Faithful v. A. Rubinstein et al.* (decided 11/1/2000). Online. Available: http://elyon1.court.gov.il/files/99/660/086/I04/99086660.i04.pdf (accessed, 3 Aug. 2008)

Arabic bibliography

'Abbasi, M. (1996) *Qura Qada Safad fi 'Ahd al-Intidab*, Nazareth: al-Hakim lil-Tiba'ah.

Abu Zahra, M. (1971) *Muhadarat fi al-Waqf*, 2nd edn, Cairo: Dar al-Fikr al-'Arabi.

Al-Adawi, M. (1956) *Kitab al-Ziyarat Bi-Dimashq*, ed. Salah al-Din al-Munjid, Damascus: Al-Majma' al-'Ilmi al-'Arabi.

Al-'Asali, K. J. (1990) *Mawsim al-Nabi Musa fi Filastin, Ta'rikh al-Mawsim wal-Maqam*, Amman: Jordanian University.

Al-'Awra, I. (1931) *Ta'rikh Wilayat Sulayman Basha al-'Adil*, Sidon: n. p.

Al-Isfahani, A. (1965) *Maqatil al-Talibiyyin*, ed. Kazim al-Muzaffar, 2nd edn, Najaf: Al-Haydariyya.

Arraf, Sh. (1993) *Tabaqat al-Anbiyya' wal-Awliyya' al-Salihin fil-Ard al-Muqadassa*, 2 vols., Tarshiha: Author's Edition and Ikhwan Makhul.

Ayoub, M. (1985) "Arbain" *Encyclopaedia Iranica*, II, p. 275, ed. Ehsan Yarshater, London: Boston and Henely.

Badawi, A. (1960) *Diwan al-Wazir al-Misri Talai Ibn Ruzzayk*, Cairo: Maktabat Nahdat Misr and al-Risala.

Al-Bawwab, A. H. (2003) *Mawsu'at Yafa al-Jamila*, Beirut: al-Mu'asasa al-'Arabiyya lil-Dirasat wal-Nashr.

Al-Dabbagh, M. M. (1988) *Biladuna Filastin*, 4th edn, Beirut: Dar al-Tali'a.

De-Goeije, M. J. (1906) *Bibliotheca Geographorum Arabicorum*, Leiden: E. J. Brill.

Al-Dimashqi, M. (n. d.) *Kitab Nukhbat al-Dahr fi 'Aja'ib al-Barr wal-Bahr*, Baghdad: Maktabat al-Muthanna.

Fahoum Ghanim, S. (2003) *Challenges and Changes in the History of Nazareth, the Muslim–Christian Relationships*, Nazareth: author's publication.

Farah, F. (2003) *The Living Stones, the Christian Arabs in the Holy Land*, Nazareth: Venus Press.

Hamuda, S. (1985) *Masjid Hassan Bey*, Bayt Safafa: Hassan Abu Daw.
Al-Harawi, A. (1953) *Al-Isharat Ila Ma'rifat al-Ziyarat*. Damascus: The French Institute for Arabic Studies.
Al-Hudayb, F. (1995) *Surat Yazid Ibn Mu'awiya fi al-Riwayat al-Adabiyya*, Riyad: Dar Aja.
Ibn 'Abd al-Hadi, Y. (1943) *Thimar al-Maqasid fi Dhikr al-Masajid*, Beirut: French Institute.
Ibn 'Abd al-Zahir, M. (1996) *Al-Rawda al-Bahiyya al-Zahira fi Khutat al-Muaziyya al-Qahira*, ed. Dr. Ayman Fu'ad al-Sayyid, Cairo: Dar al-'Arabiyya lil-Kitab.
Ibn al-Jawzi, S. (1964) *Tazkirat al-Khawas*, ed. al-Sayyid Muhammad Sadiq, Najaf: al-Haydariyya.
——(1995) *Al-Muntazam fi Ta'rikh al-Muluk wal-Umam*, Beirut: Dar al-Fikr.
Ibn Kathir I. (n. d.) *Al-Bidaya wal-Nihaya*, ed. Abu Milhim et al., Beirut: Dar al-Kutub al-'Ilmiyya.
Ibn Manzur, J. (1990) *Lisan al-'Arab*, Beirut: Dar al-Fikr and Dar Sadr.
Abu Mikhnaf, L. (1971) *Maqtal al-Husayn 'Alayhi al-Salam*, Beirut: Dar 'Umar Abu al-Nasr.
Ibn Nama, N. (1899) *Muthir al-Ahzan wa-Munir Subul al-Ashjan*, Tehran: Dar al-Kutub al-Islamiyya.
Ibn Shahrashub, M. (1991) *Manaqib Ali b. Abi Talib*, Beirut: Dar al-Andalus.
Ibn Shihna, M. (1990) *Ta'rikh Halab*, Tokyo: Institute for the Study of Language and Cultures of Asia and Africa – Tokyo University of Foreign Studies.
Ibn Tawus, A. (1951) *Al-Lahuf 'Ala Qatla al-Tufuf*, Najaf: al-Haydariyya.
Ibn Taymiyya, A. (903) *Minhaj al-Sunna al-Nabawiyya*, Cairo: al-Amiriyya and Bulaq.
——(1976) *Su'al fi Yazid*, ed. Salah al-Din al-Munjid, Beirut: Dar al-Kitab al-Jadid.
Ibn Tulun, M. (1986) *Qayd al-Sharid fi Akhbar Yazid*, ed. Muhammad Zinhum Azb, Cairo: Dar al-Sahwa.
Ibrahim, M. (1986) *Maraqid Al-Bayt bil-Qahira*, 4th edn. Cairo: al-'Ashira al-Muhamadiyya.
Ibrahim, Z. (2006) *Dawr al-Siyaha fi al-Tatawwur al-Ijtima'i*, Alexandria: al-Maktab al-Jami'i al-Hadith.
Idarat al-Awqaf wal-Shu'un al-Islamiyya – Qism Ihya' al-Turath al-Islami fi Bayt al-Maqdis (1985), *Al-Masjid al-Ibrahimi, Dirasa Watha'iqiyya Musawwara*, Jerusalem: Idarat al-Awqaf wal-muqaddasat al-Islamiya.
Al-Isfahani, A. (1965) *Maqatil al-Talibiyyin*, ed. Kazim al-Muzaffar, 2nd edn. Najaf: al-Haydariyya.
Jabarin, Y. (2006) "Al-Haqq wal-Madina: Azmat Shihab al-Din fi al-Nasira," *Makan*, vol. 1, pp. 7–20.
Khawarizim A. (1948) *Maqtal al-Husayn*, Najaf: al-Zahra.
Al-Khu'I, A. (2001) *Masir Ras al-Husayn wa-Mawdi' Dafnihi*, Karbala: Majallat Al-Nur.
Le Strange, G. (1896) *Description of Syria, Including* Palestine, London: Palestine Pilgrims' Text Society.
Mahir, S. (1969) *Mashhad al-Imam 'Ali fi al-Najaf wa-Ma Bihi min al-Hadaya wal-Tuhaf*, Cairo, Dar al-Ma'arif.
Mahran, M. (1990) *Al-Imam al-Husayn Ibn 'Ali*, Beirut: Dar al-Nahda al-'Arabiyya.
Al-Maqrizi, A. (1988). *Kitab al-Mawa'iz wal-I'tibar bi-Dhikr al-Khutat wal Athar al-Ma'ruf bil-Khutat al-Maqriziyya*. Beirut: Dar al-Kutub al-'Ilmiyya.

Al-Nimr, I. (1975) *Ta'rikh Jabal Nablus wal-Balqa'*, Nablus: Jam'iyyat 'Ummal al-Matabi'.

Qadri Pasha, M. (1902) *Qanun al-'Adl wa'l-Insaf lil-Qada' 'Ala Mushkilat al-Awqaf*, Cairo: n. p.

Al-Qurashi, I. (n. d.) *'Uyun al-Akhbar wa-Funun al-Athar*, ed. Mustafa Ghalib, Beirut: Dar al-Andalus.

Al-Shablanji, S. (1985) *Nur al-Absar fi Manaqib Al-Bayt al-Nabi al-Mukhtar*, Beirut: Dar al-'Ilmiyya.

Al-Shaybani, M. (1997) *Mawaqif al-Muarada fi Khilafat Yazid Ibn Mu'awiya*, Al-Madina al-Munawwara and Amman: Al-Maktaba al-Makiyya and Dar al-Bayariq.

Shubbar, J. (1969) *Adab al-Taff*, Beirut: Mu'assasat al-'Alami.

Al-Tabari, M. (1991) *Ta'rikh al-Umam wal-Muluk*, 3rd edn, Beirut: Dar al-Kutub al-'Ilmiyya.

Al-Tha'alibi, A. (n. d.) Qisas al-Anbiya' al-Musamma 'Ara'is al-Majalis, Beirut: al-Maktaba al-Thaqafiya.

Yaqut, Sh. (1979) *Mu'jam al-Buldan*, Beirut: Dar Ihya al-Turath.

Index

Abbas, Mahmoud, PLO Chairman 126, 243, 294
'Abd Al-Nabi Cemetery and *Maqam*, Jaffa 236
Abraham's Tent near Hebron 86
Absentees' property 82, 83, 87, 89, 106, 107, 112, 114, 119, 124, 244, 254
Abu Ahmad, Salman 202, 208, 216, 219, 222, 228, 229, 230
Abu Ahmad, Tawfiq 207
Grave of Bialik in Tel Aviv 84
Abu Bakr: Grave *see* Yochanan Hasandlar: Grave 69
Abu As'ad Al-Darir (Arabic: the blind): *Maqam* of 243
Abu Dis Archives 234, 243
Abuhatzera, Rabbi Yaacov *see* Baba Sali 233
Abu Hurayrah, Ali: Tomb in Yavne *see* Rabban Gamliel Tomb and Synagogue 80
Abu Nawwaf (Ahmad Salih Hamudah Zu'bi) 202, 205, 208
Acre (Arabic: 'Akka, Hebrew: 'Akko) *see* Old City of Acre 110, 124, 126
Adhan (Arabic: broadcast of Muslim call to prayer from a loudspeaker) 122, 162
Aggadah (Hebrew: legend) 96
Ahmed I, Ottoman Sultan 193
Al-Aqsa Intifada, or the Second Intifada 148, 153, 228, 238
Al-Aqsa Mosque 6, 17, 134, 180, 181, 182, 185, 187
Al-Asbahi, Khawli ibn Yazid 264, 268
Al-Ard Al-Muqaddasa (Arabic: Holy Land of Palestine) 177, 231
Al-Buraq Wall (Arabic for Western Wall), *see* Western Wall 134

Ali, Yusuf Hassan 90
Aliya le regel (Hebrew: pilgrimage) 231
Almazov, Muhammad, the grave of *see also* gravesite of Yose, Rabbi of Yokeret 69,
Arab Jews *see mizrahim* 234, 238, 244, 248
Arafat, Yasser, PLO Chairman 7, 8, 36, 212
Arens, Moshe, Israeli Defense Minister 217
Ha'Ari Hakadosh: Gravesite of Rabbi Isaac Luria in Safed 84
Ashura' Day (tenth day of Muharram) 264, 271, 283
Aviner, Gad 209
Avner Ben Ner and Mefiboshet: Tomb of 71
Avnery, Uri 224

Baba Sali: Gravesite in Netivot 25, 233, 243, 280
Balad Party, The Arab Democratic Alliance Party 219
Banat Yaqub (the Father of the Blue Stone): Tomb of 69
Baqa Al-Gharbiyya, village of 126
Bar Yochai, Rabbi Shimon: Tomb in Meron 31, 42, 69, 78, 94, 233
Barak, Ehud, Israel Prime Minister 209
Basilica of the Annunciation, Nazareth 192, 198, 201, 202, 203, 204, 213, 218, 219, 225, 227, 287.
Basula, Rabbi Moshe 167, 232
Battistelli, Giovanni, the Custos of the Holy Land 212
Battle of Karbala' 264, 271
Baybars, Mamluk Sultan Al-Malik Al-Zahir 165, 232

Bayt-Sahur *see* Bir Al-SayyidaBir Al-Sayyida, the "Well of our Lady" Bethlehem 240, 241
Beit Iksa (village near Jerusalem) 167
Beit knesset (Hebrew: synagogue) 95, 96, 99, 101, 102
Beit midrash (Hebrew: Torah study hall) 95, 96, 101
Ben Akashia Rabbi Chananya 78
Ben-Ami, Professor Shlomo, Internal Security Minister 209–13, 224, 229
Ben Chalafata, Rabbi Shimon 89
Ben-Gurion, David, Israeli Prime Minister 73, 74, 207
Benjamin: Grave of 79, 81, 82
Ben Menashe Sithon (the Ralbah), Rabbi Hayim 177
Ben Zakkai, Rabban Yochanan 69
Ben-Zvi, Yitzhak 86, 227, 291
Ben Uri, Meir 74, 86–91
Bethlehem 36, 37, 49, 71, 86, 134, 135, 140, 150, 159, 170, 198, 240, 241, 277
Bratslav Hassidim 169
Bulus Hanna, an administrator (*mutawalli*) of the Dir Al-Asad *Waqf* 108
Al-Buraq (Arabic) *see* The Western Wall 134
Bush, George W., American President 215
Bybars, Al-Malik Al-Zahir, Mamluk Sultan 232

Carmelites Cave of Elijah *see* Elijah's Cave 9, 42, 146, 149
Cave of the Annunciation in Nazareth 193
Cave of the Patriarchs (Hebrew: *Me'arat Hamachpelah*) *see* Jacob and Abraham Halls 7, 49, 67, 68, 69, 70, 71, 85, 158, 159, 160, 163, 165, 168, 174, 177, 288, 292
Chalafata, Rabbi Yose 89
Chananya village shrines 69, 78
Church of the Annunciation in Nazareth 139, 141, 193, 198, 219, 228, 291
Church of the Holy Sepulcher in Jerusalem 145, 146, 150, 154, 155
Cohanim (Hebrew: pl. of priest) 96, 97
Communist Party of Israel, Rakah, Hadash 196
Crusaders 4, 139, 159, 164, 192, 193, 202, 267
Custodian of Absentees' Property Law 1950; Amendment to Custodian of Absentees' Property Law 1965 104, 106, 112, 119, 124, 245
Cust, L.G.A. 18, 24, 41, 42, 86, 277

Dabbagh Mosque, Jaffa 236
Danin, Aharon of the Israel Lands Administration 256
Dayan, Moshe, Israeli Defense Minister 171, 177, 183
De Aveiro, Portuguese traveler 168
Dhi Al-Jawshan Al-Dababi, Shimr b. 264
Dhimmis (Arabic: status of Jews and Christians under Islam) 224
Al-Dimashqi (A Muslim Geographer) 233, 243, 294
Diodoros I, the Greek Orthodox Patriarch 212
Dir Al-Asad *Waqf* 108
Dome of the Rock 134, 183, 184, 185, 187, 189, 190, 282
Druze community in Israel *see* Nabi Shu'ayb 27, 242, 247

Edgar Construction 257
Ein Fara in Wadi Kelt 86
Ein Kerem Mosque 74
Elijah's Cave (Arabic: *Al-Khadr* or "the Green Prophet") 18, 68, 75, 76, 77, 84, 85, 86, 88, 89, 160, 161, 281
Eliyahu ha-Navi: Shrine of Prophet Elijah 236, 246
Eretz ha-Qodesh (Hebrew: Holy Land of Israel) 231
Eretz Israel ha-Shlema (Hebrew: Greater Israel) 239
Al-Fahum, Yusef Muhammad Ali, Mayor of Nazareth 195

Fahum Family *waqf*, Nazareth 193
Fahum, Atif 204, 228
Fahum-Ghanim, Siham 220
Fakhr Al-Din II, Druze Emir 193
Farah, Fuad 205, 223, 227, 228, 230
Franciscan Monastery, Nazareth 167, 195
Franciscan Custodian of the Holy Land 207
Franciscans 193, 198

Gad: Grave of 71, 79
Gamliel, Rabban: Tomb in Yavne; Rabban Gamliel Synagogue 80, 81, 84, 85

Index 299

Gaza Strip 18, 35, 42, 48, 49, 64, 184, 239, 283, 285, 287
Ge'ulat Israel Synagogue, Nes Ziona 237
Ghar Al-Anbiyya (Arabic: the Cave of the Prophets) 70
Glass, David, Director General of the Ministry of Religious Affairs 259, 263
Goldstein, Dr. Baruch: Massacre in the Abrahamic site of Hebron 37, 247
Al-Goma'a Mosque 130
Gush Emunim (Hebrew: Bloc of the Faithful) 239
Grippel, Yigal, Aviv-Jaffa deputy mayor 258
Grotto of Saint Paleagia 18, 283

Habbab, Sa'id 108
Hagai, Malachi and Zachariah: Tomb of Prophets (Arabic: *Ghar Al-Anbiyya*: the Cave of the Prophets) 70
Hagia Sophia in Istanbul 150, 151
HaGarsi, R. Yehoshua 96
Halakha (Hebrew: Jewish law in general) 94–98, 100, 102, 291
Halakhot (Hebrew: particular Jewish laws) 95, 96
Halhul 71
Hajj (Arabic: pilgrimage to Mecca) 4, 8, 18, 63, 105, 111
Hanina ben Hirkanus, Rabbi 232
Al-Haram Al-Khalili in Hebron (Arabic) *see* Cave of the Patriarchs 134
Al-Haram Al-Sharif in Jerusalem (Arabic) *see* Temple Mount 6, 7, 8, 134, 158, 159, 163, 178, 179, 181, 183, 185, 187, 188, 189, 190, 191, 206, 228, 291
Al-Harawi, 'Ali bin Abi Bakr 232, 243, 246, 267, 273, 295
Har HaBayyit see Temple Mount
Al-Hasan family, *waqf* administrators of Al-Khadir's shrine 237
Hassan Bey Al-Jabi 252
Hassan Bey Mosque in Tel Aviv 115, 143, 249, 253, 280
Hassan: Tomb of Sheikh *see* Havakkuk: Tomb of Prophet 69
Habakkuk: Tomb of Prophet; *also* Hassan: Tomb of Sheikh 69
Head of Husayn Ibn Ali, the Prophet Muhammad's grandson: legends 12, 264–73
Hebron, *see also* Al-Khalil 71, 86, 134

Henry IV, King of England 193
Heqdesh (Hebrew: Jewish religious endowment) 89, 90, 124
Herzl, Theodor: Grave in Jerusalem 84
Hezekia's Pool 86
High Court of Justice (Supreme Court of Israel) 92, 108, 124
High Islamic Sufi Council in Israel 77
Hijaz (location of the Muslim holy cities of Mecca and Medina, Saudi Arabia) 177, 232
Hilula (Hebrew: Jewish prayer festival at burial site of a saint or *tzadik*) 70, 169
Hilton Hotel Tel Aviv, *see* Hassan Bey Mosque in Tel Aviv 237, 263
Hirschberg, Dr. Haim Zeev 74, 75, 87, 89, 91, 280
Holy cities *see* Karbala, Mecca, Al-Madina Al-Munawwara 3, 15, 20, 133, 232, 284
Holy Family 76, 271
Holy Land of Palestine/Eretz Israel 160, 174
Holy places *see by name*
House of Simon the Tanner Church, Jaffa 236
Hudna (Arabic: truce) 174
Hulda the Prophetess: Tomb of 9, 70, 160
Hurvitz, Yigal. Israeli Minister of Finance 258
Husni Al-Qawasma *waqf* of the Khilwatiyya Sufi Order 126
Al-Husayni, Hajj Amin, Grand Mufti 105

Ibn Saud, Abdallah, Prince 212
Ibrahim Pasha 194
Ibrahimi Mosque in Hebron *see also* Cave of the Patriarchs 148, 177, 247
'Id Al-Shu'la (Arabic: feast of the burning light) 233
Imamiyya (Arabic: Shiite stream) 267
International Coalition for Nazareth 214, 215, 229
Isaac Hall *see* Cave of the Patriarchs, Hebron 171, 172
Islamic Movement in Israel 200, 227
Ismaili faction 267, 268
Israel Defense Forces IDF Civil Administration 158, 169, 170
Israel Lands Administration (Hebrew: *Minhal mekarke'ei yisrael*) 90, 122, 123, 202, 255, 256

300 Index

Israel National Archive 43, 106
Israeli, Professor Raphael 201, 209, 210
Istibdal (Arabic: the exchange of a *waqf* property for a substitute property that would become waqf) 117, 118, 120, 121
Istibdal bil-darahim (Arabic: an exchange of *waqf* properties for a sum of money which was used to acquire another property) 117, 118
Al-Ja'bari, Muhammad 'Ali Palestinian Mayor of Hebron 171, 175

Jabarin, Yusuf 221, 291, 295
Jacob and Abraham Halls in the Cave of the Patriarchs, Hebron 171
Jaffa 108
Jaffa Trust 255–58, 260
Al-Jami' Al-Ahmar Mosque in Safed 236
Jat, Arab village of 126
Jawliya Mosque 162, 166
Al-Jazzar, Ahmad governor (pasha) of the provinces of Sidon and Damascus 111
Al-Jazzar Mosque 104, 110, 115, 116, 126
Al-Jazzar's *waqf* 110, 111, 112, 113, 115
Jedda 133
Jeraysi, Ramiz, Deputy Mayor of Nazareth 197, 201, 203, 206, 211, 218, 219, 230
Jerusalem *see* Old City of Jerusalem 6, 18, 53, 136, 161, 191, 277
Jerusalem Institute for Israel Studies 16, 156, 173, 175, 189, 275, 279, 285, 292
Jesse's Tomb 71
Jewish National Fund JNF (Hebrew: *Keren Kayemeth LeIsrael*) 107
Jonathan son of Uziel Jonathan: Sepulcher of 232
Joseph/Yusef's Tomb near Nablus 1, 7, 15, 35, 36, 49, 85, 139, 156, 162, 238, 287
Judah (in Hebrew: Yehuda): Grave of 79, 81, 82, 83, 91
Judaization of Muslim Holy Places 72, 76, 77, 78
Ka'ba in Mecca (the most holy site for Muslims); the pilgrimage to the *Ka'ba* 4, 38, 165
Kabub, 'Abd Badawi 257, 262, 263
Kahana, Dr. S.Z., Director General of Israel's Ministry of Religious Affairs 68, 72–75, 77, 80, 84–93, 291

Kal'aji, Amram 209
Karbala, Holy City in Iraq 265, 267, 270
Katsav, Moshe, Israeli Minister of Tourism 208
Kefar 'Amuqa 232
Kever Shmuel HaNavi *see* Samuel the Prophet: Tomb of 158
Kfar Chananya 78, 89
Al-Khadr, Shrine of 236, 237
Al-Khalil (Arabic: city of Hebron) 134, 165, 239
Al-Khalili, Sheikh Muhammad, Mufti of Jerusalem 168
Khan Al-Basha 140
Khan Al-'Umdan 104, 118
Al-Khattab, 'Umar Ibn 154, 155
King David: Tomb of 68, 69, 70, 72–80, 275
Kitzur Shulchan Aruch (Hebrew: brief guide to *halakha*) 97, 101
Kivrei tzadikim see Tombs of the Righteous 72, 78, 85, 96, 97, 98, 102
Kollel (Hebrew: Jewish seminary) 167, 169, 170
Kuffa, City of 264, 268

Labor Party 126, 196, 258, 260
Lag BaOmer, Jewish festival of 70
Lahat, Shlomo, mayor of Tel Aviv 258, 263
Lancaster-Harding, G. 183
Lapid, Efrayim 209
Layish, Aharon 126, 282
Likud Party 202, 203, 209, 214, 254
Lydda (or in Hebrew city of Lod) 234, 235

Ma'abara (Hebrew: immigrant transit camp) 82
Al-Madina Al-Munawwara, Holy City of 130
Madrasas (Islamic seminaries) 105
Maharam (acronym of Rabbi Meir ben Baruch of Rottenberg) 101, 102, 103
Al-Majadala Mosque 121
Al-Makhzumi, 'Umar ibn Jabir 264
Al-Makr, Arab village near Acre 104
Manasra, Abd Al-Salam 206, 220, 228, 230
Mandatory Government of Palestine 244
Manoogian, the Armenian Patriarch 212

Index 301

Manshiyyah neighborhood of Jaffa 249, 253–56
Manzur, Sheikh 273, 295
Al-Maqasid Al-Khayriyya Al-Islamiyya (The Islamic Philanthropic Association) 257
Maqam (Arabic: traditional Muslim shrine), pl. *Maqamat* 231, 232, 233, 235, 236, 237, 239, 241, 242, 243, 245, 247, 248, 277, 294
Mar Eliyas or Shrine of St. George, Mt. Carmel 236
Maronite 56, 193
Maslaha (Arabic: advantage to the *waqf*) 117, 121
Mawsim (Arabic: annual mass Muslim pilgrimage to holy shrines) 233, 234, 235, 244, 294
Mayer, Leon Arieh 74
Mayer-Pinkerfeld Report 236
Mazra'a, village near Acre 119
Mecca, Holy City in Hijaz, Saudi Arabia 232
Al-Madina Al-Munawwara (Arabic: the Lighted City) Holy City in Hijaz, Saudi Arabia 130
Me'arat HaMachpela (Hebrew) *see* Cave of the Patriarchs 176
Megaw's Report 183, 190
Al-Musallah Al-Marwani 185
Rabbi Meir Ba'al HaNess: Tomb in Tiberias 84
Meri, Josef 231
Rabbi Meshulam from Valtira 167
Mihrab (Arabic: Muslim prayer niche) 76, 88, 160, 162
Mikdash me'at (Hebrew: a synagogue) 95
Minyan (Hebrew: prayer quorum) 32, 96
Mitzvah (Hebrew: commandment), pl. *Mitzvoth 94, 96, 99, 102*
Mapai (Labor) Party 108
Mishnah (Hebrew: first major written redaction of Jewish oral traditions) pl. 31, 95, 101, 102
Mishnayot. 95
Monastery of Mar Eliyas (Elijahu ha-Navi/Al-Khadr), Greek Orthodox, Bethlehem 240
Moshe, Basula, Rabbi 167, 232
Mosques *see by name*
Mount Carmel 9, 76, 88, 245, 281
Mount Meron 233, 243
Mount of Olives 9, 44, 45, 47, 70, 160

Mount Zion: Mount Zion Committee 6, 27, 43, 70, 72–77, 85, 86, 87, 88, 160, 167, 275
Mu'azin (Arabic: person calling for prayer) 154
Muhammad, the Muslim Prophet 4, 69, 80, 155, 164, 232, 264, 265, 269, 270
Mujir Al-Din 166
Muslim and Druze Department of the Ministry of Religious Affairs 74, 77, 81, 82, 88, 89
The Muslim Charitable Trust 255, 259
Mutawallis (Arabic: *waqf* administrators) 104, 108, 110, 112–16, 118, 120, 125
Al-Muqaddasi, Arab geographer 165, 176

Nabi Musa: Tomb of Moses near Jericho 234, 244, 294
Nabi Sa'in *waqf* affair 200
Nabi Samwil, (Arabic: Samuel the Prophet) *see* Samuel the Prophet: Tomb 162, 164–71, 174, 175, 176
Nabi Shu'ayb: the cult of 241, 242, 247
Nabi Yamin (Arabic: Tomb of Yamin) 81, 82, 90, 275
Nablus 1, 15, 17, 35, 45, 159, 176, 226, 238, 246, 296
National Committee of Arab Mayors and Local Councils in Israel 206
Naser-i-Khosro, Persian traveler 165
Nazareth *see* Old City of Nazareth 201
Nebi Huda ibn Sayyiduna Ya'qub 82
Netanyahu, Benjamin, Israeli Prime Minister 201, 203, 207, 208, 210, 223, 224
Nidhr (Arabic: vow taking) 241
Northern Islamic Movement 6, 126, 185
Al-Nuzha Mosque 236

Old City of Acre 61, 110
Old City of Jerusalem 6, 18, 53, 191, 277
Old City of Nazareth 201
Or Commission Report 205
Orthodox Arab Council in Israel 205
Oslo Accords 25, 34, 35, 47
Otniel Ben Kenaz: Tomb of 71
Ottoman Ministry of *Waqf* 110
Ottoman period 69, 105, 110, 140, 166, 175, 202, 232, 237, 245, 285
Ovadia of Bartinura 166

Index

Palestinian Arab nationalists 206
Palestinian Authority 11, 20, 25, 35, 48, 49, 64, 136, 158, 187, 212, 238
Parochet (Hebrew: Torah ark curtain) 83
'Ali Pasha, the district governor (Arabic: *Qaimaqam*) of Acre 111, 118, 119, 121
Pasha, Mahmud Ahmad 182
Peres, Gershon, the entrepreneur and contractor of the Hassan Bey transaction 256
Pilgrimage (Arabic: *Ziyara*, Hebrew: *Aliya laRegel*) 4, 8, 14–15, 20–22, 31, 35, 40, 43, 55, 63, 67–68, 70–72, 74, 78, 80–83, 85, 90, 98, 134, 164, 166–68, 176, 179, 198, 213, 232–34, 237–38, 241, 244, 246, 267–68
Pinkerfeld, Jacob 74, 75, 76, 81, 86, 87, 88, 236, 245, 280
Pope John XXIII 198
Poskim (Hebrew: Jewish jurists issuing legal rulings and interpretations) 43, 96, 97, 98, 101
Protection of Holy Places Law, 1967 42, 43, 44, 95, 98, 99.101
Public Works Department 91

Qadi (Arabic: judge) local *Shari'a* court
Qadi of Jerusalem 167, 238
Qaimaqam (Arabic: district governor) 111
Qa'war, Tannus, Mayor of Nazareth 195

Ra'am (Arab Democratic Party) 206, 213, 216–17
Rabban Gamliel: Tomb in Yavne 80, 81, 84, 85
Rabbi Akiva: Tomb in Tiberias 31, 42, 96
Rabbi Shimon bar Yochai: Tomb in Meron 31, 42, 69, 78, 89, 94, 243
Rabi'a Al-'Adawiyya (the Nun) Tomb of Rabeinu Gershom Me'Or Hagolah 18, 70, 160, 283
Rabinowitz, Joshua, mayor of Tel Aviv 256
Al-Rabita (Arab organization for the social welfare of Jaffa citizens) 253, 262
Rachel's Tomb near Bethlehem 170
Ramallah 135, 136, 230, 246
The Rambam: Tomb of (acronym of Rabbi Moshe ben Maimon) in Tiberias 94
Ramban's Cave (acronym of Rabbi Moshe ben Nachman, or Nachmanides), *see also* Ramban's Tomb 92, 93, 100, 102
Ramla 109, 113, 115, 120, 122, 164, 234
Ramon, Haim, Jerusalem Affairs Minister 209, 212
Rashbi: Cave of (acronym of Rabbi Shimeon Bar Yochai) 90
Raslan Mosque, Jaffa 236
Regulations Pertaining to the Preservation of Sites Sacred to Judaism, 5741–1981 94
Riyad, holy city of 133, 272, 295
Ron, Alik, Northern District Police Commander 204
Russian Monastery on the Mount of Olives 70
Ruth's Tomb 71

Sa'ad, Yusuf 183
Sabbah, Michel, Latin Patriarch 208, 212
Al-Sadiqi waqf 116
Safad (Hebrew: Tzfat) 232, 236, 243
Sakhrah (sacred rock) *see* Dome of the Rock 'Oʻ
St. George Shrine *see* Mar Eliyas Shrine 236, 240
Saladin, or Salah Al-Din Yusuf Ibn Ayyub 139, 164, 193, 202, 204, 269
Salah, Sheikh Ra'id of Umm Al-Fahm 205
Samuel the Prophet (Arabic: *Nabi Samwil*): Tomb of 71, 85, 86, 291
Samson's Tomb 71, 85, 86, 291
Sayf Al-Din Al-Zu'abi, Mayor of Nazareth 196
Sayyiduna 'Ali Mosque near Arsuf (Herzliya) 74
Second Intifada *see* Al-Aqsa Intifada 148, 153, 228, 238
Sephardi community in Jerusalem 168, 169
Sha'are Tzion Synagogue, in Yazur 236
Al-Sha'bi, Hajj Muhammad ibn Sheikh Khalil 111, 114, 116
Al-Sham (Greater Syria) 3, 134
Shamash (Hebrew: caretaker)Sharansky, Nathan, Israeli Interior Minister 167
Sharansky Commission 116
Shari'a (Islamic Law) 117, 118
Shari'a Court of Acre 104–16, 118–21, 125

Shavuot, Jewish Festival of Pentecost 238
Sharon, Ariel, Israeli Foreign and Prime Minister 214, 215, 216, 217, 225, 220
Shas Party, ultra-Orthodox Sephardic 202, 209
Shihab Al-Din Mosque, Affair 192, 193, 195, 197, 199, 201, 203, 205–11, 213, 215, 217, 219, 221, 223, 225, 227, 229
Shi'ite 13
Shimon the Just (Hatzadik): Tomb in the Kidron Valley 70
Shochat, Ella 233, 242, 244, 283
Shoufani, Emile, Greek Catholic Archimandrite 207
Al-Shu'la, Sheikh 233
Shulchan Aruch (Hebrew: Anthology of Jewish *Halakhah*) 96, 97, 101, 102
Sijill (Arabic: records of the *shari'a* court) 104, 237
Siksik, Zuhdi 257
Siksik Mosque (Jaffa) 236
Simat (Arabic: soup kitchen) 235
Sinan Pasha Mosque in Acre 126
Six-Day War of June 1967 150, 183
The Society for the Holy Places 88, 77, 75, 73
Sons of Jacob: Burial sites of the coastal plain region 79
Southern Islamic Movement 126
Status Quo in the Holy Places 18, 41, 86, 277
Sufi Muslims 114, 116–17, 125, 146
Suissa, Eli, Interior Minister 209
Sulayman Ibn Abd Al-Malik, Caliph 265
Supreme Court of Israel *see* High Court of Israel 29
Supreme Muslim Council 6, 7, 16, 17, 105, 106, 107, 110, 120, 170, 178, 234, 253, 280

Al-Tabari, Sheikh Musa, *Qadi* of Acre 108
Tabiyya Mosque, Jaffa 236
Takiyya (Arabic: a hall for prayer and festivities) 111
Taso Cemetery in Jaffa 236
Tel Yavne 80
The Temple/ Haram compound (Hebrew: *Har HaBayyit*) *see* Temple Mount 180

Toledano, Shmuel, Prime Minister's Adviser on Arab Affairs 256
Tombs of the Righteous 90, 91, 291
Tomb of *Tzadik a-Toachin* (the Holy Man of the Mill) 69
Tzadik, (Hebrew: sages), pl. *tzadikim* 68, 69, 72, 78, 85, 96, 97, 98, 102

Ubaydallah Ibn Ziyad 264
The Umayyad Dynasty
Umm Al-Fahm 205
Upper Nazareth (Hebrew: *Natzrat 'Illit*) 141
Al-'Uthmani, Muhammad, Chief *Qadi* 233

Vilnay, Matan 211
Vilnay, Zeev 81, 86, 90, 117, 284, 293

Wadi Hunayn Mosque 236
Walaya (Arabic: loyalty) 270
Waqf (Muslim religious endowment): The Muslim Waqf Administration and Islamic Affairs Department 238
Waqfiyya (Arabic: founding deed) 110, 111, 116, 125
War of 1948 139
Wazana, Rabbi Ya'acov 243, 290
Western Wall or Wailing Wall (known by Muslims as *Al-Buraq* Wall) 6, 134
White Mosque in Ramla 74
White Mosque in Nazareth 139, 193, 220
Al-Wihda Mosque (Jaffa) 236

Yaeger, Father David 216
Al-Yashruti, 'Ali Nur Al-Din 111
Al-Yashruti *waqf* 114, 116
Yazid Ibn Mu'awiya, Caliph 264, 272, 295, 296
Yazur Mosque 236
Yehuda Ben Baba: Gravesite near Shfaram 69, 79, 84, 125
Yeshiva (Hebrew: a Jewish seminary) 27, 238
Yishmael ben Rabbi Yose Haglili: Gravesite of Rabbi 78, 89
Yochai: Gravesite of Rabbi in Gush Chalav 89
Yochanan Hasandlar: Grave of Rabbi near Meron 69
Yose of Peki'in: Gravesite of Rabbi 69, 79, 90
Yose of Yokeret: Gravesite of Rabbi 69

304 *Index*

Zaddiq (righteous man, Hebrew) *see* tzadik 232
Zahir Al-'Umar Mosque 111, 126
Zawiyya (Arabic: a Sufi lodge) 11
Zaydan, Muhammad 206
Al-Zaydani, Zahir Al-'Umar 111
Zayta (Arab village) 126
Al-Zaytuni Mosque 126

Zayyad, Tawfiq, Mayor of Nazareth 140, 196, 201
Zedekiah's Cave 45, 86
Zikhron Ya'akov Synagogue 236
Ziyara (Arabic: pilgrimage, seasonal visit to a saint's tomb) 231, 246
Zohar (Hebrew: the central work of Kabbalah or Jewish mysticism) 31, 233

eBooks – at www.eBookstore.tandf.co.uk

A library at your fingertips!

eBooks are electronic versions of printed books. You can store them on your PC/laptop or browse them online.

They have advantages for anyone needing rapid access to a wide variety of published, copyright information.

eBooks can help your research by enabling you to bookmark chapters, annotate text and use instant searches to find specific words or phrases. Several eBook files would fit on even a small laptop or PDA.

NEW: Save money by eSubscribing: cheap, online access to any eBook for as long as you need it.

Annual subscription packages

We now offer special low-cost bulk subscriptions to packages of eBooks in certain subject areas. These are available to libraries or to individuals.

For more information please contact webmaster.ebooks@tandf.co.uk

We're continually developing the eBook concept, so keep up to date by visiting the website.

www.eBookstore.tandf.co.uk